RESISTANCE AND BETRAYAL

Resistance and Betrayal

The Death and Life of the Greatest
Hero of the French Resistance

Patrick Marnham

RANDOM HOUSE
NEW YORK

RANDOM HOUSE and colophon are registered trademarks of Random House, Inc.

This work was originally published in Great Britain as
The Death of Jean Moulin: Biography of a Ghost,
by John Murray (Publishers), London, in 2000.

Grateful acknowledgment is made to the following for permission to reproduce illus-
trations: Plates 1, 2, 3, 4, 6, 7, 8, 11, 18, 19, 23, 24, 26, 27, 28, 29, 30 and 31, Keystone/Corbis
Sygma; 9 and 10, Musée des Beaux-Arts, Béziers; 17, © Nogues/Corbis Sygma; 25,
© Robert Capa/Magnum Photos.

Library of Congress Cataloging-in-Publication Data

Marnham, Patrick.
Resistance and betrayal: the death and life of the greatest hero of the
French Resistance/Patrick Marnham.
p.   cm.
Includes bibliographical references and index.
ISBN 0-375-50608-X (alk. paper)
1. Moulin, Jean, 1899–1943. 2. World War, 1939–1945—Underground
movements—France. 3. Guerrillas—France—Biography. I. Title.
D802.F8 M263   2002
940.53′44—dc21   2001048160

Random House website address: www.atrandom.com

Printed in the United States of America on acid-free paper

2 4 6 8 9 7 5 3
First U.S. Edition

Book design by Casey Hampton

Les Français sont tellement différents les uns des autres,
comprenez-vous, tellement prêts à se déchirer! Il fallait bien
leur trouver un dénominateur commun. Ce ne pouvait être
que la patrie . . .

CHARLES DE GAULLE

(The French are so different one from another, you see,
so quick to tear each other apart. It was essential to find
some common cause. It could only be patriotism . . .)

Acknowledgments

Among witnesses of the occupation in Lyon I must first thank Dr. Frédéric Dugoujon, one of those arrested at Caluire, who provided me with a vivid account of the day in 1943 when his house was raided by the Gestapo; we were at the time sitting in the room in which he himself had been arrested. It was to be many years before I discovered that the account he gave me that day differed substantially from the account he had given at a postwar treason trial in Paris in 1947. Dr. Dugoujon also introduced me to his housekeeper, Marguerite Brossier.

Secondly I must thank the late Claude Bourdet, one of the leaders of the resistance network *Combat,* deported to Sachsenhausen, and the resister David Rousset, deported to Buchenwald, as well as his wife, Susie Rousset. Comte Jacques de Place, a former member of both the Resistance and the *Cagoule,* showed me round the Quartier St. Jean, in Lyon, using the skeleton keys he had manufactured himself during the occupation, which still turned a surprising number of locks. The sculptor Jean-Louis Faure, much of whose work has been inspired by his youthful memories of the occupation, was generous with suggestions and research material, and Madame Monique Gonthier was able to shed an unexpected light on what the occupation meant for a teenage Jewish girl in hiding. Other witnesses of the period who assisted me include Mrs. Audrey Hooper, who spent the war in Châteauroux, and the late Sam White, who, as a war correspondent, witnessed the *épuration,* or purification, in both Paris and the south of France. Like so many who have written on France I am indebted to Richard Cobb, who was a generous and patient guide on the liberation period, which he participated in, and on Lyon, which was one of his favorite cities. Professor Cobb once told me that he could never really quite believe in Jean Moulin, a judgment which deterred me from writing on the subject for some time.

In Lyon I was assisted by the historian Henri Hours, by Pierre Truche and by Maître Jacques Vergès, and by the librarians of the Bibliothèque Municipale and the archivist of the Evêché; in Paris by the librarians of the Bibliothèque Nationale, the librarian of the British Institute and by C. L. Campos, editor of the *Journal of Franco-British Studies.* I am also grateful to the director of the Musée Jean Moulin in Paris, the director of the Musée des Beaux Arts in Béziers and the director of the Fondation Jean Moulin in Bordeaux as well as to the archivists of the Délégation à la mémoire et l'information historique in the Ministère de la Défense. My thanks are also due to the staff of the London Library and to Bodley's librarian in Oxford. In Bordeaux I was assisted by Maître Bertrand Favreau, Maître Gérard Boulanger, Maître Francis Vuillemin, Maître Arno Klarsfeld and Michel Slitinsky. Like many others I am indebted to the researcher and lawyer Serge Klarsfeld for his early assistance, and to my friends Sorj Chalandon and Vibeke Knoop Rachline. Antony Beevor and Dr. Nicholas Goodrick-Clarke have both been generous with their encouragement and advice.

The first person who spoke to me about her personal experience of resistance was Anne-Marie de Bernard of the *Prosper* network, deported to Ravensbruck in 1943. She worked for a British secret intelligence network and paid a terrible price, and I would like to acknowledge her courage and strength. Her daughters, the late Moune Watson and Madame Béatrice Théry, have been most helpful to me on many occasions over the years.

None of the above are in way responsible for such errors as remain, the less so since I am sure that several of them would disagree with my conclusions.

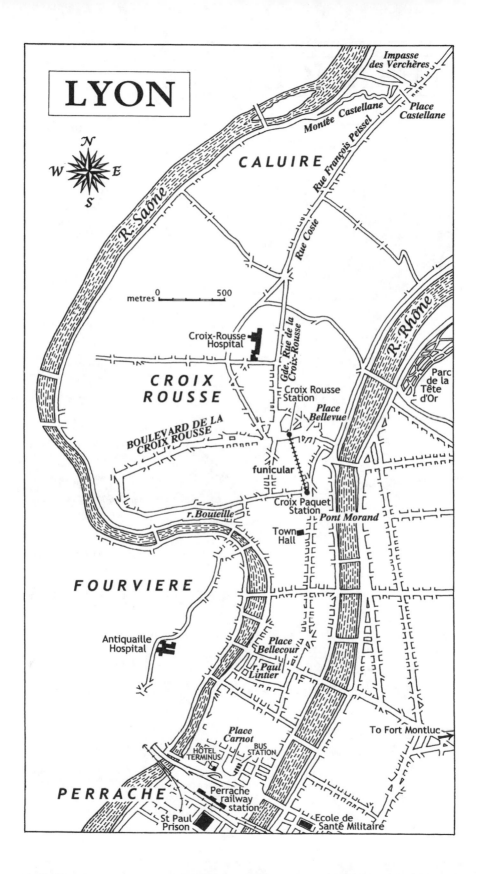

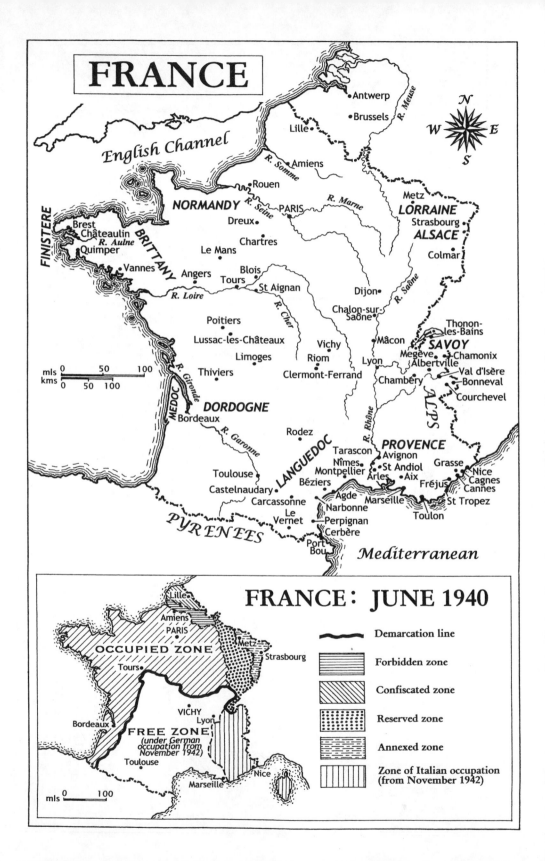

FRANCE

Antwerp
Brussels
Lille
Amiens
Rouen

English Channel

R. Meuse
R. Somme

Metz
LORRAINE
Strasbourg
ALSACE
Colmar

NORMANDY
R. Seine
PARIS
R. Marne
Dreux
Chartres

FINISTERE
Brest
Châteaulin
R. Aulne
Quimper
BRITTANY
Vannes
Angers
Blois
Tours
St Aignan
Le Mans

R. Loire
R. Cher

Dijon
R. Saône

Poitiers
Lussac-les-Châteaux
Limoges
Thiviers
Vichy
Riom
Clermont-Ferrand

Chalon-sur-Saône
Mâcon
Lyon

Thonon-les-Bains
SAVOY
Megève
Albertville
Chamonix
Chambéry
Val d'Isère
Bonneval
Courchevel

mls 0   50   100
kms 0   50 100

R. Gironde

MEDOC
Bordeaux
DORDOGNE
R. Garonne
Rodez

Toulouse
Castelnaudary
Carcassonne
Le Vernet
Béziers
Agde
Narbonne
Perpignan
Cerbère
Port Bou

LANGUEDOC

Tarascon
Nîmes
St Andiol
Montpellier
Arles
Marseille

PROVENCE
Avignon
Aix
Grasse
Fréjus
Toulon
Nice
Cagnes
Cannes
St Tropez

R. Rhône

ALPS
PYRENEES

Mediterranean

FRANCE: JUNE 1940

Lille
Amiens
PARIS
OCCUPIED ZONE
Tours
Metz
Strasbourg

Bordeaux
VICHY
Lyon
FREE ZONE
(under German occupation from November 1942)
Toulouse
Nice
Marseille

mls 0   100

▬▬▬	Demarcation line
☰	Forbidden zone
▨	Confiscated zone
⠿	Reserved zone
☰	Annexed zone
▥	Zone of Italian occupation (from November 1942)

CONTENTS

Acknowledgments... ix

Map of Lyon... xi

Map of France.. xii

Introduction... xv

PART I: THE LEGEND

  1 A Doctor's House in Caluire............................. 3

  2 Into the Panthéon....................................... 9

PART II: WAR

  3 The Prefect of Chartres................................ 19

  4 Zones.. 35

  5 Life on Half-Pay....................................... 52

PART III: LIFE

  6 A Republican Cradle.................................... 69

  7 A Secret Man, a Complex Man............................ 85

  8 Moulin Rouge.. 104

PART IV: RESISTANCE

  9 An Envoy to London.................................... 129

 10 Life Underground...................................... 144

 11 The Army of the Night................................. 161

12 Betrayal 175

13 An Urn and a Pot of Jam 187

PART V: RESURRECTION

14 The Machinery of Insurrection 201

15 Murdering History 217

16 The Doctor's Waiting Room 233

Postscript 259

Glossary 263

Chronology 267

Notes 273

Select Bibliography 277

Index 281

Introduction

Jean Moulin is remembered in France today as the great hero of the wartime Resistance. Yet few modern heroes remain so enigmatic. Sixty years on, mystery shrouds such elementary facts as his true political beliefs, the manner of his betrayal and even the time and place of his death.

In 1941, Moulin—who had been a senior civil servant before the outbreak of the war—slipped over the Spanish border out of wartime France using a passport he had forged himself to reach London and take his place as the most eminent recruit to the cause of the Free French. There he agreed to act as General de Gaulle's emissary to the Resistance and was entrusted with the mission of uniting the movement and reforging it as an instrument of national liberation. Despite his high rank he was twice smuggled back into France, where he lived underground and frequently on the run in conditions of grave danger.

By May 1943, Moulin had succeeded in creating a united resistance movement, ranging from the ultra-right to the communists, under his personal political leadership. To achieve this he had had to overcome the bitter rivalries dividing the ambitious individualists who had created the original networks. One month later Jean Moulin was betrayed to the Gestapo and captured in Lyon. Despite the torture he suffered at the hands of the SS officer Klaus Barbie, Moulin remained silent and paid for his courage with his life. Two postwar treason trials held in Paris failed to uncover the identity of his betrayer. Twenty years later, during an emotional ceremony at the Panthéon, his heroism was officially recognized and he was consecrated as a national symbol.

Jean Moulin came from what the French call a "a republican background." In the undeclared civil war that divided French society during his lifetime and that of his father before him, the Moulin family was always on the progressive side of the argument, egalitarian, anti-monarchist and anti-clerical. Moulin first achieved political influence during the 1930s, when the Spanish Civil War led to the formation of the Popular Front, an alliance between radicals, socialists, communists and other "anti-fascists."

For many thousands of European and American idealists this exhilarating intellectual adventure was brutally terminated in August 1939, with the news of the Nazi-Soviet Pact.

It was then—in Koestler's mocking simile—that the men of the Popular Front faced the bitter truth as did Jacob in Genesis, who awoke on the morning after his wedding night to find that after seven years of struggle he had won not the beautiful Rachel but her hideous sister, Leah. Jean Moulin's dedicated support for the Popular Front led to postwar accusations by fellow resisters that his commitment to communism may have survived the Pact and that he may even have been a communist agent. In 1989 Moulin's wartime radio operator, Daniel Cordier, outraged by this suggestion, defended the reputation of his old commander in the first of what was planned to be a six-volume study that must be one of the quixotic biographical monuments ever conceived. But despite Cordier's loyal efforts the arguments continue, reflecting the divisions in French society that were established a century ago and persist to this day. In such circumstances it is sometimes easier for an outsider to make out the truth.

My own interest in the life of Jean Moulin began in the early 1980s when I was writing about the political maneuvering that preceded the trial in Lyon of the man who arrested him, the former SS officer Klaus Barbie. Barbie eventually received a life sentence after being convicted of wartime crimes against humanity. Over the years Barbie made numerous contradictory statements about the raid he had conducted on the house in Caluire and "the traitors of the Resistance"; none were entirely convincing and it seems likely that when Barbie died in a French prison he revenged himself by taking the truth with him to his grave.

Perhaps the most intriguing aspect of the story of Jean Moulin is that a life that has been the subject of so many inquiries should remain so discreet.

We glimpse Moulin in a succession of silhouettes: an incident with some army recruits in Montpellier when he was aged eighteen, an encounter with a brutish gatekeeper, a fragment of verse which is all that remains of a dinner with the depraved poet Max Jacob, some drawings scribbled on a café tablecloth during the occupation of Lyon. Pieced together, such moments can form the outlines of a man's life; certainly they reveal someone whose vitality and humanity stand in strong contrast to the heroic effigy they lowered into the crypt of the Panthéon.

I

THE LEGEND

ONE

A Doctor's House in Caluire

THE HOUSE IN CALUIRE stands today exactly as it stood then, a handsome stone building on the corner of a small provincial square called the Place Castellane. Caluire is a suburb of Lyon, perched on a hill overlooking the sleepy waters of the River Saône. Raised on a terrace slightly above the level of the square, its three floors protected by a stone wall and iron railings, the house has the light gray shutters and dark green creeper of so many French villas of its period.

Today, as then, it is the property of Dr. Frédéric Dugoujon. In 1943 Lyon was under martial law, occupied by German forces, but most people tried to carry on as normally as possible. Dr. Dugoujon was among them. In common with the great majority of people he was not involved in resistance. But he had a friend who was a member of the resistance group *Libération,* and at this man's request the doctor agreed to let his house be used for a secret meeting on the afternoon of 21 June. The doctor's house was a bad choice for a meeting place. Having only one entrance it was a natural trap. Once inside, the only exit was through the front door.

The twenty-first of June was a Monday; the meeting was scheduled for 2:15 in the afternoon. It had been called by Jean Moulin, a prefect suspended on half-pay by the wartime Vichy government, who had crossed under a false identity to England, where he had been nominated by Gen-

eral de Gaulle as the political head of the Resistance. Seven other prominent members of the movement had been summoned to the meeting,
whose purpose was to discuss the appointment of a new military leader for
"the Secret Army." This was the name given to the united military resistance, an organization which was in a state of crisis following a succession
of arrests by the German security forces. Eight people was an unusually
large number for such a meeting, but it seemed that a doctor's house during surgery hours, with a steady arrival and departure of patients, would
provide effective cover.

Between 2:00 and 2:20 the doorbell at the doctor's house rang three
times and the maid admitted five young or middle-aged men who were
shown not into the ground-floor waiting room but up the stairs to a room
on the second floor. They were Colonel Albert Lacaze, a regular army officer and a member of a small independent resistance group called *France
d'Abord;* André Lassagne, the friend of Dr. Dugoujon, a professor of Italian
and a member of the network *Libération,* which was close to the French
Communist Party; Bruno Larat, who ran the COPA,* the service which
organized parachute drops and landings for the Resistance; and Henri
Aubry and René Hardy, both members of a powerful right-wing resistance
group, *Combat.* All of these men were inside the house in good time for the
meeting. Another person expected, Claude Serreulles, failed to turn up,
having lost his way and taken the wrong tramcar.

Not all those sitting in the upstairs room knew each other by sight or
even by name since they had adopted *noms de guerre.* They were aware that
they had been summoned by the head of the Resistance whom they all
knew as "Max." But "Max" did not come. So, for forty-five minutes, five
men involved in a hazardous common undertaking but more or less
strangers to each other sat together in an increasingly exposed situation.
The conspirators were unarmed, unguarded, in a house with no escape
route. It was a standard precaution in the Resistance to walk away from a
broken appointment after a short delay and start again. But on 21 June
these men were lulled into waiting, by the welcoming atmosphere of the
house, or by the reassuring routine of the surgery which they could hear
on the floor below—the ringing of the doorbell, the footsteps going backwards and forwards across the hall, the occasional noise of voices, includ-

---

* Acronyms and foreign titles are explained in the glossary on page 263.

ing the voices of women and children, the greetings given by the maid, Madame Brossier, to regular patients; normal life in all its distracting familiarity. Then as time passed, and their conversation started to go round in circles, they began to wonder what had happened to "Max."

Just before three o'clock the front doorbell rang again, twice, and Madame Brossier was confronted by three more men, all of whom she showed into the doctor's waiting room where they joined a group of six patients. One of them was "Max." The others were Raymond Aubrac, like Lassagne a member of *Libération*, and Lieutenant-Colonel Schwartzfeld, like Colonel Lacaze a member of *France d'Abord*. Although "Max" and Aubrac realized at once that they had been shown into the wrong room, and knew that by remaining they were further delaying the start of a meeting that was already forty minutes behind schedule, they stayed there for five minutes, inhibited even from discussing what to do by the presence of the doctor's bona fide patients. Perhaps they thought they were the first to arrive. Perhaps they thought that the doctor had failed to brief the maid. Perhaps they were waiting for an opportunity to talk freely. In his consulting room across the hallway Dr. Dugoujon was examining a small boy who was accompanied by his mother. A few minutes after three there was a sudden loud banging at the front door followed by a crash, and the orderly routine of the doctor's house in the Place Castellane was broken forever.

"The first I knew that something unusual was going on," said Dr. Dugoujon in 1985,

> was when I heard a noise in the hall. I left my patient and came out to find that several men in civilian clothes, armed with pistols, had burst through the front door. I don't know why they did that. If they had rung the bell the maid would have let them in. I asked them what they thought they were doing. Of course I was pretty sure I knew the answer already. There was a big brute who came toward me as though to hit me, and then a smaller man with piercing blue eyes and a sharp, pointed face who ordered me into my own waiting room with all the patients. That was my first sight of Klaus Barbie, who was the head of the Lyon Gestapo. They rounded up everyone they found in the house and pushed them into the waiting room. Then they handcuffed all the men and took us away for questioning. There

were German soldiers outside. We were all handcuffed except for a young man with fair hair.

The doctor's house had been raided by a *Sonderkommando,* a special police group recently formed in Lyon to intensify operations against the Resistance. Upstairs they burst into the room where the meeting was assembled and ordered everyone to lie on the floor. Then their leader broke off the leg of an antique Henri II table and started to beat André Lassagne. Hardy was arrested by an SS corporal called Harry Steingritt and he was the only man taken at Caluire who was not handcuffed. "I understand some German," said Dr. Dugoujon,

> and I heard them say there were no more handcuffs. So they tied a leather strap to one of his wrists and a soldier held the end of it. Outside the house when we were about to be loaded into their cars this man without handcuffs suddenly pulled the strap out of the guard's hands, punched the soldier in the stomach and ran off. He ran very fast across the square, dodging between the trees. Another soldier shouted at him and then started shooting, but the man got across the square and disappeared round the corner and none of the soldiers really searched for him.

Nonetheless one of the bullets fired had wounded Hardy in the arm.

The seven resisters arrested at Caluire, with Dr. Dugoujon and most of the patients in the waiting room, were taken first to Gestapo headquarters in the Ecole de Santé Militaire in the avenue Berthelot, where they were locked up till the evening. Then they were ordered out of their separate cells and lined up in the corridor. That was the second time Dr. Dugoujon met Klaus Barbie.

> It was the same little chap from my house that afternoon. He walked down the line and asked each one of us if we were "Max." But he didn't ask me that. To me he just said, "You had a gun in the drawer of your desk. Why?" It was true I had a gun in my desk. I said I always kept a gun in my desk, against robbers. He said it was illegal. I said I knew that. He just smiled. Not a particularly unpleasant smile. He gave the impression that he already knew all the answers to his own questions and he was only looking for confirmation. I realized that this was his professional manner. But I was also impressed by his con-

fidence that he would be able to find out everything he wanted to know in due course.

After a brief interrogation, Dr. Dugoujon was transferred to the central prison of Fort Montluc; with him went Jean Moulin, Raymond Aubrac, Lieutenant-Colonel Schwartzfeld and Colonel Lacaze.

For the resistance leaders their first night in Montluc was a bitter experience. Not only had their meeting been discovered but the Gestapo knew the code name "Max" and strongly suspected that he was among them. It was Midsummer night, the shortest night of the year, and though he was guarded by German soldiers and French prison warders, Jean Moulin must have had hopes, however slight, of escape since the Resistance in Lyon had the means to rescue prisoners. He must also have had hopes that his false identity, Jean Martel, art dealer from Nice, would hold, since he alone among those arrested carried a letter of recommendation from a doctor in Marseille for Dr. Dugoujon's attention.

Meanwhile at the Ecole de Santé Militaire the three prisoners who remained were already being beaten. They were the three younger men from the upper room, Henri Aubry, Bruno Larat and André Lassagne. Barbie started his interrogation of Lassagne with this terrible phrase: "Your 'Secret Army' is a secret for nobody, certainly not for us." On that first night Barbie selected Lassagne, as the most likely "Max," for special treatment. He was not only beaten but dragged out three times to stand before a firing squad. At one point a colleague of Barbie's entered the room and threw a bundle of resistance mail onto the desk saying, in French, "Max is among them."

As for René Hardy, after running across the Place Castellane he had hidden in a ditch and then made his way to a friend's house to seek attention for his wound. He was seen taking refuge and reported to French police who were investigating the shooting incident in the Place Castellane. They arrested him and took him late at night to the Antiquaille hospital, where he remained in police custody. When the French police investigation was complete Hardy was delivered to the Gestapo and confined in a German military hospital, the Croix-Rousse. The decision to hand him over was taken by the commissioner of French police in Lyon, René Cussonac, who was executed after the liberation of Lyon for this action among many others. Shortly after the execution of the police commissioner Hardy, too, was tried for treason. He was acquitted, but for the rest of his

life he was suspected of having betrayed the meeting at Caluire to the
Gestapo.

A man's life can sometimes be defined by his death. In the case of Jean
Moulin nobody knows when he died, or how or where. His body was never
found. After two days of inquiry the Gestapo had acquired enough information to begin Moulin's interrogation. That evening Dr. Dugoujon saw
him being dragged back to his cell with his face covered in blood. There
were three other occasions when members of the Resistance claim to have
seen him in a dying condition, once in Lyon, twice in the villa in Neuilly
outside Paris occupied by SS Major Karl Boemelburg, the head of the
Gestapo in France. What is clear is that Jean Moulin was last seen alive in
France. His dead body was first identified by a policeman two weeks later
in Frankfurt, Germany. His death certificate states that he died in Metz,
just before the German border. The most likely cause of death was multi-
ple head injuries, but it is not certain how these were inflicted, or by
whom. In the absence of certainty it is widely concluded that he died as a
hero, having refused to talk, and was beaten into a coma on the orders of
the senior Gestapo officer in Lyon, SS Lieutenant Klaus Barbie. Despite
the lack of detail Jean Moulin's case is a classic example of defining a
man's life by his death.

The ranks of the French Resistance contained thousands of men and
women who faced the same dangers as Moulin, and many were arrested
and tortured and subsequently died in German custody: 65,000 French
citizens were deported for resistance or for political reasons, of whom
only half survived to the end of the war. Many thousands more were executed in France, over one thousand outside Paris at the fort of Mont
Valérien alone. The rule for resistance members subject to German interrogation was that they should try to say nothing for two days, during
which time any information they gave could be rendered useless. A small
number of men and women managed to withstand the worst torture without breaking, and Jean Moulin seems to have been among them because it
is clear that none of the great store of invaluable information he held was
ever put to use by the Gestapo. In many cases the suffering of these men
and women could be exactly described after the war. But the fact that so
little is known about Jean Moulin's end made him an appropriate symbol
of the general suffering; for the Resistance he could play the role of the
Unknown Soldier.

TWO

Into the Panthéon

O N   A   F L I N T   C O L D   M O R N I N G   in December 1964 several hundred men and women, mostly dressed in black overcoats, gathered on the steps of the Panthéon in Paris listening to a speech by the writer and politician André Malraux.

In front of them, on an enormous platform draped in gray covers, stood a coffin containing the remains of the former prefect and resistance leader Jean Moulin. The scaffold, with its funeral sheeting cracking and straining in the icy wind, dominated the extensive space in front of the Panthéon and transformed it into the stage of an open-air opera house, reducing the coffin to the scale of a matchbox. Before the catafalque Malraux, also in a black overcoat, head bare, crouched over the microphone with wild eyes and beaky nose, resembled an elderly vulture. Directly opposite him, standing before the massed ranks of the dignitaries of France, Charles de Gaulle, the head of state, made one of his rare appearances in military uniform, looking restless and distressed. Around de Gaulle were gathered the ageing survivors, the men and women who had once formed the Resistance.

The speech Malraux made that day was the histrionic peak of his career. He sang the words in a high, almost female register, drawing out the vowels, peering over his spectacles into the mists of a tragic past, somehow managing to incarnate a movement in which he himself had scarcely distinguished himself. But his own modest wartime role did not matter. No one else in France could have played the part as well as André Malraux. Isaiah Berlin called his performance "an unforgettable evocation of what the Resistance had been." The wailing voice, like a geriatric fury, the accusatory stance with one foot advanced so that he could rock forwards for additional emphasis, the piercing eye, the hunched shoulders were all superb theatrical devices. In addition he had selected the music, and was particularly proud of the funeral march by Gossec, a forgotten Revolutionary composer, whose score he had rediscovered himself. Furthermore Malraux, agile politician, bogus fighter pilot, belated resister, long-retired man-of-action, fantasist, was a superb writer.

> Voilà donc . . . Jean Moulin . . . le chef d'un peuple de la nuit. Sans cette cérémonie combien d'enfants de France sauraient son nom? Here then lies . . . Jean Moulin . . . the leader of a people of the night. Without this ceremony how many children of France would even recognize his name?

The phrases rolled on. "It was a time when, in the depths of the countryside, we tracked the barking of dogs through the night. . . . He had an appointment with the leaders of the separate resistance groups at Caluire on 21 June. They were awaiting him. So was the Gestapo. Treachery played a part as well as fate. . . . He made none of the regiments. But he made the Army." And so on, until the superb peroration. "Think of his poor, battered face, of those lips that never spoke. That day, his last day, it was the face of France."

Charles de Gaulle remained impassive but by the time Malraux had finished, many other members of his audience, no doubt thinking of other men and women who had disappeared into the night, were reduced to tears. Then the drums beat, the band of the Garde Républicaine played the *Chant des Partisans* and the great coffin was carried through the doors of the mausoleum. At that moment it did not matter that the coffin was practically empty, or that Moulin's body had never been found, or that the ashes selected as his had been identified on an SS certificate.

The building before which Malraux was speaking was in fact a most appropriate resting place for the leader of the Armies of the Night, not just because it was the national mausoleum but because it symbolized the cause for which he had fought all his life; not the Resistance, but republican anticlericalism, or secularism as it is usually termed. The story of the Panthéon is the story of France's inability to resolve its quarrels over religion. The edifice was commissioned by a king, Louis XV, who had fallen ill in Metz in 1744. The king was afraid and he vowed to God that if he recovered he would replace the ruined abbey of Ste. Geneviève, the patron saint of Paris, with a magnificent new church. The king did recover but he died long before the building was complete, and it was not until 1789 that the new church could be dedicated, to the glory of God and the kings of France. Then, just as it was ready, the Revolution swept away the monarchy and the churches of Paris were desecrated and closed.

In 1791 the Revolutionary Assembly decided that a use must be found for the empty structure and, inspired by the death of Mirabeau, proposed that it should be transformed into "a Temple of Fame," a last resting place for the great men who had fought for Liberty. The church's bell towers were razed to the ground, its tall side windows were filled in, the cross above the dome was removed, and in gilt letters over the west doors the motto "Aux Grands Hommes la Patrie reconnaissante" (To Its Great Men, Their Country's gratitude) were fixed. Mirabeau's remains were placed inside, followed by those of Voltaire, Marat and Rousseau.

In its revolutionary origins the symbolic role of the Panthéon was clear; it replaced the basilica of St. Denis, ancient burial place of the kings of France. But after the restoration of the monarchy the church was for the first time consecrated, the secular inscription was replaced by a Latin dedication and the remains of Voltaire and Rousseau were removed to a space beneath the front steps, which was outside the consecrated area. Then, with the arrival in 1830 of Louis-Philippe, "King of the French," son of Philippe Egalité, the Panthéon was modestly renamed "the Temple of Humanity," the motto "Aux Grands Hommes . . ." was replaced, the cross was again removed and the building became a national necropolis. With each change of regime the process was repeated, with the Panthéon being recaptured and restored to its previous function. It was only in 1885, under the Third Republic, that the present compromise was reached. The church was once more deconsecrated and renamed the Panthéon, the motto was once more fixed to the pediment and the bodies of the republican heroes Victor Hugo, Emile Zola, Gambetta and Jean Jaurès were in due course transferred. But the cross was allowed to remain.

So the Panthéon, which was supposed to become a symbol of national identity, became instead a memorial to a fracture in French society inflicted by the Revolution and in two hundred years never mended. Since the days of Napoleon no military leaders have been buried in the Panthéon; following in the footsteps of the Emperor they go to the Invalides. The clergy are also excluded and there have been very few representatives of the political right. Instead of becoming a focus of the nation, "le Temple de la Patrie" became a last resting place for eminent political neutrals, like Marie Curie, or members of the French left.

The most significant ceremony held at the Panthéon during the lifetime of Jean Moulin—the most significant for him personally—was also one of the most hotly disputed. When in 1924 Jean Jaurès, the socialist leader and pacifist who had been assassinated on the eve of the outbreak of the Great War, was reinterred, two counterdemonstrations took place. One was organized, predictably enough, by the ultra-right nationalists of *Action française.* The second was organized by the Parti Communiste Français. When the communists broke away from the official procession and marched in front of it, singing the *Internationale,* their intention was to show that they were the true heirs of Jaurès. But what they actually achieved was to establish that the left could no longer consecrate one of its heroes without revealing new national divisions. It was a far cry from the day in 1885 when Victor Hugo, a staunch republican, who was among the minority of great men to be buried in the Panthéon directly and without benefit of exhumation, was honored by a cortège one million strong without a single voice being raised in dissent.

By the time Jean Moulin's ashes were transferred to the Panthéon in 1964 the custom had practically fallen into disuse, and its revival was designed to evoke the unity of 1885. The move was originally proposed by the socialist parliamentary opposition, who wanted to establish, under the presidency of Charles de Gaulle, that the left too had played a part in the Resistance, and that the man who had enlisted in the Resistance and united it had been one of theirs. The original date suggested had been a year earlier, on the twentieth anniversary of Moulin's disappearance. But de Gaulle, with his habitual skill, delayed matters until the twentieth anniversary of the liberation and then, by the unprecedented use of television and by ensuring that he himself was placed center stage dressed as a soldier, retranslated the symbolism. The ceremony no longer established that the left had played a part in the Resistance; it showed instead that de Gaulle, living embodiment of the wartime victory, had also enjoyed left-wing support.

Nonetheless, on a higher level, the secular canonization of Jean Moulin did succeed in creating a national symbol; it was not just the sanctification of one man's life. When Jean Moulin was resurrected from peacetime obscurity and recast in a heroic posture he became, through Malraux's artistry, the personification of the Resistance and the Resistance became the emblem of the whole of France.

Malraux's text was a lyrical evocation of the most romantic conception of resistance, darkness and fear and solitude and pain, his words made the more poignant by the presence before him of so many of the men and women who had experienced all that and who could vividly recall the terror inspired by the word "Gestapo." It was nonetheless bold of the speaker to place so much emphasis on torture, since at the time he spoke the subject of torture was once more topical in France. The fact that the French administration in Algeria had instituted "democratic torture"—after the Gestapo had done so much to discredit the practice—had been the subject of a pamphlet entitled *The Question*, written by a communist journalist called Henri Alleg in 1958. In this pamphlet Alleg, who supported the Algerian independence movement, recounted his own experience of torture at the hands of the French paratroops who had arrested him in Algiers and taken him to a secret barracks and prison at El-Biar outside the city in June 1957. The list of torture techniques set out by Alleg included burning of the tongue, cutting with a knife, rape and forced drinking of salt water. He also described two methods of torture notoriously used by the Gestapo in France during the occupation. One was *la baignoire*, the forcing of water into the mouth and lungs until the victim was on the point of drowning; the other was *la gégène*, the infliction of electrical shocks with a handheld generator. In two passages, Alleg's memoir specifically refers back to French experience during the occupation. Early in his ordeal the paratroops say to him: "Ici c'est la Gestapo! Tu connais la Gestapo?" Then, when his torture is nearly over, Alleg meets a sympathetic paratrooper who asks him if he has already been tortured "in the Resistance." Another of his tormentors says to him, in a quiet moment: "My father told me about the communists in the Resistance. They died, but they said nothing. That's good."[*]

---

[*] Malraux's literary reputation had of course been launched on his description of communists withstanding torture in *La Condition humaine*.

For communists like Henri Alleg, French military operations in Algeria against nationalist "terrorists" or "resisters" were seen in the context of the German occupation of France. Like the Nazi security forces, the French army ordered military doctors to supervise the inflicting of pain. They were not there to protect the victim from harm but to ensure that the techniques were applied effectively and for as long as possible. Himmler defined the general limits for the use of what he called "the third degree" in 1942, and on the whole the French army in Algeria followed Himmler. The proper targets for torture included communists, saboteurs, terrorists and members of resistance movements.

At first the claims made by Alleg were denied and the French government seized copies of his book and destroyed them. But the censorship was ineffective. The practices Alleg described were confirmed by other witnesses, some of them conscript soldiers who had been ordered to take part in inflicting torture. Eventually senior army officers also confirmed the accusations and General Massu, commander of the paratroops in Algeria, justified the use of torture in the face of terrorism.

Commenting on an earlier account of military torture in Algeria by a Catholic intellectual, Pierre-Henri Simon, which had caused little stir, the editor of *Le Monde* wrote: "From now on the French must understand that they no longer enjoy the same right to condemn the torturers of the Gestapo as they enjoyed ten years ago. . . ." But Hubert Beuve-Méry's comment made practically no impression. In 1958 France was incapable of linking French behavior in Algeria with German actions in France. In an extraordinary passage in a review of *La Question* Jean-Paul Sartre, who was among the most prominent champions of Alleg's work, wrote:

> In 1943 in the rue Lauriston, Frenchmen were screaming in agony; all France could hear them. In those days the outcome of the war was uncertain and we did not want to think about the future. Only one thing seemed impossible in any circumstances: that one day men should be made to scream by those acting in our name.

The example chosen by Sartre showed an uncharacteristic degree of amnesia. For when Frenchmen "screamed" in the rue Lauriston in 1943 they *were* being made to scream by torturers acting in France's name. The rue Lauriston in Paris was the headquarters of the *Gestapo française,* the French

auxiliaries of the Nazi SS, who followed the French prime minister Pierre
Laval in hoping for a German victory.

Malraux's speech showed that Sartre's amnesia had become a national
condition, and suggested that the barracks at El-Biar would soon be as
thoroughly forgotten as the rue Lauriston. The consecration of Jean Moulin on the steps of the Panthéon in 1964 was an essential part of this
process. Lacking a body they reburied a ghost, and a patriotic legend was
born.

II

WAR

THREE

The Prefect of Chartres

A T 2:57 A.M. (Berlin time) on 17 June 1940, General Koch-Erpach, commanding the 8th Infantry Division of the *Wehrmacht*, which was advancing from Paris toward Tours on the River Loire, ordered Major Grossmann, leader of the 84th Infantry Regiment, to march on the city of Chartres at 5:30 and comb it for enemy units. Major Grossmann's request for a longer period of sleep was successful, but at 5:10 the radio crackled out with another order from the General. Grossmann was to march on the city at 7:30 sharp, sweep it thoroughly, and then continue south along Route National 10 toward Bonneval, halting for a rest at the village of La Bourdinière, fifteen kilometers farther down the road.

According to the regimental log, Grossmann's motorcycle units, followed by tanks and armored cars, entered Chartres shortly after 0800 hours (Berlin time), in other words at seven o'clock in the morning, local time. They found tank traps, gun emplacements and pillboxes, all abandoned. The sweep took over two hours. Chartres had been shelled and bombed for days but a violent thunderstorm on the previous evening had extinguished the fires. The Cathedral of Notre Dame was unharmed but the evidence of destruction was everywhere else. An army of refugees and fleeing soldiers had passed through Chartres, looting the houses left empty by the inhabitants and throwing aside anything it could not use or carry. The streets of the city were infested with stray cats and dogs but nothing else moved. There was no water, electricity, gas, telephones or radio.

One junior officer commanding a reconnaissance unit that passed by the prefecture was met by a sight he had not seen before in the four weeks he had so far spent fighting in France. Standing in line in the courtyard of the eighteenth-century building, beneath a large French flag, were three silent figures, the central one in an unfamiliar dark blue uniform, the second wearing the soutane, the black robe of a priest, the third, an old man, in a civilian suit. The officer got out of his car and asked them who they were. The man in uniform replied that he was the prefect and that he, with the representatives of the bishop and mayor of Chartres, was ready to surrender the city. The officer replied that he was not authorized to accept the surrender, and drove on. The divisional log notes that the prefect of Chartres eventually surrendered the city to General Koch-Erpach "at 9:45." At 10:00 Major Grossmann announced that there were no French troops in Chartres and twenty minutes later the 84th Infantry Regiment continued its line of march.

The last disorganized units of French troops had in fact passed through Chartres at 3:00 A.M. that same morning. They were falling back from the north and the direction of Dreux. The noise of their tanks and trucks had woken the prefect, who had gone out into the night to discover whether these "vague silhouettes" were friend or foe. But it was too dark to see and the men said nothing so he called out, "French or German?" and several voices replied, "French." "What are you doing?" "On fout le camp . . . Tout est foutu . . . On est crevé! . . ." ("We're getting the hell out of here . . . All is lost . . . We're wiped out.") The rearguard limped through on foot and the prefect went back to sleep until he was woken at 6:00 A.M. by the arrival of the vicar-general of the diocese, Monsignor Lejards, and the city's only remaining municipal councillor, Pierre Besnard, whom he had asked to be at his side when the moment came to meet the enemy face to face.

The German arrival had been expected for two days. The last French unit based in Chartres, the 1st Battalion of the 7th Motorized Dragoons, which had been covering the French retreat, had been ordered to withdraw at midnight, after which nothing stood between the city and the enemy except scattered detachments from the 26th Regiment of Senegalese Sharpshooters. The tendency of colonial troops to stand their ground and fight, with or without their officers, causing considerable German casualties, had infuriated General Koch-Erpach and when soldiers of the 8th Division of the *Wehrmacht* captured Senegalese soldiers in the Eure-et-Loir they shot them out of hand. There had been a battle between Senegalese stragglers and men of the 8th Division outside Chartres on 16 June, at the end of which the Germans shot 165 Senegalese prisoners, and stripped the bodies of their name tags. A further fifty Senegalese were rounded up and shot near Chartainvilliers, ten kilometers northeast of Chartres.

These infantrymen, speaking little French and abandoned by their officers, usually recruited from Muslim or animist villages in the West African bush, were the last French soldiers to die in defense of the spiritual center of Christian France. The fact that so many prisoners had been executed in public, and that these war crimes had been so widely witnessed, apparently troubled General Koch-Erpach and he ordered two intelligence officers on his staff to find a solution. This order was to have dramatic consequences for the prefect of Chartres, forty-one-year-old Jean Moulin.

The Battle of France lasted seven weeks, at the end of which the *Wehrmacht* had achieved, for the price of only 27,000 dead, everything that one million German dead and four years of battle had failed to achieve in the Great War. For eight months, following the declaration of war on 3 September 1939, France under its prime minister, Edouard Daladier, and Britain led by Neville Chamberlain had stood by and watched as Germany and the Soviet Union butchered Poland. A small British Expeditionary Force (BEF), initially composed of a token four divisions, had joined a French army which enjoyed a superiority over available German forces of more than three to one. But nothing had been done. War had been declared but not waged; the Third Republic had had more than enough of waging war. Then, on 10 May, the German attack had been launched in the West with nearly three million men pouring into Holland and Belgium. Within five days Holland had been defeated and the Panzers had broken through the French lines at Sedan in northeastern France and appeared to be heading straight for Paris.

Paul Reynaud, the right-wing republican who had become prime minister on 21 March, was forced to deny that the French government was about to flee from the capital, a promise he was able to keep since the German thrust continued straight ahead toward the Channel coast instead of swinging south toward Paris as it had done in 1914. This unexpected move cut the Franco-British armies in two. Reynaud did not manage to obtain the resignation of the ineffective French commander-in-chief, General Gamelin, until 19 May, by which time it was too late. On 26 May, with the allied northwestern front in chaos, the Royal Navy began to prepare the evacuation of the BEF, by now nine divisions strong, from the northern port of Dunkirk. By 4 June, when the town's defensive perimeter, which had been held by French troops, was finally overrun, more than 337,000 British and French soldiers had been taken off the beaches and landed in England. The *Wehrmacht* then turned south and began its final attack; Paris was abandoned and declared an open city on 14 June. On 16 June Reynaud, who had retreated to the southern port of Bordeaux with his government, was outvoted on his proposal to continue the fight from Algeria and resigned. His successor, the Great War veteran and national hero Marshal Pétain, asked for an armistice on the following day and this became effective at midnight on 24 June.

In France the summer of 1940 is still remembered for the speed and ferocity of the Panzer attack, for the terrifying noise made by the Stuka dive-bombers, and for the sight of up to nine million French and Belgian civilians and soldiers fleeing southwards down the roads of France. *L'exode* (the exodus), as it was known, began to spill into Chartres on 10 June, when the long convoy of buses carrying French government personnel out of Paris to Tours, south of the River Loire, passed through the city. A retired mayor of Chartres, Maurice Vidon, watched them pass by and wrote in his journal, "The panic-stricken manner of officers from the war ministry and the air ministry who were taking their families far away from Paris gave people pause for thought." Vidon noted that the bombardment of the city's outskirts by German bombers a week earlier had had a much less serious effect on public morale.

That day Jean Moulin realized that Paris was going to fall and he persuaded one of his two mistresses at the time, Antoinette Sachs, who had come to see him in Chartres, to drive him to the capital without telling anyone since he thought that if his absence from the department were known it might create a panic. Once in Paris they went directly to his flat in the rue des Plantes, where Moulin emptied a cupboard full of files belonging to Pierre Cot, his old boss. He tied them up in a sheet and loaded them into the car. No sooner had they returned to Chartres than Moulin asked Antoinette to repeat the operation alone. It is obviously significant that his chief priority on 10 June was not Chartres or his department but preventing the archives of Cot's period at the air ministry from falling into German hands.

The idea that it was possible to make two return journeys from Chartres to Paris in one day, on 10 June 1940, might seem incredible, but there is the evidence of Simone de Beauvoir to support it. On the morning of 10 June she watched an endless procession of cars leaving Paris, and when she herself left during the course of the afternoon and drove toward Chartres there were no delays until they reached the outskirts of the city. On 11 June Moulin put Antoinette Sachs to work again. Without him in her small car it was possible to load all the files at the same time. She was directed to take them to safety. The roads having by this time become completely blocked, a ministerial pass no longer had any effect. So Moulin gave her a Red Cross pass, still recognized by the police, and she set out for the south. She reached the house of the former prime minister, Joseph Paul-Boncour, a republican-socialist, at St. Aignan on the River Cher that night, and the next day she continued her journey.

Over the next three days the people of Chartres also began to drive south, leaving behind them a ghost town dominated by the two spires of an empty cathedral. The local air base was evacuated on 12 June, which meant that the air-raid sirens stopped working and the first warning of a raid was the noise of exploding bombs. On Thursday, the thirteenth, more refugees started to arrive. They came from Rouen, only eighty miles to the north, and they had seen German troops. On the morning of 14 June, with the town on fire from repeated bombing raids, the municipal fire brigade mounted their four engines and drove out under the command of Fire Captain Cochinal, carrying with them the town clerk. They explained to anyone left to listen that it was time to save the fire engines from the danger of being destroyed by fire. The town clerk was followed by the director of public works who had requisitioned the municipal dustcart. The chief water engineer then left, having closed down the reservoir and shot the guard dog. That afternoon the city was flooded with refugees and the German air force, in the absence of antiaircraft guns, abandoned bombing raids and came in at low level to machine-gun the streets. "Terror," wrote Maurice Vidon, who never left the city, "reached new heights."

On the morning of the same day, 14 June, Moulin received an order from the minister of the interior to abandon Chartres and fall back out of German reach, together with all members of his staff who were of military age. It was the last order he received from the ministry of the interior be-

fore the armistice and the first order he flatly disobeyed. In the afternoon
the German planes, attacking an undefended city, resumed bombing and
destroyed twenty more houses with incendiary bombs, apparently doing
their best to set Chartres alight. As this terrible raid continued the medical
colonel in charge of the hospital ordered an evacuation and organized a
convoy of thirty trucks to carry his patients to safety in Vannes on the
Brittany coast. Without a fire brigade nothing could be done to put out the
fires and so they burned on until the violent thunderstorm which doused
them two days later.

Moulin was again absent for much of 14 June. He had driven north directly toward the German advance to support and encourage his friend
Maurice Viollette and his subprefect, who were based in Dreux. When he
got back in the afternoon he found his own staff in a state of panic. He
evacuated them south that night. The mayor also left that day, as did the
city's entire contingent of gendarmes. The bishop of Chartres, an old opponent of Moulin's and a partisan of Franco, also drove out. Even though
Monsignor Harscouet was an adversary of the prefect, his departure is difficult to understand. His presence alone might have proved decisive in the
event of a German threat to the cathedral, and the example he could have
given might have persuaded many people to stay, particularly among the
town's anticlericals. He set out, possibly due to a certain psychological
rigidity,* to carry out an ordination of four deacons, all of military age,
who had been evacuated out of enemy reach to the south of the department.

The ordination took place on Sunday, the sixteenth, in the village of
Montigny-le-Gannelon on the banks of the river Loir, which forms the
southern boundary of the Eure-et-Loir. The service was punctuated by
the noise of shells and bombs as the enemy approached. After the ceremony was over the bishop was dissuaded from returning directly to
Chartres by the local military commander, General Hering, previously
military governor of Paris, which he had evacuated without a shot being
fired, and Monsignor Harscouet did not regain his cathedral for several
days. In the original manuscript of his war diary, *Premier Combat,* Jean
Moulin described the ordination in the south of the diocese as "oppor-
tune," an adjective later deleted. But the fact that the bishop was absent

---

* Monsignor Harscouet was in due course to give a measured but reasonably positive
welcome to Vichy's first anti-Semitic legislation, the *Statut des Juifs.*

on official duty, which was eventually carried out under enemy bombardment, seems to place his absence in a slightly different category to that of the mayor, Monsieur Gilbert, who got as far as the coastal resort of Les Sables d'Olonne before coming to an enforced halt, 235 miles from Chartres. He returned on 27 June to a rather frosty reception.

Next morning Moulin estimated that there were only about 700 citizens left in Chartres out of a population of 23,000, but they had been replaced by thousands of refugees who were seeking food, shelter and medical attention. With the departure of the gendarmes the refugees started to loot the shops and houses. Over the next three days the prefect, with the help of Monsieur Vidon, two journalists, one military dentist, one schoolteacher, four priests and twenty-two nuns, battled on. When retreating French soldiers stole his car he requisitioned a bicycle.

He managed to keep two bakeries open and organized a system of water carriers. One of the journalists became the police force. The schoolteacher became the gravedigger. Monsieur Vidon, the retired mayor of Chartres, was responsible for shooting twenty-five stray dogs and countless cats. Cows, pigs and horses grazing in the streets were rounded up. Two pro-German agitators, one of them resembling a communist *provocateur*, appeared, and the prefect managed to shout them down as they were urging a crowd to loot the bread store. Then a battalion of Dragoons, part of the 4th Armored Division which had executed two successful counterattacks under its commander, Colonel Charles de Gaulle, in May in northern France, arrived with orders to hold the line outside the city and Moulin arranged for the arrest of the professional agitator and his female accomplice. The Dragoons were ordered back after twenty-four hours and as they drove away Monsieur Vidon noted that their trucks, too, were "loaded with loot . . . and women."

The two principal hotels of Chartres, abandoned by their owners, were filled with refugees who overflowed from the bedrooms onto the staircases and wrote messages for lost members of their families on the hotel walls. One enterprising rogue broke into the wine cellar of the Hôtel de France and, posing as the hotel manager, sold off its contents at 20 francs a bottle. Everything cost 20 francs, from ordinary table wine to vintage cognac. And so it went on, until the morning of 17 June.

Jean Moulin's account of the surrender of the city of Chartres is to be found in *Premier Combat*. At seven that morning, with Monsignor Lejards to his right and Pierre Besnard to his left, he stood in the courtyard of the prefecture. They faced the French flag which flew for the last time in four years over the gateway. Shortly afterward the first enemy troops, on motorcycles, arrived, followed by armored cars. Eventually a large car stopped and several officers got out and saluted. The oldest approached them and, in French, asked who they were. Moulin identified himself and his companions, then, "according to the rules of war," surrendered the city, adding that he would guarantee a peaceful situation if the German troops respected the civilian population. The officer gave him that assurance, put him in charge of law and order and instructed him to remain at the prefecture. He added, "Tell your people that for them the war is over."

The collected memoirs of the veterans of the German 8th Infantry Division give a slightly different account of the surrender of Chartres to that offered by Moulin.

When General Koch-Erpach led the division through the city he drove past the prefect's residence. The latter, in full uniform, was standing alone in the courtyard of his residence, inside the open gateway. When the general invited him to come forward he replied that he would only consent to surrender in his official residence. The general did not have the time to accord him this pleasure and drove on.

So, with Major Grossmann's report in the regimental log, there are three different accounts of the surrender of Chartres, but they do not necessarily contradict each other. Moulin's description of the solemn declaration must have referred to the initial meeting with the reconnaissance officer, when he was accompanied by Besnard and the vicar-general. There is no mention in Moulin's account of a German refusal to accept the surrender. The second account, the divisional log, merely records the time of General Koch-Erpach's brief conversation. When the general drove on he considered the city to have been handed over. The third account, in the divisional memoirs, adds previously unknown details of this second meeting. But it may have been the incident described there—the prefect's refusal to step forward—that provided General Koch-Erpach's intelligence officers with a possible solution to a problem they had been ordered to solve, the problem of the Senegalese prisoners.

Colonial troops had been shot down, unarmed, and these executions had to be justified. It was clear that crimes must have been committed.

Since these were black troops, that was only to be expected; rape and murder of women and children would be the sort of thing needed. And since this would need French confirmation, and since Chartres contained not only a senior French official but an insolent one . . .

Moulin's account of his treatment by German intelligence officers after the surrender of Chartres also appeared in *Premier Combat*. Following the brief meeting with the general, Moulin recalled that he changed into civilian clothes and walked around the town. He saw a baker, whom he had suspected of being a German spy, arm in arm with a German officer whose first idea it was, like any tourist, to visit the cathedral. Elsewhere refugees assisted by German soldiers were systematically looting whatever remained. Since the soldiers were forbidden to "break and enter" they directed the French looters to break in and then, once the premises were open, went in themselves to pick up "what had been abandoned and left lying around." At six in the evening Moulin returned to the prefecture to share supper with a vanload of postmen from Paris who had been helping him for several days. Just then he was told that two German officers wanted to speak to him urgently. He put on his uniform and invited them to come into his office. In excellent French they asked him to accompany them to headquarters, where the general wished to speak to him on a matter of importance.

Moulin was taken to the luxurious Hôtel de France, which had been requisitioned. He never saw General Koch-Erpach. Instead, after being kept waiting under armed guard, he was told by the two officers that French soldiers in retreat had raped and massacred women and children. These shameful crimes had been committed by black troops and in order to establish the facts a protocol had been drawn up which he was required to sign. When he refused he was taken to one of the large villas on the rue du Docteur-Maunoury where a third officer, sitting in front of a typewriter, handed him the agreement. When the prefect declined even to read it the beating began. It went on throughout the evening, for what Moulin later estimated as seven hours. At one point he was driven out of Chartres to see the evidence of the crime, nine bodies of women and children laid out in a barn, obviously victims of an air raid. When Moulin pointed this out the officers took him into a nearby shed and threw him onto the truncated corpse of a woman, claiming that this too was the work of the black troops. The beating continued until 1:00 A.M., when the prefect was taken back into town and locked into a room with a Senegalese soldier who was barefoot and in shirtsleeves. There his brutalizers left him with the remark, "Since you love negroes so much we thought you'd like to sleep with one of them."

That night Moulin decided that he would not be able to take any more beating without giving in. "I knew I was at the end of my strength and that if it started again I would finish by signing." He could hear a clock striking the hours in a bell tower. The Senegalese soldier was asleep. At 5:00 A.M., just before dawn, using a piece of broken glass he found on the floor, Moulin cut his throat. His life was saved by the arrival of a guard shortly afterward.

When the guards saw the prefect drenched in blood with an open wound at his throat they took him outside and called for help. He was treated by a German army doctor, and then by Captain Foubert, the French military dentist. Moulin discovered that he was already on the grounds of the hospital, the Hôtel-Dieu, since he had been imprisoned in the hospital gatekeeper's lodge. No sooner was his wound stitched up than the same two German officers who had tormented him on the previous day reappeared and drove him back to the Hôtel de France. From the entrance hall Moulin could hear the noise of an angry row while the officer who had beaten him up made his report. A senior officer then ordered that Moulin be driven back to his residence. The prefect's ordeal was over. After four days his temperature returned to normal and he was able to resume his work with the new *Kommandantur.* Nearly three months would pass before his wound healed.

Jean Moulin's behavior when faced with the German army at Chartres on the first day of the city's occupation made him a local hero in the department of the Eure-et-Loir, and later caused him to be hailed as one of the first French resisters. His account of his experience, written nearly a year later mainly for his sister, has become a historical document and is among the most vivid and convincing eyewitness narratives of the fall of France. His description of his mistreatment was confirmed by the German and French doctors, and by many other witnesses in Chartres, including the nuns who nursed him. The nine victims of machine-gunning at La Taye were buried on 18 June by the journalist Jules Rousselot; the "dismembered trunks of two women" were buried at the same time. In other words the essential veracity of the account is well established. But like any historical document, *Premier Combat* is a legitimate subject for critical examination, and particularly so when a man's heroic legend is (unintentionally) founded on his own account.

Moulin was not the only prefect to remain behind when the army retreated. In Lille and in Blois, to name but two other towns, the prefects stayed at their posts. But the prefect of Lille had the support of the archbishop of Lille, and together they persuaded many Lillois to remain in the city, whilst the prefect of Blois, Viellecazes, who had received orders to encourage the evacuation of the town which was about to become a battleground and a point of ambush for the German army, left when Blois had been evacuated and his task was complete. Moulin's case was different since he actually disregarded an order from Georges Mandel, the minister of the interior, and he was isolated, the only official left behind. So the question arises, why did he disobey his orders? One explanation for his decision is that Moulin was acting before the armistice in the hope and belief that the army intended to make a stand further south, on the Loire. He therefore considered that his duty was to remain with those who would be temporarily stranded behind German lines and do what he could to assist them. The fact that the mayor and the bishop of Chartres had both left would have been an additional argument for him to stay.

When Moulin instructed his staff to withdraw to the south of the department he gave them a letter to post to his mother and sister. In this letter there are two curious sentences. "When you receive this," he wrote, ". . . I will, on the orders of the government, have received the Germans and been taken prisoner." The orders he had in fact already received had been to retreat. Then he added a prophetic postscript: "If the Germans, who are capable of anything, make me say something dishonorable, you will know already that it will not be true." That comment is an uncannily exact description of what was to follow. The fact that Moulin was beaten up by the German officers who were determined that he should sign a false statement is well attested, but the circumstances in which he attracted their attention seem unusual. If the German divisional memoirs are reliable his initial defiance of General Koch-Erpach suggests a recklessly provocative attitude; it scarcely mattered, after all, whether he was standing inside or outside his garden railings when he surrendered the town, particularly since his primary concern was to protect the refugees from further mistreatment. Even by his own account Moulin's attitude toward his tormentors at the beginning of his interrogation was openly contemptuous—"My smile," he wrote, "put them in a rage. . . ." The officers who had interrogated him, and who had just arrived in Chartres, accused him of being a partisan of the war and suggested that he had stayed behind in Chartres to seek a confrontation with the enemy. In this they were perhaps correct. Moulin's decision to stay and his initial attitude to the German forces could both be explained by his subconscious need to live down his memory of the First World War, when he was accused of being "a shirker."

Moulin's subsequent narrative is made deliberately inaccurate by his inclusion of reconstructed dialogue, which is sometimes unconvincing. And his description of the route the Germans took to view the dead refugees at La Taye is back to front, which may not be surprising in view of the state he was in at the time. But there is a further peculiarity toward the end of his narrative. Having been taken back into the center of Chartres, after viewing the corpses, he was subsequently driven a few hundred yards down the rue du Docteur-Maunoury from a house which he knew, to the Hôtel-Dieu, one of the most prominent buildings in the town. He then claims that, although he passed through a railed gateway and was taken out of the car and into an isolated building near tall trees, he had no idea that he was in the hospital lodge.

After he had cut his throat and been taken into the hospital, wrote Moulin, he was quick to explain what had happened to Dr. Foubert since he was sure that his best chance of rescue lay in informing as many people as possible. One of the reasons the wound in his throat did not heal was that the scar was close to the jaw. Was it not, therefore, possible that on that terrible night Moulin—realizing exactly where he was, that is, close to the hospital—inflicted a wound which would bleed and look dangerous but which would not sever a major artery; a wound which he could survive until the guards took him to the hospital? In other words his "suicide bid" was informed by his military training and was, in reality, a desperate bid to escape. This would explain why, having cut his throat, he was able to remain conscious. It would explain why the guard came so quickly—because Moulin had already heard his steps. And it would explain why Moulin awaited the guard standing up—to give the blood time to run all over his uniform. It would also explain why he was able to walk out of his cell and, with assistance, walk the considerable distance from the lodge to the hospital. Finally it would explain why, despite the wound, he was able to talk lucidly to Dr. Foubert when he got there, and why the doctor told him shortly afterward that he was well enough to return to work.

After the war, when Laure had accepted that her brother was dead, she found the manuscript of *Premier Combat* among his papers, and it was published in 1946 with a preface by General de Gaulle. One can assume that Moulin never intended it to be published in the state he left it; despite its merits as a vivid eyewitness account it reads like a first draft, and is all the more powerful for that. But in preparing the manuscript for publication someone has made several cuts. Descriptions of the state of panic of Moulin's number two, the secretary-general, have been omitted. Another cut reads:

> I am ashamed to write that the best cars left first; that it was the so-called ruling class of the bourgeoisie who gave the appalling example. I am ashamed to write that in Dreux, four days before the Germans arrived, the senior doctor jumped into his car shouting to his patients, "Every man for himself"; that in Chartres not a single doctor, apart from the dental-surgeon Dr. Foubert, stayed, and that in Châteaudun the flight of the hospital surgeon meant that many wounded patients died through lack of treatment.

The phrase "so-called ruling class of the bourgeoisie" is of course straight out of the Marxist night-school handbook.

Moulin also criticized the horde of Parisian refugees who flooded into the Eure-et-Loir. Paris, too, had emptied out four days before the Germans arrived. Moulin wrote: "Certainly they [the Parisians] had suffered the terrible moral shock of the war ... but [most of them] had been spared the real material horrors, the dive-bombers, the machine-gunning of the refugee columns, and the wounded, the old people and the dead who have just been abandoned." Later as he passed through the Place des Epars where a French armored column was being machine-gunned from the air he wrote: "Comforting sight. Oh young men with clear eyes, looks toughened by battle, springing bare-chested like young gods from your steel armor, armored horsemen of today, friends, brothers, you carry all our hopes." Later two of the "armored horsemen" (Dragoons) told him that they feared nothing, except the French antitank guns the Germans had captured. Moulin's picture of the men of the 7th Motorized Dragoons was consistently romantic. It was Monsieur Vidon who pointed out in his diary that it was soldiers from this regiment, not the refugees and deserters, who systematically pillaged the town.

But the most significant editorial cut in the original text of *Premier Combat* comes from the section describing the town after German occupation. Shortly after he had surrendered Chartres, Moulin recounted how a German vehicle-recovery unit had requisitioned his two cars, despite his objections. "My remarks were disregarded," he wrote in the published text. In the manuscript one reads a more detailed account.

> I pointed out that this seizure was [illegal] and arbitrary. But the corporal threatened me with all sorts of hell on behalf of his officers. In fact shortly afterward he returned with an officer who bellowed at me to follow him. I refused on the grounds that the divisional staff officers who had contacted me had told me to stay at my post. They left, cursing me in German.

The omission of any account of this incident in the published version makes the brutal attack on him that followed seem unprovoked, whereas Moulin had in reality twice drawn attention to the fact that he was a potential point of resistance, the sort of public official the Germans would be well advised to break. He had, after all, previously posted notices all over the department urging the population to stand firm. "People of the Eure-et-Loir," read his notice, "Your sons are fighting victoriously against the German onslaught. Be worthy of them and stay calm. . . . Don't listen to people who are spreading panic. They are going to be punished. . . . Share my confidence. We are going to win." This instruction was published in the local paper and Moulin himself went round with a bucket of paste and a roll of bills. "I've become a bill-sticker," he said, in the days before the Germans arrived.

All over the department thousands of people read these notices and obeyed them. In fifty to a hundred villages the mayor and council stayed put, the villagers followed their lead, the butcher and baker stayed to feed the community, and refugees were given food and shelter. It was the day after the prefect's notice was posted that the government ordered the evacuation of the Chartres air base, after which the prefect was alone. It seems that the Germans were not simply interested in covering up their own atrocities; they also wanted to destroy the authority of a local champion.

The notion that they were as interested in destroying Moulin's reputation as in obtaining his signature is supported by a remark the German intelligence officer made to the nun in charge of the hospital before he took the wounded prefect away. "You didn't know, did you, Sister, that your prefect had vicious habits (*moeurs spéciales*). He wanted to spend the night with a negro, and look what's happened to him." The Senegalese soldier with the crust of bread had been allotted a nonspeaking part in a sadistic farce designed as much to tarnish Moulin's reputation as to obtain his cooperation. In recent years it has been suggested by some historians that Jean Moulin was not wholeheartedly in favor of resistance in 1940. But a careful reconstruction of events in Chartres suggests that, on the contrary, he sought the "first combat" that nearly killed him.

The fall of Chartres was a stern test for Moulin's courage and an equally stern test for the staunch anticlericalism he had inherited from his father. All the institutions of the Republic had failed. The secretary-general of the prefecture, "running in every direction like a lunatic, his gas mask flapping on his shoulder," had managed to panic the entire staff. The mayor had abandoned the town, followed by the fire brigade, the police and the civil defense. Not one local doctor remained. The old and the weak were simply left behind. And Moulin found himself with his single retired mayor, one town councillor, two journalists—all right-wingers— one schoolmaster (from a Catholic school), four priests and twenty-two nuns from four different congregations who devoted themselves to the sick, the old and the orphans, and without whom all Moulin's efforts would certainly have been ineffective.

Among the priests who stayed at their posts was Canon Delaporte, who, in the absence of the bishop, ensured that mass was said in the cathedral on Sunday, 16 June. It was a sung mass and the organ may have helped to distract the congregation from the noise of the dive-bombers and machine guns in the streets outside. Canon Delaporte was a well-known figure in Chartres and a leading authority on the cathedral's stained glass. He had supervised the removal of the glass in 1918 when the town experienced its first aerial bombardment, a crisis which had given him the opportunity to study the windows at his leisure and publish his descriptive masterpiece in 1926. In August 1939 he once more supervised the removal of the glass. It was stored in over a thousand packing cases in the cathedral crypt. Then in June 1940 Canon Delaporte decided that the priceless glass would be safer in the Dordogne for the duration of the war. By the time the final bombardment of Chartres started only half of the stained glass had been driven to safety, and Canon Delaporte's presence was no doubt partly explained by the fact that the other half was still in the crypt. Also in the crypt were over one hundred elderly citizens who had simply been abandoned in the town and who were looked after by the nuns and priests until they could be moved to a more comfortable place.

In *Premier Combat* the prefect paid the nuns the following tribute.

> Finally Chartres had the sisters of St. Paul who, in these tragic hours, attained the level of their highest traditions of heroism and goodness. Inspired by the faith of Monsignor Lejards, who was to be found wherever there was danger or suffering, they became the merciful angels of our misery.

It was a tribute not only to the individuals but to the institution of the Church, an institution he had always despised but the only institution in Chartres which had done its duty. After the armistice Jean Moulin submitted a list of recommendations to the government. Of the nine people in the entire department for whom he requested the Legion of Honor, two were priests and three were nuns, and there were thirty-five more nuns on the list of those singled out to receive official congratulations.

FOUR

Zones

WITH THE DEPARTURE from Chartres of the *Wehrmacht*'s 8th Infantry Division the flickering light shed on the figure of Jean Moulin by *Premier Combat* is extinguished, and the resister is succeeded by the more familiar shadowy profile of the conscientious regional administrator. An armistice between France and Germany came into effect on 25 June. General Koch-Erpach's intelligence officers were replaced by the new permanent *Feldkommandant*, Oberstleutnant F. K. von Gütlingen, a Prussian warrior of the old school who was embarrassed by the treatment the prefect had suffered and determined to establish correct relations between the *Wehrmacht* and the people of the Eure-et-Loir. In this he was reasonably successful, thanks to the energetic cooperation of Moulin himself.

Just after his arrival, on 27 June, Colonel von Gütlingen published a list of ten hostages who would be punished in the event of any misbehavior by the population. The hostages, all volunteers from the local population, included two councillors and Canon Delaporte, and there was some criticism of the mayor, who had just returned to Chartres but had failed to place his own name at the head of the list. Since there was no misbehavior in the town Colonel von Gütlingen decided after ten days to cancel a second list, on which the mayor's name had once more failed to appear. This time the list was headed by Pierre Besnard, who had stood beside the prefect to surrender the city.

The most significant point about Moulin's life immediately after the occupation of Chartres is that he stayed on as prefect for over four months under the Vichy regime, a surprising choice for "the first French resister." This meant that he was implicated in the early policy decisions of the Vichy government. From the prefecture in Chartres he watched the surrender of authority by the members of the National Assembly as they abolished the Third Republic and voted supreme power to Pétain on 10 July. The parliament building in Paris was closed and the capital was moved to the small health spa of Vichy, mainly noted for the number of its hotels which could house the civil service. The elected parliament was suspended and the ministers were in future responsible to no one except the head of state, Philippe Pétain. A marshal of France, the equivalent of a five-star general, Pétain had been a national hero since 1916 when he conducted the stubborn French defense during the Battle of Verdun. But at the age of eighty-four he had become vain, pessimistic and anglophobic, with a failing memory and diminished powers of concentration. As a national leader at a time of crisis his greatest failing, from a long list, was his defeatism. His political views were nationalist and anti-republican. When Franco won the Spanish Civil War in 1939 Pétain had been sent to Madrid on the assumption that he would make an acceptable French ambassador. On becoming prime minister on 16 June 1940, his one and only decision had been to make a separate peace with Germany, demanding an armistice, which Hitler accorded him after six days. Having accomplished the French surrender, Pétain serenely awaited news of Britain's defeat. One condition of the armistice had been that the ships of the French fleet, the third largest in the world, should return to their home ports, most of which were on the Atlantic coast and would therefore be under direct German control. This condition represented a serious threat to Britain's security. On 3 July, after a French naval squadron stationed in the French colony of Algeria had refused a British ultimatum to surrender or sail for neutral territory, it had been sunk at anchor in the North African port of Mers-el-Kebir by the Royal Navy with the loss of over 1,300 lives. The next day the Vichy government severed diplomatic relations with Britain and on 10 August the prime minister, Pierre Laval, announced the formation of a French volunteer air squadron to join the *Luftwaffe* in attacking

England. Moulin had become a public official in a state which had effectively changed sides.

In Chartres things slowly returned to normal, initially with German help. The public services were restored one by one, the last to return being the post and the radio. The refugees reappeared, heading in the opposite direction, the Parisians once again distinguishing themselves by their point of view. One woman, reported Maurice Vidon, had applied to the *Kommandantur* for permission to steal a car so that she could get home to her Paris apartment more quickly. "The war seems to have taught the Parisians nothing," wrote the former mayor. "Some are asking the times of trains to Paris, not having noticed that the rail bridges and track have been extensively destroyed; others have been demanding priority on the grounds that they work in a munitions factory."

One of Moulin's first tasks was to punish his own staff. He had told them to withdraw 50 kilometers to the southern administrative boundary and await instructions. In fact the great majority had simply joined *l'exode*, eventually reaching Poitiers, 320 miles away, and failed to reappear until the end of the month. Moulin treated the cases of those who reappeared later than that as "desertion" and imposed penalties ranging from one month's to six months' suspension without pay. Monsieur Ressier, the sub-prefect who had only left Dreux on Moulin's orders, had been taken on as secretary-general in Toulouse and he never returned. The panic-stricken secretary-general, Chadel, unable to face either the prefect or his colleagues, managed to escape unpunished to another post.

On 13 August the first Vichy law against "secret societies" was passed, forbidding freemasons from holding any public office. Moulin circulated the forms through his department and eventually reported that only six (unnamed) officials had admitted to being masons, and all of them had stated that they had "broken all links with these secret societies." No mention was made of Maurice Viollette, the department's leading freemason, whom Moulin had appointed subprefect of Dreux. On 17 July, five days after Pétain assumed power, Vichy published the first of its anti-Semitic laws and five more were passed before Moulin left Chartres. These laws banned "foreigners" from public service and the professions and canceled thousands of Jewish naturalizations. Among the laws passed while Moulin was at Chartres was the first *Statut des Juifs,* which gave a wider definition of Jewish identity than the one adopted in Nazi Germany. Under Vichy anyone with two Jewish grandparents was Jewish, even if they had converted to Christianity. Prefects were also instructed to intern Jewish aliens or place them under house arrest.

Moulin, like all prefects, circulated the regulations requiring all Jews in the Eure-et-Loir to declare themselves and be listed. But he carried out his instructions belatedly and without zeal. Nobody was interned, and he intervened on more than one occasion in favor of Jewish doctors and teachers who were penalized in the Eure-et-Loir. With regard to the department's communists he showed more activity. The Vichy government continued to repress the communists. The Germans sometimes intervened in their favor. On Moulin's orders two men were arrested for distributing tracts critical of Pierre Laval, and the police were instructed by the prefect to keep suspected party activists under surveillance. The party newspaper, *L'Humanité*, was still banned, though underground editions denouncing "English capitalism and its war against the people" continued to circulate. On 25 August the German authorities in Paris negotiated the release of a number of French communist leaders who had been interned by the French government in 1939, but many others remained in the camps. Finally, on 26 October, Moulin learned of Pétain's famous meeting with Hitler at the railway station at Montoire, and in the days that followed he heard the Marshal's appeal for "collaboration." He worked on. Then, on 2 November, he was informed by the German authorities that the order relieving him of his functions had been signed.

Moulin's dismissal seems to have been a response to complaints from Vichy supporters in his department. Thinking of his indulgence toward the freemasons, they accused him of "continuing to apply the policies of the Popular Front," but his departure was opposed by the Germans he had been dealing with. At the end of September Colonel von Gütlingen had been replaced by Major Ebmeir. "I wanted you to know how very agreeable our life together in your house has been for me. I have respected you as a Frenchman and you have respected me as a German officer," wrote von Gütlingen in farewell. The colonel insisted on posing to be photographed with Moulin and left him a little souvenir, a signed photograph of himself as a young man in the uniform of a lieutenant in the Kaiser's army. Major Ebmeir, a colder and more aggressive character, seems to have held Moulin in even higher regard. "Moulin is a well-informed administrator of above-average ability and a high level of culture; he shows excellent judgment and a strong sense of responsibility," he reported to

Paris. When Ebmeir heard that Moulin was to be relieved he objected and asked his superiors to refuse to let the exemplary prefect go. This request was unsuccessful. At the official ceremony marking Moulin's departure Major Ebmeir made a speech in which he said, "I congratulate you on the energy with which you have defended your people's interests and your country's honor." The second part of that remark seems to have been a direct reference to Moulin's mistreatment at the time of the occupation of Chartres.

In the flood of regrets, praise, admiration and devotion which the people of the Eure-et-Loir released when Moulin left on 14 November, two comments stand out. Sister Aimée, who had nursed Moulin when he was wounded, was summoned to the prefecture before he went. She found him making his last preparations before leaving. He told her that he had not wanted to go without saying good-bye to her and thanked her for everything she had done for him. "I will always have a happy memory of Sister Aimée," he said; an incident which she recalled in a letter written in 1979. Another acquaintance, whose daughter had died in *l'exode,* wrote to him paraphrasing Napoleon's remark to Goethe: "Monsieur le Préfet, vous êtes un homme." ("Mr. Prefect, you are a man.") And he added bitterly, "The misfortune of France is that I haven't met many since I last saw you."

The armistice signed by Germany and France on 22 June 1940 was a rather one-sided agreement. In return for being allowed to administer part of French territory without military occupation—a concession which enabled the German army to redeploy forty divisions and encouraged Pétain to announce "L'honneur est-il sauf . . ." (Honor has been saved)— France had to submit to what was virtually a German *diktat* on all other points. All German POWs were freed at once, all French POWs, who numbered 1,850,000 men, were to be held until the final German victory. Twenty-five million people were living in the occupied (northern) zone, only fourteen million in the free zone (the *zone libre,* or Vichy France). The country's natural resources were all in the north, under occupation, with the exception of wine and fruit—so Vichy France depended on Germany for its meat, milk, potatoes, wheat and sugar. The coalfields, the steel industry and most of the manufacturing areas were also in the north. The Vichy government was sovereign in the unoccupied zone. In the occupied zone the French administration, including the police, remained in place, but under German military control. No mention was made of Alsace and

Lorraine, but they were annexed anyway and their populations were ruled by *gauleiters.* In these two provinces the use of French was banned, the male population became liable for conscription in the German forces and all Jewish inhabitants were expelled.

The Third Republic was chopped into little pieces, divided into seven zones. Apart from the occupied and free zones and the annexed provinces, there was a zone of Italian occupation, running along the Alps and around Nice; a "forbidden" zone, for defense purposes, which ran the length of the Atlantic coast; a northwestern "confiscated" zone which ran along the Belgian border and was administered by the military governor of Brussels; and a northeastern buffer zone, also "forbidden," which Hitler claimed on the grounds that it had once belonged to the Holy Roman Empire and would be a useful "breadbasket" for the Reich.

While these measures were applied the population watched passively, waiting for news of Hitler's inevitable invasion of England. They were largely unaware that London had in fact become the only center of French willingness to continue the fight, with the birth of the extremely small movement of Free French, or *Français libres,* led by Charles de Gaulle.

Before the outbreak of war Colonel de Gaulle was virtually unknown outside French military circles, although within the army's high command he had established a reputation as a troublesome freethinker who was obsessed with the country's need for a modern army containing a large armored component capable of moving quickly. The wisdom of his views became evident too late as the Panzers sliced their way through General Gamelin's antique battle lines. On 7 May Colonel de Gaulle had been placed at the head of a scratch armored division. He twice led his division in counterattacks which managed to regain ground from the Panzers, before being promoted to Brigadier-General and transferred to Paris on 5 June by Paul Reynaud as undersecretary of state for war. In that post he played an important role as a link between the French and British war cabinets in the last stages of the Battle of France.

On 17 June, with Pétain in office and asking for an armistice, de Gaulle disobeyed his orders and flew to London, determined to continue the fight. On the following day he made his historic four-minute speech, *l'appel du 18 juin,* the call of 18 June, from a BBC studio in Portland Place, calling on the French outside France to refuse to surrender. "The leaders who have for many years been at the head of the armed forces of France . . . have asked the enemy for a ceasefire," said de Gaulle. "It's true that we have been overrun . . . but has the last word been spoken? Is all hope gone? Is our defeat an accomplished fact? Of course not! . . . France has not lost. . . . We are not alone. France has a vast empire behind her. We can unite with the British Empire, that rules the sea and fights on . . . [and we] can count on the immense industrial power of the United States. . . . This war is a world war. . . . I, General de Gaulle, now in London, invite the officers and soldiers of France who are now or who will soon be in London, with or without their arms, to contact me." His broadcast ended with the words, "The flame of French resistance will not be extinguished."

Very few people actually heard this speech but on 28 June Churchill issued a communiqué in which he recognized de Gaulle as the leader of all the Free Frenchmen "wherever they might be." Over the following twelve months, as de Gaulle slowly put together the nucleus of an army, navy and air force, an intelligence service and a civilian administration, his name, thanks to the BBC, became very well known indeed.

As the Free French movement was being created various branches of British Intelligence were also beginning to work with French opponents of the Vichy regime. Among these was MI6 but of equal importance was the Special Operations Executive (SOE), an agency created by Churchill in 1940 with instructions to "set Europe alight." SOE, eventually commanded by Major-General Colin Gubbins, with its headquarters in Baker Street, had two sections, "F" and "RF," that were specifically directed toward France and it soon became the most important organization for transporting and operating undercover agents inside occupied French territory. Its work was divided into gathering military intelligence, organizing hideouts and escape lines, and subversion—which in the words of SOE's historian M. R. D. Foot included "rumour-spreading and other forms of propaganda . . . minor and major sabotage and [everything] from minor attacks on troops . . . to full-blooded insurrection." But initially SOE's activities in France were limited and infrequent, and completely unknown to the general population. For most French people the only evidence that there was opposition to the Vichy government inside France, and that it was supported by Frenchmen in England, came on the evening news broadcasts of the BBC. The first counterattack was verbal.

The word "resistance" had not become a catchphrase in November 1940. There was no "Resistance," the organization did not exist. Instead there was something which would be better described as "refusal," a mental re-

fusal of facts. There was the refusal to accept military defeat and the refusal to reconcile oneself to living with an occupying army, *l'Occupant,* seen
as a giant bailiff or an impersonal force, like an infection, that had to be
overcome.

In the early days of the occupation words acquired a previously unsus-
pected power and identity. *Français* was subconsciously spelled with a
small "f," *français,* something broken, tired, spent; something abandoned
by the wayside. *Liberté, égalité, fraternité*—Liberty, Equality, Fraternity—
the words written in iron on the front of the Republic's buildings, had all
been discredited. They had led to defeat. They were now replaced by *Travail, famille, patrie*—work, family, homeland—Pétain's motto, the way forward to the new France. There were other sinister words about too; *maçons,
juifs, communistes.* And *anglais*—English—that was a very bad word. When
an entire country is humiliated it needs an excuse. *Anglais.* "Have you seen
the English?" was the witty remark of the debacle. Of course no one had;
the English had climbed into their boats and left.*

One person who did see the English was Simone de Beauvoir. Having
driven past Chartres she spent the night of 10 June in Illiers, in a house belonging to "an old man with goiter." She slept in a double bed with *l'em-
ployée* (the maid). Next day they drove on without hindrance, "as far as Le
Mans," which was "full of English." After the armistice she drove back
to Paris admiring the German soldiers in their *beaux uniformes,* which
matched the color of their *belles autos.* They used petrol "abandoned by the
English . . . who had left cigarettes, petrol etc. etc. behind them, they were
in such a hurry to flee." The theme of *les Anglais* continues for some time
in her *War Journal,* side by side with the theme of *les jeunes Allemands.* Passing through Chartres on her way home she noted, with her habitual penetration, only slight bomb damage.

There was another ominous word, *antinationales.* If a nation has been
defeated "national" becomes an injured concept in need of protection. The
authorities were therefore on the lookout for *menées* (tendencies) that were
antinationales. In fact a government department was established to hunt
down these tendencies, which could, in a serious case, lead to trial and

---

* The French legend of Dunkirk bears little resemblance to its English counterpart. As
recently as 1993 the work of respected historian Henri Michel claimed that five En-
glishmen had been embarked at Dunkirk for every Frenchman. The British figures are
338,000 men evacuated, including 123,000 Frenchmen: a ratio of 2 to 1.

imprisonment. There was another threatening word, *degaulliste*, as in "saboteur" or even "terrorist." But still no sign of "resistance" as something specific, an identity, a badge, a cause.

Then out of these new, powerful words a few began to emerge as having exceptional qualities. *Patrie*, as in *Travail, famille, patrie*, found an echo in the land of the Free French. Even in London *Liberté, égalité, fraternité* had been abandoned, so great was the distrust and loathing of the Third Republic. In London this motto had been replaced by *Honneur et patrie*, Honor and Motherland, by those French who called themselves Free, *les Français libres. Libre*, free, was another word that began to gain ground, *libre* but not as in *Liberté*, and still a very long way from *libération*. So you had *patrie*, leading to *patriotes*, as in *patriotes français*, French patriots, who formed *mouvements* or *groupements* or *mouvements patriotes*. Soon *patrie* and *patriote* were interchangeable, they were claimed by those who revered the old Marshal and those who loathed him. And somewhere, inside a few people's heads, there was this stubborn but growing idea of *refusal*, of something which they would not accept. But it was not one unacceptable thing, it was various.

It was a refusal of defeat, refusal of the occupation or refusal of Vichy, in other words it was an emotion, based on pride or patriotism or politics. Those who refused defeat were often soldiers who had fought hard, and had become tired of being ordered to fall back. Those who refused the occupation were men or women who felt sick when they looked at the *Wehrmacht* in the street. A fugitive like Arthur Koestler looked at them and knew fear. He did not see *jeunes Allemands* in their *beaux uniformes* which matched their *belles autos*. He was looking at an animal that had tracked him down and pinned him against the Pyrenees.

"I limped down the bridge," he wrote in *Scum of the Earth*,

> . . . and then I saw. I saw them at a hundred yards—the dark green tanks, rattling slowly and solemnly over the roadway like a funeral procession, and the black-clad figures standing in the open turrets with wooden faces, and the puffing black motor bikes with men in black leather and black goggles on their eyes behind them, and the burning red flags with the white circle and the black spider in the middle, flapping lazily in the heat. I leant against a doorway and was sick. . . . For they had hunted me all across the Continent, and whenever I had paused and stopped, thinking there was safety, they had

come after me. . . . They had come after me all the way from Berlin to Paris, via Vienna and Prague, and down the Atlantic coast, until in this outermost corner of France they had at last caught me up.

A *cagoulard*, Gabriel Jeantet, a French crypto-fascist, looked at the German soldiers and felt rage: "They make me want to vomit," he said. One of the first acts of resistance was that of Parisian surgeon Professor Thierry de Martel, who committed suicide in protest, on the day the Germans drove into his city.

If Moulin was not yet a "resister" what was the nature of his refusal? Was it the refusal of a soldier who had never fought and so never been defeated? Or the refusal of enemy occupation, of contamination, of the wrong-colored *beaux uniformes,* the wrong accents issuing orders? Or was it the refusal of "Vichy," of the triumph of his father's enemies over the Republic, the refusal to close an argument that had raged for 150 years? Was it, in fact, a refusal of a victory for the wrong sort of Frenchman? Or was it (in view of his prewar commitment to the Popular Front) a refusal in response to orders, on behalf of a greater cause, on behalf of *la patrie des travailleurs* and of a patriotism that declined to speak its name—until it had triumphed and abolished *la patrie*?

When genuine resistance began, the crucial distinction for most people was the main division into "occupied" and "free" zones. In Vichy France it was possible to believe that the war was over, that France was now a neutral observer of other countries' conflict and that the visitors would, *sans conteste,* be Nazi Germany. In the occupied zone opinion varied over a wider spectrum. The first real resistance was only possible in occupied France, just as the extremes of pro-Nazi collaboration were only acceptable in Paris. In both zones there was an extreme sense of unreality. So, in Bron, a suburb of Lyon, in the Vinatier mental hospital, during the occupation, 2,000 out of 2,890 patients were allowed to die of exposure and starvation. Eight hundred died in the first twenty-nine months between July 1940 and November 1942, and 1,200 in the following twenty-two months. During this period the psychiatrists who continued to supervise their patients noted that their daily calorie level had dropped by forty-four percent, and used the daily ward rounds to gather data for theses which bore titles such as "The Delirium of Want." Symptoms of this condition included eating the bark of trees in the hospital grounds, eating

fecal matter and drinking urine, habits which had not previously been observed at Vinatier. Starvation was now treated as a novel form of mental
illness. What was significant about this situation was not the shortage of
food in the hospitals of Lyon—there was a general and serious food shortage throughout the city for most of the war—but the reaction of the psychiatrists, who attempted to explain away the fact that their patients were
starving to death by means of a bland professional formula.

In Paris another psychiatrist, destined to become famous, Françoise
Dolto, absorbed by her pioneering work in the psychoanalysis of children,
was delighted to move into a comfortable apartment in the rue St. Jacques,
in the 5th arrondissement, in the summer of 1942. There was a certain
choice of fine apartments, newly vacant, in Paris that summer. Since 7
June, French Jews in the occupied zone had been obliged to wear the yellow star, the deportation of Jewish aliens had been announced by the
Vichy government on 4 July and the arrest of nearly 13,000 Jews in Paris
on 16 July had led to public protests and what one prefect's report called
"une profonde indignation." Later Dr. Dolto, asked why she had agreed to
move into an apartment vacated by Jewish tenants in these circumstances,
accused herself of an "incredible naïvety."

Other effects of the occupation were more unexpected. In Paris the
suicide rate *dropped* from 2,354 in 1938 to 720 in 1944. Meanwhile, the national birth rate rose from 13.1 percent in 1939 to 15.7 percent in 1943, despite
the loss of 1.85 million sexually active men, the POWs. And children all
over the country stopped growing. In Montpellier in 1945, the number
of schoolchildren below the prewar average height had increased by 25
percent.

Resistance movements in the free zone confined themselves to research
and propaganda from 1940 until the first part of 1942. They were not faced
with the occupying power but with a French administration which allowed
them a certain amount of freedom, which was interested in contacting
them for an exchange of views, and which punished them irregularly by
sending their more active members to relatively comfortable internment
camps. As the historian François-Georges Dreyfus has pointed out in his
Histoire de la Résistance, even in November 1942 the notorious prison of Fort
Montluc in Lyon contained more black marketeers than resisters.

Organizations such as Henri Frenay's *Combat* were designed to con-
ceive and support a "secret army," but it was a secret army which was
awaiting its marching orders and which had been raised to join the battle

when the moment came to liberate France from German occupation. It had no military quarrel with the Vichy regime until February 1942, when the pro-Pétainist ultras of the *Légion des Combattants* formed a private security service, or *service d'ordre,* the SOL (*Service d'ordre légionnaire*), an armed group of army veterans intended to track down the resistance and other opponents of Pétain's *Révolution nationale.* For most people in the Vichy zone the question of resistance did not arise because there was nothing to resist; there was just the slow dissolution of hope in Marshal Pétain's policies, and belief in Nazi victory being replaced by *attentisme,* or "wait and see."

In the occupied zone matters were different. On the one hand there was an additional excellent reason to avoid resistance, which was that it was extremely dangerous. If you were caught resisting in the free zone you faced a few months in an internment camp. In the occupied zone you faced torture, deportation and death. On the other hand there was an enemy to resist, a provocation to respond to, a telephone wire to cut, an anti-German leaflet to hand on.

The story of communist activity in the occupied zone in the months following the armistice illustrates some of the complexities of the occupation. In July 1940, immediately after the occupation of Paris, two communist delegates made an appointment with the *Propagandastaffel* to request permission to republish the party's newspaper as a reward for the PCF's support for the Nazi-Soviet Pact, a classic example of collaboration. In the hope of a favorable reply the PCF had already paid a deposit of 50,000 francs to the paper's printer, Georges Dangon, the husband of Marcelle Dangon, Pierre Cot's secretary in Paris. Despite the Nazi-Soviet Pact the request was refused and so the French Communist Party remained a proscribed organization whose members were liable to arrest by the Vichy authorities in both the Vichy and the occupied zones. During this period the "party line" was that there was nothing to choose between Hitler and Churchill, and members were forbidden to join in the anti-fascist struggle even secretly within the ranks of the French resistance.

But the fact that the PCF (down from about 200,000 to about 10,000 members) had become a conspiracy meant that when the order came from Moscow to resume the armed struggle in June 1941 the party was well placed; 10,000 was a very small political party but a very large resistance network. The communist resistance movement was officially founded in

May 1941 and baptized *le Front National.* The party's most important armed group, the *Francs-Tireurs et Partisans–Main-d'Oeuvre Immigrée* (FTP–MOI) (Sharpshooters and Partisans–Immigrant Labor Force), was probably the most ruthless and threatening of the armed movements. And since the liberation the French Communist Party has never ceased to claim credit for its resistance record. And yet, throughout the occupation, the basic line never changed; the enemy was not just fascism but international capitalism and the communist resistance was not fighting for *la patrie* but for *la patrie des travailleurs* (the workers' homeland), the greater nation of comrades that stretched across frontiers. At the beginning of the war, before the fall of France, Maurice Thorez, the secretary-general of the French party, took advantage of a period of leave in November 1939 to desert from the French army and flee to Moscow, where he remained for the duration. In his absence, as in his presence, the party was at first directed by Eugen Fried, a Slovakian Jew who had arrived in France in 1930 as the representative of the executive committee of the Comintern, with full powers.

From its early days of armed resistance the FTP–MOI followed a highly unpopular policy of assassinating individual, and frequently unarmed, German soldiers in a successful attempt to trigger a policy of German reprisals. Three hostages were shot in retaliation for communist assassinations in August 1941, fifty-two in September and ninety-eight in October. The communist resistance, realizing the unpopularity of its policy, never admitted that it was responsible for the assassinations. The logic behind this policy was that the reprisals (carried out in public) would make the Germans even more unpopular than the anonymous assassins.

After the war communist propaganda claimed that the PCF was "the party of 75,000 martyrs" (*75,000 fusillés*—executed members), a figure that was for many years widely repeated by French historians although it was entirely mythical. The total number of German soldiers assassinated in France between the armistice and D-Day was a few hundred. In reprisal 40,000 hostages were shot, and the majority of them were not communists. (Apart from other considerations the party only had 10,000 members in 1939.) Furthermore, among those most at risk from the activities of the communist resistance were other members of the resistance, particularly on the noncommunist left. The party's armed groups started settling its scores with left-wing rivals as early as September 1941. Later the leaders of the French Communist Party consistently lied about the wartime "line," not only multiplying the numbers of communists shot by a factor of approximately ten, but further claiming to have supported General de Gaulle's historic appeal for resistance made on the BBC on 18 June 1940, when its underground propagandists had in fact been distributing leaflets urging French men and women to play no part in "an imperialist war."

If Vichy continued to regard the PCF with suspicion, the occupying power played a more subtle and apparently pro-communist game. In response to L'Humanité's appeal to French workers to fraternize with German soldiers, the German authorities released several hundred communist militants from prisons in the occupied zone, and when a communist-led strike broke out in the northern coal mines over working conditions, it was the German authorities who presided over negotiations between French unions and employers.

As for the noncommunist resistance during this period, if it was not yet engaged in sabotage or paramilitary operations, it was not inactive. In the southern zone, in Lyon, Captain Henri Frenay, a thirty-five-year-old staff officer, who had escaped soon after being made a prisoner of war on 25 June 1940, had joined the Deuxième Bureau (Intelligence Service) of Vichy's defeated army. From a conservative, Catholic family who were admirers of Marshal Pétain, Frenay immediately began to recruit and organize the nucleus of a resistance movement both within the army and beyond it. Within the first year of the occupation Frenay, based in Lyon, had set in place the framework of a "secret army," set up a private intelligence service and launched an underground newspaper called Vérités (Truths). Despite his reactionary background Frenay was deeply influenced by his relationship with his mistress, Berty Albrecht, a militant feminist and socialist. By fusing with the Christian Democrat movement of François de Menthon, based in Marseille, Frenay extended the membership of his group, soon to be called Combat, across the spectrum from left-wing socialists to Catholic Pétainists who found common cause in ridding France of German occupation. Combat was eventually organized into six regional commands based on Lyon, Marseille, Montpellier, Toulouse, Limoges and Clermont-Ferrand. It also succeeded in infiltrating the Vichy administration with the Noyautage des administrations publiques (NAP) (Infiltration of the Civil Service) and was sufficiently threatening for the Vichy minister of the interior, Pierre Pucheu, to kidnap Frenay's mistress, Berty Albrecht, and then summon Frenay to Vichy, on a safe-conduct, to talk about possible cooperation.

The second largest movement in the Vichy zone was founded by a political maverick, Emmanuel d'Astier de la Vigerie, an aristocrat who had started in politics on the anti-Semitic right and then become a monarchist naval officer before joining the socialist left. In his movement, *Libération*, d'Astier de la Vigerie, according to the historian Jean-François Muracciole, was hoping to unite the trade union, socialist and communist resisters. He himself was on the road to communism; although he never took a party card he became one of Moscow's reliable fellow-travelers and played a useful role in subordinating his movement to communist control. Among those who joined *Libération* in Lyon were Serge Ravanel, a pro-communist engineer, André Lassagne and Raymond and Lucie Aubrac, all of whom were either communists or supporters of close links with the communist resistance and all of whom were to play a part in the subsequent events that led to Caluire. Emmanuel d'Astier de la Vigerie, sometimes known as *l'aristocrate rouge,* the red aristocrat, did not have as much success as Henri Frenay in recruiting members to his group or in attracting them from such a wide political spectrum. He remedied this by consistently exaggerating the membership and did this so skillfully that he was eventually appointed minister of the interior in Algeria by de Gaulle. In any event few socialists were attracted to *Libération;* it became a movement that was essentially political rather than military, and its most effective activity was the publication of its newspaper, also called *Libération.* Whereas the leaders of *Combat* wanted to raise and train a secret army, *Libération,* according to J.-F. Muracciole, worked to trigger and direct a popular uprising.

A third substantial movement in the southern zone was called *Franc-Tireur* (Sharpshooter), again after its newspaper, and again based in Lyon. Founded in 1941 by Jean-Pierre Lévy, an engineer from Alsace, it attracted former members of both the monarchist movement, *Action française,* and the PCF (the French Communist Party), but its most influential supporters were either Jewish or Protestant. *Franc-Tireur* was capable of mounting armed attacks on enemy targets, but J.-P. Lévy's main role in the struggles to come was as a mediator between the extreme wings of the resistance movement.

What did membership of any of these groups amount to in the southern zone between July 1940 and February 1942? In the first place resistance was a conscious choice, not just of an attitude toward what the Pétainist regime called "the occupying forces"—and what the resistance press still called "the enemy"—but also of political preference. The early resisters of the southern zone usually had an idea of both the name and the direction of the group they chose to join. They were recruited by friendship or by chance—because they agreed to read an unlicensed newspaper, or made pro-Gaullist remarks, or were known to be hostile to Pétain. A small minority was involved in preterrorist activities, such as concealing arms or ammunition. Others agreed to help fugitives such as political refugees or RAF airmen. A few members of the Vichy police, the administration or the armed forces were also resisters. But for the great majority of resisters in the southern zone the early months were for dreaming and plotting. The early resistance saw itself as a revolutionary movement, what Henri Frenay called "une expression politique révolutionnaire." When the war was won there would be a new France, neither the Third Republic nor Pétain's bogus National Revolution, but something that had still to be invented, that would be shaped by the struggle to come and be purified by the suffering necessary to achieve victory.

In the northern zone resistance was less abstract, since the suffering had already begun. Because the organization of resistance was so much more dangerous, and contact between the initial conspiracies was more difficult, there were many more resistance groups, and many smaller ones, than existed in the free zone down south. There were about 450,000 German troops in the occupied zone in early 1941 and a highly efficient military intelligence service, the *Abwehr*, devoted to tracking down terrorism and espionage. One of the first conspiracies was formed among the anthropologists and ethnologists of the Musée de l'Homme, which included several communists who had decided to ignore the party line. Betrayed in February 1941, most of the leaders of this group were shot in the moat of the fortress of Mont Valérien to the west of Paris.

Elsewhere, former members of *Action française* formed the curiously named *Confrérie Notre Dame* (Confraternity of Our Lady) which stretched from the Dordogne to Paris. This was founded by a Gaullist agent, Gilbert Renault, known as "Colonel Rémy," and its leaders included the socialist journalist and intellectual Pierre Brossolette. A CGT union official and civil servant, Christian Pineau, launched *Libération-Nord*, which eventually linked up with *Libération* in the Vichy zone, and Henri Frenay spread his early *Mouvement de Libération Nationale* (later *Combat*) from Vichy France into occupied France, where he recruited doctors, priests and even junior judges. In a characteristically practical manner Frenay directed them to concentrate on information about German troop movements on the Channel coast and the lines of communication with the German frontier. In due course this led to followers of Frenay providing the Admiralty in London with the information which enabled the RAF to carry out low-level bombing of the German battleships in Brest harbor.

At the Sorbonne some students and professors, philosophers and geographers formed *Défense de la France*, the Defense of France, using an illegal printing press in the cellars of the university to distribute pro-English and pro-Gaullist propaganda. Early in 1941 a group of teachers, soldiers and industrialists formed the *Organisation civile et militaire* (OCM), founded on the idea that "Britain has one chance in a thousand of winning, we must help her take that chance." Gradually, during the course of 1941, as German units were moved to the Russian front, leaving only thirty divisions, or 350,000 men, in occupation, five large groups emerged. These were the OCM, *Libération-Nord*, *Défense de la France*, the communist *Front National* and a group called *Ceux de la Résistance* (Those of the Resistance), which united the survivors of Frenay's northern group, most of whom had been betrayed to German intelligence in February 1942.

Ceux de la Résistance was perhaps the classic example of an occupied-zone resistance group. The right-wing republican and diplomat Jacques Lecompte-Boinet, its founder, started as a follower of Frenay. When the original group was betrayed he crossed the demarcation line to join *Combat* but was quickly disillusioned by *la mentalité*, the political in-fighting of Vichy France, the anglophobia, hostility to the Third Republic, military paralysis and utopian daydreaming. Disgusted by the fact that he was charged 10,000 francs by professional smugglers whenever he wanted to cross the demarcation line, he gave up visiting the southern zone and slowly built up a network of cells of ten men and women throughout the northern part of the occupied zone which specialized in intelligence, sabotage or escape lines.

Lecompte-Boinet refused to work with SOE, the British secret intelligence service, because he wanted to serve *la France libre*—Free France. At the same time he remained both pro-British and suspicious of de Gaulle. He refused to unite with the OCM because he suspected the industrialists of inflating their membership. He was on friendly terms with *Défense de la France*, but with few practical consequences. The strain of life underground made resistance leaders deeply suspicious, even of each other.

FIVE

Life on Half-Pay

O N L E A V I N G C H A R T R E S in November 1940, Moulin found himself deprived of his profession. For twenty-two years he had devoted his life to a career in local government. Now that was over; he had been retired on half-pay; his professional body no longer had any use for men of his opinions, no matter how able they were. At no time does he seem to have considered returning to his earlier vocation as artist. Political cartooning was clearly out of the question and it may be that his critical faculty discouraged him from continuing with painting and etching. But he had a small collection of excellent paintings, and enough contacts to open an art gallery. The art market was active in Paris during the occupation and art dealers can build up quite a large stock in troubled times. Furthermore, an art dealer has to travel. At some point after leaving Chartres, Moulin began to develop a project for an alternative life.

The principal purpose of that life remains unclear. M. R. D. Foot in *Six Faces of Courage* has described the version which has passed into legend, and which accords with Moulin's own account.

He went back to St. Andiol, and settled down ostensibly like a good Voltairean to cultivate his garden . . . [he] appeared to be an affable man in early middle age . . . idling away his time in the pleasantest part of unoccupied France. . . . He was in fact extremely busy, sounding out the possibilities of political resistance. . . . All through these months Moulin went on quietly, gently, unobtrusively, irresistibly, encouraging people to resist, and finding out how resistance could and could not work.

In fact there seems to be little evidence that Moulin did anything of the sort. Although he had decided, even before leaving Chartres, to prepare a second, false identity, the curious thing about his life between November 1940 and September 1941 is how little effort he made to contact the various resistance movements that were beginning to emerge.

In Chartres, Moulin had issued himself a bogus identity card in the name of Joseph Jean Mercier (who signed himself "Jos."), born at Péronne on 20 July 1896, that is, one month later and three years earlier than the correct date. The photograph showed him wearing horn-rimmed spectacles. The choice of pseudonym with the same initials may have been to avoid problems arising because he carried a monogrammed wallet or diary, the similarity with his genuine birthday would have been to help an apprentice spy remember his assumed one; Péronne was a town in the Somme which he knew because he had once administered it. Its registry records had been completely destroyed during the Great War. Curiously he also altered his prefectoral identity card, issued by the personnel department of the ministry of the interior in Paris in September 1939, and identifying him as prefect of the Eure-et-Loir. To this he added a photograph of himself wearing a moustache and with an apparently unscarred throat. In other words it would seem that Moulin may have been preparing to take a false identity even before the fall of France.

Moulin's movements between 16 November 1940 and 9 September 1941 have been divided by Daniel Cordier into four periods. Initially he was in Paris for two weeks. Then he crossed the demarcation line between the occupied zone and Vichy France on 1 December, using an *Ausweis*, a German pass which Major Ebmeir had issued him in Chartres. Once across he was not officially allowed to return. During that period he had no need to adopt a false identity and he would have wanted to get his presence south of the line well attested. He stayed in the unoccupied zone for four months establishing his real identity as a retired prefect, while setting up a false identity in Marseille that would enable him to obtain exit papers.

Then on 8 April 1941 he returned to Paris, crossing the line illegally for the first time, again staying for about two weeks. He then recrossed illegally into Vichy France, where he remained for five months before receiving the Spanish and Portuguese visas he needed in order to leave France.

Moulin had arrived in Paris from Chartres in November 1940, armed with a certain amount of information about the embryonic resistance movement. Like all prefects he had been informed by the Vichy ministry of the interior that Lyon, Marseille, Clermont-Ferrand and Paris were the chief centers of dissent. Admiral Darlan, the head of the French navy, whose headquarters had been at Maintenon in the Eure-et-Loir before the debacle, was by now the Vichy prime minister, and Moulin, who had met him at Maintenon, was under no illusions about his pro-Nazi and anti-English views. On the wireless Moulin would have listened, in breach of the law, to the BBC news of the progress of the Battle of Britain and the Blitz, and might well have recognized the voice of his old friend André Labarthe, who broadcast regularly from London in 1940.

On reaching Paris, Moulin went to his apartment in the rue des Plantes and called an old friend, Pierre Meunier. Meunier had been a pre-war colleague of the first ministry, on the staff of onetime minister Pierre Cot. In September Meunier had called on the prefect in Chartres and had agreed to contact any remaining members of *la bande de Cot*. Pierre Cot himself, a noted left-winger, had escaped to the United States. Nonetheless, Meunier and the former prefect made an early call on Cot's personal secretary, Marcelle Dangon, whose husband was a member of the PCF and the printer responsible for *L'Humanité*. In Cot's absence Madame Dangon dealt with his professional affairs and forwarded his letters, a complicated task which she performed throughout the occupation. Moulin was therefore in correspondence with his old boss from the autumn of 1940.

Among his former associates in Cot's office the customs official Gaston Cusin was the most advanced in his plans for resistance. In September Cusin conceived the embryo of what was to become one of the leading resistance groups in the occupied zone, *Libération-Nord*, which recruited its leaders from the ranks of the CGT trade union and pro-socialist civil servants. Moulin had a succession of meetings with Cusin in left-bank cafés including the Deux Magots, the place where he and Cusin had formerly met to plan the Spanish arms-smuggling operation. Cusin, together with Christian Pineau, a bureaucrat in the ministry of food, was concentrating on propaganda with an underground newspaper, *Libération,** and had reactivated his network of customs officers for wartime duties. Meunier later said that together with another former Cot aide, Robert Chambeiron, he first formed a small group called *Frédéric* and then established contact with two other groups later to become significant, *Ceux de la Libération,* a socialist group specializing in intelligence and aid to fugitives, and *Ceux de la Résistance.*

Another person Moulin met during this fortnight in Paris was Maurice Panier, a former militant of the "anti-fascist" RUP peace movement and veteran of the Comintern. Panier, too, had traveled to see him while he was working in Chartres, and it is probable that Moulin knew he was in regular contact with the Soviet secret service, in the form of Harry Robinson.

All these men—Meunier, Cusin, Dangon, Cot, Chambeiron, Panier and Robinson—had shared Moulin's support for the Popular Front, and had on occasion conspired together on its behalf.

The fact that Moulin should have taken the trouble to travel to Paris to meet this group of prewar Popular Front associates immediately after he stopped working for Vichy is obviously significant. Of those mentioned, Pierre Cot had denounced the Nazi-Soviet Pact and interrupted or broken his contact with the Comintern in August 1939. But Meunier, Gaston Cusin and Chambeiron, though critical of the pact, had not condemned it. Marcelle Dangon's husband continued to work with *L'Humanité,* the French Communist Party newspaper, after the pact. Panier was among those who, in Koestler's blistering phrase, had understood that "real anti-Fascism meant supporting the Fascists." He remained a dedicated Soviet agent, as did another of Moulin's friends, André Labarthe, who had been reactivated by the GRU in July shortly after his arrival in London and ordered to spy on de Gaulle.

Harry Robinson, with whom by several accounts Moulin was on cordial terms, remained in charge of the "Red Orchestra," which, after Stalin's purge of the GPU–NKVD in 1938 and 1939 and the hemorrhage of support that followed the pact, was attempting to regain its former level of efficiency. The record of Robinson's transmissions to Moscow in the second half of 1940 shows that on four occasions he passed military information

---

* Unrelated to the southern group of that name.

from the Eure-et-Loir. It is not known whether this information came from Moulin, Panier or some third source.

To place Moulin's visit to Paris in its least patriotic light, one could summarize it as follows: his first contact with the "resistance" was with a cell controlled by Soviet intelligence. He met Maurice Panier, a full-time GRU agent, who had already traveled to see him in Chartres. Panier's controller was Harry Robinson, the GRU resident in France who during the "Phony War" (from September 1939 to May 1940) had also been the controller of Kim Philby, then a war correspondent in Paris attached to the BEF. On returning to London, Philby was swiftly recruited into the Secret Intelligence Service (MI6) and seconded to work with the newly formed SOE, whose duties included sending agents into France. In London, Philby remained in contact with Robinson, via Moscow.

Apart from his meetings with former colleagues from the Cot clan, Moulin is known to have spent one night at the apartment of his mistress, Madame Lloyd, at 32 rue de Lübeck, a house with two entrances on different streets. According to his former wife, Marguerite Cerruti, he spent another night with her in her mother's apartment in the rue Littré, after a chance encounter at the Montparnasse brasserie La Coupole. For those who see in Moulin a patriotic resister from day one, he had, by the time he left Paris and crossed the demarcation line, set up an information cell which would one day enable him to coordinate the resistance movements of the occupied zone. For those who believe that he was actually working for Soviet intelligence, he had contacted the right people to make that work most effective. By any analysis, it seems unlikely that he was merely taking the opportunity to say good-bye to his circle of Parisian friends before an absence of unknown duration.

On arriving in Vichy France on 1 December Jean Moulin traveled to Montpellier to visit his mother and sister. Laure noted that he was still unable to talk normally, and tended to choke when he was eating; the scar on his throat was still livid. It was while staying in Montpellier that Moulin wrote *Premier Combat,* his account of the German occupation of Chartres. It was at this time also that he signed a notarized agreement with his sister under which he would inherit the shares, savings and furniture left by his father, while she took the land and buildings—an arrangement that was the opposite of the usual one since it meant breaking the family connection with St. Andiol, but it gave Moulin what he needed, cash. He also began an energetic correspondence with the ministry of the interior in Vichy on the subject of his pension, which he regarded as too low.*

On 7 December Moulin took the train to Toulouse to visit Ressier, formerly his subprefect at Dreux who was now secretary-general for the Haute-Garonne. Moulin was not there to talk over old times. He remembered how Ressier had refused to leave his post until ordered out and judged that his once loyal deputy would be prepared to help again. In Toulouse he sent a message into the prefecture asking Ressier to join him in town. They met in a café, where Moulin asked to be issued an exit permit. Ressier refused. Worse, he subsequently reported the matter to the prefect of Toulouse and an account of Moulin's plan to leave the country was circulated to the Vichy border police. This police report made no mention of Moulin's false identity, which he had been too wary to communicate to his former deputy.

The solidarity of the former prefect and his deputy was a thing of the past, and Ressier, who had not been dismissed by the Vichy regime, and whose career was progressing satisfactorily, remained a dutiful public servant, as he had been in Dreux. Whatever virus it was that had turned the onetime "youngest prefect in France" into a refuser, an "antinationalist," a potential "terrorist," a possible fugitive, left the overwhelming majority of Frenchmen of his persuasion—radical, republican, anti-Catholic, patriotic, anti-fascist—the obedient servants of the new antirepublican regime. However, by denouncing Moulin to the police Ressier showed himself to be more than an obedient public servant; he was clearly a man who believed in the Marshal's program for a national revolution and was actively combatting the "antinational tendencies." In December 1940 Philippe Pétain was at the height of his prestige. From the Hôtel du Parc in the spa town of Vichy he deployed his "supreme power" as head of state, governing by decree. These decrees began in the royal manner, "We, Philippe Pétain, Marshal of France. . . ." His regime was recognized by every country in the world with the exception of Great Britain. The elected chambers, the ministers and the local authorities were all abolished. Following the famous meeting at Montoire, when Pétain was photographed shaking

---

* The official who replied to him, Maurice Sabatier, was married to one of his maternal cousins. Later, Sabatier was to become the Vichy prefect of the Gironde, based in Bordeaux. Many years after the war, Sabatier was charged with being an accomplice in the deportation of Jews from Bordeaux. He died before he could be tried.

Hitler's hand, he echoed German demands for "correct relations" by demanding collaboration with Germany, and the great majority of the French people were happy to follow him. On 18 November Pétain had been greeted in front of a huge enthusiastic crowd by the Cardinal Archbishop of Lyon, Primate of France, with the words, "Pétain is France and France, today, is Pétain. . . ." The Marshal's photograph hung in every school classroom in the country, and with his twinkling blue eyes, white moustache and military bearing, Pétain became the focus of national adulation.

Moulin, out of step with this cult, now showed a surprising facility for the skills of his new trade. It might well be asked where a prefect of the republic learned his "tradecraft"; where he learned to use the same initials, a similar birth date; where he learned to select a town hall whose records had been destroyed. Following his choice in 1934 of 26 rue des Plantes in Paris, a building with two entrances on different streets, the apartment he chose to share with Laure in Montpellier was also in a building with two entrances on different streets. He had chosen it in the summer of 1937, though it had meant several journeys from Paris to do so. It seemed Moulin had a natural talent for duplicity.

In the winter of 1940 Jean Moulin called on the subprefecture at Grasse on a quiet Saturday afternoon and made his way to the office issuing exit permits. Here he posed a question which he knew the junior clerk would need to take advice on, waited until he was alone in the room and then opened the desk, took out the official rubber stamp and stamped his passport with the required permit.

Between 7 December, the date of his fruitless visit to Ressier in Toulouse, and 11 December, Moulin spent the night in Marseille in a *hôtel de passe* with another old friend and former flatmate Louis Dolivet. It was Dolivet, a senior Comintern agent, who had lauched the RUP and who had been at the center of the Soviet prewar penetration of Pierre Cot's air ministry. Dolivet had devoted the previous weeks to helping Noel Field, the American diplomat and Soviet agent, to organize an escape line for communist refugees trapped in the Vichy zone and wanted by the police. Under the terms of the armistice agreement these fugitives were all due to be handed over to the Gestapo. Dolivet used his contacts to help Field. These contacts included the consuls of China, Czechoslovakia and Colombia in Marseille, as well as senior French army officers and former members of Pierre Cot's cabinet. Dolivet himself left France on 12 December. By his own account he had obtained a passport from a personal contact in the prefecture in, oddly enough, Toulouse; he had also obtained an exit permit and no fewer than three foreign entry visas—for Colombia, the United States and Brazil. He even had permission from the Banque de France to export U.S. $500 and 3,000 francs.

The scene of Moulin and Dolivet bidding each other farewell in a cheap hotel in Marseille is personally and politically ambiguous. Dolivet's explanation, that they had chosen a *hôtel de passe* because it was less likely to be subject to a random check by the police, raises two objections. First, there was no particular reason why either of them should have feared a police raid; second, such establishments were in fact raided more frequently than conventional hotels, although they did not require their guests to fill in the usual record card, the *fiche de police*. Dolivet recalled that before going to sleep he heard Moulin wondering aloud about the fidelity or otherwise of Madame Lloyd. He suspected her of having had an affair with Edgar Mowrer, a celebrated correspondent working for the *Chicago Daily News*. The parting of ways came at dawn. For Dolivet it was the Algiers ferry, the train for Casablanca, the boat for Lisbon, then New York, freedom, marriage and obscurity. He was never to see Moulin again.

The fact that Dolivet, with his superb contacts, should have set out leaving Moulin without exit permit or entry visa strongly suggests that, although Moulin was considering leaving France and was beginning to make the necessary arrangements, he had not reached a final decision about the nature of his resistance in December 1940. But the close friendship between the two also suggests that, just as Moulin must have known that men like Meunier and Panier were continuing to work for the Comintern, so he must have known what Dolivet knew, that Field was a Soviet agent. In other words, both north and south of the line Moulin was in contact with Soviet intelligence and his first links with the resistance were with the communist resistance-in-waiting. Furthermore, his first move was to create a false identity and wait with them.

Through his contacts with Meunier, Panier and possibly Harry Robinson, Moulin learned not only that Soviet intelligence remained active in France but what its chief objective was. For despite the success of the Molotov-Ribbentrop agreement, Soviet intelligence remained convinced that sooner or later Hitler would attack the Soviet Union. According to the memoirs of the Soviet intelligence director Pavel Soudoplatov, the NKVD analysts were convinced that Hitler would not launch this attack simultaneously with an invasion of Britain. It followed that in the months between the German invasion of France in May 1940 and the German invasion of Russia in June 1941, military and strategic information from occupied France was a leading priority for Soviet intelligence. Harry Robinson's reports to Moscow during this period regularly cover German troop movements around France. The departure of a large number of leave-trains from the Channel coastline to Germany was seen as a sign of no imminent cross-Channel invasion. The arrival of long-range artillery and airborne troops was seen as confirmation that "Operation Sealion," the German code name for the cross-Channel invasion, was still being prepared.

The military airport outside Chartres had been occupied by the *Luftwaffe,* who used it as a base for the heavy bombers of *Luftflotte 2* (the 2nd Airfleet), commanded by Field Marshal Kesselring, whose headquarters were at St. Cloud outside Paris. Another of Robinson's priorities between July 1940 and May 1941, when Goering finally admitted that the *Luftwaffe* was unable to gain control of British airspace, was German aircraft losses and morale. If, before the fall of France, Moulin had knowingly passed information about French military affairs to the Soviet Union, an ally of Nazi Germany, it would have been treason—to France; and it would mean that he was a Soviet agent. In fact none of the Robinson papers released so far contain any information about French military matters obtained before the defeat, although Robinson did obtain such information afterward.

If Moulin had been among Robinson's sources, would that have made him a Soviet agent? The answer must be yes, unless he, too, believed that Hitler would sooner or later break the pact and attack the Soviet Union. Whatever doubts Moulin may have entertained about the ultimate purpose of communist resistance, it would have been perfectly legitimate, even in 1940, to encourage all anti-Nazi resistance efforts. Even if Moulin was aware of the real activities of Robinson, Meunier, Panier and Noel Field and passively or actively assisted them, that is not conclusive evidence that he was either a fellow-traveler or a Soviet agent. The fact that he later concealed his contact with that circle is more significant.

Before his departure from France in September 1941 Moulin made very little attempt to associate himself with the growing movements of resistance present in the Vichy zone. In St. Andiol and Montpellier he remained to all appearances Jean Moulin, retired prefect and art collector, planning to open his own gallery and in correspondence with the ministry of the interior about his pension.

From the southern zone he occasionally corresponded with Pierre Cot, via Marcelle Dangon, and he saw a great deal of another mistress, Antoinette Sachs, and of Henri Manhès, a freemason and veteran of the Cot cabinet, like Pierre Meunier in the northern zone. Manhès, a military officer and veteran of the Spanish Civil War, and a senior member of the *Grand Orient* masonic group, was ten years older than Moulin and was to become his confidential agent. Whatever Moulin's true intentions may have been he confided them in Manhès. But all we can be certain of today is that during this period, when away from home, Moulin became Joseph Mercier, holder of a false identity card, a false passport and a falsified exit permit. He still had no foreign entry visa, and he made no application for the essential Portuguese transit visa until February 1941. In the same month he contacted the U.S. intelligence resident in Marseille, the vice-consul Hugh Fullerton, who broke the regulations in knowingly giving him a U.S. entry visa in his real name even though his French exit visa and passport were in the name of "Mercier." On 7 March a Marseille bank received U.S. $3,000* for Moulin sent by Pierre Cot from New York, and Cot's wife, Néna, paid for his passage from Lisbon on 14 March. The SOE office in New York was warned of his imminent arrival. But still Moulin made no move to leave France.

"Joseph Mercier" had two women in his life in 1941, his closest companion, Antoinette Sachs, and Jane Boullen, a nurse he had first met in Amiens who had crossed to the Vichy zone after being arrested by the Germans and who was now working at French air staff headquarters in Aix-en-Provence. With two women to occupy his time, two identities, a book to write, a mysterious itinerary and a watching brief in at least three conspiracies—freemasonry, Soviet intelligence and "the movement of patriots"—Moulin between November 1940 and September 1941 would have been kept reasonably busy.

Antoinette Sachs used to meet him at short notice when he telephoned her at Beauvallon, near St. Tropez. On one occasion, as recounted by Pierre Péan in *Vies et morts de Jean Moulin*, she cycled out on the road from Ste. Maxime and found him waiting for her wearing sunglasses, with a hat

---

* $3,000 was the equivalent of a year and a half's salary for the prefect of Chartres.

crammed onto his head, a scarf covering the lower part of his face. "How did you recognize me?" he asked in surprise. With Antoinette Sachs he sometimes traveled to Marseille, the magnet and jumping-off point for all the fugitives of southern France. They took separate rooms at the Hôtel Moderne. Even there he would leave her with his room key and disappear for days while she untidied his bed to make it look as though he were using it. One of the few things that are clear about Moulin's life in 1941 is that for a man on half-pay he seems to have had plenty of money.

In April 1941 Jean Moulin, for reasons unknown, decided to travel back to Paris for a short and potentially risky visit of less than two weeks. It was the first time he would have to rely on his new false identity and the journey would involve his first illegal crossing of the demarcation line; the penalties he faced if he was identified by the German police were clearly on a scale different from any sanctions that might be imposed by Vichy.

He crossed the line with the help of the former radical prime minister Joseph Paul-Boncour, whose property in St. Aignan in the Loir-et-Cher now stood on either side of the border. Moulin, who frequently saw Major Henri Manhès in his house in Cagnes, in Provence, also saw him in Paris; Manhès had by then agreed to cross the demarcation line on his behalf to maintain contact with those northern conspirators Moulin had talked to immediately after his dismissal. In Paris, Moulin once again saw Meunier, Chambeiron and, almost certainly, Harry Robinson. On 15 April, when Moulin had been in Paris for six days, the second paragraph of Robinson's message to Moscow read: "I have every reason to believe that the Americans are organizing an intelligence service. In connection with this, one of their informers who is currently in Paris, a former colleague of Pierre Cot, was able to get here by using false documents provided by an American agency. . . ." But if "the informer" referred to was supposed to be Moulin, the description does not identify him as an informer of Harry's. Someone seems to have convinced Robinson that Moulin was working for the Americans.

Daniel Cordier has concluded that because Moulin subsequently made no mention of meeting resisters in Paris in April, it means that he saw none, a reasonable conclusion if one excludes Meunier and Chambeiron from the category of resisters, as well as the GPU agents Robinson and Panier. The significant point is the date. In April 1941 French communists played no part in resistance, though they were beginning to form secret networks. After the war Henri Manhès and Maurice Panier stated that they had joined the *Frédéric* network, founded on 10 July 1940. But the official resistance records established shortly thereafter that *Frédéric* was launched on 1 January 1942—the date on which Moulin returned to France on his first official mission. The correction seems to cast doubt on Meunier's postwar claim to have been in contact with noncommunist, northern resistance groups as early as July 1940. In fact it shows that Cot's clan was in 1945 determined to conceal the fact that it had been following the communist party line in 1940.

Moulin returned from Paris to the Vichy zone in the middle of April, once more crossing through the grounds of Paul-Boncour's property at St. Aignan-sur-Cher. In the Hôtel Moderne at Marseille he found a summons waiting for him from the prosecutor's office at the Supreme Court at Riom. Dated 23 April and redirected to St. Andiol on 25 April, and then to Montpellier, it required Moulin to attend on 5 May to be questioned as a possible witness in the trial for treason of his old boss Pierre Cot. According to Antoinette Sachs, Moulin, in honor of the occasion, shaved off his moustache to match his legal identity card, but not all of it as he had to regrow it to match his illegal identity card. The results were not entirely satisfactory; at Riom he bumped into one of his former secretaries, who was struck by his unusually scruffy appearance. The record of his sworn statement to the Riom prosecutor shows that he defended Pierre Cot without reservation, describing him as "one of the most misjudged men of his time . . . whose patriotism was beyond question." He was allocated 140 francs expenses and was able to catch the last train back to Marseille, where Antoinette Sachs was waiting for him with his false papers. They made their way back to the Hôtel Moderne in single file.

While Jean Moulin was proceeding, apparently indecisively, about his business in 1941, another man engaged in inquiring into the extent of resistance, who was not French but who had been sent from the United States by Pierre Cot and Louis Dolivet, was working with more success. Howard Lee Brooks was a minister of the Unitarian Church who represented both the USC (Unitarian Services Committee), a humanitarian group active in Vichy France, and the OSS (the Office of Strategic Services, forerunner of the CIA). The USC was, in fact, a U.S. Communist Party "front." Arriving at the end of May 1941, armed with no more than a list of introductions from Dolivet, which was largely out of date, Pastor Brooks had nonetheless succeeded by the end of July in identifying and contacting all three of the main resistance groups in the southern zone, *Franc-Tireur, Libération* and *Combat* (then known as *Libération Nationale*). It is hard to believe that if Moulin had been interested in doing the same he could not have managed in nine months, with all his contacts, what Pastor Brooks achieved in only two months. Nevertheless, it was Pastor Brooks who, having met Moulin, introduced him to the de facto head of the French resistance in Vichy France and the head of *Combat,* Captain Henri Frenay. This was to be Moulin's first meeting with the leader of an operational resistance network.

The meeting made so little impression on Frenay that in later years he could no longer clearly remember whether it took place in April or August. But since the introduction was effected by Pastor Brooks, and since Brooks and Frenay did not meet until July, the date usually accepted today is late July. By that time Frenay, a regular army intelligence officer, who had started to build his movement immediately after the armistice in June 1940, had gone as far as he could without outside backing. In July 1941 his extensive secret network had three priorities: regular contact with British intelligence, arms and money. He later modified the first point to include contact with the Free French in London as an alternative option. Moulin was recommended to him as "a senior civil servant who planned to leave shortly for London" and who could act as an emissary from the *Résistance de l'intérieure* (the Resistance within France) to the British and General de Gaulle. Frenay was impressed, at their 1941 meeting, by Moulin's ignorance of the resistance. "He knew nothing about it," he later recalled.

The meeting took place in the house of a Marseille doctor by the name of Recordier at 67 rue de Rome. Frenay, who had no reason to suppose that Moulin, once abroad, would return to France, remembered that his visitor asked for as much information as possible and used a pencil to note the answers in a little *carnet* balanced on his knee. Frenay also told him what he could of other movements, in particular about François de Menthon, a right-wing, Catholic professor of law in Lyon who led a small group in Marseille called *Liberté,* and about "a movement called *Libération,*" whose leaders he himself had not met. François de Menthon was the only other resistance leader Moulin interviewed before he set out for London.

On 22 June 1941 Hitler invaded the Soviet Union. In May, on Moscow's instructions, the French Communist Party had at last taken steps to set up its own resistance movement, whose political arm was named the *Front National.*

On 19 and 20 August Moulin obtained his Spanish and Portuguese transit visas from the consulates in Marseille. On 9 September he boarded the train for Barcelona. The main line from Marseille to Avignon ran within sight of St. Andiol, but before reaching that point Moulin's train forked westward at the junction for Arles. That line runs through both Montpellier and Béziers, two towns that had loomed large in his past, then south to Narbonne, Perpignan and the frontier crossing at Cerbère–Port Bou. Had he set out from Toulouse, Moulin would have taken the line that passes Le Vernet concentration camp, which Pastor Brooks had visited, looking for clients among the 2,000 veterans of the International Brigade. On 10 April, while Moulin was in Paris, 150 of these veterans had been shot down by the police at Le Vernet; they had rioted in desperation, knowing that their only alternative was identification and selection by the Gestapo, interrogation, perhaps torture, then deportation and death.

When "Monsieur Mercier" was stamped into Spain at Port Bou it was only the third time in his life that Jean Moulin had left France. Apart from ski trips to the Tyrol and a weekend in London he had never traveled abroad. He had never been to Germany, Spain or Italy. He had never been to Corsica or Tahiti or Algeria or Bordeaux. Yet when he left France it was with the profile of a man far more committed to the defense of the Soviet Union he had never visited than he was to the cause of patriotic resistance. His first contacts with resistance had been with the communist resistance-in-waiting, and his initial reaction was to wait with them. He made no clear move to leave France until the ending of the Nazi-Soviet Pact. On reaching London he concealed his communist links. And after the war his pro-communist comrades altered the official records to conceal the fact that their group had come into existence as early as 1940.

III

LIFE

SIX

A Republican Cradle

JEAN MOULIN WAS RAISED in the belief that he was the great-grandson of "a Revolutionary soldier," that is, a direct descendant of one of those who had fought to defend the French republic in its infancy. According to his wartime companion and biographer Daniel Cordier, he was actually the great-grandson of a Napoleonic sailor who had only been five years old when the Revolution broke out, and who returned to his village in 1815, on the fall of the Emperor, to find that he had long been given up for dead and his property divided. Jean Moulin was further assured that his grandfather Alphonse, the village barber, had once been thrown into prison for his political opinions, that is, for defending republicanism. But this story was based on an incident when Alphonse became overexcited at a public meeting and insulted President MacMahon during the political crisis of May 1877. In consequence Alphonse was arrested by gendarmes and held in custody for forty-eight hours while he regained his composure. In both cases the facts, as improved by Jean's father, Antonin, were all of a piece with his own political convictions and would have helped to convince Jean that he was descended from a line of republican, progressive, anticlerical activists. The family history was in reality a little more complicated.

Alphonse Moulin was not only a barber, he was also a competent businessman. Making use of information gathered in the barber's shop he set himself up as an *agent d'affaires*, essentially a property dealer, and gained enough money from this occupation to give his son, Antonin, an extended education, much of which was provided by a Catholic school.

On leaving school Antonin attended the university of Aix-en-Provence and qualified to teach French history and literature in high school at the age of twenty, the same age as some of his pupils, so becoming the first member of the family to embark on adult life without having to undertake manual labor (the previous generations of Moulins had worked as master weavers). Two years after starting in his profession he was transferred to Béziers.

Béziers, at the time of Antonin Moulin's arrival in 1880, was the second city, after Montpellier, of the department of the Hérault. The surrounding region produced more wine, and more bad wine, than any other part of France. Its society was dominated by the rich merchants and *vignerons*, whose wealth was measured by the number of liters their land produced each year. At the turn of the century the town's population was 52,000. From Béziers one could talk to Paris by telephone for two francs a call, there were two mechanical garages in the town capable of undertaking any necessary car repairs—both equipped with inspection pits—and the principal Hôtel du Nord on the Boulevard de la Citadelle possessed a photographic darkroom for the use of its guests.

Into this vigorous and forward-looking milieu Antonin Moulin, confident of his future, fitted comfortably. He soon occupied a prominent position in the most important school in the town and intended in due course to occupy a similar prominence in the town itself. Two years after his arrival in Béziers Antonin Moulin's father died, leaving him the family property, a small farm in St. Andiol. Following his father's death Antonin made regular requests to be transferred to a school in his region of origin, probably for form's sake and with very little hope of success. For some reason, possibly a lack of money or a lack of confidence, Antonin had never continued his studies to take the *aggrégation*, which if he had passed would have qualified him to teach in the university. This omission may have been used against him when his request for a transfer was repeatedly refused.

The fact that he worked so far from his home meant that Antonin spent every available moment of leave in St. Andiol. In 1883, one year after the death of his father, he married Blanche Pègue, eighteen years old and ten years younger than he, whom he had known since childhood. On a morning in 1870 the barber's shop in St. Andiol had received the news that the village baker, Pierre Pègue, had hanged himself from a beam in the loft of his house, leaving a young widow, Clarisse, and two little daughters. This experience turned Clarisse Pègue into an authoritarian and dominating figure whose daughters were disinclined to oppose her. Blanche had the reputation of being a good housekeeper, but she remained under her mother's influence even after she was married, and Clarisse Pègue acquired the habit, despite her daughter's long annual visits to St. Andiol, of spending one of the winter months in her daughter's small apartment in Béziers.

A marriage between a man who had been brought up as an only child by his father and a woman ten years younger under the influence of an authoritarian mother might seem doomed to disaster; in fact, the marriage of Antonin Moulin and Blanche Pègue was a happy one. A baby girl was born and died in 1886, but in 1887 Blanche gave birth to a son, Joseph, and five years later to a daughter, Laure. Both Antonin and his wife spoke Provençal, and as he established himself in Béziers Antonin began to publish poems written in Provençal in the local press and to write plays. He became acquainted with the celebrated Provençal writers Mistral and Alphonse Daudet, both of whom lived close to St. Andiol. Then, as time passed, his literary interest gave way to politics.

Antonin Moulin was first elected to the town council in 1884 and made his mark during an outbreak of cholera in and around Béziers when he was one of the few councillors prepared to visit the sick in their houses. Early on he formed two important friendships in the town, which were also political alliances. The first was with Alphonse Mas, a member of the Radical Party, who was to become mayor of Béziers and a deputy in the National Assembly. The other was with an even more prominent figure, Louis Laferre, one of the founders of the Parti Radical, also a deputy and a future government minister. More important, Laferre was president of *le Grand Orient*, the largest masonic group in France. The two decades that bridged the nineteenth and twentieth centuries were the golden age of French freemasonry, a period when the majority of government ministers, in whatever ministry, were masons and when the brotherhood, with its 500 lodges and 20,000 to 30,000 members, formed what one historian has called "the only influential political network covering the entire country." As a result Laferre was one of the most powerful backstage figures in French politics.

Antonin Moulin extended his personal influence on local affairs after he became secretary of the municipal library and chairman of the library's purchasing committee. This was a key position for someone interested in forming opinions and setting standards in a provincial town where few people had the means to make a library of their own. His choice of new titles for the library's collection was significant enough, but his power to exclude books was even more satisfactory. Not content with the control he enjoyed as a teacher, elected representative and librarian, Antonin Moulin pursued a further career as a journalist and public lecturer. In each of these activities he achieved local prominence; it was the classic success story of a provincial notable.

In 1870 France's long period of peace was brutally terminated with the revival of imperial ambitions under Napoleon III and the national humiliation that followed at the hands of Bismarck. The Republic which succeeded that disaster, and in which both Antonin and Jean Moulin passed most of their lives, was destined from its conception to recapture the lost provinces of Alsace and Lorraine, to replace defeat one day with victory—in short, to make war. This victory would not only restore France's territorial integrity, it would confirm the virtue of republicanism and the depravity of republicanism's enemies. A citizen, Louis-Napoleon Bonaparte, had been elected to lead a republic. He had usurped the Republic, proclaimed himself emperor, ridiculed and humiliated his country and led it to defeat. The Republic had been restored and would in due course rectify his mistakes. Little wonder that in Moulin family legend, an imperial sailor had become a "republican soldier."

When Antonin Moulin justified his decision to enter politics he referred to duty and the public interest. If men of goodwill and moral stature did not act, he said, "the affairs of the commune would be controlled by the ambitious and the incompetent." But Antonin's great political hero was Gambetta, the man who saved the nation's honor in 1870 because he was the only socialist leader who wanted to continue the fight against Prussia after France's defeat in the Battle of Sedan. And the rhetoric Antonin used, when rhetoric was called for, which in Béziers was quite frequently, was almost imperial in its splendor; his own ideals and those of his party would only finally be achieved by fighting for "la plus grande gloire de notre immortelle république"—for the greater glory of France.

The most important national issue in which Antonin Moulin became involved during this period was the case of Captain Dreyfus. Alfred Dreyfus, a French artillery officer, was convicted of spying for the German embassy in Paris and deported for life to Devil's Island in February 1895. Dreyfus was of Alsatian Jewish stock and from the start the case against him was tinged with anti-Semitism. The conviction of Dreyfus by a military court did not at first attract widespread attention, but in 1896 the Dreyfus case became "the Dreyfus Affair" with the publication in the press of the main piece of prosecution evidence, which proved to be flimsy. It was at this stage that public opinion divided between those who instinctively defended the honor of the army and those who were convinced that Dreyfus had been chosen as a scapegoat because he was Jewish. Antonin Moulin became a convinced "Dreyfusard" in 1896. The Dreyfus Affair divided parties, friends and families. It led to a growing anti-Semitism among nationalists, royalists and partisans of the army and the Church, and to a growing conviction among the Dreyfusards that the opponents of Dreyfus were the enemies of the Republic. In 1898 the Dreyfusards decided that the principles menaced by the persecution of Dreyfus needed to be institutionalized and they founded *la Ligue des Droits de l'Homme,* the League of Human Rights. Antonin Moulin was among those who inaugurated the Béziers branch of the league in 1899, and two years later he became its president.

In September 1898 Antonin and Blanche made an exceptional journey together to Marseille to celebrate the wedding of one of his former pupils. It was the end of the long summer holidays and a joyous occasion, but it was also a time of national political tension. In Paris, on 31 August, an army intelligence officer, Colonel Henry, had cut his throat after being convicted of adding forged evidence to the Dreyfus file to strengthen the prosecution case, and the battle cries of "anti-Semite" and "antipatriot" were ringing louder than ever. On 26 September the government ordered a revision of the trial. Meanwhile on the White Nile at Fashoda, the English general Kitchener, fresh from his victory at Omdurman, was confronting a tiny French military expedition led by Capitaine Jean-Baptiste Marchand, who was proposing, with 150 native troops, to annex the entire Sudan. Egged on by the popular press in both countries, the French and British governments were being pushed into war. For French patriots the excitement aroused by the events of that autumn was at its height and nine months later, on the anniversary of the wedding night, both the bride and

Blanche Moulin gave birth. The Moulins called their fourth and last child Jean.

In Béziers, in the years following the birth of Jean, the family lived on the third floor of an apartment building overlooking the Champ de Mars, the town's parade ground. Their street was called the rue d'Alsace, named after the lost province which would one day be returned. Theirs was a new building, sunny and clean. From the balcony the children could watch the life of the great space below. The square was bordered on one side by the army barracks and was the scene of traveling fairs, circuses and weekly markets. In the far distance on a clear day they could just make out the sparkle of the Mediterranean sea. The apartment had one bedroom and two small reception rooms. Jean's parents slept in the bedroom, where he had been born, and his cot was kept there, too. His older brother slept in the *salon,* his sister, Laure, slept in an alcove off her father's study, and for most of the time she shared the alcove with one of her female cousins. So six people usually inhabited this one-bedroom flat. Among the cousins was Jeanne Sabatier, who was nine years old when Jean was born and who became his godmother.

The christening took place at St. Andiol, Jean being the first member of his family for five generations not to have been born there. He was subsequently raised by his mother in the Catholic faith and in due course made his first communion and was confirmed. The fact that, as a freethinker, Antonin Moulin permitted this has been advanced as evidence of his tolerant spirit, but the situation was commonplace. Having chosen to marry a Catholic wife in church, Antonin had promised to raise their children as Catholics. In due course he expected them to abandon their faith, as he had done. It was more unusual for an anticlerical leader like Antonin to accompany his wife to church every Sunday, but he continued to do this even after he was criticized for such a public display of tolerance by opponents within his own party.

He may have acquired this habit because, as a prominent local politician, it was useful for him to listen to the *curé*'s weekly sermons, which would regularly have taken a political direction. Or he may have done so in order to accompany his children along a path that was, initially at least, of importance to them. And there was the question of his mother-in-law, Clarisse Pègue, a lifelong Catholic with a strong influence over his wife. For Antonin Moulin to show himself as supportive and tolerant toward the family's religion was a shrewd limitation of his mother-in-law's influence. But there was also the possibility that Antonin Moulin was one of those anticlericals who are strengthened in their conviction by regular contact with the belief they have rejected. He never entirely abandoned a curiosity about an afterlife and sometimes suggested that anticlericalism was a duty reluctantly shouldered as a response to the French Church's reactionary antirepublicanism.

During Jean Moulin's early childhood Antonin's political career continued to prosper. In 1902, after sitting for most of eighteen years on the Béziers town council, he had joined the local masonic lodge, which was affiliated to the *Grand Orient,* where he was welcomed as a leading champion of anticlericalism. The eulogy supporting his application stated that "his warm love for the Republic was only equaled by his profound aversion for clericalism." In October 1904 a national scandal broke out known as the *affaire des fiches* (the index scandal). A question in the Chamber of Deputies revealed that the *Grand Orient* had been compiling an index of "untrustworthy" army officers based on the fact that they went to church. The minister of war was forced to resign, but Louis Laferre, who was the sitting president of the *Grand Orient,* justified the index, which had been designed to purge the senior ranks of the officer corps of any Catholic connections. He believed that "an army officer who goes to church cannot be trusted . . . and should not be promoted." Antonin Moulin loyally defended his friend and patron, but privately disapproved of the index.

However, the picture of Antonin Moulin as an unusually tolerant anticlerical is slightly modified by his attitude toward the religious congregations. These had become the target of radical anger during the Dreyfus Affair and Antonin had the additional motive of loathing them for their supposedly obscurantist role in education. The majority of citizens in Béziers supported secular over religious education and, encouraged by this, Antonin Moulin made the campaign against religious congregations, and in particular the teaching orders of nuns in Béziers itself, into a personal crusade. In a succession of editorials in the radical paper *L'Union Républicaine* he argued that they should quite simply be abolished and, encouraged by Laferre, he was capable of endorsing "a hatred" for the religious orders.

In the crowded little flat in the rue d'Alsace Jean Moulin, oblivious of the great ideological divisions of the day, enjoyed an uneventful, well-regulated childhood. The fact that money was short was not a cause of hardship. The worst that happened was that his toys tended to be handed on from his older brother, Joseph, having been repaired or redecorated by Antonin. In later life Moulin said that Father Christmas was the only truly sympathetic fairy-tale character he had known, and that among his happiest memories was falling asleep on Christmas Eve to dream of lead soldiers, Noah's arks and clockwork horses. There was a family crisis in March 1907, when Joseph died of peritonitis, aged nineteen. Jean remembered the loss of his brother as the loss of his chief playmate. His father was deeply affected by this death and regretted having neglected family life in pursuit of his political interests. Antonin decided in consequence to devote more time to Jean, and the youngest child's position as the focus of his father's attention gradually became more onerous.

The high point of the year for the Moulin family was the traditionally long summer holidays when father and children were free at the same time to leave Béziers for St. Andiol. There, Antonin led Laure, Jean and their female cousins on all-day bicycle expeditions across Provence, picnicking, visiting monuments and museums and speaking Provençal, the language which those members of the Moulin clan living in St. Andiol spoke fluently. There were also tennis tournaments, river-bathing parties and excursions in a pony cart and all the diversions which children cooped up in Béziers could find when they were released at the height of the summer into a village where so many of the farms, orchards and meadows belonged to members of their family. From early on Jean displayed a talent for drawing; otherwise he was a normally boisterous child, usually near the top of his class at school, who regularly received good reports from his teachers.

In 1907, two months after Joseph's death, Béziers unexpectedly became the scene of a national crisis, and the drama opened just below the Moulin family's windows. Following years of overproduction, competition from Algerian growers and the introduction of fraudulent "wines" made from chemicals and costing very little to produce, the price of wine collapsed and thousands of small wine growers in the Languedoc were ruined. On Sunday, 12 May, 150,000 men and women gathered in Béziers, many of them assembling on the Champ de Mars before marching through the streets of the city. A telegram of support from the poet Mistral was read out—in Provençal, like many of the banners. Jean and his sister, Laure, were confined by their father to the house but were allowed to watch events from the safety of the balcony. That evening and for the remainder of the week many of the demonstrators refused to leave the city. The unrest spread right across the Languedoc, and in Béziers after five days a riot broke out when the mayor, Suchon, refused to pay the rail fares of wine growers who wished to travel by train to Perpignan, which was to be the scene of the next mass demonstration. The police station inside the town hall of Béziers was set on fire and the police records were destroyed.

Throughout that summer the demonstrations held in Perpignan, Carcassonne and Nîmes increased in size. In Montpellier in June, 500,000 people gathered in protest. The region was effectively placed under martial law, and in Narbonne on 20 June the long-awaited crisis was reached. Following the arrival of 300 trains in twelve hours, another riot broke out, the subprefecture was stormed and set alight and troops opened fire, killing six rioters. At this moment the center of the crisis switched back to its point of origin. When news of events in Narbonne, fifteen miles away, reached Béziers, the 17th Infantry Regiment, based in the town, mutinied.

Unlike other regiments stationed in the Languedoc, the 17th was largely recruited from the families of local peasants, and they were incensed that the army had been used against their own people. The mutineers disobeyed their officers and marched on Béziers from Agde, where they had been redeployed as a precautionary measure. On arriving at their home barracks they broke into the armory and, marching out at battalion strength, bearing arms, they pitched their tents in the Allée Paul-Riquet, one of the principal avenues of the town. Their officers followed them and first ordered them and then pleaded with them to return to barracks.

Photographs show the troops standing beneath the trees, smoking and laughing, with their long rifles symbolically reversed, while women move among them bearing refreshments. At the same time a rumor spread that the gendarmes were marching on the town and the infantrymen, who, thanks to the generosity of the townspeople, were soon passably drunk, started discharging their weapons into the air, causing civilians to panic. Fortunately neither gendarmes nor a neighboring regiment that was still obeying orders appeared on the scene and later in the day the mutineers—following the arrival of a telegram from Paris signed by the prime minister, Georges Clemenceau, which promised no individual reprisals— retired to barracks and were disarmed.

Unfortunately the text of Clemenceau's telegram had been altered by an enthusiastic town councillor, and although the men of the 17th Infantry

Regiment were not subjected to direct reprisals for this mutiny, the regiment was shortly afterward dispatched on active service to a fortress in Tunisia, where its ranks were decimated by enteric fever within months of arriving. Twenty percent of its members died, leading to protests from the Béziers branch of the League of Human Rights. In the following year the 17th Infantry Regiment was disbanded and its surviving members were discharged.*

All these events were watched with interest by Jean, whose balcony also overlooked the barracks and who, on the day of the mutiny, had been sent home from school when the school buildings were occupied by soldiers discreetly deployed to surprise and overcome the mutineers should that prove necessary. His father wrote several articles in the local press pleading for clemency for the mutineers, many of whom, he claimed, had been forced to take part at bayonet-point, and several of whom were his former pupils and the classmates of his dead son.

It was in the following year that Jean Moulin, aged nine, began for the first time in his life to receive bad reports from school. This may have been the consequence of the disturbance provoked by his brother's death, or it may have had a more direct cause. Until then he had always been a model pupil who worked hard, behaved well and achieved high marks. Now his behavior in class deteriorated sharply. In the years that followed, matters did not improve; as he moved from junior high school to high school he became identified with his father, who was not only a figure of authority in the school but a prominent and controversial figure in the political life of the town. Graham Greene, who was also the son of a schoolmaster—in his case the headmaster—described in *A Sort of Life,* his memoir, the conflicts that this position could arouse in the mind of an adolescent boy.

> I was a foreigner and a suspect, quite literally a hunted creature, known to have dubious associations. Was my father not the headmaster? I was like the son of a quisling in a country under occupation. . . . My older brother, Raymond, was a school prefect and head of the house—in other words one of Quisling's collaborators. I was surrounded by the forces of the resistance, and yet I couldn't join them

---

* Its successor, also raised from Béziers, was butchered at Montfauçon, northwest of Verdun, in 1916, when an assault on a German strongpoint led by 300 members of the 17th left seven survivors.

without betraying my father and my brother. . . . [There was a] conflict of loyalties, loyalties to my age group, loyalty to my father and brother.

Greene was bullied for eight terms until, on the edge of a nervous breakdown, he was withdrawn from school and sent to see a psychiatrist.

Jean Moulin seems to have found a quicker solution in simply abandoning one side, his father's side, and joining "the resistance," that is in becoming not only badly behaved but a ringleader and lord of misrule.

At home, too, Jean's behavior deteriorated. He took to teasing a small female cousin who lodged with the family and who eventually became so unhappy that she had to be sent home. This bullying may have been a response to treatment he was himself receiving at school. When Jean returned home in the evening he refused to do his homework. His father became exasperated with him, and on one occasion smacked him for being inattentive while under supervision. This quite uncharacteristic incident caused a shock in the household, and the boy wept.

In any event, by the time he reached the age of fifteen, Jean had become one of the worst-behaved boys in the Lycée Henri IV. One of his father's colleagues was obliged to write in a school report that the son of the professor of French and history was "given chiefly to idleness and dissipation." At the age of sixteen, two years before the final examination, the *baccalauréat,* Jean narrowly escaped the ultimate disgrace of being held back with the class dunces to work through the entire year's curriculum again in the company of younger boys from the class below. He only avoided this indignity by submitting to a summer's cramming from his father and passing a special examination at the beginning of the new school year.

In 1913 Antonin had been "promoted" from the town council to the general assembly of the department of the Hérault, which sat in regular eight-day sessions in Montpellier in an imposing council chamber in the prefecture; its meetings were jointly presided over by the prefect. Antonin Moulin's election was part of a radical landslide and placed him beside Louis Laferre in an elected chamber. By this time the Parti Radical had developed two tendencies, one ultra-progressive and socialistic, the other more conservative and looking for its inspiration to the republican tradition. Antonin belonged to the second group. The local right-wing press ran a series of articles abusing the professor and accusing him of electoral fraud. The attacks were the more damaging and difficult to bear because they were published in *L'Union Républicaine*, the paper to which Antonin had been a valued contributor for many years but which had acquired a new publisher.

At the age of fourteen Jean remained as disenchanted with politics as he was with schoolwork. When he was not causing trouble with his friends at school he spent his time drawing in his exercise books and gazing inattentively out of the classroom window, through which over the River Orb could be seen the smudged blue line of the distant Cévennes mountains. He could sit working on one drawing for an hour or more. At home he would try to persuade his older sister to do his homework for him. He started to study German, but abandoned it and switched to English.

The summer of 1914 found the Moulin family following their usual program, setting out on the train to Avignon to spend two months in their house in St. Andiol. The newspapers were reporting the trial in Paris of Madame Caillaux, wife of former prime minister Joseph Caillaux, who was both a powerful ally of the Radical Party and an ally of the socialist and antimilitarist leader Jean Jaurès. Earlier in the year the editor of *Le Figaro*, hoping to discredit Caillaux, who was considered to be insufficiently bellicose, threatened to publish letters exchanged between him and his current wife before he had divorced his first wife. The minister's wife, Henrietta, dealt with this matter by calling on the editor in his office and shooting him dead. She was acquitted of murder by an assize jury on 28 July, a verdict which was applauded by radicals all over France, and one which may help to explain why France has never acquired a gutter press worthy of the name. But while the case was pending Caillaux was obliged to resign and his absence from the government seriously weakened the influence of Jaurès, who was himself assassinated by a nationalist visionary three days after the acquittal of Madame Caillaux and the day before France mobilized for war. By the beginning of August, with all Europe on the brink of war, the original cause of the crisis, the assassination of the Archduke Franz Ferdinand which had taken place on 28 June in Sarajevo, had long since dropped out of the news. When the proclamations of general mobilization were posted on 1 August Jean Moulin was aged fifteen, but his world had ended forever; his country was submerged in a crisis that would last for exactly thirty years and would in due course take his life and that of over 1.5 million members of his generation.

As France's colonial troops, having landed in Marseille, marched up the *route nationale* toward the front, St. Andiol as usual had a grandstand seat. The village was decked in national flags and each regiment as it marched through led by its band was applauded by the people. For the first time for many years there were no shouts of "Vive la République!" The battle cry had become "Vive la patrie! Vive la France!" Shortly after the troops had passed a sadder column, of refugees, from the north of the country arrived and Jean helped to prepare his grandmother's empty farmhouse to lodge a mother alone with five children. With these distractions the summer holidays were even more exciting than usual. By the time they were over the Germans had crossed the River Meuse, entered northern France and threatened to take Paris. Only the victory on the Marne, which seemed miraculous, prevented people from pointing out that the Republic, like the Empire it replaced, had managed to get the country invaded by the *Boches.*

In the early years of the war Jean Moulin's schoolwork showed a conventional reaction to the news reports that were available in Béziers. On one occasion, after the bombing of Rheims Cathedral, he wrote that he experienced "a violent shiver of hatred" for those he elsewhere described as "the brute unchained." Asked to choose a hero for an essay he selected Vercingetorix, an inappropriate choice—as Cordier notes—since this Gallic chief rose up against, but failed to repel, an invader and was paraded in triumph by Caesar through Rome. Jean received only $7^{1/2}$ out of 20 for his essay on Vercingetorix. A more original attitude was revealed by an essay on "armchair strategists," who abounded in the cafés of every provincial town. He wrote in this essay that it was not necessary to have been a soldier to qualify as an armchair strategist and made one of them say, "*Oui, monsieur,* on the morning after the battle of the Marne I wrote to General Joffre setting out his most sensible course of action, and he hasn't even bothered to reply." His father, who spent many hours in the cafés of Béziers taking the pulse of local opinion, would no doubt have recognized this portrait.

In one of the most successful surviving cartoons from his schooldays Jean recorded the popular attitude to *embusqués,* or shirkers. The drawing shows a tall, elegant young officer strolling down the street, dressed in spotless uniform, with polished leather riding-boots, gloves and monocle, being observed by a group of children, the smallest of whom is carrying a toy gun. The caption reads: "There goes another one who knows how to hoard France's reserves." Jean got his own back on his critical teachers by executing talented caricatures. The science master, Monsieur Maury, was shown at full length on the squared paper of a science exercise book as a disheveled and paunchy soldier, resting the butt of his rifle on his splayed boot. The caption ran: "Our last line of defense." Jean had to be careful to keep these drawings from his father, since caricatures of the French professor's colleagues were not permitted in the apartment.

In the summers of 1916 and 1917 Jean took his *baccalauréat* exam and passed both parts without great distinction. He was to all appearances an idle young man endowed with enough intelligence to cruise through an exam after making a last-minute effort, who on 20 June 1917, when he reached the age of eighteen, seemed ideal material for the army. In fact, following his father's intervention, Jean did not volunteer and he was a year too young to be drafted. Instead he was employed by the prefect of the Hérault as an assistant and registered as a student at the law faculty of Montpellier University. For Antonin, who had already lost one son under twenty and who as a member of the general assembly worked with the prefect regularly, the matter was not difficult to arrange; the immediate advantage was that Jean was not involved in the battle of the Chemin des Dames. Antonin Moulin's connections as a counsellor, a radical and a freemason were to be of similar use to his son on many occasions over the years to come.

It was after the disaster of the Chemin des Dames, an uninspired replay of the allied attack on the Somme, with French infantry being massacred by German machine guns, that the soldiers started to mutiny and desert. Throughout France the gendarmes, acting as military police, were responsible for hunting them down, and these manhunts were directed by the prefects. From his insignificant post in the prefect's outer office in Montpellier Jean Moulin was perfectly placed to observe these tragedies in their exact detail. The remoter parts of the French countryside were a refuge for thousands of deserters, and this was particularly true of southern France and departments near the Spanish border like the Hérault. Members of the military garrison in Montpellier, which was a training depot for recruits, were given another bad example by quacks and dealers in potions guaranteed to produce simulated illness leading to a medical discharge. In 1917 an umbrella repairman was sentenced in Montpellier to two years' imprisonment for selling a fluid guaranteed to produce swollen joints and open wounds to soldiers of the 142nd Infantry.

The civilian population found other lucrative means of hampering the war effort. Railway employees from Béziers, taking advantage of their free travel passes, were reported to be traveling to Castelnaudary in the department of the Aude, buying up the total stock of eggs in the town's market and returning to Béziers to resell them at a handsome profit. This perfectly legal trade was the cause of angry protests in Castelnaudary, whose egg producers did not possess free rail passes. More seriously, the prefect had to intervene in the Béziers wine market to prevent the deputy mayor of the town and two leading merchants from buying up wine in order to sell large quantities at an inflated price to the army. One evening Moulin had a humiliating reminder of how soldiers regarded young men in his privileged position. While out walking with a group of fellow students, all smartly dressed, they were set on by a band of conscripts shouting "*fils à papa*" (Daddy's boys) and "*embusqués*" (shirkers). A crowd gathered who were sympathetic to the soldiers, and the students were forced to take refuge in a café, where the waiters locked the doors.

In April 1918 Jean Moulin was brusquely torn from his university refuge when the French government, faced with the German army's last big push of the war, brought forward the age of the draft. Given the choice of the Artillery or the Engineers, he joined the 2nd Engineers and trained as a military engineer in Montpellier. He spent five months there, an unusually long training period, during which time he suffered from food poisoning and flea bites and learned to drink wine for the first time in his life. His sister, Laure, brought him extra provisions and chocolate. In July the allied counterattack began but Moulin's battalion was not called forward until 18 September. The journey across France took a week. It was Moulin's first sortie out of Provence and on the train he was comforted to meet another recruit who could speak Provençal. At journey's end they found themselves in the Vosges, in Lorraine, near Charmes, where the line had been stable since 1914.

All through the allied attacks of September and October, and the steady allied advance, Moulin's unit remained at the rear, its members playing football, undertaking cross-country runs and visiting the cinema. General Foch, the commander-in-chief, laid plans for a major offensive in Lorraine on 13 November but the armistice came two days earlier and the war ended without Jean Moulin ever coming under fire. This extraordinary good fortune, as his mother would certainly have described it, left him with feelings of regret and inadequacy, of not having played his part, for the rest of his life.

The most terrible war ever fought on French soil had ended but Moulin was not demobilized. The army at last had need of him and of men like him, from units which had never seen action. Shortly after the ceasefire the Engineers were put to work burying the bodies of soldiers who had died in the last battles near Metz. The first prisoners of war started to return and Moulin was shocked by the skeletal state of the English, who had, he wrote to his parents, been treated worse than the French. There is a photograph taken of him in November, probably after the armistice, with a comrade and two friendly girls. This almost intimate souvenir is so unusual that, as Cordier observes, it was probably not Jean who sent it home to his family. In the spring of 1919 he was posted to Paris, which he saw for the first time and where he called on some distant cousins who owned a restaurant in Montparnasse and who had a pretty daughter, Jeannette. In June 1919 he was at Verdun, where he sketched what had once been a landscape. In the year that followed the war the army made him a carpenter, a navvy and a telephone operator; as he himself said, "I was everything except a soldier." In August he got two weeks' leave, the first since his unit had been sent up eleven months before. In St. Andiol it was hot and dry. The grapes were dying on the vine. At night he could see the forest fires on the mountains of the Luberon. With his father's help he was demobilized in November.

SEVEN

A Secret Man, a Complex Man

JEAN MOULIN RETURNED from the war in which he had played no part in time to join in the first memorial ceremonies held in honor of those who had died. In Montpellier, 20,000 men and women marched to the city cemetery to hear a patriotic address. The parade was led by a rank of blind veterans. They were followed by war widows and orphans; next came the mutilated and paralyzed. Moulin occupied a modest place in the official party, as befitted a junior official in the local administration and an untried soldier. General Deville, commander of the town garrison, told the throng that 2,000 sons of Montpellier had fallen on the field of honor. (This was eighteen percent of the eligible male population, which was above the national average.) "Thanks to the elected representatives of Montpellier," said General Deville, "to its prominent citizens, and to the legal authorities, who gave a splendid example of determination and dependability, you, the people of Montpellier, came through this difficult test with flying colors in the highest interest of your country. You can be proud of the pyramid of hard work, devotion, virtue and blood which rises from French soil to heaven."

Nominally assigned to the prefecture, Moulin was actually free to devote himself to passing his law exams and to bombarding his devoted parents with postal demands for clothes, money or photographic equipment. While on secondment he was able to lead the carefree life of a student. According to Laure Moulin, in her posthumous biography of her younger brother, it was during his years as a student in Montpellier that Jean first started to become reticent about his private life. Neither she nor their parents were able to discover how he spent his time or whom he chose as his friends. With a sister's loyalty Laure associated this with his natural reserve and modesty. But his contemporaries remembered him for his flamboyant behavior, his fashionable clothes and dandified appearance. His discretion where his family was concerned was more probably due to the fact that he was leading a life which he thought would shock them, or was quite simply reveling in the opportunity to escape from the pervasive parental influence in the small and overcrowded apartment in Béziers.

Nonetheless one or two scenes from this period have been handed down. The student carnival in Montpellier in 1920 was dedicated to St. Agatha; this was due less to religious enthusiasm than to the sensational manner of her martyrdom. The carnival banner decorated with a colorful picture of the saint's breasts being cut off was painted by Moulin. Laure recalled that on another occasion her brother attended a fancy dress ball in drag, disguised *en Arlésienne,* that is, in the national female costume of Provence. In his lace bonnet and ribbons, on the arm of a taller friend, the slim figure of the prefect's assistant enjoyed a marked success among his fellow students before he removed his bonnet and revealed his identity.

In July 1921 Jean Moulin took his law degree and was accepted as a full-time member of the prefect's staff. He became deputy chief of staff, and was now qualified for a career in the corps of prefects. In his last year at university, the last days of his freedom, realizing that he would shortly have to maintain the appearance of impartiality, he joined the youth section of the Parti Radical, the nearest he ever came to making a public political commitment. Shortly after he signed up with the *Jeunesses laïques et républicaines,* the movement held a banquet which was addressed by Moulin's superior officer the prefect; there he heard his master demonstrate a superb disregard for professional impartiality, civil peace and national unity, all of which he was sworn to uphold, when, in front of his youthful audience, he said: "It was from secular schools that our soldiers drew the qualities that gave us victory. I give you the toast of France! Immortal, and inseparable from her Republic!"

One of Moulin's first duties in his new position as deputy chief of staff to Prefect Lacombe was to organize the three-day visit to Montpellier of President Alexandre Millerand which took place in November 1921. This was no minor responsibility. The president of the Republic was accompanied by five ministers, forty-six senators and deputies and five army generals. The official cortège was composed of thirty-five motorcars, and 850 people sat down for the welcoming banquet at the prefecture. Nonetheless, despite his professional preoccupations, Moulin found time to make a rather unflattering caricature of Alexandre Millerand, one of his father's particular heroes, depicting the president of the Republic with a large, hairy head and face and tiny little feet, a man well below the stature of his office as seen by the disrespectful schoolboy whose rebellious spirit survived in the young deputy chief of staff.

In the Third Republic the prefect was the representative of central government in the departments of France, and as such all-powerful. At meetings of the department's general assembly, held in the prefecture, the prefect sat beside the council's president. In addition he controlled the department's budget and was the sole link with each government ministry. The prefect was responsible for guiding or directing his department in the government's interests; and he was responsible for nourishing his department from the government's bounty. Jean Moulin's twenty-year career in the supposedly impartial but in fact highly politicized corps of prefects was marked by a succession of rapid promotions. These were due to his ferocious ambition, to his outstanding ability as an administrator—acknowledged by his supporters and opponents alike—and to his personal connections and the influence of his father—what the French call *le piston*—which he deployed with skill and determination. From November 1917 to June 1940 the Third Republic endured thirty-five different governments, but almost every administration was based on a republican, radical or socialist majority, the political family of which Antonin Moulin was a prominent regional power broker.

Moulin's professional success took place against a background of national crisis which, on more than one occasion, reached the brink of civil war. These were some of the most turbulent and violent years in France's peacetime history. The wartime "civil truce," when both republicanism and monarchism seemed to become irrelevant in face of an invasion which was repelled only after four years of struggle, was broken almost as soon as the armistice was signed in 1918. The speech which Moulin and the young radicals of Montpellier sat through in the spring of 1921 was proof of that. The hardship and anxiety of the war, the failure of the Treaty of Versailles to exact retribution from the enemy, and the economic depression of the postwar period did nothing to increase the prestige of the Third Republic, and its opponents were not slow to question its legitimacy. It was as though the ending of one conflict provoked the start of another, as though the aggression roused by the national struggle needed to find another outlet, as though the victory which had reclaimed Alsace and Lorraine and restored the frontiers of the nation had revealed a far more ominous division within those frontiers. The Republic, child of a revolution, now became the victim of the descendants of that revolution, and the unity of the war memorials, graven in stone, where monarchist and republican names were jumbled together in alphabetical order, *mort pour la France* (dead for France), was shattered in a new ideological struggle.

The first blow was struck by the left in February 1923 when "an anarchist," acting more or less alone, assassinated one of the leading figures in the monarchist movement, *Action française.* In reply the monarchists attacked and burned down the offices of two antiroyalist newspapers and mounted a punitive expedition against two leading republicans who were due to address a meeting of the League of Human Rights. One of these men, Maurice Viollette, a socialist, freemason and mayor of Dreux, who was drenched in violet ink while walking with his wife outside his apartment on the Boulevard St. Germain, later became a friend and colleague of Jean Moulin.

In February 1922 Moulin left Montpellier and went as chief of staff to the prefect of Savoy, a man called Mounier who had formerly been secretary-general at Montpellier. This was a personal appointment based on friendship, but the move to Chambéry in February 1922 nonetheless marked an important change in Moulin's life. Chambéry, the capital of the Savoy, was historically a garrison town, with its massive château providing a strongpoint that enabled whoever held it to control the Alpine passes to Italy. There was little that was familiar in this town or this region to a young man from the south. But for twenty years Moulin was not to live in Provence, or near his father, again. He continued to keep in close touch with Antonin, maintaining the imperiously dependent attitude that had developed when he first left home in 1917, and he regularly spent summer holidays in St. Andiol, but his life in Montpellier and Béziers was over. When he left Provence he also lost touch with his circle of childhood and student friends, and he had already cut his links with the friends he had made in the army.

In Chambéry Moulin took refuge first in work and then, since his work was not very demanding, in drawing and painting and increasingly in two pastimes which were not available in the provincial south, winter sports and *la vie mondaine.* The Savoy was the center of the newly fashionable ski-stations, which attracted the young Parisian élite, brilliant, sophisticated and frequently wealthy, and just the sort of contacts an ambitious young would-be prefect needed to cultivate.

In matters of lasting importance, however, Moulin remained under parental direction. In 1923, when he was twenty-four and had been absent from Provence for a little over a year, his mother and father decided that it was time he was married. The cousin he had visited in Paris, Jeannette, who was the daughter of a prosperous restaurateur, was the young person selected. Moulin was quite prepared to fit in with his father's suggestion, saying that he "probably liked Jeannette well enough to marry her," but without even waiting for this assurance from his son, Antonin had written to the prospective father-in-law setting out his scheme. Abel Auran, who had moved from Montparnasse and now owned the Restaurant du Havre near the Gare St. Lazare, replied favorably. He assured Antonin that Jeannette would bring a good dowry with her and had been provided with the sort of primary education that would suit her for a life in commerce.

Once Abel Auran met Moulin, however, he changed his mind. Deploying numerous arguments in case one would not suffice, he mentioned that the choir for the nuptial mass would have to include professional singers hired from the Opéra, that the church wedding would cost up to 18,000 francs, that Moulin's salary of 7,000 francs a year was insufficient to support a wife, and that if the wedding was to take place Jean would have to leave the service of the state and set up as some sort of businessman in Paris. Discouraged by the inflexibility of Abel Auran's reaction Jean threw in the towel, but Antonin, who did not give up easily, continued to urge his son's case. To no avail: he received a further rebuff. The Moulins finally understood; they did not have enough money, their son did not have a bright enough future, to marry the only daughter of a Parisian restaura-teur.

Before the break with Jeannette became definitive, Moulin tried to calculate when he might expect promotion. He told his father that the earliest he could expect to be appointed subprefect, so gaining a 3,000-franc pay-raise, would be in 1926 at the age of twenty-seven. "There are no examples of *sous-préfets* promoted younger than that, except for one who was the son of a member of parliament and the nephew of Charles Maurras," he told Antonin. The example he chose was that of a young man who had been given a leg up and who was also well connected to the extreme-right, a double justification for Moulin to use connections himself. And he used them to such effect that in October 1925, at the age of twenty-six, he was promoted to subprefect of Albertville, thereby becoming the youngest subprefect in France. At the time this promotion took place the minister of the interior was Camille Chautemps, who was both a radical-socialist and a senior freemason. It is probable that Moulin himself had by this time become a mason. He attended civil service meetings reserved for masons, and his promotion followed representations to a masonic minister made by a masonic deputy, Laferre, at the request of his masonic father. Whether or not he had been inducted, he was certainly seen as a friend and ally of the brotherhood and probably enjoyed more or less the same level of esteem as if he had been a member. Cordier has found no documentary trace of his membership but many of the French lodges destroyed their records before the arrival of the Nazi police in 1940.

One of the few frank and perceptive descriptions of Jean Moulin at this time was given by one of his friends:

> He had a pleasant face, which remained almost adolescent for many years. He had a sallow complexion and sometimes during a heated discussion his cheeks would grow pale. I am obliged to say that he did not always display a very pleasant character. During political discussions he would strain, often successfully, to impose his point of view. At school we would have called him, without any spiteful intentions, "a whinger." We both came from a background where politics was as popular a subject with the peasants as it was with professors. In those days it was people's daily conversational fare. In wine-growing country tongues are less bridled and we have a taste for subtle argument. He was certainly ambitious, but then we all were. . . . Moulin was just as secretive about his love-life as he was about administrative affairs. He cultivated a sense of mystery and if you saw him chatting with a friend he always looked as though he was plotting something. He was very sure of himself.

Just before his promotion Moulin slightly improved his official service record by adding a note in which he stated that he had been deputy, rather than assistant, to the private office of the prefect of the Hérault from his arrival in September 1917. The note did not falsify the record, since the correct description also remained on the file, but it added an alternative version which might swing the balance if, at any time in the future, he were to be in competition with a slightly better-qualified rival for some coveted post.

At Albertville, for the first time in his life, Moulin was running his own show. Apart from the fact that he did not have his own staff it was like having a prefecture in miniature to control, except that he reported to his departmental prefect rather than to the ministries in Paris. The job was regarded as a proving ground for high-flyers; an unimpressive subprefect might well be promoted further, but he would never reach the rank of prefect. Moulin's territory was ideal. For a start he was still within the department of his old boss, Mounier, prefect of Savoy, who would cover for him in the case of a potential disaster. Furthermore, his subdepartment bordered Switzerland, which offered the possibility of administrative problems with a national dimension. And he was even closer to the fashionable ski resorts with their influential contacts. The roads to Courchevel, Méribel and Val d'Isère all passed through Albertville, and both Chamonix and Megève were nearby.

Apart from being able to act on his own initiative Moulin was able, for the first time, to play a representative part in the cultural and social life of his district. For the first time he attended official receptions in the gorgeous blue uniform the Republic reserved for its favored servants: cocked hat with black ostrich feathers, braided military frock coat and embossed sharkskin dispatch case to hand. In Chambéry he had begun to exhibit his pictures—under a pseudonym, naturally, personal and professional discretion going hand in hand. Now, in the little town of Albertville, "Romanin"—as he signed himself—began to make more confident watercolors of the landscapes that lay all around. Among his new friends was an eighteen-year-old Parisian music student, Marguerite Cerruti, who encouraged him to send some of his cartoons of high society to the humorous magazine *Rire.*

His time at Albertville was also marked by an episode which revealed the limits of both his power and his self-confidence. His office was a splendid *hôtel particulier,* or mansion, built in the mid–nineteenth century. The house had two wings and a private park but there was no central heating;

he later remembered it as being one of the coldest buildings he ever lived in. It had the further disadvantage of being in the care of a truculent and insubordinate superintendent and gardener, who may have resented having to work for a young man of twenty-six. As time passed, Moulin's authority over this surly individual evaporated. The gardener first refused to tidy up his appearance, declining to attach a collar to his shirt even when the subprefect was expecting official visitors who would have to be admitted through the lodge. On one occasion Moulin summoned the gardener to give him some money to settle a bill, but his wife, arriving in her husband's place, explained that he was so drunk that he could not be roused and that it would be rash to entrust him with any sum of money. The gardener got drunker. After a while he refused to open the gates to visitors who arrived later than seven in the evening. "Carry on ringing the bell as long as you wish," he told one guest. "You'll be lucky if anyone hears you." When reprimanded by his superior, he would use abusive language and swear at him.

Despite a long series of complaints to the prefect in Chambéry, Moulin was unable to restore order. At first he asked for the gardener to be hauled before a disciplinary committee; then he suggested that he might be transferred, or even, in the last resort, dismissed. Nothing worked; the gardener, too, was connected, and to someone with a great deal more influence than the prefect. With his meticulous reports of the gardener's long succession of social atrocities Moulin showed how easily he could find himself out of his depth. After a while the gardener's wife, and then his daughter, began to insult the Republic's youngest subprefect. "In my opinion," wrote Moulin in his official complaint, "this employee dishonors the personnel of the departmental administration. . . . He is scruffy, rude, foul-mouthed and drunk. . . . He should be dismissed." He stayed, and Moulin had to learn to live with him.

In June 1926 Jean Moulin told his parents that he had become engaged to a girl they had never met, Marguerite Cerruti, and that he intended to get married as soon as he could. This news came as a considerable shock to Antonin and Blanche, who could not understand why Jean had presented them with a fait accompli, and whose views on the correct way for him to become engaged had been demonstrated during the affair of Jeannette. But their reproaches fell on deaf ears. Their son had been conducting an affair with Marguerite for six months, frequently in Paris, where she was studying to become a professional singer. In announcing their engagement he was, at the age of twenty-seven, demonstrating his talent for dissimulation as well as taking responsibility for his own personal future, this time unsupervised by his father.

There was, however, one serious obstacle to overcome, the opposition of Marguerite's mother, a wealthy war widow of Chambéry who had high social ambitions for her daughter and who was a well-established member of the local bourgeoisie. Madame Cerruti had no objection to Moulin in gold braid as a dancing partner for her daughter—the couple had met at a ball at the prefecture in Chambéry—but once the secret liaison was revealed Madame went to war. In response to Antonin's polite letter giving his consent to the marriage and asking for hers, she imposed a one-month silence. She refused to discuss the marriage contract (she was Marguerite's trustee) or to give her consent for the union, and Marguerite was still too young to marry without her mother's consent. Replacing his father in the front line, Jean applied the full force of his charm, his stubbornness and his diplomatic skill to overcome his mother-in-law's resistance. In August he officially broke the engagement, placing the entire responsibility on Madame Cerruti's shoulders.

Realizing that she had been outmaneuvered—her daughter would inherit the estate at the age of twenty-one—Madame Cerruti gave in with extremely bad grace, and changed tactics. If she could not prevent her daughter from being stolen from her, she could perhaps let her go and get her back later. The wedding was celebrated on 27 September 1926, three weeks after Jean's "final deadline," and only three days before both Antonin and Laure had to be back in Montpellier. Jean had been forced to agree to both a civil and a religious ceremony. The atmosphere at the wedding feast was so poisonous that in front of the guests, who included his witness, the prefect Mounier, Jean broke down and wept. Laure wrote that the sight of her brother's tears cast a chill over the occasion and seemed like "a bad omen." Madame Cerruti had already written to her son-in-law, "I wish Marguerite's father was still alive so that he could describe your conduct to you in the terms you deserve. Your much loathed Mother-in-law."

After a wedding like that, marriage itself could only be a relief, and at first all went well. Jean managed to borrow enough money from his sister, now a schoolteacher, to buy a new car. Marguerite could distract herself in furnishing and redecorating her new home. But the period of happiness was brief. Cordier has summarized the problem as a marriage between "the artist Romanin and the professional singer Marguerite Cerruti, in which the singer proved incapable of becoming a subprefect's wife." The fact that the courtship had taken place in Paris supports this view, but other factors played a part. Laure initially described Marguerite as "pretty but a bit fat," Marguerite saw her sister-in-law as "graceless, thin-lipped and intolerant." To balance the couple's social incompatibility there was the physical pleasure they took in each other's company; one of Moulin's colleagues described Marguerite as "blond, chubby and good to look at" and Jean made a nude drawing of her that confirms this description. But beyond the excitement of their courtship they seem to have had little in common. Marguerite recalled the many occasions she had been invited to listen to Jean's "brilliant" historical disquisitions, a habit acquired from his father which he indulged even during their clandestine rendezvous in Paris. After a while the round of official banquets, speeches, bridge parties and inaugurations began to pall on a young girl who had dreamed of dominating a concert hall. And, biding her time in Chambéry, there was her mother, by now feeling malevolent enough to threaten to use her right-wing contacts to block her son-in-law's future advancement.

Moulin felt sufficiently concerned about his wife's happiness by March 1928 to take her to Paris and arrange for her to resume her professional singing lessons. As they were about to set out for the station to take the train back to Albertville Marguerite invented a pretext to stay on for a few more days, leaving her husband to return alone. She then disappeared, leaving no address, and they never lived together again. In a final scene, in Madame Cerruti's apartment in Chambéry, Marguerite (whose mother had spent many months suggesting that her husband was unfaithful to her) told Jean, "My mother was right. You only married me for my money." Moulin replied, "You know that is untrue." Many years later Marguerite blamed her mother for the failure of her marriage. They were divorced, on the grounds of Marguerite's desertion, in June, just two years after Moulin had announced his engagement and a few months before Marguerite's twenty-first birthday, when her mother would have lost control of her estate.

Moulin's reaction to the failure of his marriage was as discreet as his engagement had been, and it was only as he was filing an application for divorce in Chambéry that he wrote to tell his family that the marriage was over. Up till then he had deliberately misled them about Marguerite's whereabouts, evidence that he had until the last moment been hoping for a reconciliation. When that hope faded Moulin faced a double humiliation. He had once again been rejected by the bourgeoisie he despised but aspired to join.

Throughout this personal crisis Moulin found a refuge in his work. Legislative elections were held in April 1928, and these were the first he had had to supervise alone. It was a more exacting task since the elections were held under a new system of proportional representation designed by the radical government to minimize the communist vote. The question of how far the radicals should ally themselves with the extreme-left had already divided Jean and his father. Antonin excluded the possibility of such an alliance, Jean regarded these views as old-fashioned and out of touch. In supervising political events in Albertville during this period Moulin made an uncharacteristic faux pas by publicly supporting one of the candidates, a socialist. The subsequent press criticism obliged him to justify his conduct to the prefect.

The 1928 elections in Savoy were chiefly notable for the victory in Chambéry of a young lawyer from Paris called Pierre Cot, who won the seat for Moulin's party, le Parti Radical-Socialiste, the Radical-Socialists, against the sitting right-wing candidate. Jean Moulin had first met Pierre Cot in 1925 in Chambéry, probably when the two young men were pursuing a joint passion for skiing and nightclubs. Cot was four years older, a decorated war veteran and at that time a budding right-wing politician from a Catholic background. As he searched for a seat in the Chamber of Deputies Cot's views moved to the left, settling in line with those of the Radical-Socialist Party (that is, the left-wing, noncommunist republicans) when he saw an opening in Savoy.

Cot was athletic, energetic, charming and ambitious. In a letter to his father Moulin described him as "young and brilliant"; in part because of his military record, he would always remain someone Moulin looked up to. Cot saw Moulin, at that time the prefect's chief of staff, as "young and artistic," and the two were well matched, Cot's gifts as an outstanding public speaker and leader of men being complemented by Moulin's administrative skill and application. They spent an increasing amount of time together, playing tennis, swimming, skiing and practicing, separately, the shimmy and the foxtrot, essential skills for young men setting out to conquer female hearts in Val d'Isère or Aix-les-Bains in the 1920s.

Starting well to the right of Moulin, Cot first engaged with Moulin's politics, advocating educational secularism, republicanism and human rights, and then continued on toward the left, becoming both a pacifist and a partisan of a defensive alliance with the Soviet Union. Moulin, once attached, followed Cot's lead. But in Albertville, when Cot's career was just under way, Moulin was still far from the extreme left. The best indicator of his political opinions is his published cartoons. As these became more successful, the favorite targets of his humor were the bourgeoisie and local notables and politicians, including left-wing politicians. They, together with foreigners (Germans, Americans, Africans, Arabs) and modern abstract painters, were all treated in the same slightly stereotypical manner. The socialist politician Louis Rothschild, who had taken the political alias of Georges Mandel, would not have been flattered in 1928 by the humorous study Moulin made of his head.

In January 1930, thanks once again to connections, Moulin was promoted a grade to subprefect second class and dispatched across France to the subprefecture of Châteaulin, near the great fishing port of Quimper, in Finistère, and with this move to Brittany he came up against some of the harsher realities of the subprefect's life. He no longer occupied a glamorous and socially prominent post, bordered by an international frontier, administering some of the most spectacular scenery in France. The jokes about preferring Paris "snow" (cocaine) and fashionable suntans made little sense in Châteaulin, a fervently Catholic district, a sort of Siberian wilderness for a clever young anticlerical looking for a ladder to the top. The neighboring villages bore names like St. Nic, St. Côme and Ste. Marie, and in Châteaulin itself, where all that moved was the River Aulne, the liveliest inhabitants were the salmon leaping their way upriver. The subprefecture in Châteaulin did not just lack central heating, it had no gas supply and no bathroom; wood was the only available fuel and that had to be chopped. Moulin may have comforted himself that he was now surrounded by the landscape of Gauguin, but for the dandified wit of a fashionable ski resort this was thin comfort. He missed the company of the attractive and influential crowd who gathered in Chambéry. On his arrival in Quimper he noted despondently that several members of the general assembly attended meetings dressed in Breton national costume. One of his first official tasks was to circulate an order prohibiting the sale of pornography; he had fallen among bigots, he must respect their views.

Jean Moulin remained at Châteaulin for three years, and while there one of his few consolations was the occasional presence at Quimper, only thirty miles away, of the poet and artist Max Jacob. Son of the sole bourgeois Jewish family in Quimper—his father was a prominent antiques dealer—Max Jacob was a convert to Catholicism, a conversion in which none of his Catholic neighbors in Quimper professed to believe. He was also a flamboyant member of bohemian society; wherever he went he took with him a strong whiff of corruption and Montparnasse, whose international reputation for creative license he had done much to establish. Alternately a rake and a repentant sinner who would retreat to the abbey church of St. Benoît-sur-Loire to repair his soul, Jacob was both a buffoon and a sincere patron of art with superb Parisian contacts. On his visits to Quimper he held court at the Café de l'Epée, where he presided over a circle of poetry enthusiasts.

During the day Max Jacob could be seen wandering around the town, following the tide as it flowed upriver from the port, and striking a pose whenever he passed his reflection in a shop window. He enjoyed the company of intelligent and sensitive young men and was less inclined to seduce them at the first opportunity—a relaxation of his wartime habit, when he had made himself the terror of the Swedish sailors who drank at Marie Vassilieff's canteen in Montparnasse. Jacob may have met Moulin by chance since the subprefect used to sketch on the banks of the River Odet along which Jacob followed the tide, or they may have been introduced by a mutual friend, the poet and aesthete Saint-Pol-Roux. In any event his visits to Quimper would have alleviated Moulin's boredom; they regularly spent time together and Max Jacob wrote a short and ambiguous poem in Moulin's honor one evening after they had dined in an old watermill at Pont-Aven near Quimper.* Jacob approved of "Romanin's"

---

* *Je suis ce soir, la chose est claire,*
L'heureux meunier du Finistère.
J'ai le moulin de Pont-Aven
Et le Moulin de Châteaulin.

(Tonight I am, the fact is clear,
The luckiest miller in Finistère.
I hold the mill of Pont-Aven
And I hold the Mill [*Moulin*] of Châteaulin.)

work, encouraged him to persevere and introduced him to Montparnasse, where Jean Moulin would eventually rent an apartment.

For most of his period in Brittany Moulin's political protector was the local notable Charles Daniélou, a left-wing radical deputy and repeatedly a minister, whose daughter had married a childhood friend of his. But he also kept in touch with Pierre Cot, and in December 1932 it was Cot who summoned him to Paris as a member of his first ministerial cabinet; Moulin was offered the post of deputy chief of staff by the newly promoted undersecretary of state for foreign affairs. The government fell within five weeks and Cot lost his position; Moulin then declined to join him in the air ministry, preferring, on Daniélou's insistence, to return to Châteaulin on condition that he was promoted to subprefect first class. The subprefect defended the deputy's interests in his constituency and provided discreet assistance at election time; the deputy, in turn, worked to promote a loyal subprefect. Two men, vaguely linked by a family connection, put their talents and influence to work for their mutual good. Moulin's promotion to first class was an essential preliminary to mounting the next rung of the ladder, secretary-general.

The decision to decline Cot's offer could not have been easy. Cot had entered the air ministry in a blaze of publicity; since his initial election in Chambéry in 1928 he had become the leader of the "Young Turks" of the republican movement, closely allied to the socialists at home and advocating a foreign policy that was both pacifist and pro-Soviet in response to the perceived threat of a third conflict with Germany. The announcement, by the radical-socialist prime minister Edouard Daladier, of Cot's promotion to the newly formed air ministry was seen as "a provocation" by the French right. So Moulin's decision to turn down the chance to be associated with this bold move, and to abandon the pleasures of a ministerial post in Paris for the obscure problems of the people of Finistère, is a clear measure of his priorities: professional advancement before political ambition. Back on duty he wrote to a friend, "It's not a bad thing to leave one's 'hole' now and again. And if the hole is called Châteaulin, it's essential."

His habitual escape route was by the night-train to Montparnasse, a district of Paris which began to exert a powerful attraction. When he was not in Montparnasse he took the night-train to Megève, only twenty miles from Albertville, where he could ski and dance in nightclubs and where the discreet young administrator and sensitive Sunday painter developed a third identity, what Cordier has described as the "sous-préfet en play-boy."

Moulin's annual salary had by now risen to 38,000 francs. He bought a Citroën sports car with a folding roof and spent some time in Paris kitting himself out elegantly for the slopes. In his private correspondence he wrote of the "grosse proportion de jolies femmes" and added, "Megève smells of sex-appeal," before going on to describe his seduction of the young mistress of an absentee industrialist. First he invited her to a gala evening at some distance from Megève, brushing aside her objections about how she would get home. "A few languorous tangos, several glasses of champagne . . . At two o'clock in the morning there were no taxis, but plenty of hotel rooms. . . . 'But I have no pajamas,' 'Don't worry, I'll lend you mine.' . . . Cue the violins." It is the idle world of his cartoons come to life, spiced with perhaps just a hint of revenge, to heal the wounds of an earlier humiliation.

The spectacle provided by this well-connected and brilliant young subprefect proved to be more than the prefect of Finistère—newly appointed the year before—could stand, and early in 1933 he decided to provoke an argument that would encourage his overprivileged subordinate to apply for a transfer. The battleground was the subprefect's entitlement to a free pass for a toll-bridge he had to use when traveling around his sector. Quickly divining the real issues at stake, Moulin displayed a certain self-confidence, even arrogance, in calling his superior officer "un con" (an ass), and his transfer came through within two months. His battle with the prefect of Finistère revealed a new man, a man who felt himself well-enough protected by two ministers to treat a tiresome superior with open contempt. The negotiation of Moulin's transfer had been a delicate operation. The prefect, having removed his travel pass, so rebuking and humiliating him, had then refused him permission to leave his post and go to Paris, knowing that he wanted to interview their joint superiors in the ministry. Moulin's response was to point out that if he had to pay for the toll-bridge he would stop using his car and take the bus, which would be at public expense. At that point the prefect authorized him to travel to Paris.

For five months Moulin took refuge in the subprefecture at Thonon-les-Bains, back in Savoy and on the shores of Lake Geneva. He had kept the true nature of his problems with the prefect of Finistère from his family until the matter was settled. His father was by now seventy-five years old and his influence was exhausted—Louis Laferre had died in 1929. Moulin may have felt the time had come for him to be offering help rather than asking for it. In October 1933 he was rescued by Pierre Cot and installed as chief of staff to the dynamic minister of the air. From now on his relationship with Charles Daniélou remained friendly but distant. For the next eight years his master would be Cot.

The profile of Jean Moulin at this time, aged thirty-four, was that of a successful young administrator, a divorcé with a crowded social life who had added personal authority and professional judgment to his native ability, and who showed no sign of being burdened with a political ideology. He had abandoned his father's nineteenth-century radicalism, but he remained within the family tradition of republicanism and a firm supporter of the radical-socialist political grouping which dominated the last years of the Third Republic. He was antimonarchist, anticlerical and a supporter of the civil rights movement; he was probably a freemason but chiefly interested in party politics as a way of furthering his own ambitions.

Cot's choice of Moulin was announced in October 1933, just after the minister had returned from an official visit to the Soviet Union during which the Soviet government had privately proposed a Franco-Soviet defense pact. The death toll from the Ukraine famine had reached six million by the time of Cot's visit, but he was among the many official visitors who quite failed to notice that a state of famine was in place. Even in Moscow the famine is estimated to have raised the mortality rate by fifty percent. Italian diplomats reported frequent cases of cannibalism during this period and if Cot was offered Soviet pâté at any of the official banquets he may well have consumed human liver.

While Antonin and Jean Moulin and their thousands of fellow radicals had been struggling to build the Republic and defend it from its enemies, another political tendency had been at work, intent on destroying that Republic and replacing it with the rival concept of *la Patrie,* or the Homeland. The monarchist principle was revived by the movement *Action française,* which was conceived by Charles Maurras as a direct consequence of the Dreyfus Affair at the same time as Moulin himself had been conceived. The exhilaration which had possessed Antonin Moulin in the autumn of 1898 on hearing the news that Colonel Henry had cut his throat had caused Charles Maurras a spasm of horror. As Antonin conceived a little republican, Maurras conceived a newspaper. Maurras reasoned that Colonel Henry had committed his forgery—and so strengthened the legal case against Dreyfus—for reasons of state. For men like Maurras it was inconceivable that officers like Colonel Henry would behave dishonorably. He was convinced that the full truth about the Dreyfus Affair was being concealed in the interests of national security and concluded that the only reason most people could not see this, and the only reason why the Dreyfus case had divided France into two warring camps, was that the country was full of deracinated half-breeds incapable of understanding French problems and indifferent to France's interests. This process, according to Maurras, had been started in 1789 when the Revolutionaries destroyed France's unity by destroying its monarchy, and attempted to refound the nation on false ideas about Man and Society. The history of France had become the history of a struggle for power between competing vested interests. To reendow France with her national destiny it was necessary to restore the monarchy, which involved the destruction of the Republic. From 1898 monarchists plotted with some army officers to avenge themselves on the Dreyfusards; military honor had been outraged, and military loyalty enfeebled, by "the Affair."

Maurras, who was born eleven years after Antonin Moulin at Martigues near Marseille, only about forty miles from St. Andiol, who was, like Antonin, an admirer of Mistral, and who loved France and Provence just as much as Antonin loved France and Provence, became the intellectual guide of *Action française*. Maurras, whose father had died when he was six, was brought up "by his mother and two intelligent priests," and he suffered from one disadvantage which never troubled Antonin but which may help to explain his idiosyncratic analysis of France's twentieth-century destiny: from childhood Charles Maurras was almost stone deaf. He anchored himself to everyday reality through his writing, which eventually won him a seat at the Académie Française. But his talent and his handicap did not render him a readily sympathetic figure. After the Dreyfus Affair, Maurras's early interest in poetry, criticism and pagan classical civilization was submerged by an increasingly violent and abusive strain of political journalism, soaked in racist theorizing, which eventually made him one of the most influential Frenchmen of his time.

Action française had a youth section, known as the *Camelots du Roy*, mainly composed of students who sold the newspaper in the street, organized public demonstrations and barracked political opponents. By the adroit use of words, Maurras transformed "republicanism" into an alien concept and "monarchism" into a patriotic duty. The *Camelots* were easily excited by Maurras's rhetoric and after the Great War they developed into a national movement, sworn to oppose the republican regime and restore *un régime français.*

Besides *Action française* there were several other nationalist groups known as "the leagues," which included the *Jeunesses patriotes* (Patriotic Youths), *Solidarité française* (French Solidarity), the veterans' group *Anciens Combattants* (The Veterans) and a movement of disgruntled taxpayers bundled together as the *Fédération des Contribuables* (Federation of Contributors). There was also the *Croix de Feu* (the Cross of Fire). It would be uncharacteristic of France if the Great War had produced only one veterans' lobby. The *Croix de Feu,* unlike the *Anciens Combattants,* was originally restricted to decorated war veterans; in the early 1930s its leader, Colonel de La Rocque, started to accumulate a secret arsenal.

In 1923, when the leader of the *Camelots du Roy,* Marius Plateau, was assassinated and the *Camelots* had responded by drenching the radical freemason Maurice Viollette in violet ink, the young doctor Henri Martin had been arrested and briefly imprisoned for this outrage. After his spell in prison Dr. Martin became a student, though not a follower, of Trotsky. He was a practical man looking for practical advice and he was struck by Trotsky's dictum that an insurrection "was like a machine. To start it you needed mechanics, and only mechanics could stop it." The idea that an insurrection was a technical matter, and the study of this technology, became popular subjects for discussion at meetings of the *Camelots du Roy* and the *Croix de Feu.* A large pool of trained specialists was, of course, already available, and both movements began to seek support among the ranks of monarchist army officers.

During this period there was a third political force at work in France which was to influence the life of Jean Moulin. In 1920 the French socialist party—the Parti Socialiste, or SFIO (*Section française de l'Internationale ouvrière*)—split, one section allying itself with the Third Communist International, or "Comintern," and becoming the Parti Communiste Français, or PCF. That year, at its Second Congress, the Comintern had resolved that its component members had the duty to set up secret organizations, parallel to the official party organizations, which would work to prepare the world communist revolution. The Comintern's executive committee had already voted to establish a world information network in pursuit of the revolutionary class struggle. In 1924 a man known as Henri or "Harry" Robinson arrived in Paris from Berlin. He appeared to be an ordinary communist militant detailed to work with the French party. He was in fact a trained intelligence officer of the GRU and the Comintern. Robinson was of French Jewish extraction but had been brought up in Frankfurt. As technical director of the organization's politico-military apparatus in central and western Europe, he is today regarded as the most important single figure in the first Soviet spy ring set up in France. Robinson was never seriously troubled by the French police, despite his lack of a resident's permit, during his years in France, and his activities continued through peace and war until he was betrayed to the Gestapo in Paris in December 1942.

Robinson's spy "ring" became so extensive that it was eventually nicknamed "the Red Orchestra." As time passed he transferred to the direct service of the Soviet secret police, or GPU (later known as the KGB). From the start he worked through the French Communist Party and the Soviet embassy in Paris, using the party newspaper *L'Humanité* and the vast CGT trade union at will. He constructed a network that covered the army, navy and air force, the arms industry, government scientific laboratories, military arsenals, ports, railways, banks, the post office and many government ministries; he was a very effective spymaster. Many of his agents were recruited through the PCF, but never from among its listed members because the party had to present the appearance of independence. Flanked on one side by the Comintern's secret organization and security service, known as the OMS (the Department of International Connections), the PCF was flanked on the other by a succession of noncommunist public organizations known as "front" organizations and dedicated to "world peace," "human rights" or "anti-fascism." These attracted influential figures who would never have joined the party itself but who were prepared to ally themselves with it on a succession of issues. Such people were described by Lenin as "useful idiots" and confirmed his dictum that the West was "ready to weave the rope on which it would be hanged."

In 1932, when Pierre Cot, the charismatic leader of the "Young Turks" of the Radical-Socialist Party, first became a minister, he and his team of advisers were selected as a prime target by the Comintern.

EIGHT

Moulin Rouge

IN JANUARY 1934 Jean Moulin was a secretive man with the social habits of a libertine, a weekend painter with an acknowledged gift for caricature, attentive from a distance to his elderly parents and still without any particular political commitment beyond a generalized, radical loyalty designed to be of help in his career. Within the next six years he would be promoted twice, he would become the youngest prefect in France, receive the Legion of Honor, occupy one of the most influential positions in the administration, be denounced as a communist and in short become one of the more successful as well as reviled figures in his profession. The key to this transformation lay in the events he observed one evening in February 1934.

Serge Alexandre Stavisky was a naturalized Jew from Kiev who came to France as a refugee during his childhood and grew up to make his living as a swindler. In 1933 Stavisky, who had cultivated a wide circle of connections among radical and republican politicians, concocted a fraud based on the issue of investment bonds through the *crédit municipal* (a local authority bank) in Bayonne and in Orléans. The bonds proved to be worthless and unsupported by public moneys and at the end of the year Stavisky disappeared with over 250 million francs of investors' savings. He had been assisted by friends in the Senate and the Chamber of Deputies, as well as by journalists and the Paris public prosecutor, who happened to be the brother-in-law of Prime Minister Camille Chautemps.

News of this swindle, and its political ramifications, broke in *L'Action française:* the newspaper could hardly have designed a more appropriate villain, perfectly matched to each of its prejudices. Early in January 1934 Stavisky was discovered dead in a villa in the winter resort of Chamonix, not far from Albertville. The police said that he had shot himself; the monarchists replied that he had been murdered by the police on the instructions of the prime minister in order to ensure his silence. This dramatic sequence of events was whipped up with great skill by the editor of *L'Action française,* Léon Daudet, in order to provoke the long-awaited political crisis and start up the machinery of insurrection. "Down with Thieves!," "Down with Murderers!" ran the headlines, and the prime minister was described as "the leader of a criminal gang."

The initial results were highly satisfactory. On the night of 11 January, only three days after the discovery of Stavisky's body, there were serious riots in Paris. It was fortunate for Cot and Moulin that they had decided to go skiing in Zürs and not Chamonix. Nevertheless, *L'Action française* did everything possible to involve Cot directly in the Stavisky affair. The air minister was accused of dining with Stavisky on several occasions at the Claridge Hotel on the Champs-Elysées, and was said to have handed out free air tickets to Stavisky's cronies. Cot had a letter published denying these allegations and the paper commented, "Of what value is the denial of a minister in a government led by a liar?" As the demonstrations continued for day after day the right-wing press began to call on the people of Paris to rise and save the nation. The government fell on 27 January and the new prime minister, another radical, Daladier, in an attempt to regain control of the situation, dismissed the prefect of police, who was accused by the left of doing nothing to stop the riots and by the right of being involved with Stavisky. This move reassured the left but enraged the extreme-right, who called a demonstration for 6 February to protest the dismissal of a man they had until then been accusing of corruption. For the *Camelots du Roy* it was the opportunity they had been awaiting. Arms were distributed, plans were laid; the technicians were at their posts. The mechanism was ready to be set in motion. The people were summoned into the streets to overthrow the government that had unleashed "anarchist socialism" and "permitted a conspiracy of swindling freemasons to escape unpunished."

On the afternoon and evening of 6 February, Paris came closer to insurrection than at any time since the rising in 1871 which had established
the Commune. In the Chamber of Deputies Daladier's government faced
a crucial vote of confidence. The debate, which had opened with a brisk
exchange of insults—"Dictatorship of Freemasons!," "*Provocateur!*," "Buc-
caneer"—degenerated steadily. On being abused by the Communist Party
secretary-general, Maurice Thorez, one radical leader and former minister replied, "I have thrown you into prison once and at the next opportunity I will throw you in again." Throughout the debate the communist
deputies kept up a steady chant of "Les Soviets! Les Soviets!" while the
deputies of the extreme-right launched verbal attacks which repeatedly
spilled over into physical violence. Pierre Cot, seated on the ministers'
bench among his cabinet colleagues, was the target of special attention.
Unknown to fellow ministers he had, with Moulin's assistance, taken precautions to safeguard military air bases from being seized by extreme
right-wing officers. Then, as the debate reached its climax, gunfire was
heard from the streets outside the Palais Bourbon and Moulin left his seat
in the officials' gallery to see what was going on.

From the raised terrace behind the columns of the Chamber of
Deputies there is a clear view north across the bridge over the Seine to the
great open space of the Place de la Concorde on the opposite bank of the
river. That evening the lines of police and *gardes mobiles* (riot police) were
drawn up in ranks on the near side of the bridge and held the ground to
the mid-point of the Pont de la Concorde. The descending slope of the
bridge was a no-man's-land, littered with the debris of a Paris riot, paving
stones, cobbles, park benches, pewter figures ripped from street fountains,
as well as discarded police equipment and one or two burning barricades
and looted buses. On the far bank Moulin could see a mob of about 30,000
insurrectionists bubbling backwards and forwards across the Concorde.
For the monarchists among them this was holy ground; the guillotine
which had decapitated Louis XVI during the Revolution had been erected
at its center. Earlier in the evening the police had abandoned attempts to
regain control of the Concorde after the rioters, many of whom were
armed war veterans, had slashed the hocks of the police horses with cut-
throat razors. The shooting had started when a small group of royalists
had directed fire onto police ranks and the riot police had replied. By midnight fifteen people, four of them royalists, lay dead while 1,435 were
wounded.

As Moulin watched from the terrace, the sound of gunfire drove the royalist deputies inside the Chamber into a further paroxysm of excitement. One blind war veteran shouted: "They are breaking down the doors of Parliament! They have opened fire!" Another pointed at Daladier and cried: "You are responsible! You have spilt the blood of your fellow citizens! You have committed political suicide and drenched yourself in French blood. Did you give the order to the police to open fire? Answer!" Others shouted: "A government of murderers! Resign! Resign!" and all the time the communists continued their hypnotic, semi-hysterical mantra, "Les Soviets! Les Soviets!" The debate was closed by the president of the assembly but it was 2:30 in the morning before the Chamber could be cleared. By that time renewed police charges had driven the royalists out of the Place de la Concorde and up the Champs-Elysées. Three infantry battalions which had been brought into the center of Paris to support the police remained concealed and did not have to be deployed. The initial fire from the royalists had not been followed up.

For experienced observers among the insurrectionists the conclusion was clear; their leaders had betrayed them. The technicians had started the juggernaut but the drivers had failed to put it into gear. At the height of the fighting, when it seemed the police lines must break and the Chamber be taken by storm, Charles Maurras had refused to allow armed groups of *Camelots du Roy* to move forward, arguing that verbal attacks would eventually win the day. When this refusal was known, many of his followers, including a frustrated young man named Pierre de Bénouville, became disillusioned with *Action française* and started to seek a more direct solution. These "extreme" extremists saw no future in a movement whose leaders urged the French people to rise up and, when they had risen, instructed them to sit down again. Acting at first within the ranks of the *Camelots,* but against the orders and without the knowledge of their leadership, they turned to direct action, bomb attacks and the assassination of selected targets. They also forged links with sympathetic army officers and eventually formed a conspiracy named the CSAR (*Comité secret d'action révolutionnaire*), mockingly nicknamed "*la Cagoule*"—the Hood.

If the royalists regarded the events of 6 February as a failure, Moulin was more impressed. Before his appalled eyes the Republic had tottered. He had seen his country's leaders lose control of events, he had seen a mob on the point of overrunning parliament, he had seen his hereditary enemies shooting down the representatives of civil order and on the point of overturning democratic rule. On several occasions during the debate Pierre Cot had been called to the telephone only to listen to anonymous death threats. By the time the mob had been dispersed Moulin was emotionally drained and his colleagues found him sobbing in despair. When they tried to comfort him he would only say, "Now do you understand?"

On the following day, Daladier took the advice of several of his ministers, including Pierre Cot, and resigned. He had been informed by the new prefect of police that further trouble was likely and would have to be repressed, this time with military assistance and the risk of high civilian casualties. Cot went, too, and Moulin put himself at the disposition of the minister of the interior.

In February 1934, when the Daladier government fell, Moulin found himself, for the first time since he had left Montpellier barracks in 1918 to head for the front, without a job and with more than enough leisure time to fill. He rented a studio at 26 rue des Plantes and started to attend art school. Laure recalled that his studio was on the top floor of a modern building, the highest in the neighborhood. In a detail that was to become a personal trademark, the building had two entrances on different streets. Even today its brutalistic concrete façade is notable for an air of gloom and menace. The studio had a view over the rooftops. The building was, Laure wrote, "full of painters," an untypical situation since few of the artists of Montparnasse inhabited the newest building in their neighborhood.

For a brief interlude Moulin was able to lead the life of a bohemian. He attended life classes at schools such as the Académie Colarossi and the Grande Chaumière; he frequented the Dôme and the Rotonde. The art curator Jacques Lugand considers that his sketches of this period resemble the work of Pascin, who hanged himself *à la portugaise* from the doorknob of his studio in Pigalle in 1930, and who was known for his erotic, sprawling nudes of unusually young models. Some of Moulin's drawings were made in brothels, a setting he borrowed from Pascin's master, Toulouse-Lautrec—although Moulin chose brothels in Pigalle, which were seedier than the ones around the Opéra. Apart from an evident fascination with low-life nothing is known about Moulin's motives for these expeditions, or why he should have left Montparnasse and crossed Paris to make drawings in a brothel when his own district was teeming with artist's models who would have charged him less.

During this period, Moulin devoted quite a lot of his time to assisting his father. In old age Antonin had decided to write a life of a historical figure connected with St. Andiol, Ernestine de Castellane, châtelaine immediately after the Revolution and the second wife of Joseph Fouché, the Terrorist of Lyon and Napoleon's minister of police. Fouché married Ernestine in 1815 after he had played a significant part in the restoration of Louis XVIII and just before he underwent a final and well-deserved humiliation at royal hands. What persuaded Antonin, a lifelong antiroyalist and anticlerical, to write the biography of such an obscure Catholic aristocrat will never be known; it is a decision as mysterious as his son's sudden passion for the brothels of Pigalle. Nonetheless, Antonin's book, for which Jean, based in Paris, did some of the research, was a success. Its treatment of the theme of Fouché in old age, the son of a grocer become one of the most powerful men in Europe, finally treated with contempt as though he, the multimillionaire Duke of Otranto, had never been more than the son of a grocer, was sufficiently skillful to be rewarded with a prize from the Académie Française. Antonin was delighted by this recognition and genuinely surprised. The prize had been announced several months earlier than anticipated, and he had not even had time to start lobbying for it.*

In July 1934, after four months of *la vie bohème*, Moulin took up a position as secretary-general of the prefecture of the Somme, based at Amiens, the necessary promotion before he himself could become a prefect. Just as the prefect administered the department, his secretary-general was his chief of staff, organizing the work of the prefecture. In his two years in Amiens, Moulin had to supervise four elections, a useful concentration of administrative experience, and with his usual efficiency he organized his prefecture well enough to enable him to complete a task which he had been working on since 1932, a commission to illustrate an edition of the verse of the nineteenth-century *poète maudit* Tristan Corbière. This commission had originally been sponsored by Max Jacob. In October 1935 Moulin's eight somber etchings, signed "Romanin," were exhibited in

---

*Antonin Moulin's achievement was the private fantasy of General de Gaulle. One day, striding down St. James's in London, in 1941, de Gaulle said without warning: "The best profession in the world is librarian. Municipal librarian in a small town in Brittany. One day, as retirement draws near, one sits down to compose a monograph of eighty pages. 'Did Madame de Sévigné once pass through Pontivy?' And one becomes quite frantic, dashing off stinging letters to the vicar, who is dithering over a crucial date."

Paris and, on Max Jacob's prompting, favorably reviewed by the influential critic André Salmon. They were to be "Romanin's" last work. He never exhibited again and seems to have abandoned painting altogether at this time.

The most dramatic event in the personal life of Jean Moulin during his years in Amiens was his brush with death at a public banquet. A departmental medical conference on public health, organized in June 1935, was followed by a sumptuous lunch, after which 150 general practitioners, medical professors and hygiene inspectors were taken to hospital with food poisoning. One man died. Moulin, who wrote to his sister that he had only been slightly affected with a high temperature and had been able to attend two other banquets immediately afterward, nonetheless requested sick leave six weeks later. His complaisant doctor recommended "at least three weeks in a health spa" ("une station hydrominérale et climatique") and the secretary-general selected Evian, on the shores of Lake Geneva close to Thonon, where he invited his parents to join him. The picture this affords of an attentive son is thrown slightly out of focus by the discovery that Pierre Cot and Gaston Cusin, another political ally and friend, were both staying near Evian at the same time.

While Moulin was in Amiens there was a change in Moscow's party line which led to the creation in France of the *Front Populaire* (Popular Front)—the union of the noncommunist and communist left. This ideological tack, announced in June 1934, became celebrated because it forced Maurice Thorez, the puppet leader of the French Communist Party, to contradict a speech he had made two days previously in which he had excluded the possibility of a formal political alliance with other socialist and progressive formations. After receiving a note from Eugen Fried, the Comintern's executive committee member delegated to oversee the PCF, informing him what his new opinions were, Thorez passionately argued *for* the formation of such an alliance immediately. In Paris the moving spirits behind the acceptance of the Popular Front were the socialist (and anti-communist) leader Léon Blum and the radicals Edouard Daladier and Pierre Cot, the chief targets of monarchist hatred in the riot of 1934. Responding to the formation of the Popular Front in April 1935, Charles Maurras, writing in *L'Action française*, described Léon Blum as "a man to gun down, but in the back."

1. The schoolboy in Béziers, c. 1912.

2. Antonin, father of Jean Moulin,
schoolmaster, anticlerical and republican.

3. Blanche Pègue, Jean's mother,
a Catholic and a good housekeeper.

4. Jean (*back row, center*), still a model pupil at the Collège Henri IV, in the class of Monsieur Ain, c. 1907.

5. Jean Moulin's caricature of Monsieur Maury, the science teacher, as the nation's "last line of defense," 1915.

6. April 1918: Jean is called to the colors, but the war ends before he sees action.

LA DERNIÈRE LIGNE....

7. Law student on the beach at Valras-Plage in 1920.

8. Subprefect at Albertville, c. 1927.

9. Cartoon of the cafés of Montparnasse in the 1930s. The caption ran: "Well, at least as a Foujita look-alike he can get the Americans to buy him the odd drink."

10. "The widow prepares for a fashionable funeral at the Madeleine." The figures in the background are professional mutes. Moulin's first (broken) engagement had been due to end in a fashionable Parisian wedding.

11. Jean Moulin with his minister, Pierre Cot, at Megève in 1935.

12. Cycle tour of the Gorges du Tarn in summer 1938. Moulin is the prefect of the Aveyron. Pierre Cot (*right*) is out of office. André Labarthe (*left*), an official in the air ministry, is already a paid agent of Soviet military intelligence. Also present are Andrée Chatain (*left*) and Néna Cot.

13. Moulin with Gaston Cusin, customs official and arms smuggler.

14. Louis Dolivet

15. Henri Manhès

16. Pierre Meunier

17. Raymond Aubrac (Raymond Samuel)

18. Laure Moulin and Jean, c. 1939, outside La Lèque, the shepherd's hut they bought
in a remote corner of Les Alpilles.

19. Prefect's identity card with disguised photograph. Moulin's moustache grew quickly.

20. Antoinette Sachs, dressed down for the beach.

21. Gilberte Lloyd on the occasion of her remarriage, 1943.

22. Pierre Brossolette, in London, 1942.

23. Souvenir photograph of the prefect of Chartres with Colonel F. K. von Gütlingen and the colonel's dachshund in the gardens of the prefecture. The white scarf conceals the wound in Moulin's throat.

24. The doctor's house at Caluire.

25. August 1944. Chartres celebrates "the Purge." The mistress of a German soldier has been shaved in public. The unsmiling man in a beret carrying a bundle of clothes is the woman's father. The baby's father has departed with the retreating German army. The flag in the background is flying over the gateway of Moulin's prefecture.

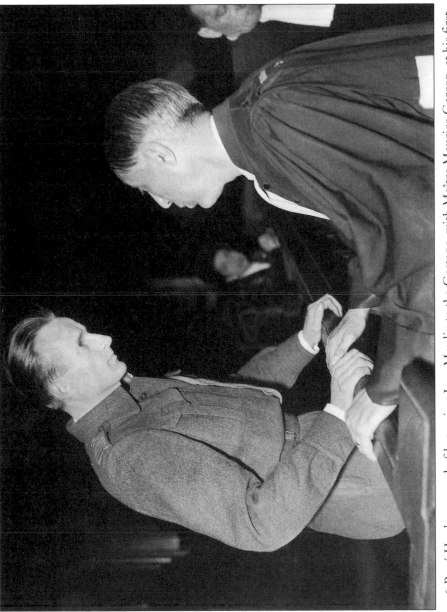
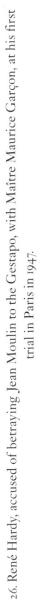

26. René Hardy, accused of betraying Jean Moulin to the Gestapo, with Maître Maurice Garçon, at his first trial in Paris in 1947.

27. Henri Frenay takes the oath before giving evidence for Hardy at the second trial.

28. Pierre de Bénouville gives evidence for Hardy at the second trial.

29. Witness for the prosecution. Lydie Bastien, Hardy's ex-mistress, "un bel animal," gives evidence against her former lover at the second trial.

30. Edmée Delettraz, who worked for both the Resistance and the Gestapo, and who betrayed Berty Albrecht, gives evidence against Hardy at the second trial.

31. Malraux's valediction on the steps of the Panthéon, 1964.

In February 1936 Blum's car was caught up in the funeral cortège of a prominent member of *Action française* that happened to be passing near the National Assembly. Blum was recognized and attacked by *Camelots du Roy* wielding iron bars. He suffered head injuries and could be taken to safety only after the intervention of workers from a nearby building site. This outrage finally prodded the right-wing radical government into activity. Charles Maurras was charged with "incitement to murder" and *Action française* and the *Camelots du Roy* were proscribed. In Paris 500,000 people marched to the Bastille "to defend the Republic," and in Amiens, where the French Communist Party (PCF) had only 600 members, a communist front meeting demanding a Popular Front government attracted 4,500 people.

Three days after the attack on Blum, when indignation in France was at its height, a Popular Front government was elected in Spain: left-wing political prisoners were released; the Falange, the movement of the extreme-right, was proscribed; its leader, José Antonio Primo de Rivera, was imprisoned and socialist movements organized mass land seizures. In addition, 160 churches and convents were destroyed and 269 members of the clergy were murdered. In France, in May 1936, the Radical Party lost heavily in the legislative elections, and there was a notable increase in the communist vote. In Amiens, in the first round, the communist candidates topped the poll. In the second round the mayor of Amiens, the only candidate whose reelection had been guaranteed by the prefect, perhaps on Moulin's advice, was defeated. In the second round five out of seven Popular Front candidates were elected, including two communists, and the radicals lost five of their six seats. A crowd of 10,000 people marched through the streets of the city singing the "*Internationale.*" Nationally the results were described as "a tidal wave" for the left. The communists increased their seats from ten to seventy-two. The socialists formed the largest group in the new parliament and gained forty-nine seats, and the radicals, who had dominated the Assembly since 1920, lost forty-three seats. Léon Blum formed a Popular Front government—the communists, having campaigned nationally for this result, were forbidden by Moscow to join a coalition—and Pierre Cot, who was once again offered the air ministry, immediately invited Moulin to rejoin him as chief of staff.

For the next two years, from June 1936 to April 1938, Moulin worked beside Cot in Paris for the interests of the Popular Front, for much of the time following secret instructions that demanded daily cooperation with Comintern agents. Throughout this period France's domestic and foreign politics were dominated by events in Spain.

Pierre Cot's policy at the air ministry was pacifist by conviction and pro-Soviet by calculation. In Cot's analysis the threat from Nazi and fascist governments in Germany and Italy could only be balanced by a Franco-Soviet alliance. This policy was widely supported in France, and Pierre Laval, as a right-wing radical prime minister, had signed a Franco-Soviet Pact in 1935. But in the face of the Nazi threat Cot abandoned his earlier attempt to link his pacifism to disarmament, and replaced his early ideal of a nonmilitarized air system with a blueprint for a modern French air force. He was in fact responsible for both military and civil aviation and Moulin was head of his civil cabinet, the military cabinet being entirely staffed by air force officers. In partnership with Cot, Moulin's views moved to the left—Cot was eventually to describe him as "the most left-wing member of my staff"—and one of his less enchanted colleagues wrote: "As soon as the left is criticized he loses all sense of judgment concerning colleagues or politicians."

Moulin now believed that republicanism and human rights were not enough. Socialist politics were necessary to defend these ideals and to defeat fascism, and in particular "international socialist" policies. His energy and intelligence soon won him a leading place among Cot's advisers. "Monsieur Moulin had a considerable influence on the minister's thinking and enjoyed very close personal relations with him," wrote another of his colleagues at that time. But it was a notorious fact in the air ministry and in the council of ministers that Moulin's influence over Cot was the opposite of stabilizing, and that it encouraged the headstrong, impulsive side of Cot's character.

Moulin's specific responsibilities included political and parliamentary relations, the press, secret funds, labor relations and Spain. On 17 July 1936 news reached Paris that a military rising against the Spanish Popular Front government had taken place in Spanish Morocco. This was quickly followed by an appeal for help from the Spanish government and Blum's immediate reaction was sympathetic. France faced the danger of being encircled by fascist regimes and support for the Spanish Republicans was the logical sequel to the cross-party policy of a pro-Soviet, anti-Nazi alliance. The Spanish wanted planes, guns and bombs to be delivered at once, in execution of an existing commercial agreement. Blum's cabinet was unanimous in consenting to this request. The Spanish air attaché in Paris then defected to Franco and leaked details of his government's shopping list to France's right-wing press, which reacted by accusing Blum of "warmongering" and "intervening in the internal affairs of another country."

Under strong pressure from the British government, led by Stanley Baldwin—whose senior ministers were to include both Neville Chamberlain and Lord Halifax—Blum abandoned support for the Spanish government and switched to a policy of "nonintervention." Then, in response to protests from Pierre Cot and other pro-Republican ministers, Blum authorized a third, secret, policy which he described as "*nonintervention élastique*." France would officially back the policy of nonintervention in Spain while secretly doing everything possible to ensure that the Spanish government received all the arms and other supplies it needed. The minister overseeing this policy was to be Pierre Cot, and the official responsible for applying it day by day was his chief of staff, Jean Moulin.

Moulin thereby became involved in an official smuggling operation in which a small team of conspirators in key departments set out to mislead and deceive, while breaking every published regulation governing trade with Spain. Moulin's closest collaborators in this operation were Gaston Cusin, who had become a customs officer and trade union militant in Bordeaux and who was also a friend of Cot's, and André Labarthe, an air ministry engineer who was, in public, a fierce supporter of the Republican cause and, in private, a paid agent of Soviet military intelligence. They were joined by André Malraux, whose novel *La Condition humaine* had just won the Prix Goncourt.* The French team worked closely with a Comintern group organized from the Soviet embassy in Paris whose leader, Louis Dolivet, was soon to become one of Jean Moulin's closest friends.

Before the nonintervention ban came into effect, on the night of 8 August 1936, the French team, primarily Moulin, Cusin and Malraux, managed to organize the transfer of a number of military aircraft into Spain. The figure accepted in France today is "about fifty." These planes, it was believed at the time, played a crucial role in the early battle for Madrid, won by the Republicans in November, a victory which endowed André Malraux with an international reputation as "a Gallic Byron," the novelist

---

* Unknown to Léon Blum, and possibly to Cot and Moulin as well, Malraux's original journey to Spain was made on behalf of the Comintern.

who engaged in dogfights with Nazi aces and emerged victorious. On the strength of this exaggerated reputation—Malraux did not hold a pilot's license and his status as a squadron leader in the Republican air force was strictly honorary—Malraux embarked on a high-profile fund-raising tour of the United States.

Following the ban on arms exports, France, according to Pierre Cot in his memoirs published in New York in 1944, exported a further 129 aircraft to Spain, of which eighty-three were military. The right-wing press gave much higher figures at the time, and argued that Cot's unofficial pro-Republican and pro-Soviet activities were bleeding France of vitally needed planes and putting the homeland in mortal danger. One of the minister's leading critics, *L'Echo de Paris,* demanded that Cot be stopped from "arming the Spanish communists" and claimed that he was "playing Hitler's game," "leading France into war" and "blackening her international reputation." In the Chamber of Deputies Cot was accused of exporting "over 400 French military aircraft to Spain"; this was at a time when the French air force possessed only 477 modern aircraft with an operational capacity. In other words the French public was led to believe that Cot and his staff at the air ministry had exported most of the French air force to defend the communist cause in Spain.

The policy of the Popular Front government toward Spain became so unpopular that in October 1940, in the anguish of military defeat, the Vichy authorities decided to try six men for treason in view of their responsibility for the fall of France. The Vichy prosecutors, working in Riom, in the Auvergne, chose two prime ministers, Léon Blum and Edouard Daladier, one general, Maurice Gamelin, one senior civil servant in the defense ministry and two air ministers, Pierre Cot and his immediate successor. A prosecution witness at the eventual trial unsuccessfully demanded that Jean Moulin should join Léon Blum and Pierre Cot in the dock. Blum, Cot and Moulin were all singled out by the prosecutors for the policy they applied between July 1936 and January 1938 with regard to military intervention in the Spanish Civil War. The eighth and last ground in the prosecution case was "deliveries of aeronautical material to the Spanish government."

Pierre Cot's arms-smuggling operation in 1937 involved not just planes but guns. The smugglers forwarded Soviet weapons and munitions from ships unloaded in France's Atlantic ports, usually Bordeaux, which were then conjured through the French railway system by Gaston Cusin before crossing the land frontier into Catalonia. These shipments had to be concealed from French frontier guards, customs officers, prefects and from the posses of French supporters of General Franco. This operation became increasingly important as Franco's forces succeeded in closing down, one by one, all the Republicans' alternative lines of supply. The land frontier between France and the Basque enclave was cut early in September 1936, the six Mediterranean ports were closed by the noninterventionist naval blockade in August 1937, and when the Basque Republican forces surrendered in October the only alternative route left open was by air. But the Republican airfields were out of range of almost all neutral or friendly airfields, outside France.

The eighteen months when Moulin was in charge of this clandestine and probably illegal operation were among the most creative and fulfilling of his career. He was the leader of a small band of brothers-in-arms, carrying out a secret policy which he believed to be both in the national interest and morally right. His "second" personality, hidden and rebellious, could be put to work in the service of his country. He could exercise the talent for conspiracy which had been foreshadowed by his secretive behavior as a student in Montpellier, and perhaps even earlier, by the conflict of loyalties imposed on him at school. As representatives of the French government, Moulin and Cusin dealt with a team of Soviet "advisers," in fact Comintern and NKVD (GPU) agents, who were made welcome in Paris and whose task it was to deliver the shipments which were to be transferred to Cusin's night-trains. Their leader, "Louis Dolivet"—born in Hungary, the son of Austrian-Jewish parents, as Ludwig Brecher—had worked for the Comintern in France since 1929 and was originally a protégé of Willi Munzenberg, the most prominent of the exiled German communists in Paris and a senior Comintern agent. Dolivet was assisted by Maurice Panier, a member of the French Communist Party who worked openly for Willi Munzenberg and secretly for Harry Robinson, the Comintern officer in Paris who also headed the GRU (Soviet military intelligence) spy ring in France. Two other important members of the conspiracy were the Swedish banker Olaf Aschberg and the Russian banker Dimitri Navachine, who from their banks in Paris funded covert Soviet activities throughout western Europe. A liaison with the Soviet embassy was established through General Vladimir Vasiltchenko, who had been nominated as Soviet air attaché in February 1936 and who was a GRU officer in personal contact with Moulin.

In order to conceal his real activities Louis Dolivet set up and manipulated a succession of front organizations, the most prominent of which was the RUP (*Rassemblement universel pour la paix*), an international anti-fascist pressure group dedicated to world peace, known in England as the "International Peace Campaign" where it was, supposedly, directed by Lord Robert Cecil and Philip Noel-Baker. The first assembly of the RUP was an immense success. Its president was Pierre Cot and among those on the platform were Jean Moulin and other members of Cot's ministerial cabinet, including two young air ministry officials, Pierre Meunier and Robert Chambeiron. Later they were joined by André Labarthe and by a professional pilot, journalist and adventurer called Henri Manhès. All these men—Cusin, Dolivet, Panier, Aschberg, Navachine, Meunier, Chambeiron, Labarthe and Manhès—were friends and colleagues of Moulin and partisans of the Republican cause in the Spanish Civil War. But they were also active Comintern or GRU agents, or future supporters or members of the French Communist Party. Also drawn into the circle of Pierre Cot by the RUP was a young American diplomat named Noel Field, who was a GRU agent, and, according to the historian Stephen Koch, one of the most important Soviet agents then active in Europe.*

The Comintern provided two other agents to assist Dolivet. One was usually known as "Herta Tempi," a German communist refugee, who was the secretary, translator and mistress of Dolivet. She was also the mistress of Noel Field. Another was frequently known as "Martha Jansen," born in Poland, later a member of the German Communist Party, a journalist and translator who was also Dolivet's mistress, as well as being the mistress of André Labarthe.

So Pierre Cot's cabinet, which was operating a conspiracy to deceive the extreme right and France's noninterventionist allies, was itself infiltrated by a deeper and more sophisticated conspiracy based in Moscow and operating through the Comintern, the GRU and the NKVD; a conspiracy capable of deploying hundreds of trained agents, of motivating thousands of peace-loving idealists, of erecting international front organi-

---

* After the war, Field claimed to have been involved in the murder of his fellow Soviet agent Ignace Reiss by an NKVD assassination squad in Switzerland in 1937.

zations, of manipulating government policy in France and Spain and of diverting and soaking up foreign government funds. The critical question about Moulin is, would it have been possible for the Comintern to gain this degree of influence within Cot's office without the knowledge and agreement of his omnicompetent chief of staff? Although there is no direct evidence, as so far revealed by Soviet archives, that Moulin was a Comintern agent, common sense suggests that both he and Pierre Cot must have known and approved of what was going on.

On 9 August 1936 Dolivet demonstrated his ability as an organizer when he managed to assemble 400,000 people in the Parc de St. Cloud on the edge of Paris to hear Léon Blum, the prime minister, speak in favor of World Peace. There seemed nothing incongruous in the fact that the Communist Party groups present at this peace meeting spent much of the time chanting "Des avions pour l'Espagne! Des canons pour l'Espagne!" (Planes for Spain! Guns for Spain!) The PCF's lobbying was highly successful. Ten thousand French volunteers joined the communist-led "International Brigade," five times more than came from Britain.

A man with the charm, ability and dedication of Dolivet, in weekly or daily contact with Moscow, could not only attract an army of political sympathizers, infiltrate a ministry and run rings around a national police and security operation, he could also attract the support of a generation of intellectuals. So it was that, when Dolivet was claiming a world membership of 400 million, the RUP enrolled men such as Frédéric Joliot-Curie, Louis Aragon, André Gide and André Malraux.* None of them had any suspicion that the policy of "anti-fascism" and "international peace" could lead directly to the Nazi-Soviet Pact, the Nazi and Soviet invasions of Poland and the Second World War. There they sat on the platform at the Mutualité, or at other venues, their intelligence, talent and achievements blazing out over the heads of the foot soldiers of idealism, in auditoriums as large as the Heysel football stadium, while Dolivet danced behind their backs, pulling the strings. Jean Moulin was on the stage at these meetings, and as time passed he must have been increasingly aware of the activity in the wings. The ambitious opportunist and the principled republican are

---

* André Gide denounced the Soviet system in 1936 in the celebrated book *Retour à l'URSS*. André Malraux never developed a closer association with French communism. Frédéric Joliot-Curie, France's leading atomic physicist, remained a faithful ally of the Soviet Union after the war. Louis Aragon was a hardline Stalinist until his death in 1982.

now joined, in silhouette, by the idealist and communist fellow-traveler. And there was a further link, which appears to put Moulin's involvement with the Comintern beyond a doubt.

There was a private club also set up by Dolivet, with the financial backing of Olaf Aschberg, called the *Cercle des Nations,* which was established in Paris in a fine town house on the rue Casimir-Périer, near the National Assembly. The committee of this club included Dolivet, Labarthe, Moulin and Pierre Meunier. The club's stated intention was to allow "members of the French and foreign élites to get to know each other in an atmosphere of mutual esteem." It was actually intended to further the cause of the RUP. The club was under French police surveillance, partly because it was installed in a house owned by Aschberg, whose links with the Soviet embassy were known, and partly because it was a popular meeting place for military officers attached to the nearby war ministry. It was also close to the headquarters of the RUP in the Place du Palais Bourbon, where Pierre Cot had set up his private office. When Moulin left the air ministry in April 1938 he was allocated an office of his own in the *Cercle des Nations.*

Louis Dolivet, meanwhile, had taken a private apartment in the same building as Moulin, but on the floor below, at 26 rue des Plantes. And since Dolivet was secretary of the RUP, and *ex-officio* landlord of Cot's private office, which was run by Pierre Meunier, he also had an entrée into the air minister's office whenever he wished. The links between the Comintern and the French air minister's inner circle could hardly have been closer. Cot arranged for the RUP to receive an annual grant of 100,000 francs from the foreign ministry. And it seems more than likely that some RUP resources were, in return, used to support Cot's private office. Such an arrangement would certainly have been known to the chief of staff. In return for his efforts Dolivet successfully applied for French nationality. This request was processed by two freemasons, one of them the minister of justice, and since Cot was not a mason we can assume that it was Moulin who set the wheels in motion for his friend.

In his years at the air ministry Jean Moulin began affairs with two women he had met in 1936 at separate official functions, both of whom were childless and both of whom were two years older than he. The first was Madame Gilberte Lloyd, a wealthy divorcée with a talent for marrying prudently who had been born in Mulhouse in Alsace during the period of

German annexation. Her family, the Riedlingers, was involved in industry and arms production and she had spent the years of the First World War in Berlin. According to Pierre Péan in *Vies et morts de Jean Moulin*, she became a naturalized French citizen in 1920 and took up residence in Paris following her second divorce in 1936. Moulin saw her in Paris, either in her splendid apartment at 32 rue de Lübeck in the 16th arrondissement or in his apartment in Montparnasse. According to Péan, Madame Lloyd was sometimes described as "the most beautiful woman in Paris."

Moulin's second conquest was Antoinette Sachs, an artist who had been a pupil of Matisse and whom he met at a dinner party given for a Soviet diplomat. With her dark hair, sidelong smile and tender voice, she was an experienced heartbreaker who was officially the mistress of the poet Paul Géraldy. Moulin saw her both in Paris and in the south, introduced her to his parents and once in 1939 asked her to marry him on the grounds that he wanted her to be the mother of his children, a proposal which she declined, ostensibly out of loyalty to Géraldy.

In March 1937, at the height of the Spanish Civil War, Jean Moulin was nominated prefect of the Aveyron, thereby becoming, at thirty-seven, the youngest prefect in France. Despite the fact that the arms-smuggling operation was at its height he left the air ministry and installed himself in Rodez, 400 miles to the south and not far from the Spanish frontier. In accepting this position Moulin apparently again gave the advantage to his professional future over any political commitment. His appointment, and departure from the ministry, coincided with the award of the Legion of Honor and gratified his father's dearest wish, to see his son a prefect.

But Moulin only remained at Rodez for seven weeks, after which Cot managed to get him seconded back to Paris as a prefect *hors cadre*, without a prefecture, and even during this brief period in Rodez, Moulin continued to act as Cot's chief of staff, spending much of the time on the night express, working. The transfer back to Paris had always been foreseen, but it took longer to arrange than anticipated. If the transfer had proved impossible, then at least one of Cot's key collaborators would have reached the rank of prefect, wielding in his department what the historian M. R. D. Foot has rightly described as more power than "anything found in England, below the permanent secretaryships of a few great ministries in Whitehall."

Back in Paris, Moulin continued to be responsible for labor relations in

the air industry, which were chaotic,* and also for civil aviation. He faced
difficulties in both these fields, and in the matter of civil aviation got into a
muddle of entirely his own making. At a time when the French military
aviation industry was so unproductive that even Neville Chamberlain, by
then the British prime minister, felt obliged to complain about its "lamen-
table state," Moulin decided to boost national morale with a series of international air races. Naturally the intention was that these should be won
by France.

The results were disastrous. In a race specifically organized to demonstrate the country's ability to outface the fascist threat, the first three
planes were Italian and the best French planes were shown to be 35 mph
slower than those made by the fascists. Moulin had to present the prizes,
Cot falling suddenly ill when he realized that his chief of staff had arranged
for him to give "three million francs of taxpayers' money to Mussolini," as
the right-wing press put it. "Now that he has established that we fly 58 kph
slower than fascism, will Cot decide to stop humiliating our young men?"
the editorial writer continued. "This race has covered the country's civil
aviation with ridicule. . . . Pierre Cot should face a court martial. . . . We
have had enough of being humiliated by the gang of rascals, profiteers and
pot-bellied cretins who rule our country."

As the year went by these continuous press attacks began to weaken
Cot's position in the government and in the Radical-Socialist Party. It became clear that France was losing the air-arms race, the planes were being
built too slowly and were outclassed when they arrived. An air force general summarized the situation by saying, "If war broke out tomorrow, our
air force would be destroyed in a few days." Cot protested, with justice,
that his budget was too small, but to no avail. On 15 January 1938 he left the
air ministry, taking with him the reputation of being "the gravedigger of
French aviation," and moved to the ministry of commerce, where he
stayed for only three months. In April he resigned for the last time.

---

* Cot's attitude to labor relations is epitomized by an incident shortly after his appointment in 1936. He had arrived at his new ministry to find that government air factory
workers, led by the communist-dominated CGT union, were on strike. In an unusual
scene at Le Bourget airport the new air minister, noticing a group of strikers outside
the building, abandoned his officials, walked over to the strikers, and, standing in front
of them, gave the Red clenched-fist salute and joined them in singing the "*Internationale.*"

On 17 April Antonin Moulin, aged eighty-one, died in St. Andiol. He was killed by a *mistral,* having caught a chill just after returning to the village for the Easter holiday, but his son had time to reach the house and talk to him before he died. Jean was sufficiently affected by his father's death to remain in St. Andiol and Montpellier for the six weeks that remained before his reinstallation in Rodez. Two days after that ceremony he received a visit from some of his Paris friends and the whole party set off on a four-day bicycle tour of the banks of the River Lot and the Gorges du Tarn. A photograph shows them lunching on a sunny café terrace. The youngest prefect in France is his customary, athletic self, in a dazzling white T-shirt with not a hair out of place. He is surrounded by Pierre Cot and his wife Néna, André Labarthe and Paul Chatain, a wealthy Grenoble business-man with whom they frequently went on holidays, skiing or cruising on Chatain's yacht in the Mediterranean. It was with Chatain that they had been skiing in Zürs when the body of Stavisky was found and the whole adventure started. This holiday snapshot is a memorial to a friendship and a political collaboration that for its instigator, Cot, had just terminated in personal failure and a political débâcle. But Moulin, promoted and decorated, had waltzed away from the crash.

The reality behind the rumors and headlines that had destroyed Cot made his fall a memorable irony. As Gerald Howson has established in *Arms for Spain,* only nineteen (not fifty) French military aircraft were legally delivered to Spain by 8 August 1936; they were all unarmed and their weapons were never delivered. By the end of October these had been followed by nine illicitly exported military planes, also unarmed, seven further planes which were almost certainly unarmed, and three planes shipped in crates which may not have been assembled until February 1937. It is clear from these figures that France's contribution to the air battle for Madrid was nonexistent. As Howson writes: "there are few artefacts more useless than a fighter aircraft without its armaments." When the Republicans eventually established air superiority over Madrid in February 1937, it was with Soviet planes and, usually, Soviet pilots. By then the Republicans had acquired at least 162 Soviet fighters and forty Soviet bombers.

From one point of view the fall of Pierre Cot was a disaster of "news management." Both he and his staff knew perfectly well how few planes had actually been smuggled into Spain, but they were trapped by the logic of the secret policy of *nonintervention élastique.* On the one hand they were prevented by France's membership of the nonintervention pact from disclosing the existence of *any* secret support for the Spanish Republicans; on the other they were inhibited by guilt and embarrassment from defending themselves by revealing the paltry extent of that support insofar as it extended to military aircraft. Instead the leaders of the French Popular Front were hoist by their own petard, forced in public to take the blame for a conspiracy that had largely failed and which they denied had ever existed, while privately obliged to pretend that it had been a brilliant success. One can assume that their dilemma caused a certain amount of quiet amusement in Moscow, which had mounted the entire sinister farce of military support for the Spanish Republic during the Spanish Civil War, a tragedy which the Soviet Union regarded as the world's biggest antifascist propaganda exercise, and an opportunity to acquire the maximum amount of Spanish gold in return for the minimum number of outdated or unserviceable weapons.*

The biggest individual loser in the fall of the Popular Front was undoubtedly Pierre Cot. "The gravedigger of French aviation" was never again to be a government minister. Cot remained an impotent spectator of Munich and was further humiliated when the Nazi-Soviet Pact rendered his long-held pro-Soviet views ridiculous. He was then rejected by the Free French in London in 1940 on the grounds that his name had "become a term of abuse." Embittered by this experience he went to New York where he made contact with the Comintern in September 1940. In the United States he became a correspondent and analyst for the NKVD (GPU) case officer Vasili Zaroubine, and devoted his considerable political skill to undermining and discrediting General de Gaulle.

But Moulin, in Rodez, was able to continue his career unhindered. He had been trained all his life to head a prefecture and he knew that he could manage it with style. When he returned to the Aveyron he entered his department as a baron enters his fief. He was in need of a new boss, but the remarkable timing of his appointment to his first prefecture, one month before the Cot bobsled struck a wall of ice, suggests that, foreseeing the impact, he had already renewed his contacts with *le Grand Orient*.

The importance of this period for Moulin's reputation in France was not the actual failure of the arms-smuggling policy so much as its reputed

---

* For the story of how the Soviet Union responded to requests from the Spanish Republican government for urgent military aid, see *Arms for Spain*, by Gerald Howson.

success. From this point on the story of Moulin's life is dominated by "the Moscow question." To what extent was he aware of the Comintern conspiracy to infiltrate the cabinet of Pierre Cot? And how close were his subsequent links with Soviet intelligence? When war came, which cause would be his?

Jean Moulin arrived in Chartres in January 1939, after spending just eleven months as prefect of the Aveyron. The move did not involve a promotion, but Chartres was only one hour by train from Paris, a great advantage both socially and professionally. The transfer had been requested by Moulin and sponsored by Maurice Viollette, mayor of Dreux, ex-minister in Léon Blum's government, president of the general assembly of the Eure-et-Loir, prominent member of the *Grand Orient,* and friend of Moulin since 1927. Viollette's influence was sufficiently strong to overcome the objections of the mayor of Chartres, the right-wing senator Raymond Gilbert, who opposed Moulin's appointment.

In Rodez, Moulin's efficiency and charm had made him a popular figure, even with his political opponents. In a letter to his mother he complained about the "corvée" (chore) of greeting Cardinal Verdier, the archbishop of Paris, on an official visit, but in public his attentions to the cardinal were highly correct. As the Republican forces collapsed in Spain, 500,000 Republican refugees flooded over the border into France. They included communists, anarchists and thousands of members of the International Brigade, revolutionaries without a state to overthrow. They were regarded with deep suspicion by the right-wing radical government of Edouard Daladier, which had succeeded the Popular Front in April 1938, and, following Hitler's invasion of Austria, had replaced the previous policy of a Franco-Soviet Pact with an Anglo-French alliance while making every effort to fulfill a belated rearmament program. When the government launched a campaign of repression against aliens throughout France, Moulin, despite his leftist sympathies, executed it loyally. In September 1938 he took the necessary steps to expel to Spain old people, children, militiamen and even political refugees, notwithstanding the steady advance of Franco's forces. The future of these people in the shrinking Catalan enclave was grim, and if they happened to be anti-Stalinists they faced the additional risk of torture and death at the hands of their communist comrades in Barcelona.

One of Moulin's first official duties on arriving in Chartres had been to attend the annual banquet organized for the town's "republicans" by the local masonic lodge. Following his speech the new prefect received the special congratulations of the lodge which regarded him, thanks to family loyalties, as a particularly welcome ally. In Chartres, Moulin continued to follow his instructions and showed no hesitation in arresting and interning aliens, communist and noncommunist alike. By then Daladier and Chamberlain had signed the Munich agreement, Hitler had broken it in March 1939, and it was becoming increasingly clear that war was imminent.

In July 1939 Moulin traveled on leave to St. Tropez and joined Pierre Cot on a cruise to the island of Porquerolles. He had last seen his former protector, under whose guidance he had helped arm some of the Republican forces he was now repatriating, at the Radical Party's congress in Marseille the previous October, when Cot had been booed and hissed by his own party for his performance at the air ministry.

After returning from the Mediterranean cruise Moulin took another short holiday with his mother and his sister Laure. They went to London for three days. Laure (who was a teacher of English) spoke the language well, but it was Moulin's first visit. In fact, apart from his skiing holidays in the Austrian Tyrol, it seems to have been the first time he had ever left France. Moulin was back at his desk to hear the news of the Nazi-Soviet Pact. This agreement was fiercely denounced by many left-wing leaders—including Pierre Cot, who described it as "a stab in the back"—and it caused a dramatic exodus from the French Communist Party. Arthur Koestler wrote about this disillusion in *Scum of the Earth*, his account of his years as a refugee in France:

> It was equally hard for a slow-thinking French Renault worker of 45 and for a little Polish Jew of 19 to realise that the messianic belief to which each in his way had devoted what was purest in him was a fake; that they had been taken in like fools, borne beating and imprisonment for nothing; lost the prospect of advancement in the factory for nothing; suffered, dreamt, quarrelled, argued for years and years— all for nothing.

All the hopes of Moulin and Cot, and the Popular Front, of the pro-communist, anti-fascist world campaign for peace, lay in shreds with the signing of the Nazi-Soviet Pact. A week later, on 1 September, Hitler invaded Poland and Stalin followed two weeks after that. France was at war.

The period of the phony war was taken by the French government as an opportunity for another attack on the extreme left and the communists. In October the thirty-five communist deputies in the National Assembly were arrested. Both openly and secretly the Communist Party was following Moscow's orders, doing everything it could to support its new Nazi allies and sabotage the French war effort. "Anti-fascism" was dead. Instead the communists distributed tracts arguing that this was a capitalist and imperialist war, that Daladier and Chamberlain were "warmongers" and just as much enemies of the people as Hitler, and that proletarians should fight the enemy at home rather than serving as capitalist cannon fodder. Acts of industrial sabotage became increasingly common. In the Eure-et-Loir, Moulin ordered police surveillance and repression of known communist agitators, particularly those working in the railway yards at Dreux.

The repression of the communist leadership in time of war during the Nazi-Soviet Pact was hardly surprising, but according to Koestler, who was himself arrested in Paris and interned at this time, "It was murderous stupidity on the part of the French government to start a police pogrom against the communist rank and file, instead of seizing this unique opportunity to win them over." There were at this time about 3.5 million aliens living in France, which was almost ten percent of the population, and Koestler was among the high proportion of them who were revolutionary leftists, men who had become utterly disillusioned with the communists as a result of Stalin's pro-Hitler policy. After being arrested in Paris in October, Koestler was sent to the Le Vernet internment camp in the Ariège, about thirty miles north of the Pyrenean frontier. This was notoriously the worst camp in France and when he got there he found that a high proportion of its prisoners were the alien remnants of the International Brigade. Moulin sent a large number of detained aliens on to Le Vernet, and in the case of Spanish refugees who were in breach of residency regulations, expelled them to Spain, where they faced imprisonment or worse under the Franco regime. On one occasion, described by Cordier, Moulin ordered the arrest of a Spanish refugee who had committed the offense of carrying a nonstandard identity card. It was signed "Stalin" and bore the motto "The Party is the State of the proletariat." The Spaniard explained that he had been obliged to accept this card because he had been a civil servant working in the Republican zone, and that if he had been in the Francoist zone he would have had to carry a Falangist card. He received a five-month prison sentence followed by deportation.

In *Scum of the Earth* Koestler recorded what it was like for an unprivileged alien to deal with the senior French administration at this time, a body which he typified as being "a mixture of ignominy, corruption and laisser-faire." Its victims considered Le Vernet to be below the level of Nazi concentration camps in the matters of food, accommodation and hygiene, and they based their comparison on experience of several camps including Dachau. In the Nazi camps, men were beaten to death quite quickly, whereas in Le Vernet they were beaten but they died slowly of brutal work, undernourishment and disease. And most of the men imprisoned there had been sent on the decision of their local prefect.

While waiting for the war to warm up, Moulin, haunted by his inactivity in 1918, made several attempts to be transferred for military service, and at one point managed to enlist as an air gunner. He was ordered to report for training to the military air base at Tours, with the rank of sergeant, but the Ministry of the Interior discovered what had happened and insisted on his immediate demobilization. So it was that when the German army eventually struck into Holland and Belgium on 10 May 1940, Moulin was once more behind his desk in Chartres.

IV

RESISTANCE

NINE

An Envoy to London

Jean moulin's clandestine journey from Marseille to London took six weeks but passed without serious incident. The train from Marseille carried him to Barcelona where he spent the night before traveling on via Madrid and crossing into Portugal on 12 September 1941. He checked into a cheap *pension* in Lisbon, the Algarve, and his first move was to report to the American embassy. On the following day he met Major L. H. Mortimore, SOE's representative at the British embassy, who immediately sent a telegram to London, announcing his arrival. Moulin told the major that he was the emissary of three major resistance organizations and wished to travel to London as soon as possible. The immediate result of this interview was disappointing. Major Mortimore received no orders to put Moulin on one of the highly coveted flights to England.

Kicking his heels in Lisbon he grew bored. He was not apparently exhilarated by the harbor, busy with the arrivals and departures of ships from all over the world, which gave other fugitives from wartime France a sense of hope and freedom. He noted only the "strong contrast between the luxuries enjoyed by the few and the misery of the majority," a stilted reaction and the curious echo of a remark Cardinal Verdier had made to him in Rodez in 1938 after a visit to Hungary. Some time after his arrival a boy robbed him of his washbag and his alarm clock, a theft which must have taken place from his hotel room. On the British embassy's advice

Moulin moved to a different *pension,* and while he was waiting for permission to leave started to type a long report on the objectives and needs of the resistance movement. It was—after his account of the occupation of Chartres, *Premier Combat,* which he had written in St. Andiol in the winter of 1940–41—his finest literary effort, a masterpiece of imprecision, overstatement, approximations and bluff. But it was beautifully judged and eventually it did the trick.

The reasons for Moulin's unusually long delay in Lisbon have never been properly explained. London knew who he was, having been alerted to his impending departure by the U.S. consulate in Marseille as early as 8 April, at which point of course Moulin had set out, not for Lisbon, but for Paris. It seems that while he was being held in Lisbon a delicate game of cat-and-mouse was being played between three parties: SOE, the Gaullist intelligence service in London—later called the BCRA (*Bureau central de renseignements et d'action*)—and Moulin himself. The official explanation for the delay, given by the SOE archivist in 1979, was "the restricted number of flights and poor weather conditions." There were other complications. General de Gaulle's representative in Lisbon was unavailable, having just been arrested by the Portuguese police; and because of a deterioration in relations between de Gaulle and Churchill in London, "Free French" business was being accorded a low priority. Nonetheless Moulin was too prominent a recruit for SOE to pass over, and an imposed delay would have emphasized who was ultimately in charge. Moulin no doubt hoped that his initial report would accelerate his transfer to London. According to Cordier it may in fact have delayed it, since its evident interest meant that Major Mortimore would have encoded it and cabled it to London, where it would have been decoded, translated and studied, without being passed to the BCRA. In response to SOE's approaches in Lisbon, Moulin said that he was keeping an open mind about which service to work for, and wished to speak to the French leadership in London before deciding. He was eventually put on the daily seaplane to Poole harbor and landed in England on 20 October.

While in Lisbon, Moulin had written to Pierre Cot a letter which he did not post until the afternoon of his arrival in England. In this letter Moulin said:

> As you have known for some time I have decided, after all, not to go to America, believing that I can serve our unhappy country better in

following another path and in remaining closer to our English friends. . . . I have learnt by various means that you, on the contrary, are much more useful in the United States, where you continue to do good work for the allied cause. To each his destiny. . . . I regret not being able to give you my address . . . but I am traveling a lot at the moment and I need some peace.

This letter could be read literally. In view of the considerable efforts and sums of money Cot had expended in getting Moulin out of France on the assumption that his former chief of staff would join him in America, Moulin owed him an explanation for the change of plan. By posting the letter from England Moulin may have been letting Cot know how far his own plans had been realized. Or he may have decided not to post the letter until he was certain that his decision to abandon his mentor had been successful. Cot's reaction to the news is not known. By this time he had been working for Soviet intelligence for over a year. It would have been normal for him to have felt some disappointment that the Free French movement, which had repudiated him as a notorious minister of the Popular Front, should have accepted one of his closest collaborators without blinking. Several phrases in Moulin's letter could well have turned the knife in the wound. "*A chacun sa destinée*" (to each his destiny) carried a hint of indifference, if not triumph. The refusal to give his address was unnecessary; Cot already had two addresses for Moulin, at St. Andiol and *chez* Madame Dangon. The withholding of an English address, and the specious reason—"I need some peace"—were an indelicate reminder that contact would not be welcome while he was establishing his credentials in London. But the fact that Moulin posted the letter from England, immediately on arrival, suggests that it may have had another purpose altogether. Knowing that it would be read by the British censor Moulin was signaling that he was now independent of Cot.

The impression made by Jean Moulin on his arrival in England in October 1941 has been summarized in *Six Faces of Courage* by M. R. D. Foot, a wartime member of the special forces and SOE's historian. A prefect shunned by Pétain had arrived to help General de Gaulle. This man had been dismissed by Vichy after refusing to implement antirepublican directives. He had subsequently worked quietly, "gathering up the reins" of resistance and encouraging people to resist. "By August 1941 he had discovered enough: he had detected four main groupings, and was empowered by the leaders of three of them to get out to London, if he could, and report what was going on to General de Gaulle." This was the first, official portrait of Jean Moulin.

Where Lisbon had failed to stimulate Moulin, Bournemouth seems to have deployed its special magic. He was exhilarated to have reached a country where Frenchmen were still in the fight and understood why he was regarded—like all new arrivals—with suspicion. On the day he arrived he was sent under armed escort to London, a journey which some of his compatriots were surprised to find they did not have to make in handcuffs. Although Moulin's transfer to London had by this time been requested by General de Gaulle he was not passed on to the Free French but taken to the interrogation center in the former Royal Patriotic School in south London. It was not unusual for French volunteers to be held there under heavy guard for a number of weeks, an experience they found uncomfortable since they had to sleep in the school dormitories, in beds designed for schoolgirls.

Once in London, Moulin was interrogated by Captain F. Eric Piquet-Wicks of the Royal Inniskilling Fusiliers, who was the acting head of the "RF" section of SOE, the section which had been set up to collaborate with Gaullist intelligence. Piquet-Wicks remembered a small man, calm, collected, unremarkable, almost placid. Other English witnesses recalled "sparkling eyes, a lively manner . . . grace of movement and almost absurdly youthful appearance. . . . Above all he had charm: simply to be in his presence was a delight." Piquet-Wicks cleared "Moulins," as his report identified him, in less than two days and was under the impression that he had signed up a new member of SOE. Moulin himself thought differently: he did not want to work *for* SOE but he had no objection to working with it. Later Moulin was taken to see Maurice Buckmaster, the head of SOE (F), the independent section operating in France, which was regarded by the Gaullists with hostility. But Buckmaster, who may have been encouraged by the strongly republican emphasis Moulin gave to his *curriculum vitae,* also failed to overcome his objections.

Apart from enjoying Moulin's company there were other reasons why SOE officers were impressed by his presence in London. The first was his former rank; as M. R. D. Foot later put it, he was "the first man of any real consequence to come out of France since June 1940; had he wanted he could have set himself up in opposition to de Gaulle. . . ." Another was his personality. A subsequent SOE note read: "He is the first person [i.e., Free Frenchman] I have met or heard of having . . . the sort of natural authority and experience which his past history gives him." A third and crucial reason was the credentials Moulin apparently carried. He was the first serious emissary to London from the French Resistance; the first delegate of three resistance movements. SOE knew this because he told them so, and they believed him because they wanted to believe him—he was exactly the kind of Frenchman they had been waiting for. Nonetheless they were deceiving themselves; in creating the identity which he assumed when he reached Lisbon, Jean Moulin was pulling an audacious confidence trick. "Joseph Mercier," a bogus law teacher from Columbia University (so bogus that he did not even speak English), had been replaced by an equally bogus "emissary from three resistance organizations."

Moulin, who claimed to be "the delegate of three movements," had in fact only been in touch with two resistance leaders, Frenay and de Menthon. Neither had appointed him their delegate; Frenay had merely briefed him on the position in his own movement and told him what he knew about two others. Frenay said that when Moulin left him in April 1941 he never expected to see him again, had no further contact with him before his departure, and assumed that even if Moulin did succeed in reaching England he would certainly not be returning to France. De Menthon was able to tell Moulin even less than Frenay; again there was no question of "delegation." Nonetheless Moulin told SOE that he represented "*Liberté, Libération* and *Libération Nationale.*" His description of *Liberté* was brief but accurate. He said that it was "chiefly" in the occupied zone, when it was entirely confined to that area. He said that *Libération* was in the occupied zone, which he knew to be untrue, and added that it was now "practically fused with *Libérte,*" which was also untrue; the two groups had very different politics. He said that *Libération Nationale* was in both zones, which was an exaggeration, but again it gave the impression of a far wider net of contacts than he actually had. Moulin also invented, for the benefit of SOE, an imaginary exodus of "bourgeois adherents" from the resistance groups at the end of the Nazi-Soviet Pact, and added an equally imaginary influx of workers. Moulin then said that the three resistance chiefs had held a meeting in July, which they had not held (even if they had held one he would probably not have known about it), and added three equally fictitious meetings since, "the last one on September 5th." He then invented a number of details about decisions taken at that meeting.

On 24 October Moulin was released from the Royal Patriotic School and driven by Captain Piquet-Wicks to the De Vere Hotel in Kensington High Street, where he would be lodged at SOE's expense. He was issued an Aliens' Registration Certificate by the Metropolitan Police on the following day. It recorded that "Joseph Jean Mercier" had no profession and wore horn-rimmed glasses. It was at the hotel that Moulin was first contacted by "Colonel Passy," the *nom de guerre* of André Dewavrin, a regular army captain and *polytechnicien* and an engineering instructor at St.-Cyr military academy who had become the head of the BCRA, the Gaullist intelligence unit. Dewavrin, like de Gaulle, had attended the élite Catholic school in Paris, the Collège Stanislas. Having volunteered for the Norwegian expeditionary force he was evacuated from Narvik through London, where he was one of the few French servicemen to leave the ranks and volunteer to fight on with the Free French. De Gaulle decided that he would be a suitable person to set up an intelligence service—Dewavrin was rumored, without evidence, to have been a member of *la Cagoule,* the extreme-right terrorist network—and his presence in London, in this influential position, was one of the reasons for Moulin's distrust of the Gaullists. This was the man who, aged thirty, twelve years younger than Moulin, was to be for some time his nominal superior and main operational contact.

In his memoirs Dewavrin described how he was confronted with "a small, solid man"—both Piquet-Wicks and Dewavrin were tall; Moulin was actually of medium height—"with pepper and salt hair and a sallow complexion. His eyes shone, he radiated physical and moral strength, energy and tenacity. When he spoke there was often the hint of a smile behind his gaze which gave away his inner thoughts and disarmed his listener." It was to Dewavrin, or Colonel Passy, that Moulin gave the text of the coded message announcing his safe arrival, to be broadcast on the BBC: "Henri Delacour se porte bien" (Henri Delacour is well).

Moulin knew that the interrogation he faced from Colonel Passy's BCRA would be at least as testing as any mounted by SOE. Furthermore he would have to be rather less imaginative in some of his claims: it would be dangerous to invent details since these might easily be demolished by other new arrivals whose identity he would not know. He had for instance told SOE, apparently in conversation, a fantastic story about his attempts to help the Spanish Republicans when he was at the air ministry. According to M. R. D. Foot, working from SOE records:

Luck gave him an opening. Many devout French catholics were as set on Franco's victory as devout republicans were on the republic's, and Moulin happened to discover that a devout catholic official in the air ministry was trying to smuggle a French air force aircraft to the Spanish rebels. As the price of his silence, Moulin browbeat him into smuggling a dozen aircraft to the Spanish republic instead. This was not an elegant proceeding, but it was efficient: Moulin felt he had struck a dozen small blows against the totalitarian menace he could see looming over France.

Something about that story, its romance, its glibness, the smooth way in which it borrows a pinch of likelihood and reverses the truth about Léon Blum's policy of *nonintervention élastique*, is worthy of the pen of Claud Cockburn writing from Spain for the *Daily Worker*. Moulin must have concocted it to conceal the fact that Blum's "elastic" nonintervention entailed working with Soviet intelligence. It is unlikely that he wheeled it out for either Passy or de Gaulle.

The basis of Moulin's deposition to Colonel Passy was once again the long memorandum he had written for SOE in Lisbon. To reassure Passy, Moulin claimed (untruthfully) to have omitted the names of resistance leaders in the version he had supplied to SOE. When he handed over a carbon copy of the report to Passy it was the first opportunity the latter had had to study it. In subsequent conversations, Moulin was more careful about embroidering his written account.

André Labarthe, Moulin's old friend and fellow arms-smuggler, who in 1940 had become one of the best-known voices on the BBC broadcasts to France, had been expelled from the Gaullist movement in January 1941, after MI5 accused him of plotting against de Gaulle. (It was Labarthe who started the rumor of Passy's connection with the *Cagoule*.) On returning to France Moulin told his sister that he had avoided Labarthe because the latter was a journalist, but he knew very well that he was a journalist who was capable of keeping a secret and this was neither a truthful explanation nor a sufficient reason. In fact news of Labarthe's misadventures in London had reached Moscow and been sent on to Harry Robinson in Paris. From Robinson via Maurice Panier, a warning may have been sent to Moulin before his departure for Lisbon. This chain of information certainly worked in the opposite direction. Moulin's ordeal in Chartres was practically unknown outside the Eure-et-Loir, and had never been published in France except for one brief and vague reference in a Provençal paper in July 1940, and no mention had been made of it outside France. Yet in June 1941 André Labarthe wrote in his non-Gaullist review *France Libre* of "a friend of mine, a Frenchman, who cut his throat in a German dungeon because he refused to betray." The most likely source of this story reaching Labarthe was the old Cot grapevine, and in 1941 it ran through Moscow.

Moulin's life in London—he was in England for ten weeks—was socially very limited because he was traveling as "Mercier," an identity which meant that when he returned to France he would be able to spend part of the time as himself in St. Andiol, Montpellier and Nice. If he were widely known to be in London then he would have to live entirely underground in France. This limitation made it more difficult for him while in England to get an objective sense of the strength and weakness of Gaullism, the degree of support the General enjoyed among the French community in exile or of the political color of his strongest supporters. Moulin would not have been reassured to hear that the Free French had abandoned *Liberté, égalité, fraternité* and replaced it with the more nationalistic *Honneur et patrie,* although his arrival coincided with a decision to restore the republican motto. In France the Gaullists were caricatured as *cagoulards,* and there were certainly some among them; the *Cagoule* had split into two factions after the armistice, the majority rejoicing and joining Pétain's inner circle.

In his report to de Gaulle on the resistance Moulin referred to this division and to Colonel Groussard, leader of the anticollaborationist *cagoulards,* who had been briefly arrested by Vichy police after returning from a visit to England. Moulin even had the effrontery to suggest that he was in touch with Groussard, and had been entrusted with a secret dossier which he had deposited in a safe place and which would be circulated should any mischance befall the colonel; it contained, according to Moulin, much damaging private information about Pétain.

Unlike some of the more plausible information in the report, this improbable detail was perfectly true. He did hold such a dossier; it had been furnished by the colonel's sister-in-law, Antoinette Sachs. Moulin may have calculated that his possession of it might protect him from the hostile intentions of any *cagoulards* in the Gaullist movement. He had every reason to be wary of them. The *Cagoule,* in the form of Groussard, had illegally arrested Prime Minister Pierre Laval in December 1940, and in its more traditional pro-Nazi form had murdered a former Popular Front minister of the interior, Marx Dormoy, in July 1941.

Quite soon after his arrival in London—the date has disappeared with de Gaulle's appointment books—Moulin was taken to see *le Symbole* himself, Brigadier-General Charles de Gaulle, a man who was nine years older than he but whose rank in the republican hierarchy was inferior (as a prefect Moulin's administrative rank was the equivalent of major-general). There was no question, however, as to who was in charge of the meeting. Moulin left no written account of the occasion but many other visitors who underwent the same ordeal have evoked it.

Christian Pineau (of *Libération-Nord*) was invited to dine with de Gaulle in a private room at the Connaught Hotel. There was a blazing log fire, brass fire-irons, a thick carpet and high leather-backed armchairs. "Immense in his uniform he walked towards me," wrote Pineau, "slowly raising his hand to reach out to mine at the very moment when we were face to face. He has the firm and unctuous gestures of an authoritarian prelate. Without saying a word he led me to an armchair, ensconced himself directly opposite and then spoke his first words. 'Speak to me of France.' (*Parlez-moi de France.*) And then de Gaulle fell silent. Imagine," said Pineau, "an examiner who sets a question on the vaguest subject in the world and then lets you talk on without giving any idea of whether you are on the right lines."

After half an hour Pineau, exhausted, came to a halt; and then the General started to speak. But his words had nothing whatsoever to do with Pineau's. He spoke of the Free French, and the soldiers in Africa and their military feats, with a mixture of pride and bitterness, the latter largely caused by the problems he faced with the British government. When he eventually asked for details about the life of the resisters he remained quite unmoved by the description of the risks they ran and the anguish they suffered. De Gaulle had a regular soldier's disregard for irregulars and this prevented him from warming to the resistance. As Cordier has pointed out, he always spelled the word with a small "r" in his speeches and memoirs. But Pineau explained his reaction differently. "It was clear that for him every fighting man who risked his life was merely doing his job ... tank drivers in the western desert and distributors of underground leaflets in the occupied zone were exposing themselves to identical dangers. The dinner was good," added Pineau, "the Bordeaux excellent."

Some hint of the reason for de Gaulle's bitterness may be found in another account of a meal with the General, this time from the pen of an English visitor, the writer and diplomat Harold Nicolson. Nicolson, who was then the political editor of the BBC, lunched with de Gaulle at the Connaught on 9 December 1941 when Moulin was still in London and at a time when he was seeing de Gaulle at regular intervals.

> Lunch with de Gaulle at the Connaught Hotel. I cannot make out whether I really like him. His arrogance and fascism annoy me. . . . He asks what I meant by saying that the French in England should "compose their differences." What he wanted me to say was that I had meant that they should all join de Gaulle. I am not prepared to say that as yet. I say that I was cross at having one Frenchman telling me that de Gaulle was surrounded by Jews and freemasons while another told me that he was surrounded by Jesuits and *cagoulards*. He does not like this at all and his *aide-de-camp* blushes. But it was not a bad thing to say.

Moulin's distrust of de Gaulle before his arrival in England is well established. Cot had by this time developed the view, which he freely expressed to his French correspondents in London, that de Gaulle was "a fascist." This was at that time a view commonly held among left-wing opponents of Pétain, who could see no advantage in backing one politically ambitious conservative general against another. Cot added that de Gaulle himself probably did not realize that he was fascist. One of Cot's letters to London was described as "private" but he added a list of socialist politicians-in-exile to whom it might be shown. It was distributed more widely than that since it was intercepted by the British censor, sent to the Foreign Office and circulated for comments. It is notable that in his letter to Cot of 19 October, in which he announces his change of destination, Moulin made no mention of de Gaulle, suggesting instead that he was going to work with "the English." He continued to treat Cot's opinions with care, writing to him even after he had joined the BCRA, "For the moment one should support de Gaulle, later we will see." And when he returned to France he said to one resistance leader, of the General, "He's a very great man. . . . But what are his real feelings about the Republic? I could not tell you. I know his official position, but . . . is he actually a democrat?"

With that comment Moulin was expressing all the republican's fear of a military *putsch*. Theirs was not an obvious partnership. Moulin was looking at a right-wing, Catholic army officer, a nationalist rather than a republican by reputation; de Gaulle was faced with an anticlerical pillar of the Popular Front, suspected of being a communist, a man who was said to be more of an idealist than a patriot. Perhaps the only thing they had in common was that both had been educated in schools where their father was a teacher, a situation which de Gaulle, too, had found a strain. Yet somehow in London Moulin seems to have fallen under the strange charm of this bizarre figure; it was a case of the seducer seduced. He later told a colleague in France that he had been so moved that he had found himself speaking in his long-forgotten southern accent. The most compelling point about de Gaulle, from Moulin's point of view, was his transparent love for France.

This love of France was sometimes expressed in unexpected ways. While Moulin was in London news arrived of the massive reprisals carried out against French hostages after the assassination of a number of German soldiers by the communist resistance. De Gaulle was opposed to the communist policy but when Pétain made an appeal to stop the assassinations de Gaulle's attitude hardened, and he called a press conference. Blaming the reprisals on the surrender of the Vichy government de Gaulle said:

> Yesterday we heard the quavering voice of the old man describing the killing of German soldiers as "the crime without a name." . . . In fact it is absolutely normal, and it is absolutely justifiable, that the Germans should be killed by the French. If the Germans do not wish to receive death at our hands they merely have to stay at home and not make war on us. Anyway, sooner or later, they are all fated to be slaughtered, either by us or by our allies.

Moulin would have read the reports of this speech the day he left the Royal Patriotic School and just before he met de Gaulle. Two days later he saw Captain Piquet-Wicks again and told him that he had chosen to volunteer for the Free French and that de Gaulle had decided to make him his delegate in the Vichy zone.

In any event the meeting had gone very well. De Gaulle had not only been impressed by Moulin's rank and experience and by the story of Chartres, he had also been won over by the idea that in occupied France, isolated French men and women about whom he knew nothing had heard his voice and sent him their envoy. He was in fact, in London in 1941, desperately isolated and his forces undermanned. In the sixteen months that had elapsed between de Gaulle's historic broadcast of 18 June 1940 and the arrival of Jean Moulin the Free French in London had made very little progress. Large numbers of French troops had landed in Britain just after the speech, including 123,000 evacuated from Dunkirk, 7,500 evacuated from Norway and 22,500 sailors whose warships had taken refuge in English ports. But of this total of 150,000 men, only 7,000 had chosen to answer de Gaulle's appeal. Furthermore the quality of recruits he had been able to attract was often low. Too many of the well-qualified or able Frenchmen who had been in London in 1940 had left, for the United States, or Switzerland, or to rejoin Vichy France. Jean Monnet, Raymond Aron, the novelist and diplomat Paul Morand and Alexis Léger (the poet Saint-John Perse) had all turned their backs on de Gaulle. When another outstanding recruit from the resistance, Pierre Brossolette, a prominent socialist intellectual and journalist, eventually reached London in April 1942 he was struck by the mediocrity of many of the men who formed de Gaulle's court. With the exception of Colonel Passy and three others, Brossolette described them as *doublures*—stand-ins. There was "unrelieved mediocrity" wherever he went; even the intelligent staffmen were "soft and timid." Whatever able men did arrive were almost all, like Moulin, sent back to France.

De Gaulle's relations with his only powerful patron, Winston Churchill, veered between the poor and the catastrophic. A large faction in the War Cabinet considered him to be an opportunist and adventurer who would never lead France. Churchill had to summon all his patience to tolerate de Gaulle's hypersensitive and morbidly suspicious behavior. In France, de Gaulle had been stripped of his rank, put on trial for treason and in his absence sentenced to death. In London most of the arguments turned on whether de Gaulle should be treated as a symbol or as an effective war leader and head of government. Churchill wanted him to concentrate on military recruitment. De Gaulle insisted that he be allowed to represent France. "We are France" was his way of putting it. His disagreement with Churchill's conduct of the war drove de Gaulle at one point to publicly accuse the British prime minister of dealing secretly with Hitler. Churchill wondered whether he had gone mad. In fact de Gaulle was responding to the intolerable burden of his isolation. As one of his supporters wrote, "We were a few French people who trailed round the streets of London like broken toys, useless and ashamed spectators of great events. . . ." But de Gaulle was incapable of shame.

Initially Moulin's chief interest for de Gaulle was the fact that he offered the first contact with the resistance movement inside Vichy France. Passy had been parachuting liaison agents into occupied France throughout 1941 but still lacked the sort of detailed information apparently offered by Moulin's report on the southern zone. Having read that report and met the prefect, de Gaulle saw no reason not to trust him. He knew that he was a man of the left, but regarded that as an additional advantage if he himself was to lead a national movement. He did not know about Moulin's former and continuing contacts with Soviet intelligence. In 1976 Passy told Henri Frenay that there would have been no question of sending Moulin back into France if his old friendship with Labarthe had been discovered.

To the information Moulin invented for de Gaulle's benefit one should add the information he had not invented which he did not impart, in particular his contact with Manhès and Meunier in the northern zone. There are various interpretations for this curious omission. Those who are convinced that Moulin was a Soviet agent conclude that his failure to disclose these contacts is further confirmation of their theory. Alternatively he may have decided to conceal his connection with former colleagues on Pierre Cot's staff because he did not wish to discredit himself with the influential right-wingers among the Gaullists. A further explanation would be that Moulin wished to have his official mission confined to the less risky zone, partly because he did not trust Colonel Passy at this stage, partly because he wished to be the master of when and where he entered the occupied zone, which would not necessarily be the case if his mission was extended there.

The Free French movement in 1941 was not really in a position to pick and choose its agents and "Corporal" Mercier's chief qualification for his task was, finally, his willingness to undertake it. The post required physical courage, the ability to act quickly on his own initiative, great determination, a sense of purpose that would carry him through the dangers he was about to face alone, administrative experience, political agility and qualities of leadership that would allow him to impose his views on a succession of strong characters. A biographical inquiry into Corporal Mercier would have revealed that he was the grandson of a man who committed suicide in the family home; in childhood he had been deeply affected by the death of his older brother. As a schoolboy he suffered a conflict of loyalties, torn between his schoolfriends, who challenged authority, and his father, who taught in the school. The boy showed artistic talent but his father, a domineering character, pushed him into an unsuitable career as a public administrator. This conflict was reflected in a youthful interest in cross-dressing.

Through his father's influence he was sheltered from military service and subsequently experienced feelings of guilt. He passively allowed his parents to arrange an engagement with a distant cousin to whom he was not closely attached and when this fell through he attempted to break away from his father's influence by marrying a young woman who was dominated by her mother; this marriage lasted less than two years. He frequently spoke of his desire to have children but generally associated with women who were unlikely to have any. His friends spoke of his warmth and enthusiasm but his actions revealed a cold, watchful and detached personality with a marked capacity for manipulation. He was obsessively secretive about his personal life, a habit he had acquired as a student when he first escaped from the daily supervision of his childhood home. Long before he needed to, he lived like a fugitive. Under pressure he showed hysterical tendencies, he was complicated, creative and volatile with a filthy temper and ruthless personal ambition. One can imagine the BCRA analyst reading this report with growing enthusiasm and stamping it *Approuvé*. By December Moulin was ready to return to the Vichy zone as de Gaulle's delegate, with the task of uniting its three resistance movements into one.

Moulin's training for his role as a secret agent was remarkably brief. He took a crash course in coding and decoding from a French specialist and was given instructions about elementary security and the use of pseudonyms. In London his pseudonym of "Corporal Mercier" concealed his false identity of Joseph Mercier. In France he was to be "M," then "Mer," then "Ker." Finally "Rex" was fixed on.*

The final stage of Moulin's training took place at the parachute school at Ringway near Manchester. Here he had to undergo a violent session of

---

* Cordier suggests that the Latin word for "king" was selected as a sign of the importance London accorded to his mission, but it seems more likely to have been an inversion of "Ker."

physical training designed for men who were twenty years younger than he was. A specialty of the general physical training course at Ringway, according to Colonel Passy, was "flying angels" from a springboard over a wooden horse, without an instructor to catch you. "There is nothing like leaping headfirst over a barrier four and a half feet high if you have spent the previous year behind a desk," wrote Passy. ". . . A few hours of this and we had been reduced to the state of crippled old men. After two days, when we were just about at the pre-coma level, they said we were fit to jump."

Passy accompanied Moulin to Ringway to test out a new parachute and noticed that after one of the sessions in the gym the prefect was vomiting with fatigue. But Moulin had always considered himself to be *sportif* and it was no doubt a point of honor with him to pass the physical test; he knew that what lay ahead of him was the nearest he would ever get to the experience of going into battle. Moulin made two parachute jumps at Ringway without injuring himself, and was then judged ready to make a night jump "blind"—that is without a reception committee—over France. In honor of the event "Corporal Mercier" was promoted to sergeant.

What neither he nor Passy nor SOE knew was that the Vichy counterespionage service had already discovered quite a lot about Jean Moulin. They knew that a man named Moulin or Mercier, who had formerly been "the prefect of the Indre-et-Loire" (*sic*), had left for England as an emissary of "the Intelligence Service," Vichy's name for both MI6 and SOE. A report dated 31 October 1941, sent to the local office of the *Surveillance du Territoire* in Marseille, warned them to look out for him. The information had been obtained following the arrest of an SOE agent who was already in France.

TEN

Life Underground

A T 3:30 A.M. ON 2 JANUARY 1942 the pilot of an RAF Whitley dropped Jean Moulin by parachute into a strong wind somewhere over Provence. The plane came in at under 1,500 feet and through the open hatch Moulin and the two agents who jumped with him could clearly see the moonlit landscape spread out below. At one point they could even make out a group of men on a road looking up toward the noise in the sky. Moulin had asked to be dropped on the north slopes of the Alpilles range of hills, near St. Andiol. Among those hills, in a remote valley not far from the ruins of the castle of Romanin, stood an old stone farmhouse that he owned, which was the ideal spot for "Sergeant Mercier" to change back into Jean Moulin. But either because the pilot made an error or because the *mistral* blew them over the wrong valley, Moulin ended up in a bog called the Marais des Baux on the southern slopes of the Alpilles, not far from the windmill of Alphonse Daudet. It took him over an hour to find his two companions, an army officer named Raymond Fassin and a student called Hervé Montjaret who had been trained as a radio operator. They had at least fifteen kilometers to walk and they had to cross the Alpilles. Moulin was already soaked—the *mistral* had turned into a hailstorm—and the radio had been damaged in the drop. In order to avoid attracting attention they decided to separate. Montjaret was promptly intercepted and questioned by a patrol of gendarmes who had been tipped off by suspicious farmers. He subsequently got lost, missed the rendezvous, found he had no back-up address and disappeared for several weeks.

Moulin and Fassin avoided pursuit and managed to reach the abandoned farmhouse, where they spent the rest of the day and the next night. Before leaving, Moulin concealed arms and money in the farmhouse, and as far as is known he never carried a gun again. On the following morning Fassin set off alone and Moulin walked the ten kilometers into St. Andiol. Food was rationed so he collected his food coupons from the town hall and then sent a telegram to his mother and sister in Montpellier. His mother, who had no idea where he had been for the previous sixteen weeks, was relieved to hear from him. Moulin's next move was truly eccentric. He went to Megève and spent ten days skiing with the Chatains. He had eighteen months left to live.

In Moulin's absence the Resistance had changed considerably. In sixteen weeks Frenay, from his base in Lyon, had succeeded in reestablishing links with two of the biggest northern groups, *Libération-Nord* and the right-wing OCM. He had also refused an invitation from SOE or MI6—he never knew which—to sign up with them.[*] Frenay had also started to mobilize his "Secret Army" and had organized a number of small commandos, known as *groupes francs,* which were capable of carrying out military operations.

The United States had entered the war on 7 December following the Japanese attack on Pearl Harbor. One consequence of this was that de Gaulle acquired a new opponent—President Roosevelt, who developed a dislike and distrust of the leader of the Free French that was to last for the rest of his life. As soon as the United States entered the war an intelligence team from the OSS, led by Allen Dulles, was dispatched to Switzerland. Dulles immediately set about penetrating whatever networks he could find. It was Frenay who first uncovered and then rejected an attempt by the Americans to finance *Combat* and draw it away from de Gaulle's sphere of influence. But the most important development in Moulin's absence had been the Communist Party's belated mobilization.

The history of the Resistance in France has been seriously distorted by the failure to acknowledge the fundamentally disruptive role played by

---

[*] Presumably the invitation came from SOE (F) and was the first response to the report Moulin had filed from Lisbon.

the French Communist Party in the resistance movement. Directed, as always, from Moscow, the clandestine leadership of the PCF had continued to denounce de Gaulle as "a reactionary crypto-fascist" until 21 June 1941. Then with the ending of the Nazi-Soviet Pact the party launched a determined attempt to take over the direction of the national resistance and eventually cut it off from the Free French in London. Communist resistance was not confined to the *Front National* and the FTP–MOI. Communists and their allies were already infiltrating many other groups with the aim of influencing and eventually controlling policy. By January 1942 they were well established in *Libération-Sud,* where Emmanuel d'Astier de la Vigerie, the *aristocrate rouge,* was always happy to welcome them. But they had also succeeded in infiltrating *Combat,* one of whose leading members, Marcel Degliame, was an undeclared member of the party. After the war Degliame told Frenay that his mission had been to coordinate the activities of undeclared communists working inside the resistance of the southern zone. And in the third southern zone group, the broadly based *Franc-Tireur,* another communist agent, Yves Farge, was also beginning to play a prominent role. One of Allen Dulles's first approaches had been made to someone he had known as a young man and as a family friend, Noel Field, who had by then moved from Marseille to Switzerland. Dulles was apparently unaware that Field was a Soviet agent and assassin and used him as one of his first points of contact with the French resistance. The OSS's new man in Berne took the view that all anti-Nazi conspiracies were of equal use, which as far as the communists were concerned was a grave mistake. Thanks to Dulles's trust in Noel Field the French communists were able to follow the OSS's early moves.

Meanwhile the FTP–MOI had continued its policy of assassinating German troops in order to provoke reprisals and stimulate popular hatred of the occupying forces. The communists developed this policy on 4 September 1941 by assassinating one of their own dissidents, Marcel Gitton, a former national party secretary and member of the politburo, who left the PCF at the time of the pact and subsequently made a direct appeal to communist workers to support the Vichy regime. He was shot down in a Paris suburb—the beginning of a process of settling internal party scores by assassination which continued for the next three years. The historical link between the French Revolution, the mother of all revolutions, and the "Red revolution" had been emphasized with pride in France ever since October 1917, and for the 10,000 hard-core members of the PCF still present in the ranks in 1941 the approach of a new terror—a French Red terror—provoked keen anticipation. In 1998 the eminent historian Emmanuel Le Roy Ladurie, recalling his youthful days in the PCF, said: "We had the same taste for bloodletting as the *petits-bourgeois* on the French Revolution's committees of public safety." To all appearances enrolled in the patriotic struggle, the communist resistance was in fact following a separate agenda that would eventually lead it to adopt a position of open hostility toward the rest of the resistance. Moulin's role in this struggle remains mysterious, though establishing what it was provides the key to an understanding of his life, and to the French resistance.

After a short visit to his family, Moulin, or "Rex," set out, logically enough, in search of Henri Frenay, the man whose emissary he had claimed to be, his only important point of contact in the resistance and the man to whom he had now, thanks to a remarkable feat of political agility, become the emissary of General de Gaulle. He was to spend most of the next eighteen months traveling and began to know the unreal, exhausting, daily schedule of the professional resister. Jacques Baumel has described how he himself was inducted. Having agreed to serve with *Combat* full-time he was given forty-eight hours to bid farewell to his family and friends and disappear from Marseille, without explanation, for the duration of the war. He only saw his parents three times in the next three years. Two days later Baumel turned up at the Gare St.-Charles carrying a cardboard suitcase holding a towel, a sponge bag, two books and a change of clothes. He was handed a large envelope containing his new identity documents and advised to learn every detail of the contents by heart. He boarded the first train for Lyon and opened the envelope. He discovered that his name was now Jacques Brémond, that he was no longer a doctor but a commercial traveler and that he lived in Maubeuge, a town he had scarcely heard of. Now he must learn the names of its main streets, the mayor, a pharmacist, a baker, the name of a bistro.

Baumel-Brémond, code name "Rossini," learned his tradecraft quickly. Faced by a police barrier he had to force himself to go directly toward it, never to double back. He had to remember to walk on the same side of the road as the oncoming traffic, so that a car could not approach him unnoticed from behind. Check constantly for a tail, never crumple up messages—tear the paper into tiny pieces and scatter them over very long distances. Never enter a nightclub or a black market restaurant or a first-class railway carriage, they were raided all the time. Keep all the rules every day and, with luck, you might last three years as Jacques Baumel lasted. Colonel Rémy of the *Confraternity of Our Lady* broke all the rules every day and was never troubled. Other men and women kept all the rules for three days and were arrested anyway.

> We lived every day with the threat of betrayal [wrote Baumel]. It was more or less our daily diet. . . . We jumped at the slightest noise outside the window, we froze every time the doorbell rang, we automatically registered every noise in the house. It was in Lyon that I discovered every house has its own music; the private music of the instruments played by each member of the tenants' orchestra. A well-tuned ear picks out the new instruments or the false notes or the silences that have not been written into the score. . . . The strain drove men mad. You never get used to the threat of betrayal. I watched as groups, cells or entire networks were destroyed by a mixture of bad security and one unfortunate radio operator who gave away perhaps three names and two addresses after being horribly tortured. . . .

Moulin worked out a system for traveling around the southern zone which was based on an imaginary straight line running east-west through Avignon. South of this line he retained his real identity and lived in public; north of it he went underground. To the north he traveled under a pseudonym, with false papers, but he identified himself within the resistance by his code name, "Rex." Most of his journeys across the line were on the train from Marseille to Lyon, and since police controls at railway stations were frequent, this meant that he had to travel either with two sets of papers or with a courier who could carry the second set. In setting out to look for Frenay, Moulin had no courier. To pass the night without being disturbed, resisters would spend it on a train, in a third-class carriage. Night-trains, as Baumel recalled, were

> packed. People snoring, moaning, coughing in their sleep. Those without a seat piled up in the corridors, dozing, using their suitcases as a pillow. There was a strong smell of the barracks; thin wine, poor food, bad tobacco and German privates who had failed to find a seat in their reserved carriages. People rarely spoke to them, but for a few hours they shared our sleep. It was a curious sight as night fell, to see

these collapsed warriors, their tunics unbuttoned, sleeping untroubled among French citizens.

Of Moulin's original companions, Fassin had embarked on a lone quest for suitable landing grounds and hiding places for parachuted arms, while Montjaret was still missing.

Moulin decided to start his inquiries at Marseille with Dr. Recordier, in whose house he had originally met Frenay six months earlier. The doctor told him that Frenay was in Paris, but a meeting was arranged about a week later in Marseille in a small apartment belonging to the sister of one of the members of *Combat*, Georges Bidault. There, in front of Frenay's eyes, "like a conjuror," Moulin produced a microfilm from a matchbox; it was the document which invested him with his extraordinary authority, a letter from General de Gaulle. Frenay said that at the time the sight of this seemed miraculous, so strong was the impression they suddenly had of direct contact with *la France libre*. "For eighteen months," wrote Frenay many years later,

> with derisory resources, alone, we had organized ourselves as well as we could; alone we had invented our means of action; alone, and with unbelievable difficulty, we had published our newspapers and distributed more and more copies, and here at last the miracle had taken place. The man to whom six months earlier I had explained our capabilities and our targets and my desire to join forces with de Gaulle, had returned from a London at war, bearing with him the liaison we had so ardently desired and the finances which we had so cruelly lacked. Our joy was immense!

The exhilaration for Frenay was tempered almost at once by the realization that he would from now on be dependent for all contact with London, not on de Gaulle, but on the General's emissary.

The gifts which "Rex" bore were in the first place money, which the resistance needed urgently (and which was advanced by the British government), and second, regular liaison with London. Arms and agents were to be parachuted or landed, the Secret Army was to be built up and prepared for the day when de Gaulle ordered it into action. With all this Frenay had no quarrel. But he was shaken to be told that the price was a complete separation between the political and military wings of the resistance, a condition insisted on by the British government to which de Gaulle had willingly agreed. Frenay realized the depth of distrust which the British and the Free French had for the resistance, and feared that it would prevent the movement from becoming the inspiration and anvil of liberated France. He did not want to see it reduced to a network of spies and saboteurs. However, he supported the move toward fusion of the dozens of armed groups within the resistance, and decided to work with Moulin in the hope of imposing his own views and those of the other southern resistance leaders in due course.

There now began a yearlong struggle between Moulin—the delegate of General de Gaulle and coordinator of the resistance in the southern zone—and Frenay, d'Astier and Lévy, the three principal leaders of the southern resistance groups. The return of Jean Moulin marked the end of the resistance's age of innocence. During the course of 1942 the resistance developed and began to take on a more uniform appearance. It became possible to distinguish between "networks" and "movements." The first were military groups engaged in gathering information, sabotage and setting up escape lines. They worked in close contact with the central military staff of the resistance. The second were political groups intent on organizing and galvanizing public opinion. Only the communist resistance fused its political and military activities into one organization, and used military action for strictly political purposes.

During this period the pure impulse of the original engagement was lost; from now on resistance was stained by a political struggle, and meetings of the leadership were punctuated by clashes that echoed the mutual contempt and hatred of the Third Republic. The advantage swayed back and forth until the end of 1942, alliances between the four protagonists were made and broken and remade, depending on which particular issue was in dispute at the time. The mission entrusted to Jean Moulin by de Gaulle was essentially to dissolve the initial structure of resistance and bring it to heel—a task which came close to identifying him as "the enemy of the Resistance." This was a doubly hazardous role but, by the end of the year Moulin, who was the ablest politician at work, and one of the few people active in the internal resistance in 1942 who had the potential for a national political future, had achieved solid progress. Four common services had been set up: the SOAM (*Service des opérations aériennes et maritimes*) for parachute drops and landing, the WT (wireless transmissions), the BIP (*Bureau d'information et de presse*) for intelligence and propaganda and the CGE (*Comité général d'études*), a "think-tank" which was to play an influential role in drawing up the blueprint for France's new political system. A young man called Georges Bidault, a future prime minister who had established a high reputation as a journalist before the war, ran the BIP.

It was shortly after meeting Frenay that Moulin made his first contact with *Libération,* but not with its leader, d'Astier. Instead he met the movement's director of military operations, Raymond "Aubrac"—a communist secret agent, or "submarine," who was openly suspicious of de Gaulle and saw no particular urgency about meeting his delegate. Nonetheless they met in Lyon in February, in the arcade of the municipal theater, at night. Later d'Astier and Moulin started a stormy relationship, frequently conducted on an island in the River Rhône where Moulin insisted on walking around throughout conversations which sometimes lasted for several hours because, said d'Astier, spitefully, "a table and two chairs made him feel nervous."

The personality of Emmanuel d'Astier de la Vigerie was one of the more disruptive components of the French Resistance. D'Astier was a seductive aristocrat, dripping with malice, who spent much of his time trying to wreck every positive move his compatriots decided to take. He was obsessed with the past and personal life of "Rex," whom he spent much time discrediting in the eyes of right-wing resisters. His friends, particularly his communist friends, were attracted by his intelligence and generosity. Others were disconcerted by his evident pleasure in making trouble, irrespective of the consequences.

In the first ten months of living under the Vichy regime, before he went to England, Moulin had found time to lead a surprisingly normal life. His affair with Antoinette Sachs progressed in its customary on-off way. It continued to draw its dynamism from the friction between a woman with "the best address book in Paris" and a man whom nobody knew. It was, naturally, conducted in secret, although no more secretly than in time of peace. Among those who knew about it were Henri Manhès and his wife, who provided Moulin with a discreetly placed apartment in Nice. According to Antoinette Sachs's notebook they were together on the night of 30 July, "broke up" on 31 July and were together again shortly afterward. Whether or not Antoinette wanted to marry Moulin she evidently considered him a permanent part of her life, and had become more than ever indispensable to him since the start of his underground existence. And the prewar address book, which she had conceived as a social asset, had become a political weapon. Apart from Colonel Groussard, the *cagoulard* resister, it included the names of half the ministers of the Third Republic and many of their senior staff, as well as the names of many who had since gone to work for Vichy.

Following Moulin's return from England, Antoinette was perhaps the only person, apart from Henri Manhès, who had an extensive knowledge of his movements in both his identities, which placed her in a position as dangerous as it was privileged. In the southern zone she was still the one who routinely covered for him, shadowed him, provided him with a letter-box, a hideout, companionship and physical passion. She was quick-witted, brave and long-suffering, and yet in the final analysis she, too, knew remarkably little about what he was actually up to. On one day she described their relationship as one of "laughter and comradeship," on another in a gently erotic poem she described him as "her master and her prey." She was probably his ideal companion but one with whom, for profound emotional reasons, he was incapable of sharing his life publicly. He seems to have been both heavily dependent on her and profoundly detached. Because of her married name—Kohn-Sachs—her wartime identity card was stamped *Juif*, which put her in danger of deportation, so she had to apply to Vichy's General Commission for Jewish Affairs for a certificate of "nonadherence to the Jewish race," which was issued in November 1941 when Moulin was in England. This was one of the few identity documents she carried which showed her true date of birth—she was almost exactly two years older than Moulin; presumably in a matter of life and death she was prepared to make an exception because in general her identity documents knocked ten years off her age, and it is evidence of both her charm and her quick-wittedness that she was capable of presenting an official pass which suggested that she had been issued with a driving license at the age of nine.

Moulin's habit of dividing his personal life into compartments continued throughout the occupation. His pursuit of Gilberte Lloyd, who was still living in the rue de Lübeck in Paris, also continued. He saw her in November 1940 and in April 1941, and her own connections, which, with her family background, would probably have included members of the German general staff, enabled her to obtain an *Ausweis* for visits to the southern zone. She was in Vichy on 19 May 1941. And he saw her when he crossed into the occupied zone in July 1942. When Gilberte wanted to write to him she used the address of Henri Manhès, and she knew enough to inquire for "Joseph Mercier."

In January 1942, at Megève, Moulin had met a third woman with whom he claimed to be in love, Colette Pons, who was aged only twenty-one, married but separated from her husband, and who had since become unofficially engaged to a banker who was in London with the Free French. Moulin arranged to meet Colette in Nice, where he began a courtship which was so energetic that she eventually disappeared without leaving an address and tried to get an exit visa to join her future husband. Moulin continued his pursuit by correspondence and eventually, through a mutual friend, persuaded her to meet him again. The upshot was that, having failed to get an exit visa, she agreed during the summer of 1942 to manage the art gallery which he planned to open in Nice. This gallery would provide him with a cover for his secret activities. Finding the premises, which were required, as usual, to have two entrances on different streets (as well as a small apartment on the first floor), took some time but Moulin, despite his other preoccupations, supervised the details closely; the gallery was designed to be run as a profitable business in addition to providing a cover.

Antoinette Sachs, a former pupil of Soutine and Léger, agreed to supervise Colette's work at the gallery. Moulin gave Antoinette 100,000 francs to buy pictures and for this sum she was able to find two paintings by Degas, a Suzanne Valadon and a Raoul Dufy. Moulin's facility at dissimulation is shown by the fact that he concealed from each of these women—who seem to have had a mutually suspicious relationship—the true nature of his interest in the other. Antoinette thought that Colette was *la petite jeune,* a secretary whom Moulin had found in Nice to caretake the business while he was away; she had no idea that Moulin had developed an obsessive interest in Colette. Colette thought that Antoinette was an old flame who was still a bit jealous of him, and she was unaware of the extent of Moulin's continuing dependence on Sachs. Needless to say neither Antoinette nor Colette knew anything about the existence of "Madame Lloyd" in Paris.

Refreshed by his visit to Megève, "Rex" had set to work in February 1942 when, after meeting Frenay and Aubrac, he traveled to Bargemon, high up in the hills behind Fréjus, where Henri Manhès had a *pension.* It was here that he finally met up with Montjaret, his radio operator, three weeks after the parachute landing that had separated them. On the following day they were joined by Manhès himself, who had returned from Paris. Montjaret was excluded from most of the conversations between the two older men, and it was another two weeks before he was able to start transmitting to London. By then Manhès, the confidential agent, had returned to Paris, following Moulin's instruction, on a mission which, in Frenay's words, "no one had authorized, which was in defiance of his orders [from London] and which he concealed from both de Gaulle and the resistance for twelve months." In 1942 Moulin was, of course, invested as de Gaulle's delegate to the resistance with authority in the Vichy zone alone.

The precise role of Henri Manhès from February to November 1942 is unknown, but he was funded by Moulin and used the money to support and increasingly to control a number of occupied zone resistance groups. One of these groups, according to Jacques Baynac, in *Les Secrets de l'affaire Jean Moulin,* was based in the Pas-de-Calais at St. Pol-sur-Ternoise and was formed from the union of members of the right-wing OCM and the communist FTP; its leaders included Jean Cremet, whose work for the PCF and the Comintern had caused him to flee from France in 1927. But the link is highly speculative and based on the supposed itinerary of a single liaison agent. It is however a fact that one of Moulin's friends in Amiens, whom he saw again in Chartres in June 1940, Dr. Mans, was in touch with Jean Cremet in St. Pol-sur-Ternoise. Manhès is also known to have contacted three of the leading noncommunist northern groups, *Ceux de la Résistance, Ceux de la Libération* and *Libération-Nord.* The reaction of the leader of *Ceux de la Résistance,* Jacques Lecompte-Boinet, to Moulin's emissary is interesting. Manhès offered invaluable aid, a link with the air operations from London, funds, weapons and arms, but Lecompte-Boinet remained wary. He considered Manhès too "political" and, like his associates Pierre Meunier and Robert Chambeiron, far too close to the Communist Party. He was careful not to reject Manhès, but equally careful to maintain the freedom of operation of his group.

None of Manhès's northern links were revealed to Frenay or any other of the southern resistance leaders, although Frenay was already in contact with both *Libération-Nord* and the OCM. When making his contacts Manhès introduced himself, without any authority, as "the delegate of de Gaulle in the northern zone." Frenay later concluded that Moulin's discretion was explained by the need to conceal the fact that he was working toward communist control of the resistance, although it seems equally possible that he was in fact imposing de Gaulle's control on both northern and southern movements, and bypassing any possible interference from Frenay.

Frenay had other and better reasons to object to Moulin's methods. The first was that Moulin had been instructed by London to allocate a radio operator and a liaison officer to each of the three southern groups, thereby offering them direct communications with London and the possibility of mounting independent military operations. In any event, when these agents arrived, Moulin diverted them to other work. Daniel Cordier, who was supposed to assist Georges Bidault in his intelligence and propaganda service, was instead instructed to become Moulin's personal secretary. Two other agents were sent into the occupied zone to work with Henri Manhès. At the same time Moulin "suborned" Bidault's loyalties, persuading him to join the communist *Front National*, which was just moving into the southern zone, without telling Frenay, and then with the help of Lucie Aubrac of *Libération* (wife of Raymond), providing the BIP with a secretariat that was partly communist. Frenay interpreted this after the war firstly as a step toward controlling the resistance instead of coordinating it, which it was, and secondly as a means of assisting communist infiltration of noncommunist groups, which it may or may not have been.

Many years later Frenay discovered that the reports Moulin was sending from the southern zone to Colonel Passy were deliberately misleading. While Moulin had been in England Frenay had been approached by a French officer working for U.S. intelligence, General La Laurencie, who offered aid and assistance. When Frenay discovered that La Laurencie was being manipulated by the American OSS, forerunner of the CIA, which was engaged in an early attempt to gain a toehold in the resistance and weaken the influence of de Gaulle, he broke contact with him and warned other groups to do the same. In a message sent to London on 7 April, Moulin claimed to have discovered this situation himself and to have been instrumental in ending it, thereby giving the impression that *Combat* had been disloyal to de Gaulle until his own intervention had brought it to heel. In another message Moulin described sabotage operations and anti-Vichy demonstrations routinely organized by *Combat*'s *groupes francs* as having been initiated by Moulin in response to instructions received from Passy. Such tactics were only possible, of course, as a result of Moulin's monopoly of radio communications. But they do at least raise a question mark over de Gaulle's posthumous comment about the prefect of Chartres: "He was as straight as a die."

In February 1942 the Vichy secret police enjoyed a considerable success in arresting several leaders of *Combat,* including Berty Albrecht, who had become Frenay's mistress and social conscience. But some of the Vichy leaders realized that it would be wise to establish secret contact with the Resistance. The police therefore released Albrecht on condition that Frenay himself agreed to come to Vichy for talks, which, with the agreement of *Combat*'s leadership, he did. Frenay twice traveled on a safe-conduct to meet the Vichy minister of the interior, Pucheu, who asked him to stop attacking Vichy. By this time Frenay's original hopes in Pétain had dwindled away and he refused any form of cooperation; Berty Albrecht was promptly rearrested and imprisoned. And Frenay was accused, notably by d'Astier and the communists of *Libération,* of betraying the resistance. While this was going on Moulin played a characteristically subtle game, publicly supporting Frenay but privately, in messages to the BCRA in London, noting that Frenay's stubborn loyalty to Pétain had regrettably led to him making contact with the Vichy authorities. The comment was again clearly bound to provoke de Gaulle's suspicions of *Combat.*

This was all the more regrettable since *Combat* was, together with the Communist FTP, the most effective resistance group as well as being the one least penetrated by communist agents. Its newspaper was printing 80,000 copies a week by the end of 1942. It was the first group to recruit senior members of Vichy's civil service, the first to organize young fugitives from the STO and the first to draw up a blueprint for sabotaging the national railway network. Originally based on the army intelligence service, with which Frenay maintained good relations, *Combat* attracted a high quality of leaders from across the political spectrum, stopping short of the *Cagoule* on the right and the communists on the left. It was a thoroughly professional model of resistance which de Gaulle would have had difficulty criticizing had he ever been able to discover what it was.

Two months later Moulin, too, was summoned to Vichy, but under his real identity. The highly accurate police report identifying Moulin as a British agent code named "Mercier" had disappeared into the labyrinthine files of the Vichy bureaucracy, where it remained until after the liberation, and in February 1942 the French government was hoping for the former prefect's support. Meanwhile, Pierre Laval had returned to power as Pétain's prime minister. Laval was an ingenious and unpopular politician who had convinced himself that he could outwit the leaders of the

German occupation. In fact, he was slowly forced to take responsibility for a list of damaging concessions: full cooperation with the Gestapo, the deportation of Jewish children (an idea of his own) and the STO—a compulsory labor program obliging French workers to serve in the factories of Nazi Germany. Laval's return finally led Frenay to make a savage and unequivocal attack on Vichy and Pétain; in reply, Laval wanted to recruit the prefects dismissed by Vichy in 1940. Moulin declined Laval's offer but took advantage of the occasion to ask once again for his pension rights to be improved. The meeting was polite and Laval gave the necessary instructions to increase his pension, although they were never carried out.

At the end of June, a month after his meeting with Moulin, Laval made his fatal speech—the speech which would lead him to the firing squad in 1945—in which he said, "I desire a German victory because without it tomorrow Bolshevism will be everywhere." One by one the leaders of Vichy were piling up the stones which would cover their own graves. In February the first public rally of the SOL (*Service d'ordre légionnaire*) had taken place in Nice; this eventually provided Vichy with a paramilitary force inspired by the fascist movements' Iron Guards, which could be deployed against "terrorists and the enemies of the regime." It was recruited from the ex-servicemen's organization—the national veterans' legion—and led by Joseph Darnand, one of France's most celebrated heroes of the Great War, who would in due course join the *Waffen SS*. Later known as the *Milice*, it was to become the most dangerous enemy of the resistance.

Meanwhile, among the most fervent early supporters of Vichy another current of opinion was beginning to run. While the PCF had been liberated by the dissolution of the Nazi-Soviet Pact to join the resistance, the right-wing *Cagoule*, which in 1940 had expelled its minority of Gaullist supporters, was beginning to feel the strain of German occupation. Since it was essentially a nationalist and patriotic movement, to whose members the word "collaboration" carried no special magic in any circumstances, it now began to look for a way out of the impasse into which Pétain had led France. It remained as anti-Gaullist and anti-British as ever, but had no special anti-American views and saw the entry of the United States into the war in December 1941 as the beginnings of a solution. On 17 April 1942 a *Cagoule* commando succeeded in freeing General Henri Giraud from the fortress of Koenigstein in Germany where he was being held as a prisoner of war. Giraud, who was aged sixty-three, had been taken prisoner in May 1940 in northern France, while commanding the 7th Army. His escape,

which involved descending a wall and a cliff face 350 feet above the River
Elbe, by rope, and traveling 500 miles to the Swiss frontier, was hailed as "a
triumph for the resistance," but it was a triumph for a non-Gaullist "resistance" which was organized by a group of army officers who were also
loyal to Pétain. Via Switzerland Giraud managed to reach the southern
zone, where he remained in hiding while Laval's government, under great
pressure from the furious German authorities, tried to persuade him to
give himself up. Giraud met both Pétain and the German ambassador to
Paris, Otto Abetz, and eventually agreed to return to prison if the Germans would release all of France's married POWs. When this offer was refused, negotiations ended and Giraud made a public declaration of loyalty
to Pétain, while announcing that he intended to lead "the Resistance in
Europe" and had no intention of going to London.

Giraud was approached directly by the U.S. government. Roosevelt's
strong dislike of de Gaulle increased when they met and he found the
leader of the Free French to be vain, pretentious and hysterical. It can,
perhaps, partly be explained by the fact that Roosevelt was being briefed
by advisers in contact with Pierre Cot and by the OSS, whose bureau chief
Allen Dulles was receiving information from Noel Field. Both Field and
Cot were controlled by Soviet intelligence. Furthermore, Roosevelt had
always maintained excellent relations, through the U.S. ambassador to
Vichy, with Marshal Pétain, and regarded the leader of the collaboration
as the legitimate leader of occupied France. With the help of *Cagoule* emissaries, contact between Giraud and the U.S. government was quickly established and in June 1942 a marriage was announced that seemed to have
been made in heaven. The Americans had acquired an anti-Gaullist resistance leader who had "no political ambitions," apart from returning
France to democracy, and the most ferociously anti-communist political
group in occupied France had found a way to associate itself with resistance and an allied victory while blocking the communists and spurning
the British. *Libération* and the *Front National,* as well as most other resistance leaders, rejected Giraud's leadership. But *Combat* and the OCM sent
envoys to meet Giraud, and the newspaper *Combat* treated his escape as an
important news story. For de Gaulle in London, marginalized and isolated, the support of the resistance movement in France had suddenly become of the first importance.

While these developments were taking place relations between Frenay,
unaware of Moulin's tactical maneuvering, and the delegate of General de

Gaulle remained good. Insofar as the resistance in the southern zone had a significant military capacity, it was contained within Frenay's organization and—freed by the funds Moulin offered—Frenay was able to enjoy the way in which life underground had been transformed. "During the first six or eight months of 1942," he wrote in 1977 in *L'Enigme Jean Moulin*, "our relations . . . were excellent. We met frequently usually in Lyon or its suburbs where he, like the rest of us, had established his headquarters. . . . Through him, thanks to him, we had our link with London. . . . His presence among us was a source of great comfort and on the material level things had changed as well."

Until 1942 money had been Frenay's most pressing concern. He had had to borrow from his friends and relations, sometimes taking serious risks in approaching people he scarcely knew. "Practically no one was paid," he wrote. "Not even expenses could be reimbursed, we ate little and the food was poor . . . almost all our resources went on the newspaper and we lacked the means to develop it. With the arrival of 'Rex' all these problems disappeared." Frenay was able to recruit full-time agents whom he called *permanents*, the men and women who left everything, including their children and their jobs, in order to take up a clandestine existence and risk their lives as specialists in one or other of *Combat*'s activities. He was now able to pay them and, since the blueprint was already in place, his organization expanded rapidly.

Throughout 1942 Frenay tried to persuade d'Astier and Jean-Pierre Lévy to fuse *Libération* and *Franc-Tireur* with *Combat* and to enroll their armed groups in the Secret Army. Both refused because, concluded Frenay, they did not wish to see their movements dominated by *Combat*. Instead they agreed to set up a coordinating structure which would have a similar effect. Since this plan seemed to be exactly what de Gaulle had asked the resistance to do, Frenay was surprised that Moulin did not support him more vigorously, and concluded, naively perhaps, that if fusion was established Moulin would have concluded his mission and abolished his own role. Eventually, to resolve the argument, it was agreed that all four men should go to London and reach a decision with Passy and de Gaulle. Frenay and d'Astier boarded a *caïque* in a rocky inlet near Cassis on 17 September, which took them to Gibraltar and the plane for England. But Moulin and Lévy abandoned their plans to leave after the failure of a succession of planes and boats to make the rendezvous.

Despite the personal incompatibility of the two resistance leaders—

Frenay was appalled to discover d'Astier sprawled in his London hotel room with the daughter of a former Soviet ambassador, stupefied with drugs, when he was supposed to be attending an important meeting—their mission was a success. In November Frenay and d'Astier returned from London with new instructions from de Gaulle, which were put into effect at once. A coordinating committee was set up in the southern zone. The three "historic" leaders of the southern resistance and Moulin each had one vote, and Moulin had a casting vote in the case of deadlock. The committee would design the interim political and economic administration of France after the liberation; it would nominate prefects and police chiefs and newspaper and radio editors. It would direct a united paramilitary force based on Frenay's Secret Army, and all other resistance groups in the southern zone would be invited to affiliate with one or other of the three main groups. The decision was set out in a note bearing de Gaulle's signature.

It was a major victory for Frenay and for his vision of the role of the resistance; it was also a major victory for the resistance as a whole. Furthermore, the new instructions contained a reminder to Moulin that his authority was limited to the southern zone. But, unfortunately for Frenay, by the time he and d'Astier were able to meet Moulin and present him with this letter in Lyon on 18 November, the situation in Vichy France had completely changed. Nine days earlier, in response to "Operation Torch" (the landing of U.S. and British forces in North Africa), the *Wehrmacht* had crossed the demarcation line and the Gestapo had moved into Lyon. This event marked a milestone in Vichy's decline. Pétain's supporters could no longer claim that "collaboration" was shielding France from the worst horrors of occupation. Breaking all the conditions of the armistice, the German army disbanded the French army units remaining in the southern zone and provoked the scuttling of the French fleet in Toulon harbor. The hunt for Jews was stepped up, the compulsory labor program was imposed and hunger and want became commonplace in the towns as the army of occupation plundered the French economy. Laval's claim to be able to manipulate the victors of 1940 was exposed as a sham and many of the most able supporters of the Vichy regime began to make discreet contacts with the Resistance.

ELEVEN

The Army of the Night

FROM A SECRET ADDRESS in Paris in 1943, Pierre Brossolette, journalist and intellectual turned resister, who had been the quarry of a Gestapo manhunt for seven weeks, wrote to Colonel Passy in London: "For the last eight days I have been on 'full alert.' It seems that they are taking a particularly close interest in me at the moment, using every possible form of snare and check. . . . Fortunately night falls early. It's the early curfew that saves us. If it were August we would all be behind bars. . . . So,—Vive la Nuit!" Brossolette was arrested some weeks later, when the nights were still long, and after repeated torture committed suicide at the police headquarters in the avenue Foch to avoid breaking down. Another resister, the professional soldier Maurice Chevance-Bertin, when asked after the war about those days and nights, said: "What I remember best is four years of being constantly exhausted by fear."

There were three categories of resister. First there were the family men or women who lived at home and distributed pamphlets and sheltered agents and equipment while carrying on with their ordinary lives. They usually lasted a few months before being arrested. Then came the full-time resisters who were married with children. They were more vulnerable than people without close ties. The third category entered the Resistance like monks responding to their vocation and giving up all personal considerations. Baumel noticed many communists in this category.

Their only hope of emotional contact was in a passing episode with the person closest to them, their secretary or liaison agent. Resisters in this third category were the most difficult people to break. "A father," noted Baumel, "who has been beaten up and who is then told that his wife or daughter is going to be sent to a military brothel on the Eastern Front is faced with a difficult choice."

There was a curious state of mind recognized at the time by many resisters in occupied France; the longer they were hunted by the German police and their French auxiliaries, the more reckless they grew. The fear they faced every day wore them out. They watched their comrades picked off one by one and knew it could only be a matter of time before their turn came. Sometimes they even felt relief when they were arrested, because they no longer had to fear arrest. And this feeling of relief explained why some were so easily persuaded to talk. Their initial determination ebbed away as they became transfixed by the death that was tracking them down.

If their friends noticed, they might arrange for those who were worn out to be smuggled to safety, although it was difficult to get out of occupied France. The RAF used light aircraft for night landings on rough ground once a month over the period of the full moon, although even these infrequent opportunities were canceled by bad weather. The Lysander could land on a strip 300 yards long, with its motor cut, like a ghost machine. But the maximum number of passengers in a Lysander was three; the Hudson carried ten but made more noise, needed a firmer landing ground and was more likely to be noticed. Otherwise there were the fast patrol boats and submarines of the Royal Navy, deployed on moonless nights off remote stretches of the Brittany coast. This method was better for drop-offs than for pickups; the coastline was heavily patrolled and it was one thing to scramble ashore and make a run for it, quite another to confirm a rendezvous with a rubber dinghy somewhere out on a dark sea.

In these circumstances most resisters were forced to carry on until mischance, exhaustion or betrayal brought the hunt to an end. Farce and tragedy went hand in hand. Colonel Rémy once distinguished himself by dragging a large package on to a small boat trying to take him off the Brittany coast on a stormy night. A capsize was narrowly avoided. The parcel contained a potted azalea he wished to present to Madame de Gaulle. On another stormy night the boat did capsize, and Pierre Brossolette was, in consequence, captured and tortured to the point of suicide.

Six weeks before he was arrested Jean Moulin wrote to General de

Gaulle: "I am a wanted man now for both Vichy and the Gestapo. . . . I need a deputy in each zone. . . . My task becomes more and more difficult but I am determined to hang on for as long as I can." One month later he wrote, "Send me the military personnel I have asked for so many times. . . . Nothing has been done. . . . The officers of the Secret Army have suffered heavy losses. Those who remain have all had their cover blown." And six days before the meeting at the doctor's house in Caluire he sent a final appeal for help. "Now it's the Secret Army which needs to be saved. I beg you, General, do what I have the honor to request. With great devotion . . ."

The night the *Wehrmacht* crossed the demarcation line in November 1942 and entered the Vichy zone, Lyon—"the capital of the Resistance"— became as dangerous as Paris. By that time many of the resisters based in Vichy had acquired settled habits. As early as 1941, when Frenay and François de Menthon started to print their underground newspapers there, Lyon had begun to attract embryonic resistance movements. In 1942 the newspapers of *Libération* and *Franc-Tireur* were also edited and printed there. By 28 September 1942 the reputation of Lyon as a center of resistance had become sufficiently notorious for the Germans to send 280 police under an SS major called Karl Boemelburg to hunt for illegal radio transmitters in the Lyon region. Most of these men were army technicians but when German forces occupied Lyon two months later they came with a full detachment of *Sipo–SD*, the German security police.

The German manhunt designed to destroy the French resistance had become steadily more determined since 21 August 1941. It was on that day that the communists implemented their assassination policy with the shooting of an unarmed German naval cadet at a Paris metro station. At that time all police activity in France was directed by the *Wehrmacht*'s high command, which responded with a policy of reprisal killings that proved ineffective; the communist assassinations continued. In December 1941 Hitler published *Nacht und Nebel,* the decree which punished hostile action against German forces in occupied territory with death. "Night and Fog" (a phrase borrowed from Goethe) was the name given to this punishment because the guilty were to be deported to the Fatherland and executed there, no news about them being given either to their families or to the Red Cross. So the deterrent effect of the death penalty was increased by the uncertainty of its victims' fate. Then in May 1942 the German army ceded ultimate control of police operations to the RSHA (Reich Security

Service) which in France had previously been restricted to the surveillance of immigrants, communists and Jews.

The new service was directed by SS General Karl Oberg, who was comfortably installed by Reinhard Heydrich in a spacious headquarters in Paris on the Boulevard Lannes, overlooking the Bois de Boulogne. Oberg's organization, most of which was established at nine separate addresses on the nearby avenue Foch, absorbed the army's existing police services including the uniformed personnel of the GFP (Field Police). In addition Oberg had 2,000 professional members of the RSHA, who were frequently recruited from the SS. Finally the members of the RSHA could call on up to 8,000 full-time French agents, who worked beside them in civilian clothes, armed and carrying German police identification. When these auxiliaries arrested their fellow countrymen they habitually announced themselves as *Police allemande.* The RSHA was organized into seven sections, each with its own area of responsibility, and deployed across France in units known as "*KdS*" (*Kommandos Sipo–SD*). In November 1942 a *KdS* of six sections was sent to Lyon. Section IV, popularly known as "the Gestapo," was responsible for antiresistance and in Lyon was led by SS Lieutenant Klaus Barbie. He had 200 men under his command, all but a dozen of whom were French volunteers. After the war, Barbie remembered the glory of it: "I was only a lieutenant," he said, "but I had more power than a general."

Like any police force the Gestapo relied on information. Routine police work provided much of this, telephone taps, tailing, round-ups and searches, random barrier controls and paid informers. It also received a huge amount of information from anonymous tip-offs, known as "denunciations," many of which proved to be reliable. If the denunciations were signed then their authors were paid. Living conditions in France during the occupation were sufficiently difficult for payment to be an effective means of obtaining information. Already by November 1941 the standard ration card in the city of Lyon restricted people to 1,160 calories a day, which was half the prewar average. Sugar, ersatz coffee, bread, meat, butter, cooking oil and cheese were rationed. Flour, rice and chocolate were unavailable. There were only occasional supplies of fruit, vegetables and eggs, all at inflated prices. Milk was sold at nearly three times its prewar price and was restricted to pregnant women and children. Crows were on sale in the food market at 10 francs each. Soap was reserved for those doing unusually dirty work. Some people, particularly old people, starved to death. Those who could afford black market prices dealt with what they called the "Bof" (*Beurre, oeufs, fromage*)—"the swine who sold the food." One English woman married to a French doctor watched her husband set to work on a length of two-year-old "rosette de Lyon" *saucisson* and break his jaw.

> January 1943, Lyon is dying of hunger and cold. No coal, the apartments icy, we wash in cold water. Rendezvous in the Place Bellecour with my liaison chief, the most important and the most exposed link in our chain. She arrives gray with cold, her eyes red, her fingers swollen in the cutting wind. She is the wife of one of our deported comrades. I take her into a café for a glass of something burning hot. We sit on a bench and she starts to talk. She is visibly afraid. Her hands tremble, and she keeps glancing at neighboring tables. . . . She talks of food, the ration has just been cut again, 125g of bread a day, 60g of meat (a week), nothing in the market except turnips and swedes. . . . No spuds, no milk, even for children. She is having trouble finding new recruits. She knows we have no news of her husband.

The daily routine, evoked by Jacques Baumel.

The Gestapo also obtained information as a result of the fear inspired by its brutal methods, which were authorized by German law. The fundamental principle was laid down by Wilhelm Frick, minister of the interior in 1933. "Law is what serves the *Volk*. Crime is what harms the *Volk*." In June 1942 Himmler authorized "the third degree" (torture) to obtain information. It could be used without prior approval against communists, Jehovah's Witnesses, saboteurs, terrorists and members of resistance movements. All in all, the Gestapo detachment sent to Lyon possessed the means necessary to carry out its task. But in addition it had the help, and frequently the rivalry, of the *Abwehr*, German military intelligence, which had its own structure of informers. The *Abwehr* held an extensive archive of information about French affairs, which it had been compiling with the help of French agents since before the war, and which it sometimes shared with the RSHA.

In Lyon, Barbie's section IV was first set up in the Hôtel Terminus, by the Perrache central railway station. Torture chambers and cells were constructed in the hotel cellars. Later, section IV moved to more spacious accommodations in the Ecole de Santé Militaire, the former Military

School of Medicine. There was also an "information bureau," staffed by French auxiliaries in the great central square of Lyon, the Place Bellecour on the corner of the rue Paul Lintier, the little street in which Barbie requisitioned a private office. The information bureau was set up after another section, No. VI, was overwhelmed with the flood of signed denunciations. Among those who worked at the bureau was a man named Falkenstein, a *Bof* who specialized in supplying German soldiers. He was caught by section V of the *KdS,* which dealt with German army crime. On his way to be interrogated, in the prison van traveling between Fort Montluc and the interrogation center at the Ecole de Santé Militaire, Falkenstein had a lucky break. The van broke down and one of the prisoners tried to escape. Falkenstein ran after him *and dragged him back.* Section V then employed him as an informer inside the prison. After some time Falkenstein identified and denounced one of the warders who were taking messages out for the prisoners, many of whom were resisters.

At that point Falkenstein was freed and given a job with Barbie's section IV, assisting in the information bureau. There he worked for "Monsieur Jacquin," the head of the bureau, and assisted Tony Saunier, the accountant who requisitioned Jewish property for the *Sipo–SD* on a commission of fifteen percent. Falkenstein also made himself useful to Francis André, known as "the bath attendant," or *gueule tordue* (twisted face—he had suffered a serious cosmetic injury while serving as a member of the Communist Party's security service before the war). André, who specialized in questioning people while half-drowning them in a bathtub, was executed after the liberation for a nominal list of 150 murders. But Falkenstein was never punished. After a few months at the information bureau he returned to the black market, was rearrested and reimprisoned. He was freed when Lyon was liberated, together with the surviving members of the Resistance, and by the time they had worked out who he was, he had disappeared. Like other cynics he may have reasoned that since the black market was repressed by both the Vichy and the German police it was a patriotic activity.

Soon after the occupation of the Vichy zone the Gestapo began to enjoy a long run of success against the Resistance. The first breakthrough came in March 1943, when a random Vichy police *contrôle* led to the arrest of a courier working for *Combat.* The result was that the names of the Secret Army's leadership, with pseudonyms, code names and functions, as well as a 143-page report by Frenay on the state of the armed resistance in the southern zone, was passed by the Vichy police to the Gestapo. Then, on 27 April, in Marseille, one of the Gestapo's most efficient units arrested and "turned" a member of *Combat* called Jean Multon, also known as "Lunel." Without being tortured Multon agreed to tell the Gestapo everything he knew about his group. Other members of *Combat* discovered what had happened and Frenay gave an order for Multon to be executed, but he was too well guarded. Early in June, having done the maximum amount of damage in Marseille, Multon was sent "on loan" to the Gestapo of Lyon.

For the last seven months of his life, between November 1942 and June 1943, as the German police closed in, Jean Moulin was engaged in the most complicated task he had ever undertaken, attempting to unite and direct the competing interests and explosive personalities who made up the French Resistance. The coordinating committee which had been set up in the southern zone on 27 November 1942, following Frenay and d'Astier's return from London, was followed by the creation of a solidly united ad-ministration, the MUR (*Mouvements unis de résistance*), organized by its for-midable secretary, Jacques Baumel, a medical intern from Marseille who had abandoned his studies in 1941 to join *Combat*. The birth of the MUR, which swallowed the identities of *Combat*, *Libération-Sud* and *Franc-Tireur*, was delayed by the reluctance of all three of its leading members to lose their autonomy, and by the reluctance of the leaders of *Combat* to lose con-trol of their military capability. The MUR was intended to be the political master of the Secret Army, and *Combat* supplied seventy-five percent of the manpower of the Secret Army; it therefore seemed logical to Frenay that the paramilitary organization he had created should be under his com-mand.

Among *les petits soldats* (the rank and file of the Resistance), who were impelled by naïve motives of patriotism and in many cases belonged to more than one group, as they eventually discovered, the objections to fu-sion were incomprehensible. But d'Astier and Lévy flatly refused to place their movements (*Libération* and *Franc-Tireur*) under Frenay, claiming that he was "right-wing," which was true, and "authoritarian," which might have seemed less of a disadvantage. The compromise reached was that a serving general, Charles Delestraint, once de Gaulle's commanding offi-cer, became military commander of the Secret Army but remained in the-ory under the direction of Frenay, who was the "military delegate" to the

MUR. D'Astier was the political delegate and Lévy was in charge of information and intelligence. The final compromise seemed well balanced and in the struggle that preceded it Frenay and Moulin were, briefly and for the last time, on the same side.

But the truce was short-lived. For however elegantly presented the reconciliation might be, the kernel of the argument remained. It was not just a question of who was to command the Resistance; the real issue concerned the nature and purpose of the movement. "Rex's" mission had not just been to unite the Resistance and link it to the Free French. He had been sent to dissolve the Resistance as it existed in January 1942 and remold it as an instrument to serve de Gaulle's project for the liberation of France. De Gaulle regarded an autonomous Resistance as a dangerous obstacle to his plans. He had no sympathy for Frenay's semi-mystical belief, shared by many of the *petits soldats,* that from the sacrifice of the Resistance a new France would emerge. For de Gaulle the Resistance was of no importance, until it could influence the destiny of France. He showed little imaginative insight into the predicament of the individual resisters until after the war, when he met hundreds who had returned from deportation. Realizing, nonetheless, that the symbolic role of the Resistance was crucial, and that its military role was of growing importance, de Gaulle was determined to recruit the Resistance (or the "resistance" as he invariably spelled it) under his banner. He abandoned the formula *Français libres* (Free French) and replaced it with *Français combattants* (Fighting French). The Fighting French were composed of the exterior and interior resistance, and he expected the highest military standards of loyalty and discipline from each. Moulin's real task, as his personal representative, was to take whatever steps were necessary inside occupied France to achieve those standards. By the beginning of 1943 the "Free French" (as they were still known in English) had approximately 260,000 men under arms, mainly stationed in North and West Africa, as well as 40 air force squadrons, 25 warships and 17 submarines. These forces were trained and equipped by the British and American armies. If de Gaulle's reliance on the British for status and information continued until well after D-Day he was at least able to establish the strength of his claims to leadership by outmaneuvering Roosevelt's protégé, General Giraud, in Algiers and by establishing, through the work of Jean Moulin, his command of the Resistance.

On 11 February 1943, on the eve of departing for London to report on the success of "Mission Rex" and receive new orders, Moulin called a meeting of the executive committee of the MUR. Once again a fierce argument broke out, this time over the question of how to deal with the thousands of young men who were about to "take to the *maquis*" (bush) to avoid the STO, the Vichy forced labor program. Frenay and d'Astier saw this as an obvious chance to gain an important number of new recruits; Moulin suspected them of intending to build a second Secret Army outside his personal control. In response to their demands for a heavy budget increase Moulin cut their allowance by forty percent, explaining that he was removing those funds which were intended for the Secret Army. In future these would be managed by the army's own staff under the authority of its commander, General Delestraint; in other words Moulin would have direct financial control over all military spending.

Moulin's professional training as a prefect had given him a mastery of the use of budgets as a means of control. In throttling the Resistance's finances he was doing what both London and Washington had, at various times, done to de Gaulle. Funds were provided, a dependency was established, then the tap was turned off. It was a simple matter for him to arrange. The money arrived in bundles of banknotes, great packages of them parachuted at night by the RAF with the weapons and radio transmitters. Moulin controlled the delivery of this money, its distribution and the way it was spent. His decision was evidence of his ruthlessness; for no sooner was the MUR in place than Moulin was ready to set to work again, sapping the power of the Resistance's leaders to the point where they would either obey orders or be pushed aside.

If Moulin enjoyed a degree of success in 1942 in herding the southern zone resistance movements into his net, he did not apparently achieve the same results with the French Communist Party. The PCF, having followed Moscow's instructions to work as closely as possible with the noncommunist resistance, had gone some way toward infiltrating and controlling it. Starting with the *Front National,* a movement which, as its name suggested, was apparently broadly based and which never acknowledged its true communist allegiance, communists—either undeclared members of the party, or fellow-travelers, or in some cases Soviet agents, all generically termed "submarines"—riddled the membership of every movement they could penetrate. Since they were often talented and always well trained they rose quickly to influential positions. Several of the key appointments in this infiltration operation were made during the course of 1942 by Moulin. First Georges Bidault, who was nominally a Christian Democrat loyal to *Combat,* was persuaded to join the *Front National* secretly, and further persuaded to take a communist secretary, Annie Hervé, to assist him at the BIP, the resistance propaganda agency. Pascal Copeau, a communist "submarine" who was deputy leader of *Libération-Sud,* became a close collaborator of Moulin's. Yves Farge, another "submarine," was selected by Moulin to prepare a major—and ultimately disastrous—resistance uprising on the plateau of Vercors.

During this period in 1942 de Gaulle's emissaries met with great difficulty in trying to contact the PCF leadership. So well concealed were the communists, and so professional was their underground organization, that it was many months before a formal link could be set up. The man who eventually achieved this was a member of the Gaullist intelligence service named François Faure.

Under the leadership of "Colonel Rémy"—one of Colonel Passy's first recruits—the BCRA had created a Free French resistance network in both zones called the *Confrérie Notre Dame* (CND). Faure was among its agents and he, through personal friendship, made contact with the leadership of the Communist Party in March 1942. The FTP, the armed wing of the *Front National,* then asked Faure to return to London to establish an official link with the Free French. The FTP claimed to have information that would interest the British and said they were in a position to paralyze supply lines to the Russian front; in return they wanted a radio operator who could set up a permanent link with London. This offer was welcomed enthusiastically by the BCRA and the British agencies. Faure was sent back to France and a liaison officer was parachuted with him on 28 May. But both Faure and the liaison officer were arrested by the Gestapo shortly after arriving, and contact with the FTP could not be reestablished.

Meanwhile, Moulin, as we have seen, had been in touch, through Manhès, Pierre Meunier and others, with both the communist underground and Soviet intelligence agents in the northern zone in 1940, 1941 and 1942, but had never mentioned any of his northern zone activities to London. So it was by chance that in July, after the arrest of Faure, he was asked by London to reestablish Faure's link. In consequence he made a

brief visit to what was still the occupied zone from 2 to 19 July. On 25 July
he told London that he had so far failed to make contact with the PCF but
that he had been in contact with Soviet intelligence agents in the northern
zone. Since Moulin had contact with the PCF through Madame Dangon
and her husband, and with the PCF and Soviet intelligence through Meunier, Chambeiron, Panier and Manhès, his answer seems to have been misleading. Furthermore, it is noteworthy that he asked for no separate links
to be formed with the PCF while he was at work, in order "to simplify
matters."

This request was ignored and in November contact was finally reestablished—not by Moulin—with a representative of the PCF's central committee. On 11 January 1943 the Communist Party's delegate, Fernand
Grenier, arrived in London. Two weeks later, on 26 January, Colonel Passy
received a message that a man called Henri Manhès, who had just arrived
from France, was claiming to be Moulin's "delegate in the northern zone"
and was asking to see him. Moulin was not supposed to be operating in the
northern zone and had been reminded of this as recently as November
1942. Now here was Manhès going further and stating that as Moulin's delegate he had been in touch with the northern zone communists.

All this gave Passy pause for thought, and he decided to take the highly
irregular step of being parachuted into the occupied zone to see what was
going on. It was as though the head of MI6 had decided to drive up the avenue Foch for a tour of inspection. He was accompanied on this mission by
a senior SOE "shadow," Yeo-Thomas, an RAF officer who spoke rapid and
faultless French with a strong Parisian accent. Forest Yeo-Thomas was an
ideal SOE agent, being a military officer not lacking in courage (he was
eventually awarded the George Cross) and capable of working alone in
enemy territory on his own initiative. His SOE file card described him
as "more French than British in outlook," a barbed compliment, whereas
to his friend Colonel Passy he was "as French as he was English," which
was a wholehearted compliment. Passy was also accompanied by a formi-
dable recruit to the BCRA, Pierre Brossolette, an uncompromising anti-
communist who was one of the most talented men to have worked for de
Gaulle and someone whom Moulin quickly perceived as a dangerous
rival.

Pierre Brossolette came from a background very similar to Jean Moulin's. Both were born into families with an established republican tradition,
both were the children of antimonarchist, anticlerical schoolmasters, both

attended their father's schools, both fathers were the dominant parent, both boys were highly intelligent; but Brossolette, four years younger, worked a lot harder at school and, living in Paris, he entered the republic's academic fast stream, the Lycée Louis-le-Grand and the Ecole Normale Supérieure, from which in 1925 he graduated second in his class, behind Georges Bidault. Then, when he might have chosen any available university position in the country, Brossolette decided to become a journalist. Politically he associated himself with the "Young Turks" of the radical-republican movement; he also joined the *Grande Loge de France,* the country's second largest group of freemasons. In the 1930s he flirted with pacifism, supported the League of Nations and joined the SFIO (Socialist Party). His prominence as a journalist, in both radio and the press—before the war he was the most celebrated anti-fascist journalist in France—made him one of the favored targets of the extreme-right and a well-known public figure. He married young and was never attracted by communism.

Early in 1941 Brossolette, from his bookshop in Paris, started to write for the underground journal of one of the very earliest resistance groups, formed by three members of the staff of the Musée de l'Homme. The group was broken in the spring of 1941, when many of Brossolette's comrades were arrested and shot at Mont Valérien. In April 1942, having made contact with Colonel Rémy, Brossolette was flown to London and recruited directly into the BCRA.

In London Brossolette quickly gained the reputation of being one of the very few men who were intellectually and temperamentally capable of standing up to de Gaulle. From June to September he undertook his first clandestine mission in France, during which, unknown to Moulin, he traveled through both the occupied and Vichy zones. He contacted Rémy, one of the most talented agents ever sent into occupied France but who had become both unrealistic and a megalomaniac. The colonel was apparently unaware that his CND network was falling to pieces around him; on several occasions he himself had narrowly escaped arrest; he had also developed a careless habit of turning up for the wrong rendezvous at the wrong time. Meanwhile he was repeatedly disobeying ("modifying" was the favored word) his orders while simultaneously proposing grandiose schemes for the future. By this time Colonel Rémy had been involved in undercover work in France for nearly two years and Brossolette suggested that his superior be given a rest; Rémy was flown out shortly afterward.

The chief object of Brossolette's mission was to talk leading socialist politicians into leaving France and joining de Gaulle. In three months he managed to persuade André Philip and Louis Vallon to leave, and they were immediately given ministerial status on reaching London. Brossolette also converted a prominent Pétainist supporter, Charles Vallin, and made contact with pro-Gaullist leaders of the Catholic Church. Brossolette himself did not return to England until his three "trophies" and their families, and his own family, had all been taken to safety. On his return to London Brossolette broke cover and started to broadcast to France. On 22 September 1942 the announcer introduced him as a star of the Resistance who had declared his loyalty to de Gaulle. "For two years Pierre Brossolette has battled beside the French fighting inside France. Now he is in London . . ." And Brossolette chose to sing the praises of the resistance "foot soldiers" who died in obscurity. He compared them not to soldiers but to the ship's stokers working below decks on the Atlantic convoys until their ship went down. "They are fighting beside you, although you do not always know it. . . . They are among you tonight, my brothers-in-arms. Let us salute them together. . . . For they are the stokers of glory (*les soutiers de la gloire*)!"

In the latter part of 1942 serious differences developed between Moulin, isolated in France, having to wait for days or weeks for replies to his coded messages, with his radio operators being tracked steadily by the German police, and Brossolette in London, at Passy's elbow in BCRA headquarters and with privileged access to de Gaulle. Moulin wanted to abolish the redundant distinction between northern and southern zones, since both were now occupied; this would enable him to become de Gaulle's delegate to the entire Resistance. Brossolette wanted to maintain the distinction, since the movements had separate histories, and he wanted to be sent as de Gaulle's delegate to the northern zone. Moulin discovered that it was Brossolette who had written the instruction, carried by Frenay in November 1942, reminding him that he was restricted to the southern zone. Then, just when links with the Communist Party were being formed, came Passy's discovery that Moulin had been operating, through his own delegate Manhès, in the northern zone for a year. The thin line between "modifying" and "disobeying" orders seemed to have been crossed. This was the background to the "Mission brumaire," the code name for the journey undertaken by Passy, Brossolette and Yeo-Thomas in January 1943.

Brossolette arrived on 26 January and Passy followed on 26 February.

Moulin, with his habitual tactical skill, chose to return to London from 13 February to 21 March, by which time he had been in the field for a year and six weeks. The official reason for his return was to bring General Delestraint, the newly appointed military commander of the Secret Army, to talk to de Gaulle and meet Passy and the British. But Moulin also timed his London visit to coincide with the absence of Brossolette; furthermore he was able first to meet Passy with de Gaulle, and then to be in London after Passy's departure. He may also have been expecting to confer with his indispensable colleague Henri Manhès, whom he had sent to London on 26 January. In the event Manhès climbed out of the plane Moulin and Delestraint were preparing to board. When Manhès saw Moulin among the figures crouched on the edge of the field waiting to board the plane he shouted, "Wait! Don't go, Jean, don't go." Moulin hesitated but the French liaison officer in charge of the flight said, "I've got my orders," and pushed Moulin through the plane door. By the time Moulin had returned on 21 March, Manhès had been under Gestapo interrogation in the avenue Foch for ten days.

TWELVE

Betrayal

MOULIN'S VISIT TO LONDON was crowned with success. In the absence of Brossolette, de Gaulle was happy to renew his confidence in his delegate to the Resistance. Following the U.S. landings in North Africa in November 1942 and President Roosevelt's choice of the pro-Pétainist General Giraud as commander in Algiers, de Gaulle, too, was faced with a major rival, and the unification and "de Gaullification" of the "interior resistance" had become one of his priorities. On 14 February 1943, in a ceremony at his private residence in Hampstead, the leader of the Free French made "Sergeant Mercier"—whom he later described as being "filled to the depths of his soul with the love of France"—a Companion of the Order of the Liberation, the highest honor he could bestow. Colonel Passy, who observed the scene, described it as follows.

> Once again I see Moulin, white-faced, in the grip of an emotion which we all shared, upright in front of the General, who said to him in almost a murmur, "Stand to attention," and then continued in that characteristic broken, chanting style—"Sergeant Mercier, we acknowledge you as our Companion in Honor and Victory, for the Liberation of France." And while de Gaulle gave him the customary embrace, a tear of gratitude, pride and unshakeable determination ran down the pale cheek of our comrade Moulin. And since he had

raised his face to look up to the General we could once more see the traces of the razor wound he had inflicted on himself in 1940 to avoid giving in under enemy torture.

In the days that followed de Gaulle gave Moulin a new mission and increased powers. "Rex" would henceforth be known as "Max." The distinction between the two zones would be maintained, but "Max" would be de Gaulle's delegate to both. Moulin had turned the tables on his critics and taken advantage of their absence beyond the screen of coded messages to carry his point. His task now was to construct, as soon as possible, a unified political body, a national council, for the whole of the Resistance. This council would declare its loyalty to de Gaulle and thereby confirm the latter's legitimacy as the leader of all the French who had continued the fight both within and outside France. Without this support, de Gaulle's chances of imposing himself and his movement—untainted by Pétainism and collaboration—over the claims of Giraud and the hostility of President Roosevelt would be slim.

In order for the proposed new body, the *Conseil national de la résistance* (CNR, or National Resistance Council), to enjoy some democratic credibility it would have to include not just representatives of the main underground movements but representatives of the trades unions and political parties. Brossolette, Frenay and practically the entire leadership of the internal resistance were fiercely opposed to any status being given to any of the old political groupings; if the Resistance had had any purpose, apart from the expulsion of the occupying forces, it had been to make a clean sweep of the men, ideas and parties of the Third Republic, which together had led France to disaster.

Until February 1943 Moulin was also opposed to the reintroduction of the political parties. But his visit to London coincided with a major crisis in Anglo-French relations. Faced with the challenge from Giraud, de Gaulle had been forbidden by Churchill to fly to Algeria, and was on the point of being abandoned by the allies. When Moulin realized the urgency of de Gaulle's need, and saw the strength and unity of the opposition, he also realized the tactical advantage he would gain by switching his opinion. By imposing the parties on the Resistance he would serve de Gaulle, reestablish himself as his single representative and isolate his own opponents. Nobody knew better than Moulin the difficulties of the task, but within two months of his return he had succeeded in presiding over the CNR's first meeting, although it now seems possible that in setting out like this against everyone else he signed his death warrant.

From the end of April to the end of May 1943 a major offensive against Jean Moulin built up among the Free French in London which was supported by visiting resistance leaders from France. These latter included Emmanuel d'Astier, who declared that Moulin had acquired excessive power, that he was abusing it, that he was spending resistance funds without accounting for them, that he was failing to keep in touch with the separate resistance groups and treating their leaders as a colonial officer treated "native chieftains," and that he was reimposing the discredited political parties of the Third Republic against the wishes of the entire Resistance. The leader of the northern zone OCM, less verbose, described Moulin as "a dictator." Frenay complained that the Resistance was becoming bureaucratized by desk-wallahs from London, and that the Gaullist movement was mounting a takeover bid for the *Résistance intérieure*.

When Passy and Brossolette returned to London on 15 April they delivered a critical report to de Gaulle about Moulin's performance; they said that he overawed General Delestraint and was about to make a series of grave errors in his attempts to unite the northern zone movements. Moulin, informed of their criticism, countered by reporting directly to de Gaulle, hoping to bypass the BCRA. Brossolette or Passy responded by further delaying the reinforcements Moulin had requested. Claude Serreulles, who had been due to join his staff as an administrator and secretary in February, eventually arrived on 19 June.

While this offensive was being mounted Moulin, back in France, was faced with a succession of personal setbacks and professional crises. In his absence, on 13 March, the Secret Army courier had been arrested by French police at the railway station at Bourg-en-Bresse, forty miles north of Lyon. This arrest had been followed by the seizure of the archives of the Secret Army with its battle plan and the names and code names of its military hierarchy. In the days that followed several of its leading figures were arrested and held in French police custody. They included Serge Asher, Maurice Kriegel and Raymond Samuel. All three were undeclared communist militants who had joined *Libération-Sud* and been allocated important military roles. In the Resistance, Kriegel was known as "Valrimont,"

Asher was known as "Ravanel" and Samuel was known as "Aubrac." Having been questioned by French police they were sent over to the Hôtel Terminus to be interrogated by the Gestapo.

Moulin's second problem concerned Henri Frenay. He had left Frenay, six weeks earlier, with a truncated budget and in his absence Frenay had decided to resolve the problem in Switzerland. Allen Dulles of the OSS, working steadily in Berne to penetrate and direct the French Resistance, was no longer confined to contacts made for him by Noel Field. He had also been in touch with the *Cagoule*. So it was that, with the help of a relatively new recruit to *Combat*, Pierre de Bénouville, an extreme right-winger who sympathized with the *Cagoule*, Henri Frenay was able to reach an agreement with the OSS. In future the Americans would make up the budget shortfall imposed by Moulin, provide the MUR with an independent radio link from Switzerland and supply the weapons and explosives that Frenay needed. In return Frenay was required to share with the Americans in Berne all the information he sent to London. De Bénouville, returning from Berne with the glad tidings, danced round Frenay shouting, "Bravo Henri—Patron. C'est dans la poche." ("Bravo Henri—Boss. It is in the bag!") He was carrying a suitcase that contained one million francs.

Moulin therefore returned from London, on 21 March 1943, to find that the united military organization in the southern zone which he had set up before his departure was under intense pressure from the Gestapo in Lyon, while the military director of the MUR, Frenay, was in the middle of establishing his independence from Gaullist control. Moulin's response was devastating. From now on, he said, at a meeting on 24 March, the MUR would become either redundant or subordinate to the new National Resistance Council. He himself would be president of this council and its military commander would be General Delestraint. In the new "Secret Army" Frenay would have more or less the same status as a brigade commander. Frenay's reply was to refuse all cooperation with Moulin's plans and, together with d'Astier and J.-P. Lévy, to refuse to sit on the new national council side by side with the representatives of the Third Republic's political parties.

Frenay later described the meeting where these matters were discussed as the most tumultuous and violent they had ever had. He recalled returning to his hideout at Cluny, in Burgundy, exhausted and discouraged. Was *Combat* now "at war" with Moulin? he wondered. "Would we now have to use our strength against our own side? Would we now have to *resist* and battle against them too?" When it became apparent that no further compromise was possible, Frenay decided to go to London to demand Moulin's recall. The Secret Army, which now numbered approximately eighty thousand men and women, was at this stage still engaged in its four original tasks of intelligence, propaganda, assistance to fugitives and terrorism. In Lyon, which since the German occupation of November 1942 had become a city in the front line of resistance, thirty-four resistance newspaper titles were published illegally and circulated in secret. Police records show that the number of bombings and attempted assassinations against both German and collaborationist targets increased from 10 in 1942 to 127 in 1943; 300 Frenchmen were known to have died in these attacks and 22 Germans. Although Frenay considered the Secret Army to be underarmed it was probably capable of more action than it undertook, but its main priority remained recruitment, training and planning for the moment when it could assist regular allied forces to liberate France. A random selection of attacks carried out in the spring of 1943 included a bomb in the German army's luggage office at the Perrache railway station, a soldier shot outside the Hotel Massena, the wounding of a sentry guarding the German army's artillery depot and a German telephone line cut. These minor actions, each of which led to reprisals, kept the issue of resistance alive.

Moulin's next problem was personal. In the spring of 1943 he lost the support of Antoinette Sachs, who, harassed by the *Commissariat Général aux Questions Juives,* was forced to take refuge with her sister in Switzerland, where she would remain for the rest of the occupation. He had also broken with Gilberte Lloyd. In January, unable to see him as often as she wished, Madame Lloyd had tired of waiting and told Moulin that she wanted to get married. The fact that she was prepared to put this pressure on him at that time suggests that she had little concern for the importance of his responsibilities. Moulin's reply that he could not marry her because they had left it too late to have children (she was forty-five) was unconvincing. On 23 March 1943, at the *mairie* of the 16th arrondissement, Gilberte married a wealthy industrialist and widower who had an apartment on the avenue Foch and whom she had met on the train between Paris and Vichy; he had wooed her with black market cigarettes. Pierre Meunier said that Moulin was extremely depressed by Gilberte's defection.

Moulin was left with Colette Pons, whom he saw in Nice where she was running the Galérie Romanin. This had been opened in February 1943, just before Moulin's departure for London. He had devoted a surprising amount of time to this business. The opening was attended by prominent members of the German and French administrations in the city of Nice. As Baumel points out, none of these figures linked Jean Moulin, art dealer of Nice, with the "terrorist" of Lyon. The first shows included work by Utrillo, Marie Laurencin, Dufy and Matisse. It is not clear where Moulin raised the capital to fund these purchases. When Frenay heard about it he described the whole enterprise as a reckless distraction.

In addition to Antoinette and Gilberte there was a further loss, even more serious, since it was not just personal but professional. The arrest of Henri Manhès had taken place in Paris on 3 March as he was about to meet Robert Chambeiron, shortly after a row had broken out between Manhès and Pierre Brossolette. In the course of their "Mission brumaire" Passy and Brossolette were investigating Manhès's contacts with the various resistance groups to whom he had presented himself as "the delegate of Rex," in other words of General de Gaulle. Two days earlier, at a lunch party held in public, in a restaurant in the Neuilly district of Paris, attended by Passy and Yeo-Thomas as well as Pierre Meunier and Chambeiron, there had been a fierce clash between Manhès and Brossolette, with Meunier doing what he could to make things worse. Manhès was subsequently arrested by a French police *brigade spéciale* which was tracking communists. Caught red-handed with his records and correspondence, Manhès tried to mitigate his offense by telling the French police that he was a Gaullist, not a communist, and that he had merely been providing a letter-box for a number of Gaullist, masonic and communist resistance groups. Shortly afterward the French handed him over to the Gestapo. After the war, Manhès claimed to have been interrogated in the avenue Foch twenty-seven times before he was deported to Buchenwald.*

Passy and Brossolette, who were told of Manhès's arrest almost at once, did not pass the news back to London and Moulin did not hear of it

---

* In Buchenwald Henri Manhès, who survived the camp, was appointed deputy chief of the communist-dominated "French Prisoners' Committee." This committee, run by a communist member of the *Front National,* had powers of life or death over other prisoners. Any identified Trotskyists were listed for transfer to the slave camp of Dora, which had a 33 percent death rate. Alternatively they were sent to Buchenwald's experimental clinic.

until his return on 21 March. When he was told he said, "*Whatever happens now, I've had it.*"

It was against this background of crisis that Moulin traveled to Paris at the end of March to confront Passy and Brossolette. His state of mind at this stage can be imagined. Despite the impressive new powers conferred on him by General de Gaulle, he felt more vulnerable than ever. Manhès was under arrest; his own authority had been repudiated by the southern zone resisters; his organization in both zones was under ever-increasing Gestapo pressure; and this was his first visit to Paris since the break with Gilberte Lloyd. On 1 April, Moulin met Passy, Brossolette and Yeo-Thomas in the Bois de Boulogne to hear an account of their work. For the first time since he had met Passy in October 1941 he was on equal terms with the head of the Gaullist intelligence service. And he now outranked Brossolette comfortably. In the two months it had lasted the "Mission brumaire" had not just inquired into Moulin's links with the communists and other unannounced activities in the northern zone. Passy and Brossolette had also set up a "coordinating committee"—a sort of northern zone equivalent of the MUR—established against Moulin's wishes as part of Brossolette's plan to maintain the independence of a northern resistance zone under his own control. Since the German occupation of the southern zone, the importance of that region to the Resistance had diminished. The northern zone, which contained the capital city, the likeliest invasion landing grounds, and the probable scene of the major battlefields of the liberation, was clearly the crucial area. And in this area Brossolette, who was obviously aware of Moulin's pro-communist reputation, was determined that de Gaulle should have a resistance movement uncontaminated by communist influence.

The meeting in the clearings of the Bois de Boulogne—Moulin following his old habit of never sitting down—was the first direct confrontation between the two most able political supporters of de Gaulle. It was a clear victory for Moulin. On being told of the coordinating committee he merely observed that it should be summoned as soon as possible. That settled, he moved on to the attack, going for Brossolette on his weakest point: the way he and Passy had treated Manhès and Meunier, his trusted lieutenants. The bone of contention was the same: Brossolette had accused Moulin of "personal ambition." Manhès had challenged him about this. Now Moulin did so. Once again Brossolette denied that he had queried the integrity of Moulin's motives and demanded to be confronted with his accusers. Moulin agreed and a new appointment was made.

The final confrontation between Moulin and the members of the "Mission brumaire" took place on the following day in an apartment in the avenue des Ternes. Colonel Passy described the scene between Moulin and Brossolette as "a painful incident," and it must certainly rank as one of the least inspiring moments in the history of the French Resistance. Two men of exceptional courage and ability, both ready, in time of war, to die for their country, flew at each other's throats for a mixture of honorable and contemptible reasons. Had they lived in the age of dueling, the matter could have been settled with dignity. But they were children of the Republic, enlightened and cerebral, they had no weapons at their disposal except verbal weapons, and, exhausted by the strain of their daily lives, they failed to use these with agility.

Once again the reproach was advanced; Meunier, who seems to have played a destructive role throughout the relationship, confirmed that Brossolette had accused Moulin of "personal ambition." The row that followed lasted fifteen minutes. Despite everything Passy could do—at one point reminding them that several of the neighboring apartments were occupied by Germans—they continued at full volume, Moulin sometimes accusing Passy of being putty in the hands of his subordinate. Neither Chambeiron nor Yeo-Thomas played an active role. At the height of the argument Moulin, who had lost all self-control, turned his back on Brossolette and lowered his trousers, yelling as he exhibited his ass— "Now you can see my opinion of you." When the meeting broke up Passy murmured to Meunier, "You have a great commander, take care of him." Years later Meunier said that he was never sure whether Passy was being sarcastic, but it is worth noting that Meunier kept his account of this incident and of Passy's possibly ambiguous comment to a time when he and the colonel were the only living survivors of the scene in the avenue des Ternes; it was also a time when Passy was too ill to react to the revelations of a man whom he had once described as "sly and brutal."

Before leaving for London, Passy and Brossolette attended two more meetings with Moulin which were of a more professional nature and where everyone kept their pants on. On 3 April in Paris there was a session of Brossolette's northern zone coordinating committee, the first occasion on which the representatives of the northern resistance had met de Gaulle's personal representative. Moulin announced the impending formation of the CNR and reassured the assembled resisters that its purpose was to "establish the unity of the Fighting French behind General de Gaulle," and that it was not designed to weaken their own autonomy. On 12 April a second, more significant, meeting took place. This was a session of the coordinating committee's "general staff" and was presided over by General Delestraint. Delestraint announced that de Gaulle had ordered him to prepare the Secret Army to go into action in support of the allied landings, whenever those might take place. Until then the Resistance should not take any military action.

This instruction led to immediate protests from the two representatives of the communist armed resistance, the FTP–MOI, which had been harrying the German forces for the previous two years. They said that they had agreed to place their armed units under central command, but not to confine them to barracks. Moulin then intervened to support Delestraint, remarking that since the day the FTP–MOI had joined the Secret Army its contingents had become military units and were obliged to obey orders: "The time has come," he said, to "click your heels." The communists replied to this provocation by noting that the matter would have to be referred to their executive committee but they added that there would be no question of renouncing immediate military action; they were not there to march in step and behave themselves but to strike the enemy as hard and as frequently as they could. Brossolette then intervened and suggested that the FTP–MOI should place the greater part of its forces under Delestraint's command but should keep control of some of its troops to continue the program of "immediate action"—which, the communists claimed, absurdly enough, was "killing 500 Germans a month." (The total number of German soldiers assassinated on communist orders between 1941 and 1944 was later estimated at 200.)

This compromise saved everyone's face, but after the meeting Moulin instructed his secretary Daniel Cordier to suspend all future payments to the FTP–MOI. These had been running at a million francs a month. On the basis of commitments received from Rémy and Passy, the FTP–MOI had built up its recruiting drive among young men dodging the STO, so the effect of Moulin's decision on its operations and credibility was potentially disastrous. The decision became effective at the end of April, and led to protests from the PCF's representative in London. But the payments remained suspended for six months.

Just as Moulin had taken advantage of Brossolette's absence from London in March he now profited from his rival's absence from France. Making full use of his increased powers he secured, during the second half of April, the agreement of the main political and trade union groupings and resistance movements on the final structure of the National Resistance Council and was able on 8 May to send a telegram to de Gaulle announcing the "constitution" of the CNR. The same telegram stated that the new body, which had not yet met, would in all circumstances "recognize de Gaulle as the sole leader of the French Resistance." This telegram was sent by Moulin after he had heard a BBC news bulletin announcing de Gaulle's much-delayed departure for Algiers to meet General Giraud and attempt to form an alliance with him. The telegram was "signed" by all the organizations which were to sit on the CNR, although it was in fact no more than a précis of the discussions Moulin had been having. As soon as it was received it was doctored by the Gaullist information service in London and published in a form which made it look as though it was a report of the CNR's first meeting and as though the declaration of loyalty was the council's first decision. This alteration led to strong protests from the alleged signatories in France and from d'Astier and Lévy, who were in London and who considered that the premature publication of a doctored report put the lives of resisters in France in danger. Moulin also protested against the use that had been made of his telegram. But the fact remained that, in its published form, it enabled de Gaulle on his arrival in Algiers to represent himself to Giraud and the Americans as the legitimate patron and commander-in-chief of the Resistance of the interior.

Despite the misleading nature of Moulin's original telegram, and despite the cynical misrepresentation of his message in London, preparations for the first meeting of the CNR went ahead, and this historic event took place in central Paris on 27 May. In the first-floor room of an apartment overlooking the courtyard, at 47 rue du Four in the 6th arrondissement—an apartment that belonged to a former assistant of Pierre Cot—seventeen members of the *Conseil national de la résistance* met for their first plenary session. Apart from the president, Moulin, there were eight seats for the Resistance, six for the political parties and two for the trade unions. The three southern zone movements which had formed the MUR were represented by senior figures rather than by their "historic" founders; the five northern zone movements selected by Brossolette for his coordinating committee took up the rest of the resistance places. All other resistance groups in France were invited to associate themselves with one of the groups represented by the eight selected members. The political parties, rechristened "tendencies," included the PCF, the socialists and the radical-socialists and three right-wing parties. Of these parties only the first two had played any serious part in the Resistance, and the eight resistance groups only agreed to the inclusion of the politicians if the latter were excluded from the council's executive committee. The men selected to sit on the council were nominated by the organizations they represented; the Communist Party had two representatives, one for the PCF and one for the *Front National*. In addition the party had three other agents at the first council meeting, and the council's two secretaries were Pierre Meunier and Robert Chambeiron. Furthermore, Georges Bidault, who represented the right-wing Christian Democrats, was at that time generally in sympathy with communist policy.

Although the main purpose of the first meeting of the CNR was simply to do that—to meet, to exist—it did not pass without incident. Moulin opened proceedings by summarizing the purposes of the Resistance, which were to make war, restore the French people's right to speak, reestablish republican liberties and work with the allies for victory. Then he read a message from de Gaulle saying that it was essential that the Resistance be united and that this had now been achieved, thanks to the existence of the CNR.

He then invited Georges Bidault to speak and the representative of the Christian Democrats read out a declaration for the council's approval saying that Vichy had to be completely repudiated and that the head of France's provisional government could only be General de Gaulle. General Giraud should be appointed to the position of commander-in-chief of the Free French army. Both the official communist representatives strongly protested against the adoption of this declaration, not wanting to entrust so much power to "a political general" like de Gaulle, and arguing that the declaration was divisive and that de Gaulle and the "apolitical" Giraud should be accorded joint powers. Once again the discussion became heated and Moulin brought the meeting to a close, reminding those present that if they continued to shout they would be overheard, and insisting that it was necessary to reach a unanimous decision on Bidault's declaration. In these circumstances the two communists were forced to agree to vote for the declaration, and for the second time in six weeks PCF delegates found themselves outmaneuvered by de Gaulle's personal representative.

By June 1943 de Gaulle's final objectives for the liberation of France were threefold. He wanted (a) to avoid the imposition on liberated France of an allied military government, or AMGOT; (b) to win a seat at the conference table which dictated the terms of surrender and (c) to avoid the imposition of a puppet "Soviet" in France. Moulin is known to have shared the first objective; he did not oppose the second; the undecided question is whether or not he shared de Gaulle's third objective.

THIRTEEN

An Urn and a Pot of Jam

By 21 JUNE 1943, the day of his arrest, Jean Moulin seems to have reached the end of his strength. After the loss of Manhès, and the seizure of his records, Moulin had become convinced that the Gestapo had his real identity and his photograph. He habitually wore dark glasses, which were hardly a disguise; to these he added his brown trilby and a scarf to hide the scar on his throat, even in summer. On the day of Caluire, said Tony de Graaf, he was wearing a gray suit, without a raincoat although it was raining. He had redoubled his routine precautions, directing his secretaries, de Graaf in the southern zone and Daniel Cordier in the north, to misdate his correspondence and post it from towns where he had never been, the better to cover his tracks. By June the strain of his work, which had long since affected his behavior, had begun to affect his judgment as well. The rage he displayed in the avenue des Ternes with Brossolette could be explained by the problems he faced. To be forced to unravel the cat's cradle Brossolette had made of his own intricate network distracted him from the complicated game he was playing against his German and French opponents.

Three weeks earlier he had achieved the greatest triumph of his career. He had left the rue du Four after the first meeting of the CNR in an exalted mood. He had met Daniel Cordier at an art gallery on the Ile St.-Louis, where there was an exhibition of Kandinsky's work, then he had asked Cordier to have dinner and they had spent the evening discussing modern art. "He talked almost the whole time because he was very, very happy," wrote Cordier. "That evening he was relaxed, which was extremely rare." But the mood had not lasted.

The list of Moulin's enemies within the ranks of the Resistance had grown. There was Frenay, a right-winger, leader of *Combat,* the most powerful military organization in the southern zone, who regarded him as a menace to the independence and integrity of the Resistance. There was d'Astier, a left-winger, who accused him of abusing his power, misusing his funds and reimposing the political chaos of the Third Republic against universal opposition. There were the French agents of the American OSS, a service which regarded him as a man working to hand France over to a Gaullist military dictatorship, and there were the agents of the pro-Pétainist resistance of the right and the extreme-right which considered all former collaborators of Pierre Cot as "crypto-communists." Strangely enough both of these last groups were to some extent represented by one man, Frenay's new deputy and *Combat*'s new chief of staff, Pierre de Bénouville.

By June 1943 Moulin was heartily disliked in the Resistance inside France. In addition, in London, the directors of the BCRA, the organization on which Moulin depended totally for communication and both financial and military support, had just condemned him in the most uncompromising terms. In their final report on the "Mission brumaire," Passy and Brossolette stated that Moulin had been entrusted with excessive powers and was out of control. Although his personal loyalty was beyond question he was dependent on a bizarre entourage (Meunier and Chambeiron) who were "indoctrinating him" and he had set up an over-centralized communication system which was vulnerable to penetration and which, if misused, could imperil the existence of the Secret Army. Passy and Brossolette were clearly concerned about the possibility of communist infiltration.

And for Moulin, effectively, the enigmatic nature of his relationship with the Communist Party represented an additional danger and an additional strain. On two crucial occasions he had overruled communist delegates, which suggests that he was working against the party line. And for two months in succession he had refused payment of the communist resistance's funds. According to Robert Chambeiron, speaking in 1964 on the steps of the Panthéon: "Moulin was not a communist, but what may have led people to think he was, was that at a given moment he confided all the radio codes governing communications between the Resistance and London to me and Meunier; in other words no one could contact any resistance leader without going through Meunier or me." The question is, Why? In such circumstances and whatever his true objectives, the assistance of Henri Manhès, who was trusted by all concerned—the PCF, his fellow "submarines" and the delegate of General de Gaulle—would have been an essential part of Moulin's strategy.

Whether out of personal or professional need, the loss of Manhès was so serious for Moulin that he made at least one attempt to secure his release: this move was dangerous enough, but even more so since both he and Meunier had decided that Manhès had probably been forced to talk. In the middle of April, Moulin asked Colette Pons to spend a week with him in Paris buying pictures for the gallery in Nice. Fifty years later Colette Pons told the writer Pierre Péan that one day they happened to meet an old schoolfriend of hers who was having an affair with a member of the Gestapo. Moulin instructed her to dine with the couple and see if anything could be done to release Manhès. After dinner the Gestapo officer made inquiries and told Colette that Manhès had not been tortured because all his files had been seized when he was arrested. She also said that a bargain was struck over Manhès, but refused to tell Péan what it had been. When he heard what had happened, Moulin told her to leave Paris at once. It was 23 April.

Meanwhile, outside the houses in which the secret councils were held, the Gestapo continued its run of success. In April in Paris they arrested two junior members of Moulin's secretariat. And in Lyon, Hervé Montjaret, Moulin's original radio operator, who had been parachuted with him over St. Andiol, was arrested as he visited one of the *Délégation-Générale's* mail drops. Moulin felt himself increasingly threatened. At the end of the month he returned to St. Andiol to spend Easter with his mother and sister. It was almost the last time he was to assume his real identity. On the Tuesday after Easter he left and Laure recalled that she accompanied him to the gate. He was going to cycle to the station in Avignon.

"I am attempting something very difficult at the moment," he said. "If it works out I will cross the Channel so that people can forget about me for a time. They are getting closer and I have to double my precautions. Don't write to me even if *maman* is ill or even if she dies. They would arrest me at her funeral. I will send you a note now and again, by courier. But you must not write to me." I kissed him good-bye with more feeling than usual and followed his silhouette as it disappeared down the empty road. Then I went back into the house with a heavy heart. I never saw him again.

Between the ninth and the twenty-first of June the Gestapo broke seven resistance networks in several parts of France. Three of these were run from London by the BCRA, two were SOE networks including the ex-ensive *Prosper* network active in the remote Sologne region south of the River Loire, and the other two were Vichy army resistance networks. None had any connection with the Communist Party, although that may have been because the communists had high standards of security and re-garded noncommunist resistance groups as amateurs. Nonetheless the fact that five of the groups were run from London and that none were communist may not be coincidence.

None of the seven networks had any direct connection with the CNR or the work of Jean Moulin, but the Gestapo had been making progress in that direction, too. They had been aware of the existence of the Secret Army since March; they had its records and they had, briefly, arrested four of its leaders (Aubrac, Valrimont, Ravanel and Forestier) in the Lyon region. With the arrival from Marseille of the *Combat* traitor Multon—who was accompanied by his Gestapo minder, a policeman called Robert Moog, who was either Alsatian or German—the German police in Lyon, led by Klaus Barbie, concentrated on the hunt for the political and mili-tary leaders whom they only knew as "Max" and "Vidal," in reality Mou-lin and Delestraint. With the arrest of Montjaret on 4 April, Barbie had a line into the COPA, one of the most important support units of the Secret Army, responsible for organizing all parachute drops and landings.

The next success was the discovery of a mail drop in central Lyon, at 14 rue Bouteille, a box used by NAP–FER, the *Combat* group that had pre-pared a plan to sabotage the national railway system and had recruited heavily among the French railway workers. Next, on 16 April, came the ar-rest of an agent who was to prove as useful as Multon, Edmée Delettraz, a tall, handsome, dark-haired Belgian woman who is known to have worked for six different resistance or intelligence groups. These included Victor

Farrell, MI6's correspondent in Geneva; Colonel Groussard, the *cagoulard* resister who had arrested Pierre Laval in 1940 and who was now running the *Gilbert* network from Berne; the British *Pat O'Leary* escape line, founded by the Belgian doctor Albert Guerisse; *Serge,* one of the Vichy *Deuxième Bureau*'s resistance units, as well as a French police resistance network called *Ajax,* and the Swiss secret service. There may have been others. According to some sources Edmée Delettraz did valuable resistance work but after her arrest, when she agreed to work for the Gestapo intending to become a triple agent, she overestimated her ability and became an extremely dangerous woman to know. Edmée Delettraz was arrested at the Lyon mail drop, and was immediately duped by an ingenious montage. Just before the Gestapo arrived Robert Moog walked up to her, posing as a resister who had come to warn her of the danger. When his colleagues followed, hot on his heels, he attacked them and was beaten up so severely that both Madame Delettraz and several other people present were convinced that Moog really was in the Resistance. Shortly afterward Edmée Delettraz became Moog's mistress and from then on she seems to have been in a state of confusion as to whom she was actually working for.

The first target of Moog and Multon was not Moulin but Henri Frenay. Multon had the address of Berty Albrecht, Frenay's mistress and colleague. On 28 May, Moog used Madame Delettraz to trap Madame Albrecht at a hotel in Mâcon. In Berty Albrecht's handbag was an address used by Frenay at Cluny. Moog and Barbie raided the house immediately and found part of Frenay's records, but the leader of *Combat,* benefiting from a combination of instinct and luck, had just moved to a different hideout in Lyon. Nine days later in Fresnes prison, outside Paris, Berty Albrecht died, probably after cutting her own throat, although the Gestapo put it around at the time that she had been beheaded with an axe.

"Vidal," General Delestraint, was arrested, also by Moog and Multon and also in Paris, on 9 June as he arrived for a rendezvous with René Hardy, the head of NAP–FER. Hardy did not arrive. He himself had been arrested a few hours earlier by Moog on the night-train from Lyon on his way to the rendezvous. So two weeks after the inaugural meeting of the National Resistance Council, its army had lost its military commander. (General Charles Delestraint was eventually deported to Dachau, where he was executed in April 1945.) It was to discuss the steps that had to be taken to replace General Delestraint that Moulin summoned seven men to meet him at the house in Caluire.

Part of the cruelty of *Nacht und Nebel* was that, long after the Nazi regime had been destroyed, the effects of this policy lived on—the friends of those who had failed to return from deportation kept their hopes alive for years. Laure Moulin heard of the arrests in Caluire within a few days but it was not until the war was over that she could discover something of what had happened next.

Moulin was arrested on 21 June but two days passed before he was called for interrogation. That morning Dugoujon saw him, apparently in good health, in the exercise yard of the prison. At 2:00 P.M. Moulin was called out of his cell. Through the spyhole in his cell door the doctor saw Moulin return later that night, limping and with a bandaged head. On the following day Moulin was taken for a second interrogation and this time had to be half-lifted, half-dragged back. From this point on the accounts of Moulin's fate become, for whatever reason, contradictory and fantastic. Christian Pineau, cofounder of *Libération-Nord,* who was being held in Montluc under a false identity, and had become the prison barber, recounted a singular tale in his memoirs. He said that he had already recognized "Max" in the prison exercise yard and that some time later he was summoned from his cell at night by a German soldier and asked to attend to a man who was lying alone in the middle of the yard. This moribund form, unconscious, with a head wound, struggling to breathe, was "Max," and Pineau was instructed to shave him. Pineau was left all night beside the pitiful figure, who at one point opened his eyes and asked for water, and then muttered some words in English.*

The SS officer in charge of Moulin's interrogation, Klaus Barbie, was a professional policeman raised by an alcoholic father who beat him savagely and a devout Catholic mother whom he adored. Barbie's violent father eventually died from the consequences of wounds received in the Great War. During the boy's childhood his hometown of Trier was occupied by French colonial troops. In 1933, the year of his father's death, he abandoned the Catholic youth movement in which he had been working for the poor and joined the Hitler Youth. He later said that he had been attracted by the Nazi Party's promise to avenge the Treaty of Versailles. The writer Neal Ascherson considers that Barbie may have been working as an informer against the Catholic Church before he joined the Hitler

---

* Jean Moulin did not speak English.

Youth because in 1935, at the age of twenty-three, Barbie was promoted to an influential position in the SD, the internal security service of the SS, the Nazi Party's security force. In the SD Barbie was trained as a security police officer and underwent military training. When war broke out he was posted to Holland, where he hunted Jews, and then to Dijon, just north of the Vichy demarcation line. When German forces occupied the Vichy Zone, Barbie, who had reached the rank of lieutenant, became commander of the SIPO–SD's Department IV in the city of Lyon, effectively the Gestapo, which was responsible for the fight against the Resistance.

In Lyon, Barbie's methods of obtaining information were later said to have been characterized by an extreme level of violence, even by Gestapo standards. He used the routine methods of half-drowning in a bathtub, burning the soles of the feet, electrodes to the testicles and the insertion of needles beneath the fingernails. But he also beat his victims personally with a club or a whip and would sometimes set his black Alsatian dog on them. He was a specialist in the presentation of violence, attacking at once with great speed and energy, taunting his victims in fluent French and taking a considerable pleasure in the infliction of pain, in the power he exercised and in observing the effects of torture on each individual man or woman. Nonetheless some of those he questioned remained silent.

On 4 July Moulin was driven by Barbie to Paris, where Gestapo officers at 84 avenue Foch decided that he was too ill to question. He was then taken to the private villa of the senior Gestapo officer in France, Major Boemelburg, at Neuilly outside the city, where, according to one account, Barbie was severely criticized for Moulin's condition. There, early in July, both André Lassagne and General Delestraint were asked to identify him. Lassagne said that his head was heavily bandaged and only his eyes appeared to be alive. Asked if he knew the heavily bandaged man Delestraint replied, "How do you expect me to recognize a man in such a state?" A resistance courier called Suzette Olivier who knew "Max," and whose fingernails had been pulled out by her torturers, later said that she may have been confronted with him at the avenue Foch in the second half of July. His face was unrecognizable but she recognized his clothes. This time he was standing, silent, with a fixed stare, his head bandaged, and looked as though he had been drugged and was incapable of reacting. He kept his hands in his pockets and he never moved from his position, propped against a door.

The post office at St. Andiol was ordered to intercept all letters addressed to Moulin in his real name on 16 July, as the postmistress promptly warned his sister. Then on 19 October, in one of the more bizarre details of Moulin's legend, the Gestapo sent an envoy to Montpellier to inform Moulin's family of the former prefect's death. As one commentator has observed, this solicitude extended by the Gestapo to the family of a "terrorist" was "unique in the history of the war." Fortunately the front door was opened by Laure and not by her elderly mother. She immediately traveled to Paris, where Pierre Meunier advised her that since Moulin had been identified she could approach the Gestapo. Laure managed to obtain an interview in the avenue Foch with an officer called Heinrich Meiners, who told her that her brother had died of a heart attack while being transferred to a clinic, that his remains had been incinerated and that his ashes would be made available later. Meiners added, "Your brother believed he was doing his duty, but he was working against us. You have my condolences." Laure then met Meunier and Chambeiron in a café to give them the news, and returned to Montpellier. On 2 May 1944 a second Gestapo officer called at her apartment there and delivered the death certificate, which stated that Moulin had died in Metz on the German frontier, on 8 July 1943 at 2:00 A.M. Once again she returned to the avenue Foch but failed to get any further information. On 25 May a third Gestapo officer called at Montpellier to say that it would not be possible to return the urn or her brother's personal belongings before the end of hostilities. Blanche Moulin died in October 1947 still hoping to see her son again at a time when Laure, too, had not quite given up hope.

Almost as soon as they heard that seven men, including "Max," had been arrested at Caluire, and that René Hardy had escaped, a number of resisters decided that the meeting had been betrayed and that Hardy was the traitor. There were several reasons for suspecting Hardy. He had not been invited to the meeting. He had been the only man arrested who had not been put into handcuffs. When he was taken out of the house to the Gestapo car he apparently overcame his guard without difficulty. He then ran a considerable distance across the Place Castellane under fire from several Germans who had come out of the house, but still managed to get away and hide in a nearby ditch. There were reports that the German fire had been scattered and the subsequent search perfunctory.

In Hardy's defense was the fact that he had immediately taken refuge in a house belonging to resisters, a decision which suggested that he was not frightened of retaliation. Above all there was his wound, in the left arm. By the time he reached his refuge this had been bleeding so heavily that a doctor had been called. Then, rather than "escaping" and contacting the Gestapo later—as might have been expected if his flight had been a sham intended to conceal the fact that he was an informer—Hardy was left to his own devices and quickly arrested by the French police, who were investigating the shooting in the Place Castellane. They handed him over to the Gestapo a few days later.

But for Lucie Aubrac, Raymond Aubrac's wife, and Eugène Petit, known as "Claudius," there was no room for doubt. Claudius-Petit was *Franc-Tireur*'s representative on the CNR and a member of the MUR. Like Lucie Aubrac he was a communist agent. Arguing that Hardy was a traitor they "sought permission" from the MUR to dispose of him. According to Lucie Aubrac a source in the Vichy police informed her that Hardy had told them everything about the meeting at Caluire, before being handed over to the Gestapo. In addition, it seemed clear to Lucie Aubrac and her friends that Hardy had also been responsible for the arrest of General Delestraint in Paris on 9 June. Lucie Aubrac therefore made a pot of jam and laced it with cyanide and sent it to Hardy at the Antiquaille hospital where he was being treated under German guard. When he failed to eat the jam she regarded his suspicious caution as final confirmation of his guilt.

On 3 August Hardy, whose arm was still in a plaster cast, escaped again, this time from his room at the German military hospital in the Croix-Rousse, and left Lyon. On 25 August he was questioned on behalf of the Resistance by Charles Porte, a police inspector who had been stationed in Chartres in 1940, and who had worked for the Resistance ever since. He had sometimes acted as Moulin's bodyguard. Porte found the story of Hardy's escape from the hospital incredible, but did not accuse him of treason. With the help of his mistress, Lydie Bastien, an attractive young woman whose identity was known to the Gestapo, Hardy went into hiding and contacted his comrades in *Combat*, who continued to trust him and who sent him on several missions to Paris.

Lydie Bastien's parents were arrested by the Gestapo in Lyon on 2 September and held in Montluc prison for two months. Hardy and Lydie Bastien reached Algiers on 30 May 1944, where Hardy surrendered to

French military intelligence on the advice of Henri Frenay, whose independent spirit had by then provoked General de Gaulle to ban him from returning to France. After a lengthy interrogation Hardy was released and joined Frenay's staff on the Gaullist commission for prisoners of war and deportees.

The arrest within a period of two weeks of both the political and military heads of the Resistance sent a shock throughout the movement. At the time of his arrest Moulin had been president of the CNR, the National Resistance Council, president of the MUR—the body which united the three southern movements whose leaders had shunned the CNR—and delegate of General de Gaulle. Delestraint's arrest had been followed within half an hour by that of his deputy, Major Gastaldo. The subsequent arrest of Aubry, Aubrac, Hardy, Larat, Lacaze, Lassagne and Schwartz-feld—as well as the absence of Frenay—meant that numerous key positions on the military staff of the Secret Army became vacant. It was not just the commander of the army who had to be replaced, but also the head of COMAC (the national committee for military action) and the head of NAP–FER (the secret organization poised to sabotage the national railway system).

The movement which was by far the best placed to take advantage of this power vacuum was the *Front National,* set up by the Communist Party in 1942. Until Moulin had completed his work in uniting the French Resistance and endowing it with a national structure, there was nothing to infiltrate—apart from the fragmented individual movements and networks. But infiltration of Moulin's legacy was far more effective. Control of the CNR's executive committee or the MUR's directing committee, or the general staff of the Secret Army, meant control of the entire national movement, whose total numbers were now estimated at 100,000. It was the essential first step toward the PCF's ultimate goal, the liberation of the national territory and the institution of a French soviet and "a people's democracy." Fighting as hard as any against the Nazis, the communists were no longer fighting for a democratic France. It was this difference in an ultimate goal that placed the communist resistance apart from every other group, and raises the question today of whether the *Front National* and its armed wing the FTP–MOI should finally have been numbered among the Resistance at all.

The communist offensive had started even before Moulin's arrest with the strong minority group established on the CNR. This was enough to secure the communists a majority of three out of five on the CNR's *Bureau politique*, when that was set up in September 1943. By July the communist Pierre Hervé had become secretary-general of the MUR, and another powerful communist minority group had been infiltrated onto the COMAC. Then, following the arrest of General Pierre Dejussieu, Alfred Malleret—a communist sympathizer—was nominated head of the staff of the FFI, the resistance component of the national liberating army, and he immediately broke its rules of rotation by nominating a fellow communist, Colonel Rol-Tanguy, to succeed a third communist as head of the Paris FFI. In the northern zone in the second part of 1943 the noncommunist resistance movement suffered a devastating succession of arrests and three northern resistance chiefs were put out of action, leaving still greater room for the highly secure FTP–MOI to expand. Marcel Degliame, the communist "submarine" who had been deployed among the leaders of *Combat*, succeeded in Frenay's absence in getting himself nominated national director of another body of armed resisters, the "*corps francs* (irregulars) of the Liberation," who were to become the shock troops of the purge and who were, dynastically, all that remained after Caluire of the Secret Army.

At the end of this process of infiltration the communists had succeeded in taking over the National Resistance Council, the COMAC, the FFI, the remains of the Secret Army, NAP–FER—the network originally developed by René Hardy—the *Service Maquis*, which organized the resistance of the many thousands of fugitives from the STO forced labor program, and the *groupes francs*, the original resistance commandos. The comrades were, of course, incapable of taking over the *Délégation-Générale*, the directorate which represented de Gaulle in France and which was struggling to organize and control the entire resistance movement. But this they had no need to control, they merely had to watch it struggling. The first head of the delegation was Jean Moulin. After Caluire he was succeeded by another prefect, Emile Bollaert, who was arrested by the Vichy police and handed over to the Gestapo six months after being appointed. Bollaert was succeeded by Jacques Bingen, who committed suicide after being betrayed three months later. This succession of murderous setbacks ensured that the work of the delegation was severely hampered from June 1943 to

May 1944, less than one month before the D-Day landings and the moment of national insurrection. And the chief beneficiaries were the French communists.

The same fate—arrest and suicide—awaited Pierre Brossolette, Emile Bollaert's political director, taken with him, and General Delestraint's successor, Colonel Marchal, who also committed suicide shortly after his arrival in France and his prompt arrest by the Gestapo. Looking back on these events in 1947, de Gaulle, in a sardonic mood, said to Claude Guy: "I note that after the arrest of Jean Moulin, who was my representative, there were no more arrests on the National Resistance Council." The least that can be said is that it was extremely dangerous *not* to be pro-communist or a party member if one was active in the leadership of the French Resistance after May 1943, when the communists first moved into position on the CNR.

V

RESURRECTION

FOURTEEN

The Machinery of Insurrection

For France the occupation came to an end, in strangely symmetrical fashion, in a spasm of collective hysteria. Just as the arrival of the Germans had been preceded by the mass panic known as *l'exode*, so their departure was followed by a national shiver of horror, this time expressed not in panic but in murderous violence. This episode, known as *l'épuration* (the purging, or purification), was at one time thought to have led to the death of 100,000 people, although the maximum figure more usually given today is 30,000. The victims of this outbreak of mass murder included men and women who had committed some of the worst crimes of the collaboration—as well as thousands of others who were completely innocent of any crimes—and it culminated in the persecution and murder of many people who had distinguished themselves in the Resistance.

Perhaps the most famous image of *l'épuration* is that of the young women who had associated with—sometimes married—German soldiers having their heads shaved in front of a laughing crowd of women and children. In August 1944 Robert Capa took a famous picture of a mob surrounding a young woman whose head has been shaved. She is being marched to prison, carrying the baby whose German father has departed. She and her own father, who walks ahead of her looking at the ground, carrying the bundle of clothes she will need for the baby in prison, are the only people in the photograph who are not smiling. The surrounding crowd is in a joyful mood; the carnival of collaborators was one of the high points of the liberation; even the police who served Vichy loyally are smiling; particularly happy are the other women in the picture, who still wear their hair. Capa took this photograph in the streets of Chartres; he came on the scene by chance. In the background one can see the tricolor flying over the gateway of the prefecture for the first time since the day when Jean Moulin, standing in that gateway, surrendered the city. Here are the two popular spasms united in one street; the people of Chartres who fled from the city in 1940, abandoning their old and their sick, returned to celebrate and sacrifice a scapegoat.

Today the episode is regarded with revulsion; it is frequently explained by the momentary interval between two systems of government, an inevitable period of anarchy during which many of the worst crimes were committed by the "RMS" (resisters of the month of September)—that is, young men who had not been in the Resistance but who wished to make it appear as though they had. For such people the best way to avoid becoming a victim of the purge was to make it look as though you were among those most anxious to operate it. There is no doubt that September resisters existed and that they committed many atrocities, but the truth about *l'épuration* is that it was not just a moment of anarchy. It was also an episode foreseen and planned for months by the *Front National* as an essential step in the acquisition of power. This was Trotsky's machinery of insurrection in motion at last; where the *Camelots du Roy* had failed in 1934 the French communists in 1944 succeeded triumphantly.

The liberation of France began with the allied landings in Normandy on D-Day, 6 June 1944. The battle of Normandy lasted until 24 August, when allied forces, having destroyed the German 7th Army, advanced north along the Channel coast and east toward Paris. The French units re-formed from the French Pétainist armies stationed abroad in 1940—in French Equatorial Africa, the Levant, Morocco and Algeria—were able to take part in the battle. Paris was liberated on 25 August by the first French unit to see action, the 2nd Armored Division, supported by the American 4th Infantry Division. In the south of France, in Provence, an allied expeditionary force landed on 15 August between Toulon and Cannes, and on 18 August began to march north, up the Rhône valley, toward Lyon. Marseille was liberated on 29 August. On 3 September Lyon was liberated by the American 36th Division and the French 1st Armored Division. In the north of France the British 2nd Army liberated Lille and Brussels on 3 September and Antwerp on the following day. The allied armies which had landed in Normandy and Provence linked up at Autun, near Dijon, on 12 September. The last enemy soldiers were driven out of French territory near Colmar in southern Alsace by the French 1st Army Corps on 19 February 1945, although pockets of German occupation, garrisons on the Channel coast, held out until the unconditional surrender in May.

Throughout the battles of the liberation the allied armies were supported by units of the French Resistance. The moment so anxiously awaited by Henri Frenay and the founders of the Secret Army had arrived. De Gaulle had spoken of the need for "a national insurrection" as early as April 1942. This would ultimately be controlled and directed by the French Provisional Government in Algiers, over which he presided. The detailed plans were drawn up by the Gaullist intelligence service. Separate plans provided for the sabotage of the railways in Normandy, the national communications and electrical systems and for synchronized attacks on road bridges and crossroads. In April 1944 a regular French officer, General Koenig, became the overall commander of the Resistance, which would henceforth be known as the FFI, the French Forces of the Interior. On D-Day, 6 June, General Eisenhower, the Supreme Allied Commander, also gave the order for a national insurrection to break out in order to cause chaos and confusion throughout France. General Eisenhower later said that the Resistance had been "worth fifteen divisions," an estimate that some French historians regard as generous. Nonetheless, the Resistance took part in sabotage, harassment and attacks on lightly armed German units all over France, trapping isolated German columns and forcing them to surrender. Some of the hardest fighting took place in the Limousin, where the Resistance was ordered to impede an SS Panzer (armored) division that was being moved north to support the German 7th Army in Normandy. This led to very heavy losses in many areas so that on 12 June General Koenig ordered an interruption in guerrilla warfare. At the same time the communist-influenced COMAC ordered the FFI guerrillas to redouble their efforts. As a result the most widely used resistance tactic was the insurrection unleashed as German troops withdrew, the Vichy government collapsed and the victims of the occupation turned on the French collaborators.

The most celebrated call for insurrection was that of General de
Gaulle himself, but by "insurrection" he meant an armed uprising in support of the allied forces by trained members of the Resistance operating
under the ultimate direction of his subordinate, General Koenig. It was to
be an insurrection that would express France's joy and enable the people
to participate in their own liberation, but it would have strictly limited
aims. It was intended to confuse and dishearten the German forces; punish
the Vichy regime, eliminate its functionaries within a few hours and replace them with a new administration; thus facing the allied forces with a
fait accompli and preventing the imposition of an allied military government.

On 15 October 1943, an instruction had been issued by "the central
committee of the MUR," but clearly written by Pierre Hervé and his
communist agents, which set out the broad lines of this insurrection, as
reinterpreted. In conformity with the legitimate aspirations of the Resistance for reprisals it would begin with "the revolutionary repression
of treason." The Resistance would thereby impose "immediate revolutionary measures in the social and economic fields" on the provisional
government. During the insurrectional period the local "committees of
liberation" would exercise their delegated authority and direct all necessary measures. The slogan of the instruction was "There can be no
Liberation without insurrection." A list of traitors would be drawn up
beforehand which would include names, private addresses, business addresses and country addresses. All newspapers had been "guilty of treason" so the printing presses would be occupied. The popular action of the
masses would stand ready to apply the pressure of a general strike, and the
MUR instruction ended with a few words on the subject of "summary executions." It came down in favor of these, but set out a procedure which
should be followed "in order to avoid too much blood being shed." Once
it was diffused, this instruction inspired calls for bloody reprisals along
the suggested lines in the information bulletins of the local committees of
liberation, which were dominated by communists in many parts of the
country. And the results were memorable. It was the moment when the
communist mask slipped; when the intentions of the PCF toward a liberated France became apparent, and the means the communists were prepared to use were displayed for all to see.

To place *l'épuration* in context one has to recall the extreme violence that preceded it in the last days of the occupation. The most notorious example was the massacre at Oradour-sur-Glane. In a village in the Limousin, where nothing had ever happened, a unit of the SS "Das Reich" division, moving toward Normandy and harassed by the Resistance, drove into the main street, locked all the women and children into the church, rounded up all the men and shot them. Then the SS soldiers set fire to the church: 642 people died. Other villages were treated in the same way by other German units; the prisons were emptied and their occupants shot. A succession of atrocities were carried out by the *Milice*, the paramilitary body of French militiamen raised to fight the Resistance. The *Milice* took no prisoners; wounded resisters were shot even in hospitals, in some cases after being submitted to atrocious tortures. As the *Wehrmacht* started to withdraw, the actions of their supporters in the *Milice* became more and more extreme; they included bank robbery, rape and pillage and on occasion led to *miliciens* being shot by their own officers. Then, as the balance of power swung in favor of the Resistance, the same process continued, only the uniforms of the criminals changed. The disorder reached its height in departments which "liberated themselves," that is in areas where the occupying forces simply withdrew, leaving no recognized authority behind them.

In the Limousin the FFI (*Forces françaises de l'intérieure*—the title given to resisters and *maquisards* who obeyed the order to enroll in the liberating forces) were led by Georges Guingouin, the leader of the local communist FTP, one of the most decorated and hated figures in the Resistance, later known as "the Tito of the Limousin." Under his direction the region was divided into fiefs in which gangsters masquerading as patriots imposed a reign of terror under which practically everyone was vulnerable. Taking their inspiration from the Spanish Civil War—many of them were veterans of the International Brigades, and of Spanish, Italian, Polish or Hungarian origin—his men awarded each other imaginary ranks such as "colonel" or "major," described their marauding as "campaigns" and referred to the Dordogne "front" or the Médoc "front." They moved around the country in armed bands, invariably in cars and trucks, sometimes identifying themselves on their arrival with cries of "We are the masters now! We are the GPU [KGB]!" In one of their earlier and more original actions they arrested three officers of the Secret Army who were preparing a nighttime landing ground for an RAF arms drop by parachute. They then shot their fellow, but noncommunist, members of the Resistance, describing them as *cagoulards*.*

The class war was declared in the Limousin and the appropriate victims selected; Baron Henri Reille-Soult, a British intelligence agent, was shot by the *maquis* in Lussac-les-Châteaux. The parish priest of Lussac was dragged from his presbytery, forced to confess aloud to another priest in the hearing of *maquisards* and then shot. In the Dordogne, four parish priests and a nun who was a nurse at the hospital in Thiviers were tortured and shot. Representatives of the bourgeoisie such as doctors, lawyers, wine-growers and mayors were executed without trial or even charges; if they were absent their wives or mothers were shot in their place. In one case a young woman who had belonged to the *Milice* but had resigned from it one year earlier—that is, almost as soon as it was formed—was taken from her wedding ceremony and shot by the *maquis,* in her wedding dress; the killers then sat down to eat the wedding breakfast. Women who had never been suspected of any compromising behavior were publicly humiliated, stripped and tortured over a period of time before they died. And the mistreatment sometimes continued after they had died; the exact details of what they had suffered were published in the local press after the "purification" was over.

The few brave police officers or gendarmes who tried to intervene, usually on behalf of women or children, risked a slow death on the steps of the police station. And when these crimes, which were widely witnessed, led to complaints and subsequent prosecution, not a single leader of the FTP–MOI of the Limousin was punished. On the contrary they were transferred into the regular army and frequently decorated for their heroism in the face of the enemy—sometimes justifiably. "Colonel" Guingouin, communist and torturer, received the *Rosette de la Résistance,* the *Croix de guerre* with bar, the Legion of Honor and was finally enrolled in the élite company of the *Compagnons de la Libération,* nominated by the PCF

---

* Here, as elsewhere in France, prefects who (like Jean Moulin) had interned communists in 1940 were hunted down and shot. Inspector Porte, Moulin's bodyguard, who had arrested communists in Chartres in 1940, was denounced by his Vichy police colleagues after he joined the Resistance and was deported to Buchenwald in 1944. On his return he was denounced by the communists who controlled the "Committee of Liberation" in the Eure-et-Loir, and had to go into hiding again. He was lucky to escape with his life and had to maintain a false identity until 1951.

to take one of the places allotted by de Gaulle to the communist resistance. But he had won those medals in action against German Panzers. He was certainly not a last-minute member of the Resistance. The colonel was subsequently elected mayor of Limoges and then became a village schoolteacher. Finally arrested and charged with a single murder, he was acquitted in 1954—his counsel was Roland Dumas, François Mitterrand's lawyer and a future minister of justice, foreign minister and president of the Constitutional Council—after which he returned to his schoolhouse where he no doubt imposed a strict interpretation of secular education and instilled the principles of the republic. In due course, at his funeral, he will be given a resistance guard of honor. While he was at the height of his power in Limoges, a report from the local prefect said, "Here the war has given way to a civil war." The fact that the revolution did not take place was because men like Guingouin were not able to impose their will in areas less remote than the Limousin.

In Paris after the liberation, when the city was under the control of the French 2nd Armored Division and the American 4th Infantry Division, an insurrection was nonetheless proposed by the communist "Colonel" Rol-Tanguy—who, apparently expecting an allied bombardment, had established his headquarters thirty feet underground, in the city's sewers. As de Gaulle was forming his first provisional government, and before he was able to impose the rule of law, resistance torture chambers (by no means all of them run by communists) were being set up in many parts of the city and collaborators, and others, were being rounded up for questioning. Colonel Rol-Tanguy's FTP took over the Dental Institute, newly vacated by the Germans, where they started by bursting the eardrums and gouging out the eyes of a cabinetmaker and suspected collaborator. A twenty-year-old Nazi supporter was taken to the second floor of the institute to be tortured; he jumped from the window but only managed to break both his legs. He was taken back into the Dental Institute and thrown onto a straw mattress where he was left for the night without treatment. Next morning the FTP decided to shoot him and stood him up against a wall, but he was unable to remain standing for long enough to be shot, so they put him back on the stretcher and shot him there. A woman whose husband had been thrown under a tank by members of the FTP insulted his killers. She was taken to the institute and questioned, but she continued to insult them and mock them even as they beat her with truncheons. She turned out to be the wife of a dental surgeon, and a very embarrassing witness, so they decided to shoot her. An eyewitness later said that as they took aim she stuck out her tongue at the firing squad. Some days afterward the FTP announced that she and her husband had been the victims of mistaken identity.

Colonel Rol-Tanguy did his best, but the presence of two divisions of regular allied soldiers was too much for him; the FTP of Paris, having failed to mount an insurrection, had to content themselves with a settling of personal accounts. Among those they selected for punishment was the socialist mayor of the suburb of Puteaux, who had introduced a government bill in parliament before the war suspending communist deputies after the Nazi-Soviet Pact; he was shot in the street. And when they failed to find another of their political opponents, the mayor of Bobigny, they shot his son instead. Another enemy dispatched was a young Paris worker named Mathieu Buchholz, who was killed on 11 September. He was a member of the Trotskyist group *La Lutte de Classes*.

In January 1944 the *Comité français de libération nationale* (CFLN), the Gaullist government in exile, sitting in Algiers, had announced that liberated territory would in the first place be administered by seventeen regional *commissaires de la République* who would enjoy all the powers of a regional prefect, and many more. One of the primary aims of this system was to avoid the imposition of the detested AMGOT (Allied Military Government in Occupied Territory), which would have given the United States, and—even worse—the British, the final word in France's internal affairs. The avoidance of an AMGOT, such as was established in Greece, Italy or Yugoslavia, was one of de Gaulle's primary objectives from 1941, and had become one of Jean Moulin's preoccupations as well.

The task allotted to these *commissaires* was enormous and in many cases beyond them. They were supposed to ensure a swift ending to the period of insurrection, followed by the removal of the Vichy administration and the imposition of a new one, and the lawful punishment of those who merited it. In some cases the *commissaires* were not given the military or police forces necessary to impose their authority. An example was Toulouse, where the *commissaire* was Pierre Bertaux. A supporter of the prewar Popular Front, Bertaux was by trade a professor of German literature at the University of Toulouse and he had formed his own resistance group in 1941. He had to take over his responsibilities as commissioner on short notice, in August 1944, after the original nominee was beaten to death by a passing German army patrol. Bertaux was immediately confronted with the problem of the communist resistance, whose military arm in this region was under the command of "Colonel" Serge Ravanel, one of the "submarines" of *Libération*.

In order to emphasize who held the real power in Toulouse, Ravanel responded to the news that a large German force was returning to the city by telling the commissioner of the Republic that he would henceforth be responsible for his own safety. Ravanel then left him in his office at the prefecture to face the Germans by himself. When this threat did not succeed in frightening the commissioner into retreat, Ravanel's FTP locked him out of the local radio station and then machine-gunned him in his car. When Professor Bertaux survived this they came to see him in his office and asked him what his attitude was to "the insurrection." He told them that as far as he was aware the insurrection had taken place the previous Sunday, against the German forces, and was now over. They looked at him as if he were simple, and with reason, for much of his region bordered the Limousin. In the weeks that followed, the bloodshed in Toulouse under Ravanel's direction led to the city, traditionally known as "Toulouse la rose," being renamed "Toulouse la rouge," or Red Toulouse.

In the ranks of the commissioners of the republic were several men who had worked closely with Jean Moulin. Apart from Ravanel in Toulouse, Yves Farge had been appointed to restore the city of Lyon to order, and Bordeaux was administered by Gaston Cusin, Moulin's prewar ally in the customs service. And in Marseille there was Raymond Aubrac. Aubrac did not face any of the difficulties which overwhelmed Bertaux in Toulouse. In the first place, he had no ideological quarrel with the FTP of the region; in the second place, he had adequate forces at his disposal. Just after disembarking in St. Tropez on 15 August with the French troops arriving from Corsica, Aubrac signed his first official orders. Order No. 2 announced the creation of a private security force, the FRS (*Forces républicaines de sécurité*), whose principal task was to hunt down and arrest any individuals who had collaborated with the enemy. This force was recruited from the FFI, the new name for the armed Resistance, a band which bore little relation to the *groupes francs* of the dark years of occupation. By July 1944 the Resistance in the region of Marseille had grown considerably to reach a total of 8,000. By September the total was 25,000. Most of these men were recruited from the pool of fugitives who had fled Vichy's forced labor program but had previously avoided joining the resistance. In other words the FRS was recruited from a band of rootless opportunists, violent and lawless men who had been careful to have nothing to do with the fugitive élite of the years of occupation; its task was to fight, in Aubrac's phrase, against "the enemy of the interior." So far as the commissioner of the republic in Marseille was concerned, the presence of a U.S.-French army of 500,000 men moving steadily up the Rhône valley, driving the occupying forces before it, was merely a preliminary step in the direction of liberation; the main task was to defeat the "enemy of the interior."

The powers enjoyed by a commissioner of the Republic, backed by his own private army, exceeded anything seen in peacetime, even in the hands of a president of the Republic. In practice the only limitation was territorial. Commissioner Aubrac enjoyed the right to: suspend any laws or regulations in force; take any measures judged necessary to maintain law and order, the efficient operation of public services or private enterprises or the security of the French or allied forces; suspend any elected representatives or public officials or directors of public, semi-public or subsidized undertakings and nominate their replacements; cancel any outstanding judicial sanctions; direct all criminal police investigations; freeze any bank account; enlist the services or requisition the property of anyone under the rules of martial law; delegate any of his powers to his nominated representatives; and give his decisions the force of law merely by pasting them up in a public place. But there was one important exclusion from his powers: nothing had been said about the right to set up courts or carry out punishments. Here he was restricted to powers of arrest and imprisonment pending trial. So Commissioner Aubrac took judicial powers anyway. With so many other powers at his disposal, it was unlikely that anyone would object.

Outside the main cities the commissioners were to be assisted by departmental "liberation committees" which had in effect even more frightening powers. Manned by the dominant group of local resisters, in a great number of cases communists, their duty was to prepare the national insurrection and carry it out, "destroying the enemy and the enemy's agents." After the liberation they were instructed to undertake an immediate purification by liquidating traitors and arresting suspects. The term "liquidating" is just as ambiguous in French as it is in English. In its financial sense it merely means "dissolving" or "canceling"; in its sinister, metaphorical sense it means killing without a trace. The second sense was more usually followed during the "purification" of France.

Aubrac had been appointed to his post through the influence of Emmanuel d'Astier de la Vigerie, his former boss at *Libération,* who had since become the first "provisional," that is unaccountable, minister of the interior; in other words the minister responsible for directing the entire police and administrative structure of the *épuration.* D'Astier had intrigued his way into office and de Gaulle did not put up with him for long; he replaced him on 9 September 1944 with a socialist, but by then the damage had been done.

In Marseille the public shaving of women started almost as soon as the first *maquisards* arrived. First the mobs attacked prostitutes, then they set on girls who had had German boyfriends, and then they shaved any attractive young women who fell into their clutches. As the excitement of the crowds grew the women were accused of more serious crimes such as denouncing resisters; then they were taken to the improvised prisons of Aubrac's FRS and treated worse than they had been in public. There was a report of one priest interrupting the proceedings and taking two of the girls into the presbytery, where they were safe, and giving them clothes. French regular soldiers were said to have looked on ashamed; in at least one case a French officer walked up to a *chef de maquis* directing an ad hoc firing squad and shot him dead. But such interventions were rare. When the chaplain-general of Marseille prisons, Father de Perceval, asked General de Monsabert, commander of the 2nd French Army Corps, which had liberated the city, to intervene on behalf of the thousands of men locked up without charges or trial by the FRS, the general replied that he was only interested in making war and restoring the lost honor of the French army. Then he drove on up the Rhône valley, leaving the people of Marseille to the mercy of the commissioner.

After a brisk initial engagement between the socialists of Marseille and the communists—the socialists, led by Gaston Deferre, took the town hall and *Le Provençal* (the newspaper), but advanced no further—the FRS got to work. A total of 3,000 arrests were recorded in the area of Marseille, Aix-en-Provence and Arles, the region so familiar to Jean Moulin. On 4 September, as the purification process got into its stride, Commissioner Aubrac published a new order. With a view to "countering the activities of antirepublican elements more swiftly," it would no longer be necessary to inform accused people of the charges against them or take account of their explanations. Judgment could be pronounced and executed without any preliminaries. On 6 September a liberation Court of Justice was set up; no appeals could be made against its judgment and any demands for pardon could in future only be addressed to the regional commissioner. The president of the new court was appointed by Aubrac and his name was Monsieur Couteaux ("blades").

Among the first targets of the "purification" were the police, partly because their ranks contained a number of notorious collaborators who had done great harm to the Resistance, but also because they were accustomed to operating within the legal system and therefore got in the way. In Marseille the FRS adopted a practice of murdering a number of senior police officers to discourage the rest. Inspector Leuiller was shot down in a back street, without any form of investigation taking place. Inspector Poggioli was arrested, questioned and released; all the evidence showed that he had never been a collaborator. Four days later he was taken out of his house in the middle of the night by four armed men and shot. Commissaire Manefret was arrested, questioned, released and then shot in the back, by the men who had just released him, while he was walking away toward his wife. With the regular police intimidated into staying at home they could be replaced by a "people's police," as the FRS called themselves. Aubrac's original appointments to the leadership of this body were drawn from the noncommunist resistance, but when these chiefs started to intervene and limit their own men's activities they were replaced, in Marseille and in Aix, by their communist adjutants. The communists were also in the majority on the departmental liberation committee.

In Aix-en-Provence suspected collaborators were interrogated in the Hôtel de la Mule Noire, where they were tortured if they failed to give the required answers. In November two communist members of the FRS hanged three suspects from a streetlamp in the beautiful Cours Mirabeau, which runs through the old center of Aix, in front of an excited crowd. In Digne, where suspects had got as far as being tried in court, an anonymous "Immediate Action Committee" issued death threats against their lawyers, whereupon all the defense lawyers withdrew from the case. Then the committee broke into the prison and shot two men who, having been convicted of collaboration and sentenced to death, had lodged an appeal.

In Avignon "the people's court" (an FRS lynch mob) demanded that thirty convicted ex-members of the *Milice* be handed over so that they could be "burned alive." The prison authorities refused to do this so the FRS arrested a doctor who had been accused of collaboration and tortured him to death in the street. An eye was removed with a garden fork but they actually killed him by repeatedly jumping on his stomach. It was later confirmed that Dr. Frossard was innocent of collaboration and had in fact assisted the Resistance. In Cavaillon, the market town for St. Andiol, a young woman was arrested and accused of collaboration. She was released after no evidence was found, but on her way home she was rearrested and shot by a firing squad which included a nine-year-old boy. Also in Cavaillon, the FRS shot a printer, confiscated his printing press and subsequently used it for printing Communist Party publications. In the nearby town of Tarascon, the FRS arrested a bookseller who had refused to sell communist newspapers before the war. He was also accused of complaining too loudly about the fact that his house and shop had recently been destroyed by a USAF bombing raid. He was released by the tribunal, so some weeks later an armed band abducted him during the night, together with his wife. They shot him and—after she had begged for her life on the grounds that she had a nine-year-old son—they shot his wife as well.

Many of these crimes took place some distance from Marseille, but Commissioner Aubrac was well aware of the nature of the reign of terror he had instituted. One of the principal torturers worked in his office at the prefecture in Marseille. This man was known as "Major Coco"; formerly a waiter, he worked with a colleague known as "Major Rag" (*chiffon*), a slaughterer in the abattoir.* A vivid description of what it was like to be imprisoned in the Marseille prefecture during Aubrac's tenure was given by Jean-Elie Nevière, who, having been arrested by the Gestapo on 19 February 1944, found himself rearrested by the youth branch of the FRS in October because of malice or mistaken identity. It was fifty-four days before his father managed to arrange for his release.

In those days, wrote Nevière, with some moderation, "the civil servants of the prefecture had been replaced, goodness knows how, by a crowd of completely useless characters who had crawled out from all over the place and who were incompetent and greedy, and not infrequently dishonest." That was the office staff; the staff below stairs were worse. There, in the building's cellars, the two "majors" had installed a subordi-

---

* "Coco" was a popular abbreviation for communist. During the purification the *noms de guerre* which had originally been devised by members of the Resistance or Gaullists to protect their families from Nazi or Vichy reprisals became a means of protecting those who were committing Nazi-style atrocities. The names chosen reflected a gallows humor. The judge of one of the people's courts in Limoges called himself "Gandhi," after the apostle of nonviolence.

nate officer who presided over an improvised torture chamber. This man was a one-armed homosexual sadist called Fayet but nicknamed *le Manchot* (one-arm). "The prison in the cellars of the prefecture," wrote Nevière, "closely resembled the cellars of the Hotel California which the Gestapo of Marseille had vacated only a few days earlier. The same methods of torture were used in both places." Nevière was able to watch *le Manchot* at work as he always left his office door open. He wrote that forty years later the cries of suffering still rang through his head. After watching Fayet for four days Nevière wondered whether he or someone close to him had once been tortured by the Gestapo, and decided that he must be engaged in an act of personal vengeance.

The purposes of the insurrection in Marseille were not only to spread chaos and gain political control of the region, they were also financial. The action against the printer who was executed in Cavaillon was a distant echo of what had already happened in Marseille. On 25 August, at the very beginning of the purification, the president and secretary and several other members of the board of the city's Chamber of Commerce were arrested without explanation or charge, and put in prison. They were denied access to lawyers or witnesses and held for four months. The president, Emile Régis, was not even suspected of collaboration; he had in fact taken public risks to defend his members and had also intervened on behalf of Marseille's Jews. But with its leadership in prison the business community of Marseille was more vulnerable to arbitrary sequestrations. So, on 5 October, the chairman and the managing director of the city's Docks and Warehouses Board were told that they had been fired without compensation and their business seized by order of Commissioner Aubrac. On 25 November a band of armed men took them away from their houses and beat them up. They were then held in the cellars of the prefecture while Aubrac launched a poster campaign supported by radio broadcasts appealing for witnesses against them to come forward. At this time their private bank accounts were frozen. There was a heavy response to the appeal for evidence but, unfortunately for the regional commissioner, all the witnesses gave evidence for the defense. Nonetheless the two men, Alexis and Wolff, were not released for three months. A subsequent government report declared that the commissioner (despite the wide range of his arbitrary powers) had been personally responsible for an illegal arrest and Alexis and Wolff were eventually paid a total of 1.45 million francs in compensation.

The horrors inflicted on Marseille and its region in the months immediately following the liberation did not satisfy the Liberation Committees
of the Bouches-du-Rhône, which issued a public statement on 24 November in which members recorded their dissatisfaction with the progress of
the purge. They wanted more, and Commissioner Aubrac agreed. In other
parts of France the leaders of the *épuration* tried to calm the reactions of
the mob, and succeeded in doing so. But on 17 December Aubrac published a communiqué that called for "increased vigilance." Among other
priorities the communist resistance in Marseille had scores to settle with
dissident members of the party. Several were arrested, accused of "Trot-
skyism," tortured, imprisoned in the cellars of the prefecture and then
murdered at the communists' favorite killing-ground, the Pont du Jarret.
They included the commander of the communists' own *groupes francs*.

At this stage Aubrac's region had suffered, and was still suffering, from
a wave of organized violence which had not been equaled during the occupation or within historical memory. The liberation had taken place
nearly four months earlier yet over 3,000 men and women were still in
prison, held without charge. Aubrac listed the names of some of those he
held and warned the public that unless evidence was produced quickly
they might have to be released. In the event this appeal backfired. There
was no flood of new evidence from the general public and President
Couteaux's court of justice in Marseille had to cancel two sessions in January when even the jurors failed to report for duty. That part of the local
press which was in the hands of noncommunist resisters started to attack
Aubrac, pointing out that too many people were in prison for reasons
which no one understood, and complaining that having succeeded in
catching almost no Gestapo agents the *épurateurs* were "torturing under-
lings" to make them confess to crimes they had not committed.

The terror in Marseille came to an end on 23 January 1945, when
Raymond Aubrac was dismissed and replaced by a professional prefect,
Paul Haag. De Gaulle told Haag that his job was "to reestablish republican order, and reattach a region to France which is completely out of
control." After visiting Marseille earlier de Gaulle had written: "There
is an unhealthy atmosphere of continual oppression in the city and the
communists have established an anonymous dictatorship which is very
dangerous." It had taken de Gaulle some time to come to the relief of
Marseille, but he was born in Lille. It was to take Haag nearly a year to return his butchered region to normal.

Nevière described Aubrac—not quite accurately*—as "a member of the conservative, Jewish bourgeoisie . . . who was regarded as being too close to the communists." As his subsequent career was to show, Aubrac was much closer to the PCF than that.

The *épuration* in Marseille failed in its primary object, which was to punish the guilty. The list of those who went with only nominal punishments, or completely unpunished, included two SS colonels, Müller and Schörer, the commander of the local *Milice,* Paul Durandy, and the leader of the local PPF (French fascist party, founded by the former communist Jacques Doriot), Simon Sabiani. But Aubrac had more success with his own invention, the FRS. They were in due course converted into the CRS (*Compagnie républicaine de sécurité*), which still serves today as the French riot police.

When the collaborators of Vichy argued that they had not always known what crimes were being committed in their name, they were shot anyway. In 1996, asked about his time of plenary power in Marseille, Raymond Aubrac said: "Fifty years on I still have nightmares. . . . How could I decide whether to grant or refuse a plea for pardon? Well, if I thought a pardon would lead to more disorder, I rejected it. It is scandalous, indefensible, appalling, but that's what I did. . . ." Under Aubrac, during the insurrection, the mob had the last word.

---

* After his escape from German custody in October 1943, the true identity of Raymond "Aubrac," that is, Raymond Samuel, was discovered and his parents, who were living in Lyon, were arrested and deported to Auschwitz.

FIFTEEN

Murdering History

DESPITE THE DETERMINATION and ruthlessness of men like Georges Guingouin and Raymond Aubrac, the communists did not manage to transform the insurrection into a national uprising that would establish a "people's democracy" in France. And by the time they had failed, Stalin had imposed a nonrevolutionary policy on the PCF, no longer wishing the allied armies to be diverted from their drive toward Berlin. A more conventional republic was installed by General de Gaulle, founded on a myth about France's experience of the Second World War which he himself had invented. The process started in August 1944, when de Gaulle, six months before the liberation of national territory was complete, made a historic but largely misleading speech at the Hôtel de Ville in Paris. "This is one of those moments that transcends each one of our poor lives," he said. "Paris free! Liberated by herself! Liberated by her people with the support of the armies of France, with the support of the whole of France! Of the France which fights on, the only France, the real France, the eternal France!" He then made Paris a "Companion of the Liberation," so elevating a city which had scarcely been touched by German shells or allied bombs into the capital of the fighting French. The fact that Paris had emerged unscathed from the war was one of the world conflict's happier outcomes, but it was largely due to General Weygand's decision to declare Paris an open city in June 1940, and—above all—to

General von Choltitz's refusal in August 1944 to obey Hitler's order to destroy it.

Concealing this truth was, for de Gaulle, the beginning of the process of national reconciliation. The Vichy government had held its final cabinet meeting in Paris on 17 August before leaving the city to be driven into German captivity. Marshal Pétain was taken into German custody from his residence in Vichy on 20 August. The emissary he had sent to General de Gaulle, bearing the gift of full powers as head of state, was turned away. General Dietrich von Choltitz, the military governor of Paris, surrendered the city to General Leclerc on 25 August. Following public ceremonies at the Arc de Triomphe and the cathedral of Notre Dame, de Gaulle received the leaders of the Paris resistance and the CNR and, on 31 August, the Provisional Government of the French Republic (GPRF) was transferred to Paris from Algiers, where it had been established on 3 June. De Gaulle appointed a provisional list of ministers on 5 September, drawing from all "political tendencies" as well as from the Resistance and the ranks of former deputies. The first ministerial reshuffle took place on 9 September. Two weeks later the FFI were ordered to report for duty with the regular army. This order had to be repeated on 28 October owing to fierce communist opposition. On 2 November the PCF launched its first public attack on de Gaulle, accusing him of "failing to respect the French Resistance."

On 10 November Churchill and Eden visited Paris. The USA, Great Britain and the USSR had recognized the Provisional Government of the French Republic on 23 October. Now Churchill agreed that France should be accorded its own zone of occupation in Germany and its own seat at the conference to be held shortly in London on the future of Europe. With American support the French army was once again in the front line against the *Wehrmacht*. On Churchill's insistence there would be a French judge at Nuremberg. De Gaulle's myth of *la France résistante* formed an essential part of the justification for all this. But the imposition of that myth gave the French communists carte blanche to create a myth of their own. De Gaulle had imposed a false view of France as a country of resistance. With great political skill the PCF took advantage of this falsehood to impose its own historical falsification: the communists as "the party of resistance," and ultimately as the only true resisters.

In 1947 de Gaulle mused aloud about the influence the communists had enjoyed on the CNR in the last months of the occupation and the fascination they had exercised over Georges Bidault, a democrat who had even suggested that the communists should be allowed to form a government. At ministerial meetings, de Gaulle added, the MRP (Christian Democrat) ministers drank up everything the communists suggested. "It was not that the communists were more determined," de Gaulle said, "because at that time they hid their determination; it was because, faced with the unbelievable rottenness (*vachardise incroyable*) of the others, their tactics were so much better." In France's first postwar election, held on 21 October 1945, the French Communist Party topped the poll with 26.2 percent of the vote, a result that owed much to the demonstration of naked power they had so recently put on. In areas subjected to "the Terror," nobody put much faith in the secrecy of the ballot. In Limoges, Georges Guingouin was elected mayor by "a coalition of unleashed communists and terrified bourgeois," as one of his opponents commented. In Marseille, the communist leader Jean Cristofol managed a smooth transition from the committees of liberation to the town hall and the communist vote was 32 percent, nearly one in three of the thoroughly alarmed electors of Marseille having been persuaded that "a people's democracy" was the only way. In the newly elected National Assembly the communists did what they could to maintain the terror for as long as possible. Pierre Cot was among those communist deputies and allies who voted (unsuccessfully) to remove the presidential right of pardon from de Gaulle, in an attempt to ensure that the final word remained with the politically directed courts of *l'épuration*.

Following their failure to take over the Resistance, and subsequent failure to ignite a national insurrection, the communists broke their pact with the Gaullists and effectively drove de Gaulle out of power in January 1946. The PCF remained the largest political party throughout the life of the Fourth Republic but never managed to form a government. Instead the party established an enormous power base in French industry and the regions, particularly in the north, the Paris region, the center and the southeast from Marseille to the Italian border. With a membership of over 800,000 and control of the power, mining and steel industries as well as the major national trade union, the CGT, the PCF effectively employed and housed hundreds of thousands of people. This economic and political predominance was defended by a praetorian guard of intellectuals through whom the party exercised a moral and intellectual dictatorship over the national memory. In the establishment of this dominion the saga of communist resistance—part history, part legend—played a fundamental role. The saga ignored the period of Nazi-Soviet collaboration and opened with the historical courage and self-sacrifice of the FTP–MOI during the German occupation, continued through *l'épuration,* when the truth was carefully concealed, and culminated in the myth of "the party of 75,000 martyrs." An early engagement in the campaign to establish that legend occurred immediately after the war, when the communists set out to make Henri Frenay "the most hated man in France."

In September 1944, when de Gaulle, in Paris, designated his first postliberation government, the largest resistance component in this was supplied by *Combat.* Frenay took the key post of minister of prisoners of war and deportees. The communists in the same government had only two ministers, for air and public health. Over the following nine months Frenay, whose ministry was responsible for the immense problems involved in the return to France of nearly two million POWs and deportees from the concentration camps, was singled out by the communists as "a fanatical reactionary." In destroying Frenay the communists hoped to destroy the reputation of the anti-communist resistance, which had started in 1940, and replace it with the myth of the communist resistance, which had not started for another twelve months. Simultaneously the efforts of the *Front National* were focused on control of the MLN (*Mouvement de libération nationale*), the organization founded in 1943 by the three southern resistance groups and two of the northern groups, to represent the noncommunist and non- (but not "anti-") Gaullist resistance. After the liberation the MLN, because of its independence from Gaullism, became the most credible body to represent the interests and views of a national resistance movement in the political debate which was to realize Henri Frenay's dream and "reforge" France. The communists' strategy, which was quite simply to fuse the MLN and the *Front National,* was pursued until January 1945, at which point the party's assault was finally repulsed. Frenay played a leading role in inflicting that defeat on the *Front National,* and from then on he became more than ever the cherished target of the communist press.

Antoinette Sachs returned to France from her refuge in Switzerland in September 1944 and immediately started a private inquiry into the disappearance of Jean Moulin. Like Laure, she hoped to find him alive. Among the first people she met was Dr. Dugoujon, who knew very little. From the police in Lyon she heard the story of Hardy's escape, arrest and reescape.

Both Antoinette and Laure relied for their initial information on the Aubracs. Later, they were assisted by the fact that the first German actors in the drama had been arrested, and by the steady trickle of deportees returning from the camps. André Lassagne, convinced that Hardy had betrayed Delestraint as well as Moulin, told Antoinette Sachs that the decision to hold the meeting at Caluire was made on the evening of 19 June and that he had passed the time and address to "Max" and Raymond Aubrac on 20 June. Henri Aubry of *Combat* had only been given a preliminary meeting place. Uncovering a long list of witnesses, some more relevant than others, Antoinette handed over all her evidence to the *juge d'instruction* in charge of the case which had been opened against René Hardy.

On 21 February 1945 she went to Annemasse near the Swiss frontier at Geneva to meet Edmée Delettraz. Madame Delettraz was also suspected of betraying the meeting at Caluire; she had been the mistress of the German agent "Moog," she had no alibi for the period between midday and 2:00 P.M. on 21 June 1943, and she claimed to have been ordered by Barbie to trail René Hardy to the meeting place. She was also a trusted agent of the *cagoulard* resister Colonel Groussard and the colonel's mistress was the sister of Antoinette Sachs. When Madame Delettraz came to Paris to be questioned by Hardy's *juge d'instruction* it was Antoinette who was asked by the judge to help her prepare her deposition. In other words, prompted by Antoinette Sachs, the Aubracs and André Lassagne, the prosecutors of the *épuration* decided to call a self-confessed traitor, Edmée Delettraz, as state evidence against René Hardy, who, pending his trial, had been arrested by French police in December 1944. At the time of his arrest Hardy was working directly for Frenay at the ministry for prisoners and deportees.

The communists were thus presented with the opportunity to attack Frenay, not only as a dangerous reactionary, a suspected Pétainist and an incompetent and unfeeling minister, but as a man who was misusing his undeserved reputation as a resistance leader to protect collaborators and traitors. In June 1945 the campaign against the minister reached a climax when 75,000 ex-POWs marched beneath the windows of Frenay's Paris apartment in the rue Guynemer. Led by the communist leaders Jacques Duclos and André Marty, they chanted "Frenay *out*, Frenay to the stake!" "His ministry is crawling with Vichyists, traitors and opportunists," wrote *L'Humanité*. "He is determined to sabotage the Republic." Frenay resigned in the autumn of 1945 and retired to private life; and the PCF, led at first by

Maurice Thorez, who had deserted from the French army and fled to Moscow in 1940, and later by Georges Marchais, who had volunteered to work as a skilled fitter in the Messerschmitt factory in Augsburg in 1941, continued to occupy a steadily increasing space in the official records of the Resistance.

As the prosecution case against Hardy was being prepared, Antoinette Sachs, who was continuing her obsessive private investigation, found that her most sympathetic supporters included Pierre Cot, Meunier, Chambeiron and Gaston Cusin, as well as Marcelle Dangon. In June, just after the march against Frenay in Paris, Pierre Cot published a long newspaper article about Jean Moulin, whose name, for the first time, became known. Cot's article depicted his former colleague as an orthodox fellow-traveler, and—as Péan points out—brushed aside Moulin's wartime commitment to de Gaulle. One year later, in June 1946, Laure Moulin organized the publication of *Premier Combat,* which presented "Max" to the French public as the head of the Resistance and founder of the CNR who had been tortured to death by the Germans without breaking, after being "denounced by a traitor." The book had a preface by General de Gaulle in which he described its author as his "pure and virtuous companion." "Max," wrote de Gaulle, "held no faith other than France and knew how to die heroically for her. . . . His strength of character, his clearsightedness and his strength never deserted him. May his name and his work live forever."

So Moulin was claimed as a hero by two warring factions. Meanwhile the deportees, the living ghosts of *Nacht und Nebel,* had started to come back from the camps in an unbelievable condition. Nearly one million POWs came home, as well as 700,000 forced laborers from the STO and 150,000 men from Alsace and Lorraine who had been forced to fight for Germany. And there were the men and women and children who did not come back, 74,000 Jewish deportees and 35,000 resisters. Many of those who did return died shortly afterward. But "Max" was not among them.

It was against this background that the first steps were taken to transform a man into a legend. But for a legend to be put to political use it is not enough to have died for France, to have been tortured and stayed silent and to have disappeared like El Cid into the mists of history. The legend of "Max" demanded the right traitor. And Hardy was the perfect "traitor." He was a former communist.

The trial of Hardy on the capital charge of high treason opened at the Cour de Justice in Paris in January 1947, with *L'Humanité* jumping the gun by announcing the inevitable verdict, "guilty," on the first morning of the case. However, Hardy appeared in court wearing the uniform of a lieutenant-colonel, the rank he had been accorded in the FFI in recognition of his work for *Sabotage-Fer*. Young, pale, thin, intense, he made a sympathetic figure, convincing enough to have been cast in a Hollywood movie about the Resistance. And he had the good fortune to be defended by one of the most brilliant advocates of the day, Maître Maurice Garçon, who fell upon the prosecution's first witness and totally destroyed her evidence. Madame Delettraz claimed that she had met Hardy on the morning of Caluire in the Gestapo headquarters in Lyon and together they had arranged a method by which he would lead her unnoticed to the rendezvous. Maître Garçon succeeded in establishing that Madame Delettraz had been a Gestapo agent, and revealed her connection with Colonel Groussard, who, in the early days of the occupation, when he was working for Pétain, had hunted Gaullists. Hardy flatly denied that he had been arrested on the night-train to Paris; he said he had escaped by jumping from the train.

Much of the prosecution evidence that followed was provided by Gestapo records and Maître Garçon succeeded in ridiculing most of these as well. Then he produced the defense witnesses, a long line of distinguished resistance fighters who spoke up for Hardy. They included the leaders of *Combat*, Frenay, Pierre de Bénouville and Claude Bourdet. He also produced an alibi witness for Hardy, a man called Lieutenant Bossé who was himself a legend of the Resistance since he was one of the very few survivors of a German firing squad, an experience which he had brilliantly described in a book of memoirs. Since Hardy had a distinguished resistance record, since his passionate denials of guilt carried conviction and since there was no direct evidence (Delettraz apart) that he had betrayed Caluire, he was, after a week's hearings, acquitted.

For *Combat* and for Henri Frenay, the verdict was a triumph. A distinguished reception committee waited for Hardy at the gates of Fresnes prison, scene of so much wartime suffering for the resisters, and "the Frenay gang," as the communist press routinely referred to these national heroes, was photographed in joyful celebration.

The PCF took Hardy's acquittal as a signal to redouble its efforts to establish his guilt. A meeting, or "people's tribunal," was organized in a public hall, the Salle Wagram, presided over by an aggrieved Laure Moulin, and on 25 March a writer in *L'Humanité*, while demanding that "the Resistance of the bourgeoisie" should be exposed and "Judas be punished," added that the communists had been "the first members of the Resistance." The political objectives of the campaign could hardly have been made clearer.

And then, quite unexpectedly, a few weeks after the verdict, a witness came forward who could produce documentary proof that on the night of 8 June Hardy had indeed been arrested by Robert Moog on the journey from Lyon to Paris, and had not jumped from the train as he had claimed in court. He had therefore been in Gestapo hands two weeks before Caluire; more seriously, he had concealed this fact from his comrades. Hardy was rearrested in March 1947, and admitted that he had been taken off the train by the Gestapo. But stubbornly he still denied that he had betrayed Caluire. A new trial was ordered.

After Hardy had been acquitted at the end of his first trial de Gaulle said to his aide-de-camp, Claude Guy: "The comrades of the resistance reached such depths of ignominy . . . that they betrayed their brothers. Why? To get the advantage of them at the liberation. They did that. They did it when the Germans held a knife to their throats, they did it *by using the Germans*." In an atmosphere where every resister was a two-dimensional hero, where the communists were "the first resisters" and soon afterward the "most numerous resisters" and finally "the only resisters," the real history of resistance was impossible to write.

It was not possible for the French to accept that Christian Pineau was not just the man who founded *Libération-Nord*, and who believed he had shaved a dying Jean Moulin. Pineau was also the man who spent many months in 1942 repeating his conviction that Henri Frenay was "a secret agent for Vichy military intelligence" and who tried to get Frenay flown out to England and forbidden to return. The political complexities of the Resistance had to be concealed. Pascal Copeau was not just a leader of *Libération-Sud*. He was a man who, on his own admission, shortly after infiltrating *Libération* spent many hours with Jean Moulin "plotting" a series of "dirty tricks" to eliminate Frenay from the resistance movement so that he could be replaced at the head of *Combat* by Marcel Degliame—like Copeau a communist. Raymond Aubrac was not just the military director of

Libération-Sud and a survivor of Caluire, he was also the man who urged his comrades to "eliminate Frenay and others by any available means." Aubrac had wanted to kidnap the leader of *Combat* while he was in London; asked if "Max" should be told of this plan, Aubrac advised against it. Pierre de Bénouville, a leader of *Combat* whose services to the Resistance led to his appointment as an army general, was also the author of a note to Frenay urging him to envisage "reprisals" (against fellow resisters) after the arrest of General Delestraint. When asked about this by Pierre Péan in 1998 de Bénouville replied: "We had reached a point where 'reprisals' had become the norm."

As for the communist resistance, it had remained as ruthless with its allies in the war against fascism, and with its discredited friends, as it was with its enemies. Early on the morning of 2 October 1943 the FTP–MOI carried out one of its most spectacular exploits by organizing a mass breakout of sixty-nine resistance prisoners from jail in Puy-en-Velay. The released prisoners included five Trotskyists, one of whom, realizing his mortal danger, managed to escape from his liberators. The other four, including Pietro Tresso, founder of the Italian Communist Party (Trotskyist), were taken up to the armed band known as the *maquis* "WODLI" of the Haute-Loire, where the local commissars of the communist resistance organized a show trial. Just as in the Moscow show trials the four accused were made to write down their life stories, photographed, in the style of police photographs, and then denounced before general assemblies of the *maquisards* by party prosecutors. The formal accusation was that they had "poisoned the water supply." The assemblies, transformed into popular juries, were then invited to vote for the death of their fellow resisters and the Trotskyists were dispatched, their bodies concealed in a cave. This crime was concealed by communist historians for fifty years. They poisoned the wells of truth to hide the fact that the communist resistance had committed crimes against their fellow resisters, which would have merited the death sentence if they had been discovered in 1945.

The liberation was not just a moment of victory. It was also a time when good men were executed and bad men were glorified. And many of the worst went unpunished. The traitor Jean Multon—formerly "Lunel" of the Resistance—was shot, but his evil genius Robert Moog disappeared into thin air. Even today he would be only eighty-six. Some of Barbie's "gorillas" like Steingritt were shot; but after the war Barbie was set to work for allied intelligence, and in particular by the U.S. Counter Intelligence

Corps, the CIC. He was protected by American or British soldiers whenever he was interviewed by French intelligence officers about the Hardy case, among other matters. In the dangerous disorder of postwar Germany allied intelligence quickly realized the potential value of cooperation with the ex-Nazi administration and police. The hunt for war criminals gave way to the need to impose the rule of law and establish an anti-communist democracy. The contacts and information provided by a former SS captain like Barbie were invaluable. The first task he was given by the CIC in 1947 was to penetrate Soviet front organizations in the American zone of Germany and to penetrate French intelligence in the French zone (which the Americans regarded as a branch of Soviet intelligence).*

The second trial of René Hardy opened in April 1950 before a military tribunal, since he could not be tried twice on the same charge by a civilian court. This time he faced no jury but a court of seven judges, six of them soldiers and former members of the Resistance, with a professional judge as president. Once again he was defended by Maître Garçon, who liked a challenge and this time had to explain why the court should acquit a man who had committed perjury and lied to everyone about whether or not he had been arrested by the Gestapo. Once again Frenay, who had not forgiven Hardy for his lies and his failure to follow the basic rules of resistance, gave evidence for the defense and once again many other resisters joined him, including Pierre de Bénouville. Colonel Passy also gave evidence for Hardy, as did an anonymous British officer representing MI6.

For Frenay the discovery of Hardy's deception was a serious blow. If it seemed unlikely that the leaders of *Combat* had deliberately used Hardy to remove Moulin from the scene—the arrest of Aubry would have risked the destruction of their own network—the fact that such a valued and effective member of *Combat*'s inner circle could have been working for the Gestapo without being discovered damaged the reputation of all anti-communist resistance. This was one of the absurd consequences of the

---

* In 1951, after Barbie had served his purpose, his CIC case officer gave him and his family a new identity, false passports and the means to travel to Bolivia, where he lived for the next thirty-two years. When he was eventually extradited to France to face trial for crimes against humanity in Lyon in 1986 it was for the role he had played in the deportation of Jews. The name of Jean Moulin was not mentioned once during his trial, which ended in a sentence of life imprisonment.

official resistance myth. The novelist Albert Camus touched on that absurdity when, referring to the second Hardy prosecution in the newspaper *Combat,* he wrote: "Had he stayed at home like so many other people, had he not chosen the hard road, he would live an honored man today.... We cannot be the judges of this man. He must judge himself."

But Hardy was not judging himself and in his defense Maître Garçon also called Lydie Bastien, the woman with whom Hardy had been in love at the time of Caluire and whom Frenay had long suspected of having been a Gestapo agent even before she met Hardy. Lydie Bastien was once described by the head of the French secret service as "un bel animal nonchalant aux yeux immenses" (a beautiful, nonchalant animal with enormous eyes). By the time of the second Hardy trial she had taken to posing for glamour magazines and her reputation as a femme fatale was to Hardy's advantage. His case now was that, having been arrested by Barbie, he had agreed to work for the Gestapo in order to protect Lydie and her parents, but he had given no important information in return. Asked why he had not told his comrades that he had been in Gestapo custody, an admission that would have imposed an automatic "quarantine" from the Resistance of several weeks, Hardy said that he feared they would have suspected him of betraying General Delestraint, an explanation which was all too convincing. Since Hardy had been arrested on his way to a rendezvous with Delestraint, and since the general had himself been arrested at that rendezvous, Hardy might well have been suspected of treachery, and executed, before his colleagues discovered that the rendezvous had in fact been given away by the carelessness of a colleague, Henri Aubry. Summary justice applied before the suspect had time to explain himself was a commonplace of resistance life. Arrested with a letter in his pocket addressed to Lydie Bastien at her parents' address in Lyon, desperate to protect the woman he was in love with, identified by Multon as a probable member of *Combat,* Hardy was first forced to persuade Barbie that he was prepared to cooperate, and then forced to hide his double game from *Combat.* Even if he had managed to persuade Frenay and de Bénouville of his good faith he knew that the communists in *Libération* and *Franc-Tireur* would never believe him. In these circumstances his failure to taste Lucie Aubrac's pot of jam was hardly surprising.

The case against Hardy at his second trial was in fact very little changed from the case against him at his first. There were the Gestapo documents from Marseille naming him as an informer, and the evidence of Edmée Delettraz; and now the new information that he had been arrested by the Gestapo two weeks before the meeting. Maître Garçon provided a convincing explanation of the new evidence, and dealt with the old evidence in the same way as he had three years earlier. But at the second trial there was another element in the case against Hardy, and that was the unlikely manner of his escape from Caluire. The prosecution version of Hardy's escape, which was essentially the same as the *Libération–Franc-Tireur* version put about by Lucie Aubrac within hours of the arrests— what might be called the "pot-of-poisoned jam version" (which is still the commonly accepted version today)—can be summarized as follows.

René Hardy was the chief suspect because he had been arrested and released by the Gestapo shortly before the meeting, he had concealed this arrest from his comrades, and had then attended an important resistance meeting to which he had not been invited. He was the only man at Caluire who was not handcuffed after arrest, he was the first prisoner to be taken out of the house, he escaped by overcoming his guards, as he ran away the Germans did not try very hard to shoot him down and then did not bother to mount an adequate search while he was hiding in a shallow roadside ditch by their feet. He subsequently displayed a single pistol wound in his left arm which could have been inflicted either by himself or by a German accomplice. His suspicion about the pot of jam sent to him in hospital confirmed that he had a guilty secret.* Furthermore his escape some weeks later from a German military hospital, over a high wall, was beyond the capacity of a man with one arm in a plaster cast.

The trial records and the original witness statements made to the police or to the examining magistrate have recently been reexamined and discussed by the former resister Jacques Baumel, the historian Jacques Baynac and by the ex-resister and historian Daniel Cordier. It is now possible to reconstruct a fuller version of events.

Two women patients and Dr. Dugoujon's housekeeper were taken out

---

* The beauty of Lucie Aubrac's "pot of jam" argument is that it revives the medieval logic of the ducking stool. Under this form of trial by ordeal a woman was ducked in a river, and held under the water; if she survived it was clear that she had supernatural powers and she was condemned as a witch. If she drowned then she must have been innocent. So Hardy, known to be guilty, refused to eat Lucie Aubrac's jam and confirmed his guilt. Had he eaten it, and died, at least one of the grounds for suspecting him would have been removed.

of the house and loaded into the back of a Gestapo car. Hardy then came out of the house accompanied by two guards each holding one of his wrists. One of his wrists was also attached to a chain held by the guard Steingritt. Four witnesses saw Hardy led around the back of the car to be loaded into the front. As Steingritt opened the front passenger door Hardy ducked and struck him a violent blow in the stomach, causing Steingritt to reel back; he then pulled the chain from his hand and ran off, weaving between the plane trees across the center of the Place Castellane. Even Claudius-Petit, one of those who had authorized the execution of Hardy by poisoned jam, said at the second Hardy trial that there was nothing so remarkable about this incident, and added that he had witnessed far more unlikely escapes.

As Hardy broke away one German sentry outside the house, armed with a machine-pistol, fired a burst in his direction, but the car and the trees were between him and his target. By opening fire the sentry stopped three other guards from running after Hardy across the line of fire. Only when the sentry with the machine-pistol had stopped firing could the other guards draw their pistols and run after the fugitive. By this time Hardy had a clear start of twenty yards and the four or five shots they let off in his direction while running failed to hit him. As all this was going on, a small man dressed in navy blue, Barbie, came out of the house, shouting "Schwein! Schwein!" at Steingritt, then drew his Mauser pistol and fired three shots from a stationary position at Hardy, who was by this time nearly forty yards away and on the far side of the square. The first shot missed, the second carried away Hardy's hat, the third hit him. Two witnesses saw this. One said Hardy clutched his left arm in his right hand. Another said he lurched to the right.

At this point Hardy left the square and ran down a road which descends steeply toward the River Saône. A road-mender working a hundred yards from the Place Castellane saw him plunge into one of the ditches beside the road. So far from being shallow these flood ditches are six feet deep and thickly bordered by nettles, weeds and grass. Because of the thick plant cover nobody looking at the ditch from the road would have realized how well it could conceal a man. The three Germans who followed the fugitive arrived too late to see him leap into the ditch and were faced with an empty road. Before giving up the pursuit, one of them, apparently in frustration, fired a random shot into a house overlooking the road. Then they walked back to the Place Castellane and shortly afterward returned in two cars and drove down toward the river. The road-mender meanwhile had approached Hardy in the ditch and advised him to stay where he was. After about fifteen minutes the German cars returned, driving uphill, and disappeared in the direction of the square. When they had driven past, the road-mender told Hardy that the way was clear; he advised him to follow the road downhill and jump back into the ditch if he heard a car approaching.

As to whether or not Hardy shot himself in the left forearm, the four doctors who examined him on 21 June after his arrest by the Vichy police all took the view that the bullet had not been fired from close range. They noted an entry and an exit wound and a broken radial bone. An examination of his coat sleeve showed no trace of burn marks. Only in 1949, in preparation for his second trial, did a second forensic report belatedly discover "traces" of powder on the sleeve of the jacket. On 21 June, in the evening, having taken refuge in the house of friends, members of *France d'Abord,* Hardy was arrested and held under guard in a local hospital. Lucie Aubrac gave evidence at the second trial that Hardy had told the Vichy police "everything about the meeting at Caluire" and had been described as *un mouton* (an informer). But the police officer she claimed she had spoken to was a notorious enemy of the Resistance in Lyon who was dead by the time she gave evidence. And the Lyon police records, examined since the war, show that Hardy told the French police practically nothing about the resistance meeting and certainly far less than they already knew from other sources. At the trial Raymond Aubrac said that he had always been convinced that when Barbie saw Hardy at Caluire "he was expecting to see him there." This seems unlikely since Aubrac was not present when Barbie saw Hardy at Caluire. They were in different rooms on different floors. Raymond Aubrac continued to insist that Hardy had betrayed General Delestraint as recently as 1996, many years after it had been confirmed that the Gestapo learned about Delestraint's rendezvous from the blown letter-box at 14 rue Bouteille and long after it was known that Hardy had not even been questioned by the Gestapo until two days after Delestraint's arrest.

In short, Hardy's defense was not nearly as weak as it has usually been described. At the time of his second trial he was, notoriously, the target of a political witch-hunt on the part of the French Communist Party—a party that had, in the six years since the liberation, lost much of its popular appeal. In 1950 Maître Garçon set about the chief prosecution witness,

Edmée Delettraz, with even more energy than he had shown on the first occasion, and with such success that some observers expected her to be arrested when she had finished giving evidence. But it was, nonetheless, a close-run thing. By four votes to three the judges of the military tribunal found Hardy guilty. Since a guilty verdict required a margin of two votes he was acquitted. This result enabled both sides to claim victory. The communists continued, and continue to this day, to proclaim Hardy's treachery; his supporters point out that he was acquitted twice. What is undisputed by everyone, with the possible exception of the two Aubracs, is that Hardy, who held so much military information and was in a position to betray so many members of *Combat*, gave none of them away. Jacques Baumel, the secretary of the MUR, who was watched by Barbie the day before Caluire, on the Pont Morand, owed his freedom, and probably his life, to the fact that Hardy did not betray him.

There was another reason to acquit René Hardy of the treason of Caluire, although not much was made of it at either trial. Hardy did not know the address of the house where the meeting of 21 June was to be held. If he was to betray the meeting he therefore had to be followed. Edmée Delettraz swore that he came to the Ecole de Santé Militaire and arranged with her and Barbie to set up a system, using yellow chalk and a cigarette packet, to mark his route. That was the means allegedly used by Hardy in his act of treachery. But the police *Sonderkommando* did *not* get to Caluire by following Hardy. That near-certainty is established by the fact that they arrived forty-five minutes after him. The *Sonderkommando* arrived on the heels of the men in the downstairs room, Jean Moulin, Raymond Aubrac and Lieutenant-Colonel Schwartzfeld. Of these three the only one with a police "record," the only one known to the German police, was Raymond Aubrac. If they followed anyone, they must have followed Aubrac. But the *Sonderkommando* did not get to the house by following Aubrac either. They did not get to the house by following anyone. They got to the house *because they already knew its identity*—that is, they knew they were looking for "the house of Dr. Dugoujon," a name Hardy had never heard. Barbie's *Sonderkommando*, which carried out the triumphant raid on Caluire, spent nearly an hour driving around the district looking for the right house. For Dr. Dugoujon had recently changed his address. He had moved to the Place Castellane from the nearby Impasse des Verchères. Unable to find the house after a long search, the German police eventually inquired at the town hall. From there they were directed to the old address, and from there to the Place Castellane, where they arrived at around 3:00 P.M., about one hour after they were first seen driving around Caluire.

On that rainy afternoon of 21 June, on the heights above the dying reaches of the River Saône, this party of licensed killers in their two black Citroëns resembled nothing so much as a party of *paparazzi* blundering from doorstep to doorstep, on the trail of a minor publicity starlet. The treachery of René Hardy at Caluire was a red herring from the start.

SIXTEEN

The Doctor's Waiting Room

THE MYSTERY OF THE DEATH of Jean Moulin begins with the possibility that he was *not* betrayed by René Hardy. If Hardy betrayed Caluire to the Gestapo, it was because he was being blackmailed by Barbie over the safety of Lydie Bastien. Accusing Hardy is reassuring, like blaming the pilot in an air crash. Hardy's betrayal would have been a routine matter, a human failure. That, no doubt, is the reason why so many inquiries still favor the guilt of René Hardy. For once you reject the likelihood of Hardy's guilt the other possibilities are alarming, and the façade of the mythical Resistance dissolves. The reassuring official history of *la France résistante* is replaced by several scenarios, all equally fatal to the myth. Looking for a murderer, the policeman will try to discover more about the identity of the corpse. For the biographer of Jean Moulin, the priorities are reversed; to know who he was one must find out who killed him.

Henri Frenay did not believe in Hardy's treachery. Despite his anger over Hardy's lie, he remained convinced that his deputy was innocent. Instead, he began to wonder who Jean Moulin had really been. In 1973 he published his memories of the war, *La Nuit finira* (The Night Will End), in which for the first time he asked aloud whether Moulin had been a crypto-communist. Frenay developed this theory in a second book, *L'Enigme de Jean Moulin*, published in 1977. Frenay put forward two grounds for his theory. The first was the open, postwar communism of so many of Moulin's prewar colleagues. The second was the way in which Moulin had, in Frenay's view, favored communist policy while he was de Gaulle's delegate to the Resistance. In tracing the pro-communist sympathies of Pierre Cot, Henri Manhès, Pierre Meunier and Robert Chambeiron, and relating them to the work of Moulin, Frenay was voicing the first criticism of a man who had recently been transformed into a legend. The entry into the Panthéon in 1964 had been the culminating moment in this process. Enormous monuments to Moulin's heroism had been erected in many parts of France, in the hills of Provence, in Chartres and in Angers. There were at least three museums to his memory. He was on postage stamps; Marcel Bernard's photograph—of the slim figure leaning against a wall wearing a trilby, a thick woolen scarf and an overcoat—was the central icon and was widely believed to have been taken during his days "underground." Moulin was untouchable. He was no longer a man: he had become the honor of France. In the words of the historian Pierre Vidal-Naquet, to say that he was "an agent of the Kremlin is to install treason at the heart of our recent history, not because the communist religion is more contemptible than any other but because a nation should not choose . . . liars as heroes."

In contrast to Moulin, Frenay had been all but forgotten. After the war, de Gaulle had offered to make him one of the four generals promoted from the Resistance, but this was a promotion Frenay refused (Pierre de Bénouville took his place). Frenay, with the integrity of a regular soldier, was content with the rank of colonel,* which had been his father's rank. But following the publication of *L'Enigme de Jean Moulin* all Frenay's genius as a resistance leader, his courage and his modesty, were unable to save him from a further onslaught on his reputation. The true role of *Combat* was brought into issue and he was accused of being a Pétainist and an anti-Semite. In fact one of the endearing aspects of Frenay's attack on Moulin was that it was the opposite of self-serving. By questioning the integrity of Moulin, Frenay risked raising suspicions about *Combat*'s role in the betrayal of Caluire. For if Moulin *had* been a Soviet agent, and if anyone in *Combat* had realized this during the occupation, it would have been their duty to eliminate him by one means or another. Colonel Passy's reply when he was asked after the war if the BCRA would have parachuted

---

* De Gaulle also refused promotion at the end of the war and was content to hold his final 1940 rank of brigadier-general for the rest of his life.

Moulin into France had it known of his friendship with the GRU agent André Labarthe ("There would have been no question of it"), confirms the impossibility of working with Soviet agents. At the time of Caluire, Frenay was in London, but was there anyone else in the conspiracy who might have acted against Moulin on his own initiative?

There were ten conspirators; Serreulles, Lacaze, Schwartzfeld, Larat, Lassagne, Aubry, de Bénouville, Aubrac, Dugoujon and Jean Moulin. Claude Bouchinet-Serreulles had been parachuted into France only five days earlier, on 16 June, as Moulin's deputy and the first of the reinforcements "Max" had been pleading for so urgently. Serreulles never took the road to Caluire; he was unfamiliar with Lyon, selected the wrong public transport funicular (or *ficelle*) and got lost, a blunder that probably saved his life.

Colonel Albert Lacaze, a regular officer and a member of the small Lyon network *France d'Abord,* woke up on the morning of 21 June feeling unwell. His son was in the Resistance and was on the run from the Gestapo. His daughter, Odile, was in the Resistance and was living with him at home. He himself had never been to a secret meeting in his life. But he had been invited on the previous day by a younger officer, Larat, to attend, and had immediately reacted by suggesting that the meeting be canceled. That morning he decided he was not up to it and, although he knew his own house was being watched, he first telephoned and then sent Odile with a note to the house in Caluire to tell its owner, Dr. Dugoujon, who was not in the Resistance, that he would not be able to come. Dr. Dugoujon was out, so Odile left the note with the housekeeper, Marguerite Brossier. As the morning advanced Colonel Lacaze felt better and changed his mind. He was the first to arrive, at around 2:05 P.M. After his arrest Colonel Lacaze was interrogated by the Gestapo in Paris. He claimed to know nothing about the Resistance and was released without charge the following January.

Lieutenant-Colonel Emile Schwartzfeld, a reserve officer and radio engineer, did not know of the existence of the meeting until shortly before it was due to start. Like his fellow colonel, Albert Lacaze, Schwartzfeld was a member of *France d'Abord.* He was invited to attend at the last minute in a tactical move devised by "Max" and "Aubrac"; *Combat* was bound to object to the appointment of two members of *Libération* (Aubrac himself and Lassagne) to the military leadership of the northern and southern Secret Armies. The right-wing Schwartzfeld was therefore invited to attend on condition that he would replace Lassagne as temporary leader of the southern army. After his arrest Schwartzfeld, who had limited experience of conspiracy, was taken to Paris for interrogation and deported to Struthof concentration camp, where he died in June 1944.

Bruno Larat, known as "Parisot," was a young volunteer who had succeeded Raymond Fassin as director of the COPA. He had first met Moulin in England, and had been responsible for giving him false papers, a cyanide capsule and a pistol before his parachute jump into France. After the appointment of Delestraint, Larat had worked under his command and he had been told that the general wanted Colonel Lacaze to become commanding officer of the Secret Army's *Quatrième Bureau* (logistics). Larat, who knew the address of the meeting, therefore took it upon himself to invite Colonel Lacaze, even though he had no authority to do so, and even though his own deputy, Montjaret, had recently been arrested by the Gestapo; furthermore, he was aware that his own mail drops were being monitored. Larat did not even bother to introduce Lacaze, but just sent him on ahead. Larat was shown into the meeting room at approximately 2:20 P.M. After Larat's arrest he was tortured in Lyon, transferred to Paris for further interrogation and deported. He died of prolonged ill-treatment in April 1944 in the Dora slave-labor camp.

André Lassagne, who selected the house in Caluire, was a childhood friend of Dr. Frédéric Dugoujon and it was he who was ordered by Moulin to make the necessary arrangements for the meeting of 21 June. Lassagne was professor of Italian at the Lycée du Parc in Lyon. He had fought for the Republicans in the Spanish Civil War. He was a senior member of *Libération* and although not a member of the PCF he was "close" to the party. Following the formation of the MUR in November 1942, Lassagne was appointed head of the *Deuxième Bureau* (intelligence) of the Secret Army. Before the war he had attended the reserve officers' staff college, where his tutor had been Colonel Lacaze. After they were both arrested at Caluire, Lassagne insisted that Colonel Lacaze had nothing to do with the Resistance (a difficult line to defend since they had been in the same meeting room on the first floor), so Lassagne was probably responsible for saving Lacaze's life.

As the principal organizer of Caluire, Lassagne was the architect of the disaster. Jacques Baumel, who organized over a hundred clandestine meetings in three years—none of which were discovered—had set up an unrivaled security routine. He would start with the equivalent of an airline pilot's checklist, going over pages of precautions before he was satisfied. In Lyon he had a dozen suitable addresses, none of which was used twice running. They had to be houses in quiet situations, with several exits, which were easy to watch discreetly. These houses were never used as depots or hideouts, only for meetings. They were never in the center of town, where there were too many police and informers and where those summoned had every chance of bumping into an acquaintance. The meeting house was always guarded by a commando of three or four armed men who were capable of standing their ground if the police arrived. The German police usually raided in small groups since, "in a city without cars"—there was no petrol—large groups were too conspicuous.

Baumel's procedure was to fix a date and choose an address. Those summoned received a note, in code, of the day and the time and a rendezvous point with a description of the liaison agent they were to follow onto a bus. Everyone was given a different rendezvous. When the guide left the bus they followed her—it was usually a woman—and she led them to a security agent, the first person involved who knew the address. He then led them to the house by a long and illogical route. The *groupe franc* would already be in place.

Unfortunately Baumel had nothing to do with the organization of Caluire, and André Lassagne adopted a rather different procedure. He chose a house owned by a man whose brother was in the *Milice,* and which had no back entrance. He failed to organize a surveillance team before the meeting and turned down the offer of an armed guard from the *groupes francs.* He allowed far too many people to know about the meeting in advance. He agreed to take Hardy, who had not been invited, to a secret meeting, and was chiefly responsible for not advising those present to leave after a short wait. Furthermore, Lassagne, too, had for some time had the impression that he was being followed and had been so worried before the meeting started that he had first called on Dugoujon at 1:30, at which time the doctor had noticed that Lassagne was "tense and anxious." If Caluire was discovered through error rather than treachery it was probably because, by 21 June, André Lassagne was too tired to organize a conspiracy. Nonetheless Lassagne arrived on time at 2:15 P.M., having acted as guide to Aubry and Hardy. Lassagne was a man of great courage and strength who was the first of the resisters of Caluire to be tortured, and who was treated worse than anyone, with the possible exception of Moulin. But there is no evidence that this schoolteacher broke under torture.

When the Lyon Gestapo failed to make any headway with him, Lassagne was transferred to Fresnes for further interrogation. He was later deported to Buchenwald but survived and returned after the war, only to die in 1953 as a delayed result of his mistreatment.

These five resisters, Serreulles, Lacaze, Schwartzfeld, Larat and Lassagne, three of whom were deported after the meeting, two of whom died in German hands, one of whom failed to find the meeting place, can be cleared of any suspicion of treachery at Caluire. Hardy can also be eliminated for reasons already explained. The case of the remaining two Gestapo prisoners, Henri Aubry and Raymond Aubrac, and of the *Combat* leader Pierre de Bénouville, is more complicated.

Among those who were at one time suspected of betraying Caluire was Captain Henri Aubry, sometimes known as "Thomas," a regular army officer who had started the war as a lieutenant in the colonial infantry. Aubry was one of Frenay's earliest recruits, attracted to resistance by the same patriotic motives, a refusal of defeat. Baumel described him as "quarrelsome, sentimental and easy to fool." With some experience of intelligence work he soon became one of *Combat*'s leading members. By the time the MUR was formed in 1942, Aubry was among its directors and he was appointed chief of staff to General Delestraint when the latter took over command of the Secret Army.

But despite his training and experience, Aubry committed a string of serious errors before Caluire. He continued to use a mail drop days after he was told that it had been "blown"; worse, he used it for important messages written in "clear" that should have been in code. So it was that the Gestapo learned that Delestraint had summoned Hardy to a rendezvous in Paris at the entrance to the Métro Muette at 9:15 A.M. on 9 June. After Aubry discovered that the mail box was unsafe he compounded his error by failing to warn Hardy and Delestraint. His failure to warn Hardy was the more surprising since the two men met in good time to cancel the Paris rendezvous. This series of mistakes led to the arrest, and eventual death, of General Delestraint and to the arrest of René Hardy. Subsequently, having been summoned to the meeting of Caluire, Aubry spoke about it to several of his colleagues in *Combat*, breaking another rule, which was "never discuss a meeting with someone who has not been invited to it." News of the approach of this resistance "summit" (but not of its address) began to circulate in resistance circles in Lyon, which accounts for the fact that Moulin received two separate offers to provide armed protection.

In the absence of Frenay, Aubry, with de Bénouville and Claude Bourdet, was the senior figure in *Combat*. But despite his increased responsibilities his behavior seems to have become reckless. There have been various explanations for this. The obvious one is that he was simply exhausted, like many other resistance leaders; he may also have been distracted by worry over his wife, who was seriously ill. The historian François Delpla suggests that Aubry may have suffered from a conscious or subconscious resentment against Delestraint, but Aubry's memory was unreliable on other subjects as well. He saw Moulin on 21 June at 10:00 A.M. when he "forgot" something else: to warn "Max" that Hardy would be coming to the meeting. Was this because Moulin, having heard of the incident at Chalon railway station, had ordered everyone to avoid Hardy? Was it because Aubry did not want to forewarn Moulin that *Combat* would have doubled its representation at the meeting? Whatever the reason it is impossible to believe that Aubry's last omission was accidental.

And there are other reasons for wondering about Aubry's motives. He said that he had been convinced for some time that he was being followed. After his arrest Aubry told Dr. Dugoujon, in Montluc prison, "Barbie has been following me for weeks." Yet on the day before Caluire an extraordinary scene took place—it was a Sunday morning—in the middle of Lyon on one of the bridges over the River Rhône, the Pont Morand. One can assume that the meeting place was chosen by Aubry since it was another rule of the Lyon resistance never to meet on a bridge. The city bridges were under constant surveillance and easy to seal off. One by one Aubry, Hardy, Jacques Baumel, the secretary-general of the MUR, and Gaston Deferre, a leader of the Marseille socialist resistance, as well as Aubry's secretary Madeleine Raisin, who was carrying 200,000 francs in her handbag, conducted a series of open-air meetings on the Pont Morand, all of which Barbie later claimed to have observed.

When, on the following day, Barbie confronted Aubry in the upper room at Caluire his first remark was, "What's wrong, Thomas? You don't look as cheerful as you did yesterday on the Pont Morand." "Thomas" was Aubry's resistance code name. Barbie always claimed to have followed Hardy to the Pont Morand, but it is clear, once again, that he did not do so since he saw neither Baumel nor Madame Raisin, the first two people Hardy met. Barbie only saw Aubry and another man he did not know,

Gaston Deferre, who arrived later. Since Barbie did not follow Hardy to the meeting, since he had never met Baumel, since he did not recognize Madame Raisin when she was arrested later for different reasons, since he knew nothing about Deferre, one must conclude that the only person Barbie could have followed to the Pont Morand was not Hardy but Aubry. In other words Aubry was correct; Barbie *had* been following him for some time.

If Aubry had previously been arrested and questioned by the Gestapo, as Jacques Baynac has pointed out, it would explain his curious "forgetfulness." Let us suppose that Barbie had arrested Aubry, the joint deputy head of *Combat,* the chief of staff of General Delestraint, a key figure in the military arm of the Resistance. Then he arrested Hardy, whom he regarded, correctly, as a subordinate figure. Barbie realized that by "using" Hardy, and eventually blaming Hardy for the information he was obtaining from Aubry, he could protect his real and more promising source of information. Multon, Barbie's chief informer about *Combat,* knew Aubry much better than Hardy and is more likely to have betrayed the former than the latter. When another resister, General Desmazes, was interrogated by the Gestapo in August 1943, he was told that he had been betrayed by "A.—a member of the Lyon staff of the Secret Army." Only two members of the Lyon general staff had names beginning with A; Henri Avricourt Aubry, code-named "Thomas," and Raymond Samuel, alias F. Vallet or C. Ermelin, code-named "Aubrac." A Gestapo report drawn up after Caluire referred to "one of our agents in the Resistance, 'A,' an army officer." Aubrac was a reserve officer; Aubry was a regular officer. After the war a captain in the *Abwehr* referred to the fact that a person named "Aubry" was listed in the *Abwehr* card index as an informer.

Following his arrest at Caluire, Aubry was beaten up to the point where his shoulder was dislocated. The beatings continued for forty-eight hours, after which he was marched before a firing squad. At this point he started to talk, and it was apparently when he started to talk that Jean Moulin was identified. Aubry then talked to the Gestapo in Paris for a number of months, writing a fifty-two-page report which he later said contained information he knew the Germans already had or which he had invented and knew to be unverifiable. At the end of 1943 he was released, having undertaken to continue working for the Gestapo; instead, he broke contact and rejoined the Resistance in Marseille. If, as seems likely, Barbie discovered the house in Caluire not through following someone but because he knew the address, it becomes relevant that Aubry, unlike Hardy, knew the date and time of the meeting from 19 June, already knew the house in Caluire as a resistance meeting place and knew, of course, when he was given a rendezvous at the top of the Croix-Paquet funicular, that it led to Caluire. Having your shoulder dislocated must be excruciatingly painful, but the Gestapo did worse. Following this scenario one sees Aubry, the real informer, given a "level two" beating either before or after he had revealed the identity of "Max," while Hardy, the apparent informer, in fact the screen, is treated with ostentatious consideration, and put up in a German military hospital. The scenario is finally unconvincing. Captain Aubry managed to withstand two days of beatings and proved his courage and his loyalty. If, after that period, he revealed the identity of "Max" it is more likely to have been because he had reached the physical limits of his resistance.

After the liberation Aubry, who was ashamed of his failure, confided in Raymond Aubrac. Aubrac, by then commissioner of the Republic in Marseille, rehabilitated him and played a role in ensuring that Aubry was shielded from prosecution. In view of his string of errors, Aubry may have considered himself fortunate not to have been publicly suspected of responsibility for Caluire. Protected by Aubrac, subsequently among the first of Hardy's accusers, Henri Aubry duly gave evidence for the prosecution at both trials of René Hardy, the only member of *Combat* to turn against his former comrade, and it is not difficult to see his motives in doing so.

In retirement Pierre de Bénouville amused himself by giving an increasingly complicated picture of his experience in the Resistance in 1942 and 1943, and one in which he contradicted himself with increasing frequency. De Bénouville did not go to the meeting at Caluire, but he knew about it. The enforced partnership of Jean Moulin, the former assistant of Pierre Cot, and Pierre de Bénouville, the former *Camelot du Roy*, was both a historical irony and a measure of what the Resistance was supposed to be for. De Bénouville knew who Moulin was; Moulin probably knew rather less about the background of de Bénouville but could have made his own inquiries. In any case, reticence was never a striking part of de Bénouville's character. On 6 February 1934 de Bénouville had been one of the frustrated mob of royalists who attacked the National Assembly. Two years later, in February 1936, when Léon Blum's car was set upon by an *Action française* funeral cortège, de Bénouville had been escorting the deceased dignitary's niece; he had rushed back when he realized an opportunity had arisen to beat up the socialist leader, to his eternal regret arriving too late. He is then thought to have joined, or been linked with, the *Cagoule*. Jean Filliol, the *Cagoule*'s most notorious killer, was a school friend of his (as was François Mitterrand), and de Bénouville always defended the pro-fascist group warmly. When he joined *Combat* his new colleagues had to curb their irritation at his habit of shouting "Vive le Roi! Vive la Cagoule!" at inappropriate moments. Pierre de Bénouville and Jean Moulin therefore stood at almost the opposite extremes of the Third Republic, each man representing more or less everything that the other abhorred.

After the armistice of 1940 de Bénouville contributed articles to a Pétainist, anti-Semitic newspaper in Nice and associated with Colonel Groussard, a notorious *cagoulard* working for the Vichy intelligence service. He then tried to leave France and was arrested and imprisoned for six months in Toulon, where he met René Hardy, who had also been arrested while trying to reach London to join de Gaulle. On leaving prison de Bénouville started working for a strongly anti-Gaullist SOE resistance network called *Carte*, which eventually proved to be ineffectual and largely imaginary. In December 1942, just after the U.S. landings in North Africa and the German occupation of the Vichy zone, de Bénouville met Henri Frenay through a mutual friend who ran *Combat*'s *groupes francs*. Frenay recruited this *cagoulard* because, while working with *Carte*, de Bénouville had made contact with MI6 and the OSS, the new American intelligence service based in Switzerland.

Thanks to de Bénouville's Swiss connections his rise through the ranks of *Combat* was rapid. He was the chief intermediary between *Combat* and the OSS office in Berne, run by Allen Dulles, and he was also able to keep in touch with Colonel Groussard, who was running his *Gilbert* network from Geneva. He may even have met Edmée Delettraz.

Whatever the advantages to *Combat* of de Bénouville's links with the Americans in the form of money and radio contact, it was bought at the price of a potentially dangerous association with the extreme-right and the highly untrustworthy Vichy intelligence service. In view of this, it is quite surprising that Pierre de Bénouville was apparently so little suspected of responsibility for the discovery of the meeting at Caluire. Not only did he know about the meeting, which he did not attend, but it was he who instructed René Hardy to represent *Combat* there. Furthermore de

Bénouville left Lyon on 21 June after the arrival of the Gestapo at Caluire but before news of the disaster had begun to circulate. At the second trial of Hardy (where de Bénouville was subpoenaed as a prosecution witness but remained supportive of Hardy), the judge had to intervene in order to confirm that it was de Bénouville who first suggested Hardy's presence. De Bénouville's explanation to the court was that he did not know that Hardy had been arrested by the Gestapo because Hardy had concealed it from him. He said he had sent Hardy to the meeting with "Max"* as a back-up for Aubry and to prevent "Max" from imposing a new military commander on the Secret Army against the wishes of *Combat*. Asked why he did not go himself, he said that he did not want his presence at the meeting to suggest that he was sanctioning the decisions taken there, an explanation in contradiction with the desired presence of Hardy. If Moulin could be effectively opposed at the meeting, then de Bénouville should have been present. If he could not be opposed, then there was no point in breaking every rule of security and sending Hardy. In fact, from what is now known, it is very difficult to believe that de Bénouville did *not* know that Hardy had been arrested by the Gestapo before he told him to go to Caluire.

In Frenay's absence *Combat*'s new *cagoulard* recruit had taken his leader's place on the central committee of the MUR and was in sole charge of all *Combat*'s military operations. In that powerful position de Bénouville was indeed told of Hardy's arrest on the night-train to Paris by a friend in the Resistance, Lazare Rachline, who had by chance reserved a sleeping berth in the same carriage. De Bénouville said he then met Hardy "by chance" in the street in Lyon on 17 June and asked for an explanation. Originally de Bénouville claimed that Hardy told him he had not been "arrested" but merely questioned by the police and had subsequently jumped from the train before Chalon-sur-Saône. To check this story de Bénouville invited Hardy to take a shower with him in the public bathhouse so that he could look for signs of torture on Hardy's body. Since there were no physical signs of mistreatment on Hardy, de Bénouville decided he had no reason to disbelieve him. (In fact, the information from Rachline described an incident *in the station* at Chalon, so de Bénouville could never have believed Hardy's story about jumping from the train before Chalon.)

---

* Pierre de Bénouville did not know the address of the meeting.

In 1983 Hardy claimed that on the day they took a shower together in Lyon he had told de Bénouville everything about his arrest and interrogation by the Gestapo, and that his superior officer had suggested "a pact of silence." De Bénouville denied this at the time and denounced Hardy as "a liar and a coward." (By this time General Pierre de Bénouville was an influential Gaullist deputy in the National Assembly, and Hardy was dying a slow death in obscure poverty.) The question of de Bénouville's knowledge or ignorance of Hardy's arrest is clearly crucial. As late as 1985 Frenay, Claude Bourdet and other resisters gave evidence in a libel case insisting that de Bénouville would never have sent Hardy to Caluire if he had known of Hardy's interrogation by the Gestapo. And Henri Noguères, the leading French historian of the Resistance, has written that if de Bénouville *knew* that Hardy had been arrested and released and was being watched, and decided nonetheless to hide these facts from other resistance leaders and send him to Caluire, then de Bénouville would rightly have been considered responsible for what followed.

In 1997 de Bénouville told Pierre Péan that Hardy *had* told him everything, although he has since retracted this admission. In fact an analysis of telegrams sent by de Bénouville in June 1943 and accounts of conversations with other resisters—assembled by Péan and Jacques Baynac—establishes the near-certainty that Hardy was, once again, belatedly telling the truth. On 17 June de Bénouville did know that Hardy had been arrested and interrogated for two days, and had then been released as a minor player who would in future work for the Gestapo. He also knew that Barbie had talked to Hardy about the regrettable "communist influence" on the Resistance. De Bénouville kept these facts to himself and, believing that Hardy had not given Barbie much information, he saw no reason to put him in quarantine and instead sent him to Caluire. There is evidence in *Combat's* Swiss archives to suggest that by June 1943 de Bénouville had become convinced that Moulin intended to put the Secret Army under communist control. For that reason he had arranged to receive a copy of all communications crossing the desk of General Delestraint. With Delestraint out of action he was anxious to ensure that his successor could also be spied on. He had strong reasons for blocking the appointment of a pro-communist candidate. De Bénouville left Lyon that night for Toulouse on "urgent regional business" and on the following day, 22 June, while Lassagne, Aubry, Lacaze and Larat were undergoing their first interrogation in the Ecole de Santé Militaire in Lyon, he was celebrating his wedding on a little farm 250 miles away in the Lauragais.

The theory that Jean Moulin was betrayed by right-wing members of *Combat*, working in partnership with Vichy and the semi-criminal *Cagoule*, is attractive, since it puts the Resistance straight back into the context of the Third Republic; the stage is once again dominated by the familiar stereotypes of the Popular Front and the *Cagoule*, and Moulin assumes his established role as the fellow-traveler and suspected Soviet agent who is eliminated by patriotic French crypto-fascists. But to revive this plot is to forget everything that had happened in France after August 1939: *Der Pakt*, the *débâcle*, the Gestapo's reign of terror and the new alliances and enmities that had sprung from all this. Furthermore, since Hardy did not betray Caluire, de Bénouville, perhaps to his own surprise, is actually off the hook.

Whatever may have been intended to happen in the darker corners of his mind on that rainy afternoon, *something else took place*. Did it involve Edmée Delettraz? Like de Bénouville, Madame Delettraz was a friend of the *cagoulard* resister Georges Groussard. After Edmée was caught by the Gestapo, and after she had become the mistress of Moog, she said that she returned to Colonel Groussard in Geneva and explained what had occurred and, on his orders, maintained contact with the Gestapo as a triple agent. But Colonel Groussard never confirmed this story. On the contrary, he said that when Madame Delettraz told him she had been arrested he "put her into quarantine." We are dealing here with two systematic liars. But the facts show that Edmée Delettraz, "in quarantine" or as a triple agent, deliberately led the Gestapo to Berty Albrecht on 28 May 1943. Madame Albrecht committed suicide or was murdered in Fresnes prison nine days later. Then Delettraz, by her own account, trailed René Hardy to Caluire. The problem is that the Gestapo were not, on that occasion, trailing her or René Hardy. In 1945 there was enough evidence against Madame Delettraz to secure her conviction for treason. In any event she was saved by the testimony she swore against Hardy, just as Henri Aubry was saved. So there is a mystery about the role of Edmée Delettraz, but the key to the solution is missing, and until it has been found one has to abandon the attempt to prove that the extreme-right succeeded in betraying Jean Moulin at Caluire.

And so one comes to the last of the men of Caluire, Raymond Aubrac, the future conductor of the purge, the "Terrorist" of Marseille. Aubrac, who happily is still alive, has led an interesting life. Born Raymond Samuel, into a prosperous Lyonnais family, he crowned an outstanding school career by entering the Ponts et Chaussées, an élite national *grande école* where he studied engineering. With his wife, Lucie, he was on the point of leaving France to take up a post in the United States, where he had also studied, when the war broke out. In the army he was a second-lieutenant attached to the Versailles school of military engineering. He escaped in the confusion of June 1940, shortly after being made a prisoner of war, and, still in his twenties, joined d'Astier's *Libération* in Lyon, where his wife was a professor of history at the Lycée Edgar Quinet for girls. In Lyon, Aubrac became the group's military representative. His political sympathies were pro-communist. Madame Aubrac, who had been a prewar member of the French Communist Party (PCF) youth movement, was selected in 1935 for training at the Comintern's staff college in Moscow.

Clearly if Moulin was a crypto-communist he could count on the complete loyalty of Raymond Aubrac. Aubrac was, with the communist official Pierre Hervé, the leader of the *Front National*'s attempt to take over *Libération*. Aubrac was a figure of considerable influence in the southern zone resistance, but for the directors of the FN drive to take over the entire movement he was dispensable, merely one sucker on one tentacle of the octopus.

What then was the attitude of the party and of Raymond Aubrac to Jean Moulin, the man whom (as *Combat*'s archives show) Pierre de Bénouville had identified as a communist "submarine" in June 1943, and whom someone as scrupulous as Henri Frenay denounced as "a crypto-communist" after a due period of reflection in 1977? What was the relationship between this man and the PCF, the glorious wartime "party of 75,000 martyrs"?

The truth about Moulin's sympathy for communism has never been established and perhaps it never will be. It was a long affair, the seeds of which were sown on a freezing and bloody night of February 1934, which led to a young man's passionate commitment on behalf of the Spanish Republicans, then to a long and secret collaboration with the Comintern, to a close friendship with the GRU agent André Labarthe and the Comintern director Louis Dolivet. It is probable that Moulin knew—and possible that he helped—the Soviet master-spy Harry Robinson, both before the Nazi-Soviet Pact and after the defeat of France. When Moulin was drawn toward resistance, after being dismissed by the Vichy regime in November 1940, his first move was toward the cell of pro-communist friends which had already been established in Paris—Manhès, Meunier, Chambeiron, Panier and Madame Dangon—a cell which was already, as he must have known, at work supplying information for Robinson to send to Moscow. When Moulin went to London he never mentioned his association with this cell to General de Gaulle, and when he returned to France as de Gaulle's personal representative to the southern resistance he promptly disobeyed his orders by extending his mission into the northern zone and he used the funds and agents sent to him to ensure that, unknown either to London or to southern resistance leaders, he was operating through his pro-communist associates throughout France.

The French state holds an enormous quantity of wartime archives which remain under seal today. Following the normal arrangements the final war records will be opened in 2005, that is if they are judged to be merely of relevance to state security or national defense. But if they contain information of a private nature they will not be opened until the year 2040; if they concern civil servants, they remain closed until 2060; and if they contain medical details they cannot be consulted until 2090. So it could be another ninety years before all the documentary evidence about Jean Moulin becomes available. Lacking that, one is left with probabilities, and where there is no record of what a man really thought one should judge him on his actions. And if one judges Moulin by that criterion one must conclude that Henri Frenay was wrong.

At some point between September 1941 and May 1943, Jean Moulin changed course. Perhaps he had never truly been a citizen of *la patrie des travailleurs.* Whether it was the death of his father, coming so soon after the fall of Pierre Cot, or *Der Pakt,* or his experience in Chartres, or his meeting with Charles de Gaulle, something caused him to lose faith in communism and turned him back to the religion of his childhood, to the Republic and to France. Perhaps that is why he was so distressed by the arrest of Henri Manhès. "*Whatever happens now,*" he said when he heard that news, "*I've had it.*" The key word in that exclamation is "whatever." What can he have meant by that? Given the exhausting preoccupations of daily life in the Resistance in a country occupied by the Gestapo, "whatever" must have meant "whether they catch me or not." But why should Moulin have "had it" if the Gestapo failed to catch him? He had had it because he knew that without Manhès's help, without his indispensable partner in the intricate long-distance deception he had been carrying out, he would no longer be able to deceive the French communists as to what he was really doing. Manhès was the only person, according to Laure Moulin, in whom her brother confided; in other words the only other person capable of playing the double game. Manhès knew everything; he was Moulin's link with the northern resistance, with Soviet intelligence, with the French communists and with the freemasons. After the loss of Manhès there was nothing left for Moulin but to break cover and run. And yet he still managed to deceive the party from 21 March, the date of his return from England, until the afternoon of 27 May when he abruptly overruled the objections of the two party delegates to the inaugural meeting of the National Resistance Council, and so confirmed what he had first signaled on 12 April when he had told the FTP–MOI to "click their heels." On 27 May the communist leaders became certain that Moulin was no longer responding to Moscow. He had become a patriot and a de facto Gaullist. Within four weeks an SS officer had beaten him into a semicoma.

Raymond Aubrac was, and perhaps still is, an admirable communist. After the war, Aubrac became a key member of the international communist movement's secret bureaucracy overseeing national parties in Western Europe. Having been removed from Marseille in 1945 he transferred to Paris, to a post in the ministry of reconstruction. Then in 1948 he set up an import-export business with Eastern Europe which was used to provide secret funds for the French Communist Party. In 1958 he founded the BERIM, an engineering "consultancy" of the sort that is commonly used by French political parties for the covert funding of their activities. As an engineer Aubrac traveled regularly in Africa and Eastern Europe inspecting public works projects; in 1963 he became a senior official of the FAO, the United Nations Food and Agriculture Organization. When Ho Chi Minh came to France in 1946 to negotiate peace in Indo-China, he stayed at the Aubracs' villa outside Paris, and Lucie Aubrac invited "Uncle Ho" to become godfather to her daughter "Babette," and Ho did. In 1943 Aubrac appeared to be a resister, but he was a *communist* resister; the distinction did not become apparent until September 1944, in Marseille. Could Aubrac have betrayed Moulin at Caluire? The question is absurd. Aubrac was a dedicated communist. He would have betrayed anyone the party ordered him to betray for the cause. But there is a serious objection to the suggestion that Aubrac betrayed Caluire, because it would have meant betraying himself. Nevertheless, a number of questions about Aubrac's preparations for Caluire have never been answered.

In the first place Aubrac arrived late for the meeting and we know how this happened. The expected timetable was as follows. At 1:30 "Max" was to meet his secretary, Tony de Graaf. At 1:45 he was to meet Aubrac by the No. 7 bus stop outside Perrache railway station and be taken by him to the rendezvous, which was set for thirty minutes later in Caluire. This timetable would have meant that "Max" and Aubrac would have arrived about seven minutes late for the meeting, which was within the normal margin. Lassagne swore that Aubrac already knew the address in Caluire. Aubrac and "Max" also wanted to meet first in order to discuss tactics since they were entirely in agreement over what was to be done about the replacement of General Delestraint. Aubrac was to go to Paris to become a temporary commander of the Secret Army in the northern zone. Lassagne was to be proposed for the same temporary command in the southern zone. Since *Combat* would never have agreed to two members of *Libération* having this much influence, Lieutenant-Colonel Schwartzfeld, a noncommunist regular soldier and a member of the Secret Army's staff, was to be suggested as a last-minute compromise to replace Lassagne.

What happened in fact is that "Max" never met de Graaf at 1:30. Instead Claude Serreulles turned up at that rendezvous and told de Graaf that he had just lunched with "Max," whom he had met by chance. "Max" would not now be going to meet Aubrac. Instead, Serreulles would do this and would accompany Aubrac to the top of the Croix-Paquet funicular, where "Max" would be waiting. Meanwhile de Graaf would contact Schwartzfeld and ask him if he would agree to become temporary director-general of the Secret Army in the southern zone. If the answer was "yes" de Graaf was to bring the colonel to the top of the same funicular at 2:30.

This change of timetable meant that "Max," Aubrac and now Schwartzfeld would all be at least thirty minutes late for the meeting. De Graaf set off to carry out his instructions and Serreulles set out for Perrache to meet Aubrac. But when Serreulles arrived he found that, contrary to what he had just told de Graaf, "Max" was already there, in conversation with Aubrac. Serreulles was then invited to join the meeting in Caluire and given instructions about how to get to the funicular, a feat of simple navigation which he never achieved.* After his departure "Max" and Aubrac, instead of setting out promptly for the 2:30 rendezvous, embarked on a long conversation outside Perrache, with the result that they did not reach the top of the funicular to meet Serreulles, de Graaf and Schwartzfeld until 2:40. When they got there Schwartzfeld had not arrived, but instead of pressing ahead they waited again, so extending their final late arrival at the doctor's house to forty-five minutes.

The first curiosity about Aubrac's recollection of this sequence of events is that he has always denied that he knew the address he was going to, until Moulin told him on the No. 33 tram, which ran between the top of the funicular and Caluire. But Aubrac knew the house in Caluire very well. He also knew it as one of three addresses potentially available for resistance meetings; the other two were in different districts of Lyon. He would have realized where they were going soon after leaving Perrache and before they reached the foot of the funicular. His insistence on his ignorance of the address suggests that he is reluctant to be identified as someone who knew it. Nonetheless, André Lassagne had a clear recollection that the time of the meeting was discussed with both Aubrac and Aubry, representatives of the two main opposing factions within the MUR, on 19 June, but that only the former was given the address. It would seem then that Aubrac did know the selected address for two days, but has since become anxious to conceal the fact that he had this knowledge.

The second question is, why did Aubrac never query the delay apparently imposed by Moulin? He knew the time Serreulles was given to meet them, he knew they would not make it if they lingered outside Perrache. This was followed by the second lengthy wait for Schwartzfeld. Waiting around usually made resisters nervous. And yet, in his many accounts of the approach to Caluire, Aubrac never mentions that this glaring hitch in the plans was a matter of discussion between him and "Max." If Aubrac never asked "Max" about the delay, was it because it suited his own plans?

But the chief reason for querying Aubrac's account is the strong pre-

---

* Serreulles's account of events is incoherent. (a) He tells de Graaf that he had bumped into "Max," (b) lunched with him, (c) been instructed to replace de Graaf as Aubrac's guide to an unspecified location, (d) which he is *subsequently* told how to reach, and which (e) he fails to find. Initial suspicion against Serreulles was dispelled because he had been parachuted into France only five days earlier and had had no time to be in contact with the Gestapo.

sumption that, before Barbie raided Caluire and arrested Aubrac, he knew who Aubrac was.

The Gestapo had begun to get close to the Lyon resistance in March 1943 with the arrest of a courier who got off a train at the wrong station. This arrest led to the seizure by French police of part of the archives of *Combat* and gave them a mass of detailed information about the organization of the Secret Army. That information was passed to the Gestapo. The discovery of those archives was followed by a wave of arrests in the Lyon region and among the first resisters arrested was "François Vallet," the false identity of Raymond Samuel, whose code name in the Resistance was "Aubrac." Aubrac was arrested with a man called "Fouquet," in reality Maurice Kriegel–"Valrimont," and Serge Asher, known in the Resistance as "Ravanel." Aubrac, Valrimont and Ravanel were arrested together on 13 March. All three men were senior members of *Libération*'s paramilitary section and communist "submarines." They were held in French police custody but, following an agreement known as the Oberg-Bousquet Accord—made between the head of the SS in France and Pierre Laval's police chief—they were sent over to the Gestapo for interrogation. After the war, Klaus Barbie claimed that Aubrac agreed to become an informer shortly after his arrest, an allegation which is not supported in the surviving Gestapo records and which Aubrac has always denied.

In May 1943 Ravanel and Valrimont, together with François Morin–"Forestier," the head of the general staff of the Secret Army and a member of *Combat,* who had also been arrested, made a sensational escape from the Antiquaille hospital to which they had been transferred from St. Paul prison. After the war, Lucie Aubrac wrote a largely fictional account of this event in a Marseille newspaper in which she stated that her husband had been among those liberated from the Antiquaille by a *groupe franc* dressed in German uniforms. Later she gave an entirely different version of Aubrac's liberation, stating that he was actually released after she had called on the French public prosecutor and threatened him with assassination if he did not release her husband at once. In fact, Aubrac *was* released by the French authorities two weeks before the resistance raid on the hospital, and it is not clear why. He may have been released, as his wife claims, after a threat to the public prosecutor, or he may have been released after the intervention of the Vichy intelligence service—with whom he had previously been in contact—or he may have been released for some other reason. Barbie, naturally, claimed that he was released because he had agreed to work for the Gestapo. What is certain is that Aubrac had been interrogated by the Gestapo in Lyon two months before the raid on Caluire, and subsequently released. Not many of his comrades knew this, which made his case rather like that of René Hardy.

The only plausible reason why Aubrac should have agreed to work for the Gestapo without being tortured is that they had identified him as Raymond Samuel and he wished to protect his Jewish family. But Aubrac said he was never identified during his two months of imprisonment; to the French police and to the Gestapo he remained "François Vallet," a dealer in black market sugar. After his release he changed his false identity card and he was arrested at Caluire as "Claude Ermelin." Later, in the Ecole de Santé Militaire, Aubrac said he was confronted with the same Gestapo officer who had interrogated him as "Vallet" and who recognized him. In consequence Aubrac, having been recognized as "Vallet," was forced to agree that he was not "Claude Ermelin" but "Vallet," now known to be *alias* Aubrac, military director of *Libération-Sud*, because the seized archives had been consulted and they had established that "Aubrac" and "Vallet" were the same man. Aubrac later stated that he had *not* been identified as other than "Vallet," then restated that he *had* been recognized as Aubrac. But he always insisted that he had never been recognized as Jewish, or under his real name of Raymond Samuel.

The question as to whether or not Aubrac was ever recognized as Samuel is central to whether or not he agreed to work for the Gestapo. Aubrac said that in the first week following his arrest after Caluire he was repeatedly questioned by Barbie. Barbie would have him handcuffed and would beat him with a truncheon until he fainted. This happened about twenty times. After that he was not questioned any further and, unlike everyone else arrested at Caluire, he was not transferred to Paris, a circumstance which he agrees is difficult to explain. But the interest of Aubrac's case is not what information he may or may not have given *after* Caluire, but what he may have done *before* it. Since Aubrac was a dedicated communist agent, and since there is no question of his having been tortured during his first period of imprisonment, it seems highly unlikely that he would have been acting as a Gestapo informer before Caluire, unless he had been identified as Samuel. And there is one good reason to accept Aubrac's assertion that he was never properly identified. After Caluire, Aubrac was held in Montluc prison until, in October 1943, he became one of the very few resisters to escape from German custody. The circumstances of this escape were so dramatic that they made Raymond and Lucie Aubrac into legends of the Resistance. While Aubrac was being transferred between the prison and Gestapo headquarters the prison van was attacked by Lucie Aubrac and Ravanel's *groupes francs* and the thirteen prisoners inside were liberated. In February 1944 the Aubracs were flown to England and their story was told on the BBC. By that time Aubrac's parents, Albert and Hélène Samuel, had been arrested in Lyon by a joint team of French *miliciens* and the Gestapo.

If Aubrac had been identified as Samuel, and had agreed to work for the Gestapo, he would have been released by Barbie and his parents would have served as hostages; they would have been watched or arrested. When he was reimprisoned, after Caluire, his parents would have been left in peace. Once he escaped they were of course in danger of immediate arrest. If "Aubrac" had been identified as Samuel it is hard to imagine that Lucie Aubrac and the *groupes francs* would have mounted an attempt to free Aubrac without first making sure that his parents were in a secure hiding place well away from Lyon. So, assuming that he would not have abandoned his parents, the most likely conclusion must be that Aubrac was telling the truth. He was never identified as Samuel and was never a Gestapo agent. But if he did not betray Caluire to serve the Gestapo, did he betray it to serve the communists instead? Was he ordered to betray? Something in Raymond Aubrac's behavior before the meeting, his lack of concern about the late arrival, suggests that he was not terribly anxious to get there on time. And something about his behavior afterward, his determination to pin the deed on Hardy, the facility with which, at the height of "the Terror" in Marseille, he forgave Henri Aubry and recruited him to this point of view, suggest that he himself was anxious not to be investigated too closely. Oddly enough, in the BCRA office in London in the weeks immediately after Caluire, the case was called "the Aubrac affair."

Emmanuel D'Astier once described resistance as "a childish and deadly game." Of all the games Moulin was playing the one against the PCF was the most complex. It was a game in which both players had to persuade their opponent that they were secretly on the opposite side. The PCF, bent on establishing its soviets, had to appear patriotic in public while ensuring that the delegate from de Gaulle was following the Moscow line in secret. Moulin had to persuade the party that the insurrection was his true objective and that his Gaullist program was the screen. In this desperate game of double-bluff one of Moulin's tactics was to promote communist "submarines." If he promoted them he obeyed the party and *he knew where they were*. He did this time and again, and Henri Frenay among others could never understand why.

But de Gaulle understood. During his visits to London, Moulin spent many hours talking to de Gaulle in private. Not even Colonel Passy was admitted to these meetings, an exclusion that was highly unusual. It was during those conversations that Moulin persuaded de Gaulle to trust him, no matter how odd his actions seemed. In view of how little de Gaulle knew him and of how little, politically, they had in common this was a colossal risk, but de Gaulle took it. Years later the right-winger Alain Peyrefitte, then a brilliant young minister, asked de Gaulle the usual right-wing question, "Did Jean Moulin help you to contain the communist offensive, or did he on the contrary accentuate it?" And de Gaulle exploded:

> Well, for goodness sake! He contained it! Exactly *because* he had the reputation of being a left-wing prefect, and one close to the communists, exactly *because* he had been in Pierre Cot's *cabinet*, they could not object to him. His mission was to reintegrate the communists in the national community. He was the best for that. He was as straight as a die. A right-wing prefect could never have succeeded in that task.

De Gaulle did not habitually show his feelings but he must have been haunted by Moulin's last messages: "I am a wanted man now . . . send me the personnel I have asked for so many times. . . . Nothing has been done. . . . I beg you, General, do what I have the honor to request . . ." In his last telegram Moulin added that the danger that threatened him was "partly due to the methods favored by certain movements." At the end of his life de Gaulle's delegate was at an extreme point of isolation. He was faced with the German police and the French police, with his numerous enemies within the patriotic resistance, with his rivals in the Gaullist security service and with his former comrades in the PCF. For him it was not a question of who would betray him but of how many of them would do so.

The Gestapo were able to raid the meeting at Caluire because someone had given them part of the address and the time of the meeting. That is shown by the fact that shortly after 2:00 P.M. they were driving around the district looking for "the house of Dr. Dugoujon." They received the information at the last minute; that is shown by the fact that they arrived in insufficient numbers (they had to call for extra cars), with insufficient handcuffs, and without having had the time to stake out the premises as they habitually did in Lyon. Of the five people who arrived at the doctor's house on time, the three who knew the address—Lacaze, Larat and Lassagne—had no reason to betray the meeting. Of the two who did not know the address one, Aubry, may have guessed when he was given his rendezvous. But his only reason to betray a meeting at which he was present would have been if he was already a Gestapo informer. The fact that Aubry was beaten up for two days before he started to talk does not support the idea that he was already a Gestapo informer. Four of the men arrested in the upper room became the immediate victims of an SS *Sonderkommando,* and the fifth was shot and wounded while running away. It seems that the informer was not among them.

Leaving aside Pierre de Bénouville, who was elsewhere and whose curious intervention in the roll-call of Caluire—sending Hardy—if it took place, was superfluous or ineffective, three other men knew the address of Dr. Dugoujon. If the doctor had denounced himself, we can assume that he would have given his new address. That leaves two men who arrived together at a time when the meeting should already have been broken up.

If Dr. Dugoujon had not recently moved, the Gestapo would have arrived just after the meeting started at 2:15 P.M. The *Sonderkommando* would have been raiding an undefended resistance meeting because Moulin, against all the rules of resistance, had refused offers from two separate *groupes francs* to provide an armed guard for a meeting place without a back door. If matters had followed the foreseeable course, and the Gestapo had not taken forty-five minutes to find the right house, Moulin would have arrived at Dr. Dugoujon's to find that the raid was over, or still in progress, that the resisters had been taken away or that the Gestapo were still on the premises. In the latter event Moulin might have been questioned, but he had the perfect explanation. His false identity card stated that he was "Jean Martel, artist from Nice." And he was the only person to arrive for the meeting with an effective cover; a letter in his pocket from a doctor in Nice recommending Jean Martel to the attention of Dr. Dugoujon. The Gestapo could have concluded that he was simply a patient arriving too late to be suspected of attending the resistance meeting. Aubrac and Schwartzfeld, who also arrived late, might well have been questioned. They would have had to think quickly, particularly Aubrac, who was known to the Gestapo.

Two men walk toward the house in the Place Castellane, both are worried. Both suspect the address has been given to the Gestapo. The first man, who has not passed on the address, turns the corner and sees a quiet house where everything is in order. The second man looks at the tranquil scene and realizes something has gone terribly wrong. The second man does not want to go in, but if he says that, the first man will find it suspicious. If the second man walks away just before the house is raided he will become the primary suspect. So the second man has to enter the house, as though everything is in order. Which of the two men is the second man?

There is one character in the story of Caluire whose actions have never attracted attention but whose behavior is inexplicable. Her name is Marguerite Brossier, Dr. Dugoujon's maid. As the two men push open the doctor's gate and walk up the short flight of stone steps to his front door it is still peaceful in the Place Castellane. A simpleton is sitting on one of the benches, sheltered from the light drizzle by the plane trees. There are no cars to be seen. A third man, dressed in a military overcoat and wearing a loden hat in the style of Alsace, is strolling across the square, waiting his turn to go in. In the consulting room the doctor is examining a small boy with a persistent cough. In the waiting room the clock is ticking. The waiting room is nearly full, the doctor does not accord appointments. In the upstairs room, five men who have little to say to each other also sit and wait for a meeting to begin. When the doorbell rings everybody in the house hears it but nobody reacts, except of course Madame Brossier. She opens the door and shows two men into the waiting room on the ground floor. The bell rings again and she admits a third man, wearing a loden hat, and he, too, goes into the waiting room. And that is the puzzle.

The presence of Moulin and his two companions in the first-floor waiting room rather than in the meeting room on the second floor very nearly saved Jean Moulin's life. It has always been explained by the fact that they arrived so late that the doctor's maid did not realize they had come for the meeting. But how can anyone suppose that a man of Moulin's authority, a prefect and the president of the National Resistance Council, would let himself be shown into the wrong room by a muddled receptionist when he was already late for a vital and dangerous meeting? Even Colonel Lacaze, the first to arrive, at his first conspiracy, managed to get himself shown into the right room. Furthermore, Madame Brossier was an intelligent woman, *and she knew that Raymond Aubrac was not a patient.* "Marguerite," as Lucie Aubrac has since volunteered in one of her numerous memoirs, was a friend: "We knew her well." Dr. Dugoujon's regular stand-in, Dr. Fred David, was a cousin of Raymond Aubrac's. If Marguerite Brossier showed Moulin and Aubrac into the waiting room, it must have been because *one of them asked to be taken there.* And Madame Brossier would have been instructed to show Schwartzfeld into the waiting room as well.

In the waiting room the colonel is given the last remaining seat. Has he been ushered to that seat to give him the best chance of making him look like a bona fide patient? Moulin with his letter, Schwartzfeld seated among the bona fide patients, Aubrac with the problems?

There are just a couple of minutes left now for Moulin and Aubrac to work out what is going on. What are they doing in the doctor's waiting room? If neither has betrayed the meeting and they suspect a trap they should get out. They stay. So one of them knows, and the other suspects. They are in a very imprudent position. Anyone could be in this room. In fact one of the female patients is the wife of the president of the local Pétainist *Ligue des Combattants.* She is about to get her bottom kicked by a Gestapo guard after making a furious scene when she is arrested. Let us suppose that Aubrac is the second man. The Gestapo have not arrived, but they might. If they do, the waiting room is his best chance. All he has to do is explain to Moulin why he suddenly asked Marguerite to show them in there. He does not know about Moulin's letter. He is not pleased to find Schwartzfeld has been shown in, too.

Or perhaps Moulin is the second man. The Gestapo have not arrived. When they do he has his letter and he has given the hapless colonel the slight camouflage of the last remaining seat. When, if, the Gestapo arrive Aubrac will have to take his chance. So be it. Aubrac will be ready; he is a "submarine." Moulin knows all the "submarines" in *Libération.* He helped to put them there.

There are only seconds left but the clock in this waiting room ticks slowly. If Moulin and Aubrac had been involved in a joint conspiracy to betray the meeting at Caluire they would never have gone into the house. Seeing the Gestapo had not arrived they would have turned away and told the colonel they did not like the look of it. If neither of them had betrayed it they would not be in the waiting room, they would be upstairs or out and away. They look at each other, standing by the fireplace in the waiting room, the only two people who are standing. They cannot talk; they cannot break the stifling silence of the room. They try to read each other's thoughts. Which of them is the second man? The clock ticks on. No patients are called. Dr. Dugoujon is a very thorough doctor. They are both worried, they are both suspicious, but neither of them leaves. Neither of them leaves because neither can afford to. Neither can make a suspicious move. They look at each other and they realize that it is too late.

Outside the house two black Citroëns draw up silently. Captain Henri Aubry, standing at the first-floor window, shows what André Lassagne later characterized as "his usual lucidity." Aubry describes what he sees. "Cars," he says. "There are two of them," he says. "Black." He does not react.

Postscript

THE IMAGE OF MOULIN betraying Caluire and disposing of the men who wanted to dispose of him is arresting but is not finally supported by the evidence. The *Front National* and the *Cagoule* were the only political organizations known to have been ruthless enough and cynical enough to use the Gestapo against their own opponents inside the Resistance. But if Moulin did not betray the meeting it seems that he knew the meeting had a high chance of being betrayed. The letter from the doctor in Nice, his twice-delayed arrival, his inexplicable presence in the waiting room, even the lack of security guards, all point to the fact that he was expecting trouble and doing his best to avoid or minimize the consequences.

Since, in the case of Caluire, the representative of the *Cagoule* did not succeed in playing an active role, we are left with the communists, and there were many ways in which the communists could have betrayed Jean Moulin. On 5 December 1942 the *Abwehr* in Paris arrested Léopold Trepper while he was sitting in a dentist's chair. Trepper had been appointed by Moscow in 1940 to take command of Soviet intelligence throughout occupied Europe. Trepper's cover had been established while he was working as a contractor for the *Wehrmacht*. Among those under Trepper's command was Harry Robinson. On 21 December 1942 the *Abwehr* arrested Robinson, again in Paris, this time at the Métro Ségur. Trepper, who was not tortured, is known to have talked. Robinson, who was tortured, did not.

Trepper escaped. Robinson was shot. Following his escape Trepper managed to reach a communist safe house near Paris, where he sat it out until
the liberation.

After the war, Trepper said that he believed Jean Moulin had been an
important informant of Harry Robinson's. Was that information passed to
the *Abwehr*? Did Trepper "sell" Moulin as well as betraying his lieutenant,
Robinson? Between December 1942 and June 1943 the German police
would have had plenty of time to track down the ex-prefect turned art
dealer. Yet one of the curious aspects of Caluire is that, although the operation was designed to trap "Max," the Gestapo seem to have had no idea
whom to look for. Barbie had no physical description of his quarry. After
all, only one of the men of Caluire had a scar on his throat, and Barbie
never looked for a scar. It was only after interrogating his other prisoners—
Lassagne, Aubry and Aubrac—that Barbie learned not only which prisoner was "Max" but who "Max" really was.

What is beyond any doubt is that the men controlling the communist
resistance had the strongest possible motives for removing de Gaulle's
representative from the scene and enjoyed every opportunity to do so.
Their only problem was to manage it in such a way that they would not
have to take the blame. This need, to hide the party's responsibility, makes
it less likely that Aubrac was directly involved. The communists had many
ways of feeding information to the Gestapo. Aubrac, "one sucker on one
tentacle of the octopus," could have been sacrificed to the greater good,
his presence at Caluire helping to screen the identity of the informers.

If the heroism of individuals like Jean Moulin was a reality, his canonization formed part of an "official" history that was imposed on a grateful nation after the war and which the French communists and their
supporters donned as a useful fig leaf. Writers of the left forgot their own
wartime opportunism and manned the *épuration* committees run by the
PCF, where they fell on hardcore collaborators like Charles Maurras and
Robert Brasillach, both of whom were sentenced to death. Simone de
Beauvoir forgot the days when she had worked for Vichy's Radio France
and joined the PCF claque which justified Stalin's atrocities one day and
applauded the prosecution of René Hardy the next. The Hardy trial was
one of the most absurd as well as one of the most sinister moments in the
whole process. Absurd because a man was facing the firing squad for supposedly betraying a cause—*la patrie*—that his leading accusers had be-

trayed a thousand times. Sinister because by manipulating the legend of Jean Moulin, the party Moulin had abandoned was able to put him to work after he was dead.

Even today the case against the communists goes by default. Peter Wright's book *Spycatcher* was translated into French, but the fact that Pierre Cot was listed as a Soviet agent in the "Venona" transcripts was omitted from the French edition. And as recently as 1996 Lucie Aubrac, talking on television to an audience of schoolchildren and asked whether she had been a fellow-traveler in the Resistance, was allowed to get away with the reply: "Cocos ou pas, on s'en moquait!" ("Commie or not, we didn't give a damn!")

The moral superiority assumed by the French left paralyzed the postwar right, which in many cases had even more on its conscience, and the right remained powerless to challenge the communist myth until Frenay, listening to Malraux on the steps of the Panthéon, decided to break ranks for the second time in his life and attack a national hero. There was one phrase in Malraux's eulogy—one of the most celebrated phrases, quoted everywhere—that might have been written to taunt Frenay: "He made none of the regiments, but he made the army." For of course it was not Jean Moulin who made the army. The creation of the Secret Army was entirely the work of Captain Henri Frenay.

Frenay was right to challenge the legend, even if he did so on mistaken grounds. For the truth, once faced, is much easier to accept than legends. Jean Moulin *was* a man of the left, but the right did not betray him. After his arrest Moulin disappeared, not in the direction of Moscow but into the interrogation room of an SS *Sonderkommando*. German police documents refer to the fact that Moulin was driven from Lyon to Gestapo headquarters in Paris three days after the other men of Caluire, but in such a desperate state that it was impossible to question him. He had suffered severe head injuries, and the most likely explanation is the one offered by his arresting officer, Klaus Barbie, who said that the political leader of the Resistance had managed to escape the vigilance of his guards for the few seconds necessary to throw himself down the well of the great staircase in the Ecole de Santé Militaire. So, like Pierre Brossolette and Berty Albrecht and so many other heroic French men and women, Jean Moulin ensured his own silence, preferring, in the customary phrase, "to die for France."

Glossary

Resistance networks and movements are indicated by italics.

Abwehr—German military intelligence

Action française—Nationalist and monarchist political movement, noted for anti-Semitism, inspired by writings of Charles Maurras, eventually proscribed by French Catholic Church

AMGOT—Allied Military Government in Occupied Territories

Armée secrète—The Secret Army (underground paramilitary force trained for sabotage and terrorism and held in readiness for the liberation)

BCRA—Bureau central de renseignement et d'action (Gaullist intelligence service based in London; later, the DGSS)

BEF—British Expeditionary Force (small army, nine divisions, deployed to defend France and Belgium in 1939 and evacuated from Dunkirk in June 1940)

BIP—Bureau d'information et de presse (resistance propaganda service)

BOA—Bureau des opérations aériennes (service directing air operations into wartime France)

Bof—Beurre, oeufs, fromage ("Butter, eggs, cheese"; slang term for black marketeers)

Cagoule—"The Hood"—derisive nickname for CSAR (Comité secret d'action révolutionnaire); pro-fascist, terrorist conspiracy, active prewar

Camelots du Roy—Youth section of ACTION FRANÇAISE, noted for its violence

CDLL—Ceux de la Libération (northern center-left network)

CDLR—Ceux de la Résistance (northern center-right network)

CFLN—Comité français de la libération nationale (formed in Algiers, 4 June 1943; forerunner of GPRF)

CGE—Comité général d'études (resistance think-tank that influenced form of postwar constitution)

CGT—Confédération générale du travail (communist-controlled national trade union)

CIC—U.S. Counter Intelligence Corps

CND—Confrérie Notre Dame (right-wing Gaullist resistance network)

CNR—Conseil National de la Résistance (National Resistance Council, established by Jean Moulin in Paris in May 1943)

COMAC—Commission d'action militaire (coordinator of military action)

Combat—Largest resistance group in France (southern zone, multiparty, anticommunist). Organized *l'Armée secrète.*

Comintern—Third Communist International (Moscow-based agency using terrorism, intelligence and propaganda to propagate Soviet communism worldwide)

COPA—Centre d'opérations de parachutage et d'atterrissage (service organizing parachute drops and landings into southern zone)

Corps francs—Resistance shock troops

Croix de Feu—French veterans' movement of 1930s, with secret arsenal

CSAR—See CAGOULE

Débâcle—French military collapse in 1940

Délégation-Générale—De Gaulle's central political resistance directorate in France

Deuxième Bureau—French military intelligence

DF—Défense de la France (northern right-wing, non-Gaullist movement)

Epuration—Purge of French collaborators, 1944–50

Exode—Mass panic and flight from German forces, May–June 1940

Feldgendarmerie—German military police

FFI—Forces françaises de l'intérieur (resistance forces fighting under orders of French army after liberation)

FN—Front National (political arm of the FTP–MOI used by the communists to penetrate and control noncommunist resistance movements)

France d'Abord—Right-wing, resistance network based in Lyon, independent of *Combat*

Franc-Tireur—Center-left, southern resistance group (noncommunist)

Front populaire—Popular front ("anti-fascist" coalition of communist and noncommunist left-wing political parties)

FRS—Forces républicaines de sécurité (ad hoc "police force" responsible for hundreds of atrocities in the Marseille region during *l'épuration*)

FTP–MOI—Francs-tireurs et partisans–Main-d'oeuvre immigrée (armed communist resistance, heavily manned by Jewish and immigrant veterans)

Gauleiter—Ruler, designated by Nazi Party to govern a region of the Third Reich

Gestapo—Geheime Staatspolizei (German state political police; 2,000 approximately)

Gestapo française—French auxiliaries of German police (8,000 approximately)

GFP—Geheime Feldpolizei (German army field police)

GPRF—Gouvernement provisoire de la République française (formed in Algiers, 3 June 1944)

GPU—Soviet secret service (known successively as NKVD, MVD and KGB)

Groupes francs—Armed resistance commandos

GRU—Soviet military intelligence

IS—"Intelligence Service" (French term for British agencies working in France, usually SOE or MI6)

KGB—See GPU

Libération—Leading left-wing southern resistance group (pro-communist). Also known as *Libération-Sud*

Libération-Nord—Northern socialist movement specializing in propaganda

Maquis—Slang name for bands of armed resisters, living rough in remote areas

Maquisard—Member of LE MAQUIS

Milice—French militia (paramilitary, pro-Nazi group formed to fight the Resistance; 5,000 approximately)

MLN—Mouvement de libération nationale (umbrella committee for anti-communist, non-Gaullist resistance, set up in Lyon 1943)

MRP—Mouvement républicain populaire (postwar Christian Democrats, Catholic resisters)

MUR—Mouvements unis de résistance (committee formed in Lyon to coordinate noncommunist, southern resistance groups behind de Gaulle)

NAP—Noyautage des administrations publiques (*Combat* resistance organization infiltrating Vichy civil service)

OCM—Organisation civile et militaire (large, northern right-wing network)

OMS—(Department of International Connections) Security service of the COMINTERN

ORA—Organisation de résistance de l'armée (postarmistice, army resistance)

OSS—Office of Strategic Services (U.S. intelligence, later, the CIA)

PCF—Parti communiste français (French Communist Party)

PPF—Parti populaire français (French pro-Nazi party, popular with ex-communists; total of French Nazi militants 100,000 approximately)

RSHA—Reichssicherheitshauptamt (supreme Reich security service)

RUP—Rassemblement universel pour la paix (communist front "peace" movement active in 1930s)

SD—Sicherheitsdienst (internal security service of the ss)

SFIO—Section française de l'Internationale ouvrière (French Socialist Party)

SIPO-SD—Fusion of Reich security police and the sd (supreme German security service in France)

SOAM—Service des opérations aériennes et maritimes (Resistance parachuting and coastal landing service)

SOE—Special Operations Executive (British secret agency formed in 1940 to subvert Axis forces occupying Europe)

SOL—Service d'ordre légionnaire (lightly armed forerunner of the MILICE)

SS—Schutzstaffel (guard detachment—Hitler's élite, black-shirted security force)

STO—Service du travail obligatoire (deeply unpopular Vichy government scheme to compel Frenchmen of military age to work in Germany)

TR—Travaux ruraux (underground resistance network of army officers)

USC—Unitarian Service Committee (American church "humanitarian" voluntary service; actually communist front)

WT—Wireless transmissions (Resistance secret service radio)

Chronology

1885 Marriage in the Provençal village of St. Andiol of Antonin Moulin, a schoolmaster, and Blanche Pègue, a baker's daughter. They move to the departmental capital of Béziers

1898 "Dreyfus Affair" leads to foundation of the *Ligue des Droits de l'Homme* (Human Rights League). Antonin, who is a Radical Party town councillor, eventually becomes president of the Béziers branch

1899 Birth of Jean Moulin in Béziers, youngest child of Antonin and Blanche. The child grows up with his older brother and sister in a three-room apartment in the center of town

1902 Antonin joins the Béziers lodge of the *Grand Orient*, France's largest masonic order, whose president, Louis Laferre, is a personal friend

1907 Death, aged 19, of Joseph Moulin, older brother of Jean. In Béziers 150,000 peasants from wine-making regions demonstrate on the Champ de Mars beneath the balcony of the family apartment. A riot develops and the local army garrison mutinies in support

1908 Jean Moulin, a model pupil, moves to the Lycée Henri IV, where his father is professor of history. The boy soon becomes idle, dissipated and rebellious

1913 Antonin Moulin, by now a local *notable*, is elected to the *conseil général*, the powerful departmental council of the Hérault

1914 In August, outbreak of the Great War. Thousands of troops on their way to the front march from Marseille through St. Andiol, the Moulins' ancestral village, where they spend each summer

1915   Jean begins to show considerable talent as a cartoon artist

1917   Aged 18, he scrapes a pass in his final school exam, the *baccalauréat.* Through
his father's influence his military service is delayed and he becomes a law
student at Montpellier University

1918   Jean is drafted. In September his regiment is sent to the front. The war ends
before the young men from Montpellier have seen action

1919   He is attached to the office of the prefect of Montpellier and continues his
studies

1921   He becomes a member of the *Jeunesses laïques et républicaines,* the youth
branch of his father's Parti Radical. After graduating Moulin joins the *corps
préfectoral*

1922   In February, thanks to his father's political influence, Jean is promoted. He
leaves his native Provence for good and becomes chief of staff to the prefect of Savoy. In the mountains Moulin starts to paint talented amateur watercolors

1923   Aged 24, he agrees to his parents' suggestion that he become engaged to a
distant cousin. His prospective father-in-law terminates the arrangement
after meeting him

1924   Moulin becomes a freemason and adopts his father's republican and anticlerical politics

1925   Through the influence of the *Grand Orient,* Moulin is promoted to subpre-
fect at Albertville, thereby becoming the youngest subprefect in France.
He forms an important new friendship with an up-and-coming Radical
Party politician, Pierre Cot

1926   In June, he announces his engagement to a girl of his choice, Marguerite
Cerruti, a music student. Despite her wealthy mother's opposition they are
married three months later

1928   Partly owing to the interference of his mother-in-law, Moulin's marriage
fails and the young couple are divorced

1929   Death of the radical freemason Louis Laferre, Antonin Moulin's most influential political friend and protector of Jean Moulin

1930   In January, Moulin is transferred to the subprefecture of Châteaulin in a
neglected part of Brittany, which he describes as "un trou." He meets and
makes friends with the depraved poet and artist Max Jacob, who encour-
ages the young man's artistic interests

1932   In December, Moulin is seconded to Paris to the Quai d'Orsay, where he
takes up a position in Pierre Cot's first ministerial staff. The government
falls after five weeks

1933   Back in Brittany, Moulin becomes increasingly bored and spends as much
time as possible away from his post—painting in Montparnasse or skiing in

the Alps. He quarrels with his prefect and is transferred without promotion. In October, he is rescued by Pierre Cot and becomes chief of staff to the minister for air. Cot's ministry is targeted by the Comintern, whose agents—led by Willi Munzenberg—succeed in establishing close relations with the minister and his entourage

1934　In February, in the wake of the Stavisky affair, violent riots in Paris—mounted by monarchists, *Action française* and the leaders of the extreme-right—bring about the downfall of the Radical government. Moulin takes the lease of a studio in Montparnasse and spends six months leading the life of a bohemian artist. In the autumn he is promoted to the post of secretary-general of the Somme, based in Amiens

1935　In April, the left-wing political leaders Léon Blum, Edouard Daladier and Pierre Cot form an alliance with the communists; birth of the Popular Front. Charles Maurras, the intellectual leader of *Action française,* responds with the proposal that Blum should be "shot in the back"

1936　In May, Blum forms a Popular Front government. Cot and Moulin return to the air ministry. In July, outbreak of the Spanish Civil War. Moulin is placed in charge of a secret government operation to smuggle arms into Spain to assist the Republican cause. He becomes closely associated personally and professionally with a leading Soviet agent, Louis Dolivet

1937　In March, Moulin is nominated to Rodez as prefect of the Aveyron. He is now the youngest prefect in France but for the rest of the year he works at the air ministry organizing a spectacularly unsuccessful series of international air races

1938　In January, Pierre Cot is forced to resign, having been dubbed "the gravedigger of French aviation." Cot and his team are accused by the right of destroying the French air force and placing Soviet and Spanish Republican interests above those of France. Moulin returns to his job as a prefect in Rodez. Death of Antonin Moulin, aged 81

1939　In January, Moulin is transferred to the more influential prefecture of Chartres. In August, Hitler and Stalin form the Nazi-Soviet Pact. The news leads to a massive exodus from the French Communist Party. Pierre Cot is among the supporters of the Soviet Union who denounce the pact. In September, Nazi and Soviet forces invade Poland. France and Britain go to war with Germany.

1940　German forces break through allied lines on 15 May. After days of shelling and bombing, Chartres is taken on 17 June. The prefect, Jean Moulin, is identified as a focus of local resistance. He is arrested and beaten up by German army intelligence officers who order him to sign a statement falsely accusing French troops of atrocities. To avoid giving in, Moulin cuts his throat. He survives and is released. This act of defiance makes him a local hero. Following the armistice France is divided in two, Marshal Pétain's collaborationist government moving to Vichy, which becomes the capital of the unoccupied southern zone. The northern zone, which includes Chartres, is occupied and partly administered by German forces. In November, Moulin is dismissed by the Vichy government. He travels to Paris, where he contacts members of an underground communist cell. Then he crosses the demarcation line between occupied and unoccupied France and returns to his family homes in Montpellier and St. Andiol

1941   In April, Moulin crosses the line illegally in order to see his communist contacts in Paris. In June, he is summoned by the Vichy public prosecutor to Riom, where he gives evidence on behalf of Pierre Cot, who has been charged with treason. In September, after gathering information about a number of resistance movements, Moulin manages to escape from France. In October, he reaches London. He turns down an invitation to work for the British and is recruited by Charles de Gaulle, the leader of the Free French. In his absence the French communists, following Hitler's invasion of the Soviet Union, join the Resistance

1942   In January, Moulin, whose *nom de guerre* is "Corporal Mercier" and whose code name is "Rex," is parachuted back into France as de Gaulle's delegate to the resistance in the unoccupied Vichy zone. He starts to lead a double life, as a retired prefect in St. Andiol and as a secret agent in Lyon. "Rex" quickly finds himself locked in political conflict with the leaders of the three most powerful, noncommunist, southern resistance movements, *Combat, Libération* and *Franc-Tireur.* In November, German forces invade the Vichy zone and occupy the whole of France. The Gestapo arrive in Lyon

1943   In February, Moulin flies to London to seek stronger support in his struggle to impose General de Gaulle's authority over the leaders of the Resistance. De Gaulle decorates him and extends his mission to cover the whole of the country and after only three weeks Moulin, now code-named "Max," returns to France. In May, he succeeds in founding the CNR (*Conseil national de la résistance*), the umbrella group which enlists the national Resistance in the Gaullist movement. The Gestapo carry out a succession of arrests and on 21 June, following fruitless appeals for further help from London, "Max" himself is arrested in Lyon and dies under torture, having refused to talk

1944   6 June, D-Day: allied landings in Normandy. August: liberation of Paris. December: Hardy arrested and charged with treason and the betrayal of Jean Moulin

1947 January: Hardy acquitted. Within weeks new evidence is produced show-
      ing that he has lied. He is promptly rearrested

1950 Retried by a military tribunal, Hardy is acquitted for a second time after
      the judges fail to reach the required majority

1964 De Gaulle transfers the ashes of Jean Moulin to the Panthéon

1977 Henri Frenay publicly accuses Moulin of having been a Soviet agent

1981 At his inauguration as president of the republic, François Mitterrand
      places a rose on Moulin's tomb

1987 Klaus Barbie, former Gestapo officer who arrested Jean Moulin, is kid-
      napped in Bolivia and flown to Lyon, where he is convicted of committing
      crimes against humanity for his role in the wartime deportation of Jews

Notes

Sources for the life of Jean Moulin are few and far between. He was a man with an obsessive habit of secrecy, as first noticed by his sister when he was an eighteen-year-old student in Montpellier. Whether for temperamental, personal or even political reasons, Moulin gave very little away, even to his closest friends. As far as he was concerned the entire world was on a "need to know" basis. The rare exceptions to this rule were all men (invariably communists). This background made Moulin a natural secret agent, but did little to assist his future biographers.

The controversy that broke out in 1977, following the publication of Henri Frenay's denunciation, continues today. The first volume of Daniel Cordier's six-volume defense of his former commander appeared in 1989. But for all its authority, Cordier's work did not win universal approval; he was unable to defend Moulin without denigrating Frenay, who had died in 1988. So, in 1990, Charles Benfredj, Frenay's lawyer, intervened, suggesting that Moulin had not died in Gestapo custody but had been spirited away to Moscow in 1943 and swapped for some distinguished Nazi prisoner of war. More plausibly, Thierry Wolton published documentary evidence that Pierre Cot, Moulin's prewar mentor, had been listed as an anti-Gaullist informant by Soviet intelligence during the Second World War. In 1997 Gerard Chauvy, a historian from Lyon, published a book that cast serious doubt on the credibility of Raymond Aubrac, the communist resistance commander who was arrested at Caluire with Jean Moulin and who has always been one of the most important witnesses to Moulin's fate. Chauvy's arguments were challenged by Francois Delpla, a Paris historian sympathetic to Aubrac. Raymond Aubrac and his wife, Lucie, were subsequently questioned before journalists by a panel of historians, and the late Pierre Cot was investigated and declared to be above suspicion by a special historical commission appointed by Cot's children. This intellectual conflict has come to resemble the original battles fought by the warring factions of the Resistance; the advantage has swayed back and forth, with the tenured historians deploying arguments of higher caliber and the revisionists producing the more interesting documents.

The official sources on Moulin remain, for the most part, closed. In France a mass of documents relating to the administration of his time is not due to be opened for several decades to come. In their wisdom, successive French governments have imposed delays of 30, 60, 100 and 120 years on the accessibility of various categories of official document, and departmental archives for the wartime period are invariably closed. Meanwhile, in Moscow, Nazi and Soviet archives slumber, infrequently released on a selective basis according to secret policy or the private whim of the responsible archivists. Finally, the remaining eyewitnesses of the period have contradicted themselves many times and can no longer be accepted as dependable. The following is a description of the principal sources I have, in these circumstances, relied on.

PART II: WAR

I have relied on standard works by English and American historians such as William Shirer, Alistair Horne, Robert Paxton and others (as well as the French historians Marc Bloch, Pierre Lefranc and Henri Amouroux) to establish the general context of Moulin's responsibilities as prefect of Chartres in 1939 and 1940. In addition, Arthur Koestler's memoir *Scum of the Earth* provides a disturbingly clear view of what it was like to be an illegal *émigré*, and the object of a French prefect's attentions, at this time. The 800 pages of notes in Cordier's second and third volumes provide a wealth of primary sources for the period, including the original text of *Premier Combat*.

PART III: LIFE

The original source for the early life of an obscure national hero is the memoir written by his older sister, Laure, which appeared in 1969 after the ceremony at the Panthéon had transformed her brother into a legend. The simple conviction and trust that inspired Laure Moulin's work stand in strong contrast to everything since published on the subject. A mass of detail about the early life has been added by Daniel Cordier in the first volume of his study; nobody can write about

Moulin today without relying on—or challenging—the work of Cordier. New information about Moulin's personal life has also been provided by Pierre Péan who, after discovering the private papers of the late Antoinette Sachs, published *Vies et morts de Jean Moulin.*

The most important revisionist view of Moulin's political opinions and supposed sympathy for communism is that of Thierry Wolton in *Le Grand Recrutement.* Gerald Howson's painstaking exposé of the Soviet failure to supply the Republican forces with reliable weapons during the Spanish Civil War—*Arms for Spain*—sheds considerable light on Moulin's work with Pierre Cot at the French air ministry during the heyday of the Popular Front.

PART IV: RESISTANCE

For the story of the Resistance I turned first to the work of Henri Amouroux, F.-G. Dreyfus, Roger Faligot and Rémi Kauffer, with Henri Noguerès for detailed support. In *Six Faces of Courage,* M. R. D. Foot provides a moving sketch of Moulin in London in 1941. This essay is, as far as I know, the only previous study of Jean Moulin in English and is largely based on the SOE records of the day. Professor Foot also wrote the official history of the agency which tried unsuccessfully to recruit Moulin for British intelligence in 1941. Information about the early and later life of the SS captain Klaus Barbie was provided by *The Fourth Reich* by Magnus Linklater, Isabel Hilton and Neal Ascherson.

Eyewitness accounts of the "Resistance of the interior" include the memoirs of Henri Frenay, the two Aubracs, Pierre de Bénouville, René Hardy, André Dewavrin and others. Jacques Baumel has recently published an outstanding, but little noticed, example of the genre which is of particular interest since the author worked for so long with Jean Moulin. There are also outstanding biographies of Pierre Brossolette and Berty Albrecht, while F.-G. Dreyfus was unusually candid about the internal divisions of the leadership of the Resistance.

The Battle of Normandy has been memorably described by John Keegan. For the *épuration* I have relied chiefly on Bourdrel and Novick, the former in particular providing detailed information about events in the south around Marseille and St. Andiol.

PART V: RESURRECTION

As French historiography edges cautiously toward a less docile examination of the activities of the PCF before, during and after the Second World War, the pioneering work of Annie Kriegel, François Furet and Stéphane Courtois assumes its true importance. Meanwhile, for those who cannot wait, there is the distressingly high-spirited and irreverent study by Stephen Koch, *Stalin, Willi Munzenberg and the Seduction of the Intellectuals.*

Inspired by the skepticism of Frenay, three writers hostile to the received version—Benfredj, Baynac and Chauvy—have reexamined the question of Caluire. They have been answered by Delpla and, of course, by Cordier, not as part of his six-volume series but in a separate, and seventh, volume of 1,000 pages entitled *La République des catacombes.* De Gaulle's private comments have been recorded by Guy and Peyrefitte. Among those who have influenced my view of the postwar PCF are Jean-Jacques Becker, Karel Bartosek, Antony Beevor and Artemis Cooper.

Two of those directly involved in the preparation of the fatal meeting at Caluire are happily still alive sixty-seven years later—Raymond Aubrac and Pierre de Bénouville. Like several others, I suspect that these two witnesses hold the key to the mystery of Caluire, and—like many others, including Daniel Cordier—I am convinced that both have concealed part of the truth. History and heroism make an ill-assorted couple. Both of these *résistants,* in their old age, have been fiercely criticized, and will be criticized more fiercely in years to come. It is one of the unforeseeable and unjust consequences of the exceptional courage they showed, in defense of their mutually hostile beliefs, at the time of trial.

Select Bibliography

The place of publication of the French titles listed below is Paris, and of the English titles London, unless otherwise indicated

Albrecht, Mireille, *Berty* (1986)

Alleg, Henri, *La Question* (1958)

Amoretti, Henri, *Lyon capitale: 1940–44* (1964)

Amouroux, Henri, *La Vie des Français sous l'Occupation* (1961)

———, *Les Règlements de comptes* (1991)

Andrew, C., and V. Mitrokhin, *The Mitrokhin Archive* (Allen Lane, 1999)

Aubrac, Lucie, *Ils partiront dans l'ivresse* (1984)

Aubrac, Raymond, *Où la mémoire s'attarde* (1996)

Aulas, Bernard, *Vie et mort des Lyonnais en guerre: 1939–45* (Roanne, 1974)

Azéma, Jean-Pierre, *1940: L'année terrible* (1990)

Bartosek, Karel, *Les Aveux des archives: Prague–Paris–Prague 1948–68* (1996)

Baumel, Jacques, *Résister* (1999)

Baynac, Jacques, *Les Secrets de l'affaire Jean Moulin* (1998)

Beauvoir, Simone de, *Journal de guerre, Dec. 1939–Jan. 1941* (1990)

Beevor, Antony, and Artemis Cooper, *Paris After the Liberation* (Hamish Hamilton, 1994)

Benfredj, Charles, *L'Affaire Jean Moulin* (1990)

Bénouville, Guillain de, *Sacrifice du matin* (1970)

Bernstein, S., R. Frank, S. Jansen, N. Werth, *Rapport de la commission d'historiens con-*

stituée pour examiner la nature des relations de Pierre Cot avec les autorités soviétiques
(B&Cie, 1995)

Birnbaum, Pierre, *Le Moment antisémite* (1998)

Bloch, Marc, *L'Etrange défaite* (1946)

Bourdrel, Philippe, *L'Épuration sauvage: 1944–45,* Vols. I and II (1991)

Bredin, Jean-Denis, *L'Affaire* (1983)

Brooks, Howard, *Prisoner of Hope* (New York, 1942)

Brossat, Alain, *Libération, fête folle* (1994)

————, *Les Tondues* (1992)

Broué, Pierre, and Raymond Vacheron, *Meurtres au maquis* (1997)

Brown, Anthony Cave, *La Guerre secrète,* Vols. I–II (1981)

————, *Philby père et fils* (1997)

Calef, Henri, *Jean Moulin: une vie* (1980)

Chauvy, Gérard, *Aubrac: Lyon 1944* (1997)

————, *Lyon: les années bleues* (1987)

Cobb, Richard, *French and Germans: Germans and French* (New York, 1983)

Cocteau, Jean, *Journal 1942–45* (1956)

Cointet, Michèle, *Vichy capitale: 1940–44* (1993)

————, *L'Eglise sous Vichy* (1998)

Cookridge, E. H., *Inside the SOE* (Arthur Barker, 1966)

Cordier, Daniel, *Jean Moulin: l'inconnu du Panthéon,* Vols. I–III (1989–93)

————, *La République des catacombes* (1999)

Courtois, S., et al., *Le Livre noir du communisme* (1997)

Delperrié de Bayac, Jacques, *Histoire de la milice* (1969)

Delpla, François, *Aubrac: les faits et la calomnie* (1997)

Dreyfus, François-Georges, *Histoire de la Résistance* (1996)

Dreyfus, Paul, *Histoires extraordinaires de la Résistance* (1977)

Drieu la Rochelle, Pierre, *Journal 1939–1945* (1992)

Duras, Marguerite, *La Douleur* (1985)

Elgey, Georgette, *La Fenêtre ouverte* (1973)

Faligot, Roger, and Rémi Kauffer, *As-tu vu Cremet?* (1991)

————, *Les Résistants* (1989)

Foot, M. R. D., *Six Faces of Courage* (Eyre Methuen, 1978)

————, *SOE, An Outline History, 1940–46* (Pimlico, 1999)

————, *SOE in France* (HMSO, 1966)

Franco-British Studies, Nos. 2, 7, 22 (Journal of the British Institute in Paris, 1986–96)

Fraser, Ronald, *Blood of Spain* (Allen Lane, 1979)

Frenay, Henri, *La Nuit finira* (1973)

————, *L'Enigme Jean Moulin* (1977, 1990)

Furet, François, *Le Passé d'une illusion* (1995)

Galtier-Boissière, Jean, *Mémoires d'un Parisien* (1960–63)

Gaulle, Charles de, *Mémoires de guerre*, Vols. I–III (1954)

Girardet, Raoul, *La Societé militaire de 1815 à nos jours* (1998)

Green, Julien, *La Fin d'un monde: juin 1940* (1992)

Groussard, Georges, *Services secrets: 1940–45* (1964)

Grove, Peter, *Gentleman Spy: The Life of Allen Dulles* (André Deutsch, 1995)

Guy, Claude, *En écoutant de Gaulle* (1996)

Hardy, René, *Derniers mots* (1984)

Helias, Pierre Jakez, *Le Piéton de Quimper* (1994)

Horne, Alistair, *To Lose a Battle: France 1940* (Macmillan, 1969)

Howson, Gerald, *Arms for Spain* (John Murray, 1998)

Huguenin, François, *A l'école de l'Action française* (1998)

Jacob, Max, *Lettres à Jean Cocteau* (1949)

Joseph, Gilbert, *Une si douce Occupation* (1991)

Judt, Tony, *Un passé imparfait: les intellectuels en France 1944–56* (1992)

Junger, Ernst, *Journal parisien* (1980)

Keegan, John, *Six Armies in Normandy* (Jonathan Cape, 1979)

Koch, Stephen, *Stalin, Willi Munzenberg and the Seduction of the Intellectuals* (Harper-Collins, 1995)

Koestler, Arthur, *Scum of the Earth* (Jonathan Cape, 1941)

————, *Spanish Testament* (Left Book Club, 1937)

Kriegel, Annie, and Courtois, Stéphane, *Eugen Fried* (1996)

Lacouture, Jean, *De Gaulle: le rebelle*, Vol. I (1984)

Lafont, Max, *L'Extermination douce* (1987)

Lefébure, Antoine, *Les Conversations secrètes des Français sous l'Occupation* (1993)

Lefranc, Pierre, *La France dans la guerre: 1940–45* (1990)

Levy, Jean-Pierre, *Mémoires d'un franc-tireur: 1940–44* (1998)

L'Histoire (*Paris, numero spécial, juillet—août 1998*), "Le Siècle communiste"

Libération (*Paris, 9 juillet 1997*), "Les Aubracs et les historiens"

Linklater, Magnus, et al., *The Fourth Reich* (Hodder and Stoughton, 1984)

Lugand, J., ed., *Dessins et aquarelles de Jean Moulin* (Béziers, 1993)

Manson, J., ed., *Leçons de ténèbres: résistants et déportés* (1995)

Marion, Georges, *Gaston Deferre* (1989)

Marrus, M. R., and R. O. Paxton, *Vichy France and the Jews* (New York, 1981)

Melton, H. Keith, *The Ultimate Spy* (Dorling Kindersley, 1996)

Modinc, Youri, *Mes camarades de Cambridge* (1994)

Morgan, Ted, *An Uncertain Hour: Lyon 1940–45* (Bodley Head, 1990)

Moulin, Jean, *Premier Combat* (1946)

Moulin, Laure, *Jean Moulin* (1969, 1982)

Napo, Félix, *1907: la révolte des vignerons* (Toulouse, 1971)

Nevière, Jean-Eli, *Les Nazis et nous* (Marseille, 1989)

Nicolson, Harold, *Diaries and Letters: 1930–1964* (Weidenfeld & Nicolson, 1980)

Noguères, Henri, *Histoire de la Résistance en France 1940–45,* Vols. I–III (1967)

Novick, Peter, *L'Epuration française: 1944–49* (1985)

Ory, Pascal, *Les Collaborateurs: 1940–45* (1976)

Passy, Colonel (André Dewavrin), *Souvenirs,* Vols. I–II (1947)

Péan, Pierre, *La Diabolique de Caluire* (1999)

————, *Le Mystérieux Dr. Martin* (1993)

————, *Vies et morts de Jean Moulin* (1998)

Perrault, Gilles, *Paris sous l'Occupation* (1987)

————, *Les Jardins de l'observatoire* (1995)

Peters, Edward, *Torture* (Basil Blackwell, 1985)

Peyrefitte, Alain, *C'était de Gaulle* (1994)

Piketty, Guillaume, *Pierre Brossolette* (1998)

Pourcher, Yves, *Les Jours de guerre* (1994)

Rajsfus, Maurice, *Les Français de la débâcle* (1997)

Ravanel, Serge, *L'Esprit de résistance* (1995)

Rigoulet, P., and I. Yannakakis, *Un pavé dans l'histoire* (1998)

Ruby, Marcel, *La Contre-Résistance à Lyon* (1981)

Shirer, William, *The Rise and Fall of the Third Reich,* Vol. II (New York, 1959)

Sirinelli, J.-F., ed., *Dictionnaire historique de la vie politique française au XXe siècle* (1995)

Soudoplatov, Pavel, *Missions spéciales* (1984)

Tante Marie: la véritable cuisine de famille (1986)

Théolleyre, J.-M., *Procès d'après guerre* (1985)

Trepper, Léopold, *Le Grand jeu* (1980)

Varaut, Jean-Marc, *Le Procès Pétain* (1995)

Vercors, *Le Silence de la mer* (1942)

Verrier, Anthony, *Assassination in Algiers* (New York, 1990)

Vidal-Naquet, Pierre, *Le Trait empoisonné* (1993)

Werth, Léon, *Déposition: journal 1940–44* (1992)

————, *33 Jours* (1992)

West, Nigel, *Secret War: The Story of SOE* (Hodder & Stoughton, 1992)

Wievioka, Annette, *Ils étaient juifs, résistants, communistes* (1986)

Williams, Charles, *The Last Great Frenchman* (Little, Brown, 1993)

Wolton, Thierry, *Le Grand recrutement* (1993)

————, *L'Histoire interdite* (1998)

Wright, Peter, *Spycatcher* (Viking, 1987)

Zamponi, Bouveret, and Allary Zamponi, *Jean Moulin: mémoires d'un homme sans voix* (1999)

Index

Abetz, Otto, 158
Abwehr (German military intelligence), 50, 165
Action française, L' (newspaper), 105, 107, 111
Action française, L' (party), 12, 49–50, 88, 101, 102, 105, 111, 241–2
affaire des fiches (1904), 75
Aimée, Sister (of Chartres), 39
Aix-en-Provence, 212
"Ajax" (police resistance network), 191
Albertville, 90, 91, 95–6
Albrecht, Berty, 48, 156, 191, 245, 259
Alexis (of Marseille Docks and Warehouse Board), 214
Algeria: French torture in, 13–14
Alleg, Henri: *The Question,* 13–14
Allied Military Government in Occupied Territory (AMGOT), 186, 208
Alsace, 39, 73, 74, 88
AMGOT, *see* Allied Military Government in Occupied Territory
Amiens, 109–11
Anciens Combattants (group), 102
André, Francis, 166
Anglo-French alliance, 123
Antiquaille hospital, 251
Aragon, Louis, 117 and *n*
Armored Division, 1st (French), 203

Armored Division, 2nd (French), 203, 207
Army Corps, 1st (French), 203
Aron, Raymond, 140
Aschberg, Olaf, 115–18
Asher, Serge, *see* Ravanel, Serge
Astier de la Vigerie, Emmanuel d': in Resistance, 49–50, 146; de Gaulle appoints minister of interior in Algiers, 49; conflict with JM, 149; JM meets, 151–2; character, 151*n;* accuses Frenay of betrayal, 156; Frenay seeks cooperation of, 159, 160; mission to London, 159–60; and coordinating committee, 167; and recruitment to Resistance, 169; opposes JM's status in CNR, 176–7, 188; refuses cooperation with JM, 178; as provisional minister of interior, 211; infiltrates MLN, 220; Aubrac joins, 246; on resistance as game, 253
Aubrac, Lucie, 49, 155, 195, 221, 228 and *n,* 230, 246–7, 248, 251–3, 257, 261
Aubrac, Raymond (i.e., Raymond Samuel; "François Vallet"): at Caluire meeting, 5, 221, 230–1, 235, 240, 246, 249–50, 252–3, 256–7; arrested and interrogated, 7, 178, 190, 196, 238, 245, 251–2, 260; in Resistance, 49; and JM's mission to France, 151; JM meets, 153; in post-

Aubrac, Raymond (*cont'd*)
  Liberation Marseille, 209–17; identity,
  216*n*, 240, 252; and JM's disappearance,
  220; opposes Frenay, 224; and arrest of
  Delestraint, 227; at Hardy trial, 230–1;
  protects Aubry after Liberation, 241;
  background and career, 246, 248; and
  JM's attitude to Communist Party, 246;
  commitment to communism, 248, 252;
  temporary command in northern zone,
  249; denies being informer, 251;
  released by Germans, 251–2; escape
  from Montluc, 252; accuses Hardy of
  betrayal, 253
Aubry, Henri Avricourt ("Thomas"): at
  Caluire meeting, 4, 235, 237, 250, 255,
  258; arrested, interrogated and beaten,
  7, 196, 240–1, 255, 260; and Caluire
  betrayal enquiries, 238–40, 243; followed
  by Barbie, 239–40; identifies JM to
  Gestapo, 240; testifies against Hardy,
  241, 244, 245; Aubrac wins over, 253
Auran, Jeannette, 89
Austria: Germany invades, 123
Autun, near Dijon, 203
Aveyron, 119
Avignon, 212

Baldwin, Stanley, 113
Barbie, Klaus: in raid on Caluire meeting,
  5, 229, 231, 239, 240; conducts
  interrogations, 6–7; orders beating of
  JM, 8; heads Lyon KdS section, 164–6,
  190; raids Frenay address, 191; works for
  and protected by OSS, 225–6; arrests
  and exploits Hardy, 227, 233, 240, 244;
  and Hardy's escape at Caluire, 229–31;
  watches Baumel, 231; claims Aubrac
  agrees to be informer, 251; and arrest of
  Aubrac's parents, 253; unaware of JM's
  identity, 260; on JM's end, 260
Bargemon, near Fréjus, 153
Basque Republicans, 115
Bastien, Lydie, 195, 227, 233
Baumel, Jacques ("Jacques Brémond";
  "Rossini"): recruited and trained in
  Resistance, 147–8; on pressures of
  resistance life, 161–2, 227; on conditions
  in Lyon, 165; organizes MUR, 167; on
  JM as art dealer, 180; examines Hardy
  trial records, 228; not betrayed by
  Hardy, 231; security routines, 236–7; on
  Aubry, 238; avoids Barbie, 239–40
Baynac, Jacques, 228, 240; *Les Secrets de
  l'affaire Jean Moulin*, 154
BCRA, *see Bureau central de renseignement et
  d'action*
Beauvallon, near St. Tropez, 61
Beauvoir, Simone de, 23, 42, 260
BEF, *see* British Expeditionary Force
Belgium: invaded (1940), 21–2
Bénouville, Pierre de: favors direct
  action, 107; supports Frenay in *Combat*,
  178; represents right groups, 188;
  defends Hardy, 223, 226, 227, 243–4;
  urges "reprisals," 224; de Gaulle
  promotes to General of the Resistance,
  234; and Caluire meeting, 235, 238–9,
  255; background, 241–2; knowledge of
  JM, 241; and *Cagoule*, 242; in National
  Assembly, 243; suspects JM of
  promoting communist cause, 244, 246;
  cleared of betraying Caluire, 245
Berlin, Sir Isaiah, 10
Bernard, Marcel, 234
Bertaux, Pierre, 208–9
Besnard, Pierre, 20, 26, 34
Beuve-Mery, Hubert, 14
Béziers, 70, 71, 73–7, 81–3
Bidault, Georges, 149–50, 155, 170, 185, 219
Bingen, Jacques, 197
BIP, *see Bureau d'information et de presse*
Bismarck, Prince Otto von, 72
Blois, 29
Blum, Léon, 110–13 and *n*, 114, 117, 242
Boemelburg, Major Karl, 8, 163, 193
Bollaert, Emile, 197
Bonneval, 19
Bossé, Lieut., 223
Bouchinet-Serreulles, Claude, *see*
  Serreulles, Claude
Boullen, Jane, 61
Bourdet, Claude, 223, 239, 244
Bournemouth, 132
Brasillach, Robert, 260
Brecher, Ludwig, *see* Dolivet, Louis

Britain: and Spanish Civil War, 113; alliance with France, 123; Vichy hostility to, 36; Hitler plans invasion of, 40, 59–60; despised by defeated French, 42; distrust of Resistance, 150; and funding of de Gaulle, 169

British Broadcasting Corporation (BBC): broadcasts to France, 40, 41, 48, 54, 135

British Expeditionary Force (1939–40), 21–2

Brittany, 96–8

Bron (Lyon): Vinatier mental hospital, 42

Brooks, Howard Lee, 63–4

Brossière, Marguerite, 5, 235, 256–7

Brossolette, Pierre: in *Confrérie Notre Dame*, 50; in London, 140; capture and suicide, 161, 162, 198, 261; accompanies Passy to France, 171–3; qualities and career, 171–3; differences with JM over organization of Resistance, 173–4, 176, 180–2, 187–8; disagreement with Manhès, 180; told of Manhès's arrest, 180–1; recommends communists follow Delestraint, 183; and first meeting of CNR, 185; enemies within Resistance, 188

Buchenwald, 180 and *n*

Buchholz, Mathieu, 208

Buckmaster, Maurice, 132

Bureau d'information et de presse (BIP), 150, 155, 170

Bureau central de renseignement et d'action (BCRA), 130, 134, 138, 156, 170–2, 177, 188, 190, 234–5

Cagoule, la (group: *Comité secret d'action révolutionnaire*, CSAR), 107, 134–6, 139, 157–8, 178, 242, 245, 259

Caillaux, Henrietta and Joseph, 80

Caluire (Lyon): resistance meeting in, 3–6, 193, 221, 235–7, 249–50, 255–6; arrests at, 5–8, 194, 196, 231–2; and betrayal enquiries, 223–4, 228–31, 237–43, 249–61

Camelots du Roy, 101–2, 105, 107, 111, 202

Camus, Albert, 227

Capa, Robert, 201–2

Carte (resistance network), 242

Castellane, Ernestine de (Mme. Fouché), 109

Cavaillon, 213–14

Cecil, Lord Robert, 116

Centre d'opérations de parachutage et d'atterrissage (COPA), 190

Cercle des Nations (club), 118

Cerruti, Madame (Marguerite's mother), 92, 94

Cerruti, Marguerite: engagement and marriage to JM, 91–4; appearance, 94; leaves JM, 94; on JM in wartime Paris, 56

Ceux de la Libération (movement), 55, 154

Ceux de la Résistance (movement), 51, 55, 154

CFLN, *see Comité français de libération national*

CGE, *see Comité général d'études*

CGT, *see Confédération générale du travail*

Chadel (secretary-general in Chartres), 37

Chambeiron, Robert: pro-communist sympathies, 116, 234, 247; and Lecompte-Boinet, 51; forms *Frédéric* group with Meunier, 55; and Nazi-Soviet Pact, 55; JM meets in Paris, 62; liaises between JM and Communist Party, 171; and arrest of Manhès, 180; at JM-Brossolette confrontation, 181–2; as co-secretary of CNR, 185; in JM's entourage, 188–9; JM's sister meets in Paris, 194; helps Antoinette Sachs with enquiry into JM's fate, 222

Chamberlain, Neville, 113, 120, 124–6

Chambéry (Savoy), 88, 89, 92, 94–5, 98

Chartres: surrenders to Germans, 19–21, 25–7, 28–30, 32–3; JM's prefecture in, 123–4; and French refugees (*l'exode*), 22–3; evacuated, 23–5, 28–9, 31, 32, 33; machine-gunned, 23; JM's administration in, 24–5, 32–3; looting in, 25–7, 32; JM mistreated by Germans in, 27–30, 32, 135; cathedral stained glass removed, 33–4; priests and nuns in, 33–4; under German administration, 34; returns to normal, 37; at Liberation (1944), 202

Châteaulin (Brittany), 96–8
Chatan, Paul, 121
Chautemps, Camille, 90, 105
Chemin des Dames, battle of (1917), 82
Chevance-Bertin, Maurice, 161
Choltitz, General Dietrich von, 218
Churchill, (Sir) Winston S.: recognizes de
    Gaulle as Free French leader, 41;
    French communists' view of, 46; poor
    relations with de Gaulle, 130; forbids
    de Gaulle's flight to Algiers, 176; visits
    Paris (Nov. 1944), 218
"Claudius," *see* Petit, Eugène
Clemenceau, Georges, 77
CNR, *see Conseil national de la résistance*
coordinating committee (resistance), 167
Cockburn, Claud, 135
"Coco, Major," 213
COMAC, *see Commission d'action militaire*
Combat (earlier *Mouvement de Libération
    Nationale;* resistance group):
    representatives at Caluire meeting, 4,
    234–5, 238, 243, 249; Frenay runs, 45, 50,
    159, 167, 178–9; role, 45, 50, 234;
    Lecompte-Boinet joins, 51; Pastor
    Brooks contacts, 64; Menthon and, 133;
    Frenay rejects U.S. funding of, 145;
    infiltrated by communists, 146; Baumel
    serves with, 147, 167; JM claims to be
    disloyal to de Gaulle, 155; contacts
    Giraud, 158; permanent recruits to, 159;
    courier arrested, 166; strength, 167;
    Bénouville in, 178, 238, 242; trusts
    Hardy, 195; represented in de Gaulle's
    first provisional government, 220;
    Copeau plots to oust Frenay from,
    224–5; and prosecution of Hardy,
    226–7; Aubry in, 238–40; archives, 246,
    251–2; suspected of betraying JM, 247
Combat (newspaper), 158
Comintern (3rd Communist
    International): in France, 47, 59, 102–3,
    113, 115–17, 122, 123; JM's association
    with, 116–17, 246; in USA, 122;
    denounces Nazi-Soviet Pact, 55; and
    Cot, 135
Comité français de libération national
    (CFLN), 208

Comité général d'études (CGE), 151
Comité secret d'action révolutionnaire
    (CSAR), *see Cagoule, la*
Commission d'action militaire (COMAC),
    196, 197
Commune (Paris, 1871), 106
Communist Party of France (PCF): in
    resistance movement, 4, 46, 49, 224;
    and funeral of Jaurès, 12; activities,
    102–4; and 1934 riots, 106–7; and
    Popular Front, 110–11; and RUP, 116;
    support for Spanish International
    Brigade, 117; desertions after Nazi-
    Soviet Pact, 124; repressed by
    government, 38, 125; remains proscribed
    under Germans, 46; wartime party
    line, 46–7; assassinations of German
    soldiers, 47, 183; denounces de Gaulle
    and Free French, 145; disruptive role in
    Resistance, 145–47, 225; mobilization,
    145; merges political and military
    activities, 150; and end of Nazi-Soviet
    Pact, 157; dedicated resisters in, 161–2;
    JM's relations with, 169–71, 188–9, 246,
    253–4; and first meeting of CNR, 185–6;
    trusts Manhès, 189; tight security in,
    190; goals, 196; infiltrates Resistance
    leadership, 197–8; benefits from
    Resistance arrests, 198; at Liberation,
    202–3, 206; and *l'épuration*, 207–8, 209–10,
    212–13, 260; in insurrection (1944), 209,
    217; self-promotion as party of
    resistance, 218–20; attacks de Gaulle,
    218; election success (1945), 219; and
    legend of JM, 222; and Hardy trials,
    223–4, 230–1; seeks control of Secret
    Army, 244; believes JM's defection
    from communist cause, 248; and
    Caluire betrayal, 259–60; guilt
    overlooked, 261
Compagnie républicaine de sécurité (CRS), 216
Confédération générale du travail (CGT),
    100, 219
Confrérie Notre Dame (Confraternity of
    Our Lady), 50, 148, 170
Conseil national de la résistance (CNR;
    National Resistance Council): formed,
    176, 183; JM presides at, 176–7, 196;

amalgamated with MUR, 178; enlarged,
184; first meeting, 184–5; recognizes de
Gaulle, 184–5; representatives and
composition, 185; and arrested groups,
190; communists in, 196–8, 248; and first
provisional government, 218
COPA, *see Centre d'opérations de parachutage
et de'atterrissage*
Copeau, Pascal, 170, 224
Corbière, Tristan, 109
Cordier, Daniel, 53, 62, 69, 81, 84, 94, 99,
125, 130, 137, 155, 183, 187–8, 228
Cot, Néna (Pierre's wife), 61, 121
Cot, Pierre: appoints JM *chef de cabinet,*
95–6, 98, 100; political views, 95; wins
Chambéry seat (1928), 95; visits USSR,
100; targeted by Comintern, 103; skiing,
105; and Stavisky scandal, 105; and 1934
unrest, 106–7; advises Daladier to
resign, 108; at Evian, 108; supports
Popular Front, 110; resumes Air
Ministry post, 111; plans modern air
force, 112; supports Franco-Soviet
alliance, 112; and French policy on
Spain, 113; and Gamelin, 114; as
president of RUP, 116; cabinet
infiltrated by Soviet agents, 116, 122–3;
has JM seconded back to Paris from
Aveyron, 119; and international air
races, 120; resigns, 120; solidarity with
striking workers, 120; fall, disgrace and
move to USA, 122, 184, 247; and supply
of aircraft to Spain, 122; denounces
Nazi-Soviet Pact, 55, 124; JM joins for
Mediterranean cruise, 124; JM removes
files in Paris (1940), 22; employs
Marcelle Dangon as secretary, 46; in
USA, 54, 63, 130; correspondence with
JM, 61, 131; sends dollars to JM, 61; tried
for treason, 63; JM writes to from
Lisbon, 130; and JM's decision to go
to England, 131; connections with
Comintern, 135; mistrusts de Gaulle,
138; JM conceals membership of staff,
141; advises U.S. government, 158; votes
to remove presidential right of pardon
from de Gaulle, 219; helps with
investigation into JM's disappearance,

222; pro-communist sympathies, 233;
name omitted from French edition of
Spycatcher, 261
Couteaux, M. (president of Marseille
court), 212, 215
Cremet, Jean, 154
Cristofol, Jean, 219
Croix de Feu (group), 102
CSAR, *see Comité secret d'action
révolutionnaire*
Curie, Marie, 12
Cusin, Gaston, 54–5, 110, 111–16, 209, 222
Cussonac, René, 7

D-Day (Normandy, 1944), 202
Daladier, Edouard, 96, 105–6, 107–8, 110,
114, 123–6
Dangon, Georges, 46
Dangon, Marcelle, 46, 54–5, 61, 138, 171,
247
Daniélou, Charles, 98
Darlan, Admiral Jean, 54
Darnand, Joseph, 157
Daudet, Alphonse, 71, 144
Daudet, Léon, 105
David, Dr. Fred, 257
Défense de la France (group), 51
Deferre, Gaston, 211, 240
Degliame, Marcel, 146, 197, 224
Dejussieu, General Pierre, 197
Delaporte, Canon (of Chartres), 33–4
Délégation-Générale, 197
Delestraint, General Charles: as head of
Secret Army, 168–9, 174, 177, 178, 183, 238;
pursued and arrested, 191–3, 195–6, 221,
225–6, 231, 238, 249; deported and
executed, 192*n;* Aubry and, 240;
Bénouville and, 244
Delettraz, Edmée, 191–2, 221, 223, 228, 231,
242, 245
Delpla, François, 239
Desmazes, General Marie-Alphonse-
René-Adrien, 240
Deville, General Louis-Georges, 85
Dewavrin, André ("Colonel Passy"): sees
JM in London, 134–5, 140–1, 143;
receives reports from JM, 155; and
Frenay, 159; letter from Brossolette, 161;

Dewavrin, André (*cont'd*)
mission in occupied France, 171, 173–4, 180; on Yeo-Thomas, 171; discovers JM's operations in north, 173–4; relations with Brossolette, 173–4; on JM's award of honor, 175; criticizes JM, 177, 188; investigates Manhès, 180; JM confronts in Paris, 180–2; defends Hardy at trial, 226; on sending JM to France, 234
Digne, 212
Dolivet, Louis (i.e., Ludwig Brecher), 54–5, 58–9, 63, 113, 115–18, 247
Dolto, Françoise, 45
Doriot, Jacques, 216
Dormoy, Marx, 137
Dreux, 31, 37, 125
Dreyfus, Alfred: affair of, 72–3, 75, 101–2
Dreyfus, François-Georges: *Histoire de la Résistance,* 45
Duclos, Jacques, 221
Dugoujon, Dr. Frédéric, 3–8, 192, 220, 231, 235–7, 239, 255, 257–8
Dulles, Allen, 145–6, 158, 178, 242
Dumas, Roland, 207
Dunkirk evacuation (1940), 22, 42*n*
Durandy, Paul, 216

Ebmeir, Major, 38–9, 53
Echo de Paris, L' (newspaper), 114
Eden, Anthony (*later* 1st Earl of Avon), 218
Eisenhower, General Dwight D., 203
épuration, l', 201–2, 204–16, 218–20, 261
Evian, 110
exode, l' (of French refugees, 1940), 22

Falange (Spain), 111
Falkenstein (Lyon black marketeer), 166
Farge, Yves, 146, 170, 209
Farrel, Victor, 190–1
Fascism, 111
Fashoda incident (1898), 73
Fassin, Raymond, 144–5, 149, 236
Faure, François, 170–1, 173
Fayet (*le Manchot*), 214
Fédération des Contribuables (group), 102
FFI, *see Forces françaises de l'intérieur*
Field, Noel, 58–60, 116, 158, 178

Figaro, Le (newspaper): editor shot (1914), 80
Fighting French, *see* Free French
Filliol, Jean, 242
First World War: outbreak and conduct of, 80; ends, 83–4
Foch, Marshal Ferdinand, 83
Foot, M.R.D., 41, 119, 134; *Six Faces of Courage,* 52, 131–2
Forces françaises de l'intérieur (FFI), 197, 205, 209; ordered to report for duty with regular army, 218
Forces républicaines de sécurité (FRS), 209–13, 216
Foubert, Captain (military dentist), 28, 31
Fouché, Joseph, Duke of Otranto, 109
"Fouquet," *see* Kriegel, Maurice
Franc-Tireur (movement), 49, 64, 146, 159, 167, 227, 228
France d'Abord (resistance group), 4–5, 230, 235
France: inter-war unrest, 87–8, 105–7; relations with USSR, 101, 112; falls (1940), 19, 21–2; alliance with Britain, 123; 1940 armistice, 34, 39–40; Third Republic abolished, 35; partitioned (1940), 40; reaction to German occupation, 42–4, 46; vocabulary under occupation, 42–3; social effects of occupation, 45; Liberation and end of German occupation (1944), 201–4; Allied southern landings in (August 1944), 202; insurrection (1944), 204–5, 206–11, 217; first provisional government (1944), 206–11, 217–18, 220; *see also* Resistance (French); Vichy
France-Libre (review), 136
Franco, General Francisco, 113, 115, 123
Franco-Prussian War (1870), 69
Franco-Soviet Pact (1935), 112, 123
Francs-Tireurs et Partisans (FTP; armed wing of *Front National*), 170, 206–9
Francs-Tireurs et Partisans-Main d'Oeuvre Immigré (FTP-MOI), 47, 146, 154, 182–3, 197, 220, 225, 248
Franz Ferdinand, Archduke of Austria, 80
Frédéric (group), 55, 63
Free French (*Français libres; later* Fighting

French or *Français combattants*): in
London, 40, 235; movement develops,
41; vocabulary, 43; Lecompte-Boinet
supports, 51; Frenay's contact with, 64;
low priority in London, 130; motto
(*Honneur et patrie*), 136; limited choice
of agents, 141; Communist Party's
isolation from, 146; and Degliame, 146;
distrust of Resistance, 150; attacks
Vichy government, 156–7; adopts new
name, 168; opposition to JM, 177;
Giraud appointed to command, 185;
recruits Aubry, 238

freemasonry, 37, 71, 75, 90, 118, 122, 123–4,
172

Frenay, Captain Henri: in Resistance, 45,
48–51; JM meets, 64, 153; contact with
Free French, 64; and JM in London,
133; and JM's return to France from
England, 141; organizes resistance
groups, 145; rejects U.S. help, 145; JM
seeks to contact, 147–8; in Paris, 149;
JM overrides, 154–5; unaware of
Manhès's links with northern groups,
154; meets Vichy minister Pucheu,
156; relations with JM, 158–9; financial
situation, 159; mission to London,
159–60; and new Resistance
administration, 160; prints
underground newspaper, 163;
Gestapo discovers reports, 166–7;
and coordinating committee, 167;
status in MUR, 167; ideology, 168; and
recruitment to Resistance, 168; carries
Brossolette's instructions to JM, 173;
opposes reorganization of Resistance,
176; agreement with and funding from
OSS, 178; refuses cooperation with JM,
178, 188; on JM as art dealer, 180; as
target for Multon, 191; Hardy works for,
196, 221; and communist infiltration of
Resistance leadership, 197; Communist
Party disparages, 220–1; defends Hardy
in trial, 223, 227; Pineau claims to be
Vichy agent, 224; disbelieves Hardy's
treachery, 233; suspicions of JM as
crypto-communist, 233–4, 246–7, 254;
Bénouville meets, 242; Bénouville

deputizes for, 243; challenges legend of
JM, 261; as creator of Secret Army, 261;
L'Enigme Jean Moulin, 159, 233; *La Nuit
finira*, 233

French Revolution, 146–7

Fried, Eugen, 47, 110, 248

Front National, le (communist
organization), 47, 51, 65, 146, 155, 158,
169, 170, 196, 202, 220, 246, 259

Frossard, Dr., 213

FRS, *see Forces républicaines de sécurité*

FTP, *see Francs-Tireurs et Partisans*

FTP-MOI, *see Francs-Tireurs et Partisans-
Main d'Oeuvre Immigré*

Fullerton, Hugh, 61

Gambetta, Léon, 11, 72

Gamelin, General Maurice, 22, 40, 114

Garçon, Maître Maurice, 223, 226–8, 230

Gastaldo, Major, 196

Gauguin, Paul, 96

Gaulle, Charles de: nominates JM as
political head of Resistance, 3–4; at
JM's Panthéon funeral, 9–10, 12;
idealizes profession of librarian, 109;
Cot seeks to discredit, 122; resists
German offensive, 25; writes preface to
JM's *Premier Combat*, 31, 222; leads Free
French in London, 40–1; military ideas
and practice, 40–1; appeal to France
(June 18, 1940), 40, 48; appoints
d'Astier Minister of Interior in Algeria,
49; Lecompte-Boinet's attitude to, 51;
Labarthe spies on, 55, 135; JM acts as
emissary to, 64, 147; and JM's delay in
Lisbon, 130; poor relations with
Churchill, 130; and JM's visit to
England, 131–2, 135; employs Dewavrin,
134; JM meets and reports to, 136–40;
support for in England, 136, 140;
manner, 137–9; Communist Party
denounces, 146; Roosevelt mistrusts,
145, 158; gives letter of authority to JM
for mission in France, 149–50; JM
conceals actions from, 154; OSS
attempts to weaken influence, 155;
praises JM's integrity, 155; rivalry with
Giraud, 158, 175–6; and Frenay, 159–60;

Gaulle, Charles de (*cont'd*)
approves new Resistance organization, 160; receives letters from JM, 162–3; on role and funding of Resistance, 168; relations with Brossolette, 172–3; meets JM on 1943 visit to London, 174; forbidden to fly to Algiers, 176; confers powers on JM, 180; issues orders to Delestraint, 183; CNR recognizes as sole leader of Resistance, 184–5; meets Giraud in Algiers, 184; objectives for liberation of France, 185; JM as delegate for, 196; comments on no arrests after JM's, 198; calls for French insurrection, 204; forms first provisional republican government (GPRF), 207, 217–18, 220; opposes AMGOT, 208; dismisses d'Astier, 211; and administration of Marseille, 215; attitude to communists, 218–19; right of pardon, 219; on communist betrayals, 224; retains rank of Brigadier, 234*n*; not told of JM's relations with communist cell, 247; trusts JM's containment of communist offensive, 254
Géraldy, Paul, 119
German Field Police (GFP), 164
Germany: use of torture, 13–14, 165; conquers France (1940), 19, 21–2; takes Chartres, 20–1; invades Poland, 124; 1940 armistice with France, 34, 39; reprisals for assassination of soldiers, 47, 139, 146, 163, 183; invades USSR, 60, 64; occupies Vichy zone (1942), 160, 163; anti-resistance measures, 163–4; atrocities, 204–5; *see also* Nazi-Soviet Pact
Gestapo: uses torture, 13–14, 165; in Lyon, 160, 164–6; successes and arrests, 189–90; informs family of JM's death, 194; and retrial of Hardy, 227–8; beats up and interrogates Aubry, 240–1; interrogates Hardy, 243; interrogates Aubrac, 251; knowledge of Lyon resistance, 251; in raid on Caluire, 254–5, 257
Gestapo française, 14

GFP, *see* German Field Police
Gide, André, 117 and *n*
"Gilbert" network, 191, 242
Gilbert, Raymond, 25, 123
Giraud, General Henri, 157–8, 175–6, 184–5
Gitton, Marcel, 146
Goering, Hermann, 60
Goethe, Johann Wolfgang von, 39
GPU (*later* KGB), 103
Graaf, Tony de, 187, 249
Grand Loge de France, 172
Grand Orient, Le (Masonic group), 61, 71, 75, 122, 123
Grasse, 58
Greene, Graham: *A Sort of Life,* 78
Grenier, Fernand, 171
Grossmann, Major, 19–20, 26
groupes francs, 145, 155, 197, 253, 255
Groussard, Colonel Georges, 136–7, 152, 191, 223, 242, 245
GRU (Soviet military intelligence), 55, 116, 235
Gubbins, Major-General Colin, 41
Guérisse, Albert, 191
Guingouin, Georges, 205, 206–7, 217, 219
Gütlingen, Oberstleutnant F. K. von, 35, 38
Guy, Claude, 198, 224

Haag, Paul, 215
Halifax, Edward Frederick Lindley Wood, 1st Earl of, 113
Hardy, René: at Caluire meeting, 4, 220–1, 237, 239, 244, 245; escape and arrest at Caluire, 6–7, 194–6, 229–30, 238, 240, 243; wounded while escaping, 6; suspected of betrayal, 7, 195, 253; arrested on way to meet Delestraint, 191; develops NAP-FER, 191, 197; released and joins Frenay's staff, 195–6, 221; second escape from hospital, 195; first trial and acquittal, 222–3, 260; second trial and acquittal, 224–31, 241, 243, 260; treachery disproved, 233–4, 238, 245; Bénouville meets, 242;

interrogated by Gestapo, 243–4, 251;
released by Germans, 252
Harscouet, Monsignor Raoul-Octave-
Marie-Jean, Bishop of Chartres, 24
and *n*
Henry, Colonel Hubert, 73, 101
Hering, General Pierre, 24
Hervé, Annie, 170
Hervé, Pierre, 197, 204, 246
Heydrich, Reinhard, 164
Himmler, Heinrich, 14, 165
Hitler, Adolf, 38, 40, 46, 59–60, 64, 123–5,
163
Ho Chi Minh, 248
Holland: invaded (1940), 21
Howson, Gerald: *Arms for Spain*, 121, 122*n*
Hugo, Victor, 11, 12
Humanité, L' (newspaper), 38, 48, 54–5, 103,
221, 223

Infantry Regiment, 17th, 77–8
International Brigade (Spanish Civil
War), 65, 117, 123, 125
International Peace Campaign, 116
Italy: part-occupation of France, 40

Jacob, Max, 97, 109
"Jacquin, Monsieur" (Lyon), 166
"Jansen, Martha," 116
Jaurès, Jean, 11, 12, 80
Jeantet, Gabriel, 44
Jeunesses laïques et républicaines, 86
Jeunesses patriotes, 102
Jews: Vichy law on status of, 24, 37–8;
expelled from Alsace-Lorraine, 39–40;
deported, 45, 57*n*; wear yellow star, 45
Joffre, General Joseph-Jacques-Césaire,
81
Joliot-Curie, Frédéric, 117 and *n*

KdS, *see Kommando Sipo-SD*
Kesselring, Field Marshal Albert, 60
Kitchener, General Horatio Herbert
(*later* Earl), 73
Koch, Stephen, 116
Koch-Erpach, General, 19–21, 26–7, 29, 35
Koenig, General Marie-Pierre, 204

Koestler, Arthur, 55, 125; *Scum of the Earth*,
43–4, 124, 126
Kommando Sipo-SD (KdS), 164–6
Kriegel, Maurice ("Valrimont";
"Fouquet"), 177, 190, 251–2

Labarthe, André, 54–5, 113, 116, 118, 121,
135–6, 141, 235, 247
Lacaze, Colonel Albert: at Caluire
meeting, 4, 235–6, 238, 255, 257; arrested
and interrogated, 7, 196, 245
Lacaze, Odile (Albert's daughter), 235
Lacombe (prefect of Montpellier), 86
Laferre, Louis, 71, 75, 79, 90, 100
La Laurencie, General Benoît-Léon
Fornel de, 155
Languedoc: wine crisis in (1907), 76–7
Larat, Bruno: at Caluire meeting, 4,
235–6, 238, 255; arrested and beaten, 7,
196, 245
La Rocque, Colonel François de, 102
Lassagne, André: at Caluire meeting, 4,
221, 235–6, 250, 255, 258; arrested,
interrogated and beaten, 5, 196, 245,
260; in Resistance, 49; asked to identify
JM, 193; on Aubrac at Caluire, 249;
proposed as temporary commander in
south, 249
Laval, Pierre, 15, 36–7, 112, 136, 156–8, 191
"leagues, the" (nationalist groups), 102
Leclerc, General (Philippe-Marie de
Hauteclocque, called), 218
Lecompte-Boinet, Jacques, 51
Léger, Alexis (Saint-Jean Perse), 140
Légion des Combattants (organization), 46
Lejards, Monsignor, 20, 25–6
Lenin, Vladimir Ilich, 103
Le Roy Ladurie, Emmanuel, 147
Leuiller, Inspector, 212
Le Vernet internment camp, 65, 125–6
Lévy, Jean-Pierre, 49, 150, 159, 167–8, 178
Libération (resistance group), 3, 49–50, 55,
64, 133, 145, 151, 156, 158–9, 163, 167, 227,
228, 235–6, 246, 249
Libération Nationale, see Combat
Libération-Nord (resistance group), 50–1,
54, 137, 154, 224

Libération-Sud (resistance group), 146, 167, 170, 177, 224, 225

Liberté (group), 64, 133

Ligue des Droits de l'Homme, La, 73, 78, 88

Lille, 31

Limoges, 219

Limousin, 205–7

Lisbon: JM delayed in, 129–32

Lloyd, Gilberte, 56, 59, 118–19, 152–3, 179

London: JM reaches, 133–40

Lorraine, 40, 88

Louis XV, king of France, 11

Louis XVIII, king of France, 109

Louis-Philippe, king of the French, 11

Luftwaffe: fails to gain supremacy over Britain, 60

Lugand, Jacques, 108

Lussac-les-Châteaux (Limousin), 205

Lutte des Classes, La (group), 208

Lyon: under martial law, 3; German Sonderkommando unit in, 5–6; Gestapo move into, 160, 164–6; as resistance center, 163; Barbie in, 164–6; food shortages, 164–5; German anti-resistance activities in, 190; liberated (1944), 202–3; post-Liberation administration, 209; Gestapo knowledge of resistance in, 251; *see also* Bron

MacMahon, Marie-Edmé-Patrice-Maurice de, 69

Madrid: battle for, 113

Malleret, Alfred, 197

Malraux, André: eulogy of JM, 9–10, 13–15, 261; and supply of aircraft to Spain, 113; supports RUP, 117; *La Condition humaine,* 13n, 113

Mandel, Georges, *see* Rothschild, Louis

Manefret, Commissaire, 212

Manhès, Henri: pro-communist sympathies, 116, 154, 234, 247; and Lecompte-Boinet, 154; as JM's confidential agent, 61; contacts northern groups, 62–3, 154; JM withholds contact with from de Gaulle, 141; and JM's relations with Antoinette Sachs and Gilberte Lloyd, 151–2; organizes resistance groups, 153–4; and JM's operations in north, 170–1, 173; and JM's relations with Communist Party, 170–1; interrogated by Gestapo, 174; in London, 174; arrested, 180, 187, 189, 247; in Buchenwald, 180 and *n;* JM defends, 180–1; JM attempts release of, 189; trusted by all parties, 189

Mans, Dr., 154

Marat, Jean-Paul, 11

Marchais, Georges, 222

Marchal, Colonel Pierre, 198

Marchant, Captain Jean-Baptiste, 73

Marne, battle of the (1914), 81

Marseille: JM meets Dolivet in, 58–9; Antoinette Sachs provides false papers for JM in, 63; liberated (1944), 202; post-Liberation administration and *l'épuration,* 209, 211–16; communist vote in (1945), 219

"Martel, Jean," *see* Moulin, Jean

Martel, Thiery de, 44

Martin, Dr. Henri, 102

Marty, André, 221

Mas, Alphonse, 71

Massu, General Jacques, 14

Matisse, Henri, 119

Maurras, Charles, 90, 100–101, 107, 110–11, 260

Maury, M. (science teacher), 82

"Max," *see* Moulin, Jean

Megève, 98–9

Meiners, Heinrich, 194

Menthon, François de, 48, 64, 133, 163

Mercier, Joseph-Jean: as JM's false identity, 53

Mers el-Kebir, 36

Meunier, Pierre: pro-communist sympathies, 116, 234; runs Cot's private office, 118; and Lecompte-Boinet, 154; and JM's knowledge of Soviet intelligence activities, 59–60; JM meets in Paris, 62; JM withholds contact with from de Gaulle, 141; and JM's relations with Communist Party, 170–1; and JM's

confrontation with Brossolette, 180–2;
as co-secretary of CNR, 185; in JM's
entourage, 188; believes Manhès forced
to talk, 189; JM's sister meets in Paris,
194

MI5 (British counterintelligence), 135

MI6 (Secret Intelligence Service), 41, 56,
242

Michel, Henri, 42

Milice (French anti-Resistance
militiamen), 205, 212

Millerand, Alexandre, 86–7

MIR, *see Mouvements unis de la résistance*

Mirabeau, Honoré-Gabriel Riqueti,
Comte de, 11

Mission brumaire, 173, 180–2, 188

Mistral, Frédéric, 71, 76, 101

Mitterrand, François, 242

Möller, SS Colonel, 216

Molotov-Ribbentrop Pact, *see* Nazi-
Soviet Pact

monarchists, 101, 105–7

Monnet, Jean, 140

Monsabert, General Joseph-Jean
Goislard de, 211

Montfaucon, 78n

Montjaret, Hervé, 144–5, 149, 153–4, 189,
236

Montluc prison, 192, 252–3

Montparnasse, 98, 108, 119

Montpellier, 45, 56, 60–1, 82, 85–7, 121

Moog, Robert, 190–1, 221, 224, 225, 245

Morand, Paul, 140

Morin-Forestier, François, 191, 251

Mortimore, Major L. H., 129–30

Moulin, Alphonse (JM's grandfather),
69–70

Moulin, Antonin (JM's father):
background and career, 69–73, 74–5,
79–80; marriage, 70–1; as Dreyfusard,
73; attitude to religions, 74–6;
freemasonry, 75; and JM's upbringing,
76, 79; accused of electoral fraud, 80; in
First World War, 81; protects JM in
war, 82; influences JM's career, 87–8;
JM separated from, 88; plans JM's
marriage, 89; and JM's marriage to

Marguerite, 89–90; political views and
ideals, 95, 100–101; aging, 99; writes life
of Ernestine de Castellane, 109; joins
JM in Evian, 110; and JM's
appointment as prefect, 119; death, 121,
247

Moulin, Blanche (*née* Pègue; JM's
mother): marriage, 70; relations with
mother, 71; trip to Marseille, 73; plans
JM's marriage, 89; and JM's
engagement to Marguerite, 92–3; joins
JM in Evian, 110; letter from JM in
wartime Chartres, 29; JM visits in
wartime, 56; JM contacts on return
from London, 145; death, 194

Moulin, Jean ("Jean Martel"; "Max"):
convenes and attends Caluire meeting,
3–5, 191, 230, 231, 235, 238–9, 243, 246,
249–50, 256–7; arrested, imprisoned
and interrogated, 6, 191–3, 196, 246, 261;
mystery of death, 8, 233, 261; Panthéon
funeral and consecration, 9–10, 12, 15,
234, 261; legend of, 12, 15, 222, 260;
family and upbringing, 69–70, 72, 74–6;
birth and christening, 73, 74; confirmed
as Catholic, 74; witnesses Béziers wine
crisis, 76–7; school misbehavior, 78–9;
and outbreak of First World War, 80–1;
anti-German views, 81; cartoons and
caricatures, 81–2, 87, 96; passes
baccalauréat, 82; first works in *préfecture*,
82, 85; studies law, 82, 85; service in
First World War, 83–4; demobilized,
84, 85; reticence and secrecy, 85–6, 90,
104, 142, 154; career in *préfecture*, 86–7,
89–91, 95–6, 98, 104, 109, 119; law degree,
86; student life, 86; drawing and
painting, 88, 91; moves to Chambéry, 88;
marriage suit rejected, 89; salary, 89, 99,
61n; sports and pastimes, 89, 91, 95,
98–9, 121; appearance and manner, 90,
91, 132, 134; and freemasonry, 90, 118,
123–4; moves to Albertville, 90–1;
difficulty with insubordinate gardener,
91–2, 99; engagement and marriage to
Marguerite Cerruti, 92–4; marriage
failure and divorce, 94–5; Cot appoints

Moulin, Jean (*cont'd*)
chef de cabinet, 95–6, 98, 100; political
views and sympathies, 95–6, 100, 104,
112, 233–4, 246; moves to Châteaulin, 96,
98; buys car, 99; transferred from
Finistère, 99; political influences on,
102; skiing, 105; and 1934 riots, 106–8;
drawings in brothels, 108; loses post,
108; attends art school in
Montparnasse, 108; in Amiens, 109;
helps father with biography of E. de
Castellane, 109; illustrates Corbière
poems, 109; abandons painting, 110;
food poisoning, 108; rejoins Cot as *chef
du cabinet* (1936–8), 111; supports
communist candidate in Amiens, 111;
influence on Cot, 112; and French
policy on Spain, 113; and Vichy treason
trials, 114; in charge of arms supplies to
Spain, 115; supports RUP, 116, 117, 118;
and Comintern conspiracy, 116–18, 123,
247; love affairs, 61, 118–19, 151–3;
awarded *légion d'honneur,* 119; nominated
prefect of Aveyron, 119; seconded back
to Paris, 119–20; and father's death, 121;
organizes international air races, 120;
reinstalled at Rodez (Aveyron), 121, 122,
123; surrenders Chartres, 19–20, 25–6, 32;
expels Spanish refugees, 123; as prefect
of Chartres, 123–4; holiday with sister
in London, 124; tries to enlist in
Second World War, 126; orders
repression of communist agitators, 125;
at fall of Paris, 22–3; evacuates Chartres
staff, 23–4, 29; wartime administration
in Chartres, 24–5, 32–4, 36, 37;
mistreated by Germans in Chartres,
27–30, 32, 135; refuses to concede
Senegalese crimes, 26–8; remains in
Chartres, 28–9, 33; attempts suicide, 30;
condemns anti-Jewish laws, 37–8;
dismissed (October 1940), 38–9;
German respect for, 38; reaction to
German occupation, 44; on half pay,
52; crosses Vichy line, 54, 62, 170–1;
false identity (as J. J. Mercier), 53, 57,
61, 142, 143; in occupied Paris, 54–8,
61–3; inheritance, 56; negotiates

pension, 56; requests visa to leave
France, 57; illicitly stamps own
passport, 59; as putative Soviet agent,
59–60, 141; financial resources, 62;
summoned as witness in Cot treason
trial, 63; as emissary to de Gaulle, 64;
meets Frenay, 64; ignorance of
Resistance, 64; conceals communist
links, 65; leaves France for London, 65,
129; delayed in Lisbon, 129–30; writes
report on Resistance aims and needs,
129–30; arrives in England, 130–1; claims
to represent resistance groups, 132–3;
questioned in London, 133–5; reports to
de Gaulle in London, 136–41; returns to
France from England, 141–2, 144–5;
psychological makeup, 141–2; training
as agent, 142; Vichy information on,
143; early movements on return to
France, 145; and Communist Party's
role in resistance, 147; system of
traveling, 148; struggle with Resistance
leaders, 149–51; role of mission in
France, 150; runs art gallery in Nice,
153, 180; unauthorized actions, 154, 155;
overrides Frenay, 154–6; summoned to
Vichy and declines offer, 156–7; in new
Resistance administration in south, 160;
appeals for help to de Gaulle, 162–3;
attempts to unite and coordinate
resistance movements, 167–8; controls
Resistance budget, 169; relations with
Communist Party, 169–70, 244, 253–4;
differences with Brossolette over
organization of Resistance, 173–4, 187;
operates in north, 173; visits London
(February/March 1943), 173–4; de
Gaulle appoints Companion of Order
of Liberation, 175; changes opinion on
recognition of old political parties in
Resistance, 176–7; Fighting French and
Resistance opposition to, 177;
amalgamates MUR and CNR, 178;
criticized by Passy and Brossolette, 177;
confronts Dewavrin and Brossolette in
Paris, 180–2; loses lovers, 179; heads
CNR, 182–3; instructs communist
groups to follow orders, 183; and CNR

recognition of de Gaulle, 184; and de Gaulle's objectives for liberation of France, 185; presides at first meeting of CNR, 185; suffers strain, 187; Germans pursue, 190; heads *Délégation-Générale*, 197; opposes AMGOT, 208; postwar enquiries into disappearance, 220–2; Copeau plots with, 224; suspected of communist sympathies, 233–4, 246–7; identified to Gestapo by Aubry, 240–1; abandons communist sympathies for patriotism, 248; refuses armed guard at Caluire, 255; betrayal at Caluire, 259; *Premier Combat*, 24–7, 29, 31–2, 34, 84, 130, 222

Moulin, Joseph (JM's brother), 71, 76

Moulin, Laure (JM's sister): family life, 71; childhood, 74, 76–7; helps JM in First World War, 83; on JM's reticence, 86; and JM's wedding, 93; on JM's Paris studio, 108; London holiday with JM, 124; and JM's mistreatment in Chartres, 28; letter from JM on remaining in Chartres, 29; finds manuscript of JM's *Premier Combat*, 31; JM visits in wartime, 56; and JM's wartime visit to London, 135; JM contacts on return from London, 145; JM pays last visit to, 189; learns of Caluire arrests, 192; warned of Gestapo interception of JM's mail, 193–4; informed of JM's death and cremation, 194; travels to Paris, 194; postwar investigation into JM's disappearance, 220; publishes JM's *Premier Combat*, 222; and trial of Hardy, 224; on JM's confiding in Manhès, 248

Mounier (Prefect of Savoy), 88, 91

Mouvement de Libération Nationale, see Combat

Mouvements unis de la résistance (MUR): formed, 167–8; JM controls, 169, 196; subordinated to CNR, 178; at first meeting of CNR, 185; and Hardy's supposed treachery, 195; communist representation in, 197; issues instructions on insurrection, 204; and Caluire meeting, 236; Aubry in, 238

Mowrer, Edgar, 59

Multon, Jean ("Lunel"), 167, 190–1, 225, 227, 240

Munich Agreement (1938), 124

Munzenberg, Willy, 115

Muracciole, J.-F., 49

Musée de l'Homme (Paris), 50, 172

Mussolini, Benito, 120

National Assembly (French), 219

Nacht und Nebel (German decree), 163, 192, 222

NAP-FER (*Combat* unit), 190, 191, 196, 197

Napoleon I (Bonaparte), Emperor of France, 39

Napoleon III, Emperor of the French, 72

Navachine, Dimitri, 115–16

Nazi-Soviet Pact ("Der Pakt"; 1939), 55, 59, 65, 122, 124–5, 245, 247; ends, 135, 146, 157

Nazism: Cot perceives as threat, 112

Nevière, Jean-Elie, 213, 216

Nice: JM's art gallery in, 153, 179–80

Nicolson, (Sir) Harold, 138

NKVD (Soviet secret force), 115–16

Noel-Baker, Philip (*later* Baron), 116

North Africa: Allied landings in (1942), 160, 175

Noyautage de l'Administration Publique (NAP), 48

Oberg, General Karl, 164

Oberg-Bousquet Accord, 251

OCM, *see Organisation civile et militaire*

Office of Strategic Services (OSS), 63, 145–6, 155, 158, 178, 188, 242

Olivier, Suzette, 193

OMS (Comintern's Department of International Links), 103

Oradour-sur-Glane, 205

Organisation civile et militaire (OCM), 51, 154, 158

OSS, *see* Office of Strategic Services

Pakt, Der, see Nazi-Soviet Pact

Panier, Maurice, 55, 56, 59, 60, 62, 115–16, 135, 171, 247

Panthéon (Paris): JM's funeral in, 9–12, 15, 234, 261
Parc de St. Cloud (Paris): Blum's peace speech at, 117
Paris: riots (1934), 105–7; falls (1940), 22–3; evacuated, 31; suicide rate drops under occupation, 45; as center of dissent, 54; JM in during occupation, 54–8, 62–3; liberated (1944), 202, 217–18; insurrection in (1944), 207; declared open city (1940), 217; *see also* Montparnasse
Parti Radical, 79, 86, 111
Parti Socialiste, 102
Pascin, Julius, 108
Passy, Colonel *see* Dewavrin, André
"Pat O'Leary" escape line, 191
Paul-Boncour, Joseph, 62–3
PCF, *see* Communist Party of France
Péan, Pierre, 189, 225, 244; *Vies et Morts de Jean Moulin*, 61, 119
Pearl Harbor, 145
Pègue, Clarisse (JM's maternal grandmother), 71, 74
Pègue, Pierre (JM's maternal grandfather), 71
Perceval, Father de, 211
Péronne, 53
Perse, Saint-Jean, *see* Léger, Alexis
Pétain, Marshal Philippe: and armistice (1940), 22, 39–40; granted supreme powers, 36; meets Hitler, 38; motto (*Travaille, famille, patrie*), 42–3; policies, 46, 57–8; and Resistance, 49–50; JM claims information on, 136; left-wing view of, 138; appeals against assassination of German soldiers, 139; Frenay loses faith in, 156; taken into custody (1944), 218
Petit, Eugène ("Claudius"), 195, 229
Peyrefitte, Alain, 254
Philby, Kim, 56
Philip, André, 173
Pineau, Christian, 50, 54, 137
Piquet-Wicks, Captain F. Eric, 132–4
piston system, 87, 90, 92, 98, 192, 224
Plateau, Marius, 102
Poggioli, Inspector, 212

Poland: invaded (1939), 124–5
police: purged in *l'épuration*, 211
Pons, Colette, 153, 179–80, 189
Popular Front (*Front populaire*), 110–11, 114, 122, 124, 245
Porte, Charles, 195, 206n
Primo de Rivera, José Antonio, 111
"Prosper" network, 190
Provençal, Le (newspaper), 211
Pucheu, Pierre, 48, 156
Puy-en-Velay, 225

Quimper, 96–7

Rachline, Lazare, 243
Radical-Socialist Party, 95, 103
"Rag, Major," 213
Raisin, Madeleine, 239–40
Rassemblement universel pour la paix (RUP), 55, 58, 116
Ravanel, Serge (Serge Asher), 49, 177, 191, 209, 251–3
Recordier, Dr. Marcel, 64, 149
"Red Orchestra" (spy ring), 55, 103
Regis, Emile, 214
Reich, Das (German army SS Division), 205
Reich Security Service (RSHA), 163–4
Reille-Soult, Baron Henri, 206
Reiss, Ignace, 116n
Renault, Gilbert ("Colonel Rémy"), 50, 148, 162, 170, 172
Résistance de l'intérieur, 64
Resistance (French): develops, 41–2, 44–6, 48–51, 54; struggle for control of, 149–50, 224–5; categories of members, 161–2; members' behavior, 162; reorganized and coordinated, 167; de Gaulle's attitude to, 168; funding, 169; arrests, 197–8; supports Allied armies in Liberation, 204; supports popular insurrection, 204–5; represented in de Gaulle's first provisional government, 218–19; myth of, 233; *see also* Secret Army
Resisters of the Month of September (RMS), 202
Ressier, M. (subprefect), 37, 57–8

Reynaud, Paul, 21–2
Riedlinger family, 119
Riom (Auvergne), 63, 114
Rire (magazine), 91
RMS, *see* Resisters of the Month of
   September
Robinson, Henry ("Harry"): as Comintern
   intelligence officer in Paris, 55, 103;
   Panier works for, 56, 115; Philby reports
   to, 56; and JM's knowledge of Soviet
   intelligence activities, 59–60, 62;
   reports to Moscow, 59–60; JM meets in
   Paris, 62; told of Labarthe's activities,
   135; JM's relations with, 247; arrested
   and shot, 259–60
Rodez, 119–21, 122, 123
Rol-Tanguy, Colonel Henri, 197, 207, 208
Roosevelt, Franklin Delano: hostility
   toward de Gaulle, 145, 158; chooses
   Giraud as commander in Algiers, 175
Rothschild, Louis (Georges Mandel), 29,
   96
Rousseau, Jean-Jacques, 11
Rousselot, Jules, 28
Royal Air Force (RAF): airmen helped by
   resistance groups, 50; clandestine
   missions, 162
Royal Navy: in Dunkirk evacuation, 22;
   cripples French fleet at Mers el-Kebir,
   36; clandestine missions, 162
Royal Patriotic School (London), 132, 134,
   139
RSHA, *see* Reich Security Service
RUP, *see* Rassemblement universel pour la paix
Russia, *see* Soviet Russia

Sabatier, Jeanne (JM's cousin), 74
Sabatier, Maurice, 57*n*
Sabiani, Simon, 216
Sabotage-Fer, 223
Sachs, Antoinette, 22, 61–3, 119, 136, 151–3,
   179–80, 220–2
St. Andiol, near Avignon, 56, 60, 69–71, 74,
   76, 81, 84, 88, 121, 189, 193
Salmon, André, 110
Samuel, Babette (Lucie and Raymond
   Aubrac's daughter), 248
Samuel, Raymond, *see* Aubrac, Raymond

Sarajevo, 80
Sartre, Jean-Paul, 14
Saunier, Tony, 166
Savoy, 88, 91, 95
Schörer, SS Colonel, 216
Schwartzfeld, Lieut.-Colonel: at Caluire
   meeting, 5, 231, 235, 238, 249–50, 256–7;
   arrested, 7, 196
"Sealion, Operation," 60
Second World War: outbreak, 124
Secret Army (French): formed, 4, 7; built
   up from London, 149, 160; German
   knowledge of, 166–7, 190; reorganized,
   166–7, 236; arrests and seizures, 177, 196;
   remnants, 197; Bénouville suspects
   communist control of, 244; *see also*
   Resistance (French)
Section française de l'Internationale ouvrière
   (SFIO), 102
Senegalese troops: shot in French retreat,
   20–1, 27–8
"Serge" (resistance worker), 191
Serreulles, Claude, 4, 177, 238, 249, 250*n*
Service d'Ordre Légionnaire (SOL), 46, 157
Service du Travail obligatoire (STO;
   German forced labor program), 169,
   183, 197, 222
Service Maquis, 197
SFIO, *see* Section française de l'Internationale
   ouvrière
Simon, Pierre-Henri, 14
Sipo-SD (German security police), 163,
   166
SOE, *see* Special Operations Executive
SOL, *see* Service d'Ordre Légionnaire
Solidarité française (group), 102
Sorbonne (Paris), 51
Soviet Russia: relations with France, 100;
   spy ring in France, 103; sets up Popular
   Front, 110; pact with France (1935), 112,
   123; arms supply for Spain, 114–15, 121;
   receives intelligence from wartime
   France, 56, 59–60; Germany invades
   (1941), 60, 64–5; *see also* Nazi-Soviet
   Pact
Spain: effect of political events on France,
   111–13; Popular Front Government in,
   111–12; Civil War, 113–14, 116; supply of

Spain (*cont'd*)
  aircraft and arms to, 113–15, 121, 122*n*, 135;
  French volunteers in, 117; Republican
  refugees in France, 123–5
Special Operations Executive (SOE), 41,
  51, 56, 129–30, 132–5, 190
Statut des juifs, 24*n*, 37
Stalin, Josef V., 55, 125, 217, 260
Stavisky, Serge Alexandre, 104–5, 121
Steingritt, Corporal Harry, 6, 225, 229
STO, *see Service du Travail obligatoire*
Suchon (Mayor of Béziers), 77
Sudan: Anglo-French rivalry in, 73
Switzerland: OSS team in, 145, 178

Tanguy, Henri, *see* Rol-Tanguy, Colonel
  Henri
Tarascon, 213
Taye, La, 28–30
"Tempi, Herta," 116
Thonon-les-Bains, 99, 108
Thorez, Maurice, 47, 106, 110, 222
"Torch, Operation" (1942), 160, 175–6
Toulouse, 57, 58, 59, 208, 209
Toulouse-Lautrec, Henri de, 108
Trepper, Leopold, 259–60
Tresso, Pietro, 225
Trotsky, Léon, 102, 202
Trotskyists: purged by Communist Party,
  225

Ukraine: famine, 100
Union Républicaine, L' (newspaper), 75, 80
Unitarian Services Committee (USC), 63
United States of America: enters war, 145,
  157; links with Giraud, 158; and funding
  of de Gaulle, 169
USC, *see* Unitarian Services Committee

Vallin, Charles, 173
Vallon, Louis, 173

"Valrimont," *see* Kriegel, Maurice
Varadier, Aglaë de, 234
Vasiltchenko, Vladimir, 116
Vassilieff, Marie, 97
Vercingetorix, 81
Vercors, 170
Verdier, Cardinal Jean, Archbishop of
  Paris, 123, 129
Vérités (underground newspaper), 48
Versailles, Treaty of (1918), 87
Vichy: government holds treason trials,
  114; anti-Semitic laws, 24*n*, 37–8, 45;
  administration, 34; as capital of
  unoccupied France, 36; law against
  "secret societies," 37; suppresses
  communism, 38; economic
  dependence, 39–40; infiltration of
  administration, 48; resisters in, 49–50;
  information on JM, 143; negotiates
  with JM and Frenay, 155–7; mobilizes
  against Resistance, 157; zone occupied
  by Germans (1942), 160, 163–4;
  government collapses (1944), 203–4,
  217–18; collaborators shot, 216
Vidal-Naquet, Pierre, 234
Vidon, Maurice, 22, 23–4, 32, 37
Viellecazes (prefect of Blois), 29
Viollette, Maurice, 24, 37, 88, 102, 123
Voltaire, François Marie Arouet de, 11

Weygand, General Maxime, 217
Wolff (of Marseille Docks and
  Warehouse Board), 214
Wright, Peter: *Spycatcher,* 261

Yeo-Thomas, Forest Frederick Edward,
  171, 173, 180–2

Zaroubine, Vasili, 122
Zola, Emile, 11

About the Author

PATRICK MARNHAM lived for twelve years in Paris and covered three French war crimes trials for the British and American press. His previous books include *So Far from God,* winner of the Thomas Cook Prize; *The Man Who Wasn't Maigret: A Portrait of Georges Simenon,* winner of the Marsh Prize for biography and an Edgar Allan Poe Award finalist; and *Dreaming with His Eyes Open: A Life of Diego Rivera.*

About the Type

The text of this book was set in Janson, a misnamed type-face designed in about 1690 by Nicholas Kis, a Hungarian in Amsterdam. In 1919 the matrices became the property of the Stempel Foundry in Frankfurt. It is an old-style book face of excellent clarity and sharpness. Janson serifs are concave and splayed; the contrast between thick and thin strokes is marked.